Moot Plays of Corneille

OTHER BOOKS BY LACY LOCKERT

•

(Vanderbilt University Press)

Criticism

STUDIES IN FRENCH-CLASSICAL TRAGEDY

Translations

THE CHIEF RIVALS OF CORNEILLE AND RACINE

•

(Princeton University Press)

Translations

THE INFERNO OF DANTE

THE BEST PLAYS OF RACINE

THE CHIEF PLAYS OF CORNEILLE

RACINE'S MID-CAREER TRAGEDIES

MOOT PLAYS OF
Corneille

TRANSLATED INTO ENGLISH BLANK VERSE
WITH INTRODUCTIONS

BY

LACY LOCKERT

Nashville

THE VANDERBILT UNIVERSITY PRESS

1959

CONTENTS

"Let us simply take the trouble to read him, and not restrict ourselves to the four tragedies studied in the class-room—only two of which, after all, the *Cid* and *Polyeucte*, are unquestionably masterpieces."

—Robert Brasillach in his *Pierre Corneille*, p. 491.

PREFACE

The work of Corneille in the field of serious or non-comic drama, unlike that of Racine after his novitiate, has never been admired in its entirety. *Théodore* and *Pertharite*—to say nothing of the mis-classified *Agésilas*—were immediate and utter failures. *Sophonisbe* and *Pulchérie* and *Suréna* fared little better. Of the rest, ten (the *Cid, Horace, Cinna, Poly-eucte, Pompée, Rodogune, Héraclius, Nicomède, Œdipe,* and *Sertorius*) were considered notable tragedies in the earlier part of the eighteenth century. In the nineteenth, the first four of these were generally regarded as Corneille's master-pieces, quite in a class by themselves above all his other plays, with *Nicomède* and *Rodogune* coming nearest to them. At the start of the twentieth, *Nicomède* was threatening to sup-plant *Cinna* in the esteem of critics; and *Rodogune* had greatly declined in favor, especially in the eyes of the highest authorities, though a certain fame was still enjoyed by it and *Pompée* and *Sertorius.*

More recently, however, there has been a general challen-ging of traditional ideas about Corneille,[1] including the tradi-tional appraisals of his plays. Some tragedies that were formerly extolled are now little liked; others, which had never before been thought well of, are now acclaimed by critics as real masterpieces. Amid such changes—and such divergences—in evaluation, the student of drama who is lacking in knowl-edge of French, but who has an inquiring mind and a critical sense perhaps superior to that of many people who are better linguists, may wish that he could judge for himself. This, through the medium of translations, it is entirely possible for him to do.

A play can be appraised in a good translation almost as well as in its own language. Very few of the many writers who have discussed Ibsen have read him—or could read him—in Norwegian. Their inability to do so has not prevented them from forming confident opinions about him, or from express-ing these opinions in books. True, when a drama is written

---

[1] Cf. *Le sentiment de l'amour dans l'œuvre de Pierre Corneille,* by Octave Nadal, Paris, 1948, pp. 283-286.

in verse, there is an added difficulty. Poetry is not really translatable; and the precise quality and intensity of the emotions depicted will not be rightly conveyed by a less eloquent expression of them than that in the original. But practically everything else that is involved in our estimate of plays—construction, conduct of scenes, dramatic effects, characterization, ideas—can be reproduced in a translation without any considerable loss. Where only one author is concerned and the question is in part not the absolute merit of certain dramas but their relative merit as compared with each other, it is all the more feasible to form a correct judgment from translations, especially if these are in every instance by the same hand. And though Corneille was a genuine poet, his poetry is of a rhetorical sort which makes it easily allowed for by the imagination, and its excellence is not so different from play to play as to be a serious imponderable when one does not have a first-hand acquaintance with it in the French.

In my book *The Chief Plays of Corneille,* which presents to English readers the six most famous tragedies of this dramatist (but not necessarily the six best ones), I have translated the *Cid, Horace, Cinna, Polyeucte, Rodogune,* and *Nicomède.* Of these, the *Cid* and *Polyeucte* are still accorded an unquestioned primacy; the right of *Nicomède,* also, to a high rating is recognized by everyone, and that of *Horace* has been denied, so far as I know, by none but Brasillach. Others have agreed with him, however, in disparaging *Cinna;* and *Rodogune,* as I have said, is no longer ranked among the best plays of its author.

Œdipe has for several generations been seen to be among his very worst—the most artificial, mannered tragedy that he ever wrote. *Sophonisbe* is like a caricature of his work subsequent to the *Cid.* *Tite et Bérénice* is a singularly unattractive play, of interest only because of its connection with Racine's *Bérénice.* *Agésilas,* wrongly called a tragedy, is merely an unsuccessful attempt at a new kind of light comedy. No one will come to the defense of *Théodore* or *Pertharite.* All of these dramas would belong in a volume with the engaging title of *The Worst Plays of Corneille.*

To my mind, the once-lauded *Pompée* and *Sertorius* also would belong in it! There would be few dissenters today from

that estimate of *Pompée;* its lack of any real plot, the pre-
posterous "gallantry" which it ascribes to so well-known a
figure as Julius Caesar, its constant rhetoric, and the essential
unreasonableness and unloveliness of its formerly-admired,
vengeful Cornelia have finally condemned it. But it has, even
yet, an occasional champion; and *Sertorius*—better constructed, at least—is still a much mooted play. Both, therefore,
are included in the present volume, which makes accessible
to people who cannot read the French originals those dramas
of Corneille, comedies aside, whose degree of excellence can
be a subject of dispute. Some of them have been said by some
recent critics to be superior to everything else of his but the
Cid and *Polyeucte.* May not some of them be, at any rate,
better than the famous *Cinna?* May not most of them be
better than the famous *Rodogune?* The English reader can
now judge for himself.

I have translated these plays into the same elastic blank
verse of Fletcher and other late-Elizabethan dramatists
that I used in *The Chief Plays of Corneille* and in *The Chief
Rivals of Corneille and Racine.* The short Introductions that
are prefixed to each play are largely made up of translated
quotations from a few critics selected to show the differing
views that have been held as to their merit in modern times—
i.e., in the last eighty-five years. These views are, of course,
simply specimen judgments; I have not sought to draw from
the whole field of criticism on the subject. To reduce to a
minimum the footnotes which might otherwise obtrude on the
reader's attention and distract him in his perusal of the text,
I list here the authors most frequently quoted and the book
by each of them to which the page-references in the footnotes
refer:

Brasillach, Robert: *Pierre Corneille,* Arthème Fayard, Paris, 1938.
Couton, Georges: *la Vieillesse de Corneille,* Maloine, Paris, 1949.
Dorchain, A.: *Pierre Corneille,* Garnier, Paris, 1918.
Faguet, Emile: *En lisant Corneille,* Hachette, Paris, 1914.
Hémon, Félix: *Théâtre de Pierre Corneille,* Delagrave, Paris, 1887,
    vol. iv; *Cours de Littérature,* Delagrave, Paris, 1930 ed.
Lancaster, Henry Carrington: *A History of French Dramatic
    Literature in the Seventeenth Century,* Johns Hopkins Univer-

sity Press, Baltimore, Part II, 1932; Part III, 1938; Part IV, 1940; Part V, 1942.

Lanson, Gustave: *Corneille,* Hachette, Paris, 5th ed., 1919; *Esquisse d'une Histoire de la Tragédie française,* Columbia University Press, New York, 1920.

Lemaître, Jules: the chapter "Pierre Corneille" in L. Petit de Julleville's *Histoire de la Langue et de la Littérature française,* Armand Colin, Paris, 5th ed., 1924, vol. iv.

Merlet, Gustave: *Etudes Littéraires sur les Classiques français,* Hachette, Paris, 1882 ed., vol. i.

Petit de Julleville: *Théâtre choisi de Corneille,* Hachette, Paris, n. d.

Schlumberger, Jean: *Plaisir à Corneille,* Gallimard, Paris, 1936.

In the Introductions, after the quoted criticisms I append comments of my own. These are usually taken, either verbatim or slightly altered, from my *Studies in French-classical Tragedy.*

Dr. C. Maxwell Lancaster of Vanderbilt University has in this book, as in former ones, checked my translations. I am much indebted to him for his kindness.

La Mort de Pompée

(THE DEATH OF POMPEY)

INTRODUCTION

The fate of Corneille's *la Mort de Pompée* (1642-1643) has been a strange one. In the dramatist's own day this tragedy seems to have been, next to *Cinna* (which it sought to rival [1]), the most highly esteemed by "the judicious," just as *Polyeucte* is their favorite today, although the *Cid*, then as now, was preferred by the public at large. When on January 2, 1685, Racine addressed the French Academy on the occasion of the admission to it of Thomas Corneille to fill the place left vacant by the death of Thomas' great brother, he said: "The stage resounds still with the applause which was elicited at their first appearance by the *Cid, Horace, Cinna, Pompée—* all those masterpieces" whose fame "will live forever on the lips of men." One may well wonder whether this enumeration of Corneille's "masterpieces," which omits *Polyeucte* and includes *Pompée*, simply records the consensus of critical opinion at that time—a proper and sufficient thing to do in such circumstances—or whether it represents also the opinion of Racine himself, whose own achievement indicates literary ideals of so different a nature.[2]

At any rate, from that day to this the reputation of *la Mort de Pompée* has steadily declined. At the Comédie Française it was played more frequently than *Polyeucte, Héraclius,* or *Nicomède* between 1680 and 1700, but only eleven times in the whole period 1815-1900. Its lack of dramatic qualities was well recognized in the latter part of the nineteenth century, though its traditional fame still preserved for it a qualified respect. Gustave Merlet said that despite its "historical insight and oratorical merits of the first order, we shall rank this play only at a certain distance below the masterpieces

[1] In his dedicatory epistle prefixed to *le Menteur,* he explained: "I have written *Pompée* to satisfy those who found the verses of *Polyeucte* not so potent as those of *Cinna,* and to show them that I could easily attain to loftiness again when the subject matter would permit."

[2] It is a curious fact that Thomas Corneille, under the subject "Rouen" in his *Dictionnaire universel géographique et historique,* in speaking of the work of his illustrious brother, mentions as notable plays which added to the great dramatist's fame after the *Cid* five tragedies: *Horace, Cinna, Polyeucte, Rodogune,* and *Héraclius*—but not *Pompée.* Did this master of melodramatic situation leave out so fervently admired a play because he could not stomach its deficiencies of plot and action? Naturally, he admired the sensational melodramas *Rodogune* and *Héraclius.*

3

which are admired without reservations." [3] Félix Hémon
declared: *"La Mort de Pompée* is a fine historical pageant
rather than a gripping drama; the very beauties which one
sees resplendent in it, and which are not mediocre, have
a certain heaviness and a slight coldness, despite the mag-
nificence—sometimes studied and forced—of the style." [4]
Similarly, Petit de Julleville: *"Pompée* . . . seems a fine frag-
ment of a historical poem rather than a real drama. . . . The
heroic steadfastness of Cornelia . . . is displayed in admirable
scenes where the sublimity of the style cloaks and conceals
somewhat strained feelings. Unfortunately, the episodic love
of Caesar for Cleopatra lends a slight frigidity to the action." [5]

Greater critics were less hesitant to condemn this play un-
reservedly. Jules Lemaître calls it "the grandiose declaiming
of a poet who never perceived the difference between Virgil
and Lucan." [6] And according to Emile Faguet, shortly after
the turn of the century, *"Pompée* . . . is a very mediocre
tragedy. . . . The two-fold nature of the plot is obvious. . . .
The two-fold nature of the interest is equally so . . . The play
is, moreover, full of rhetoric and declamation. It is, if not
filled, at least too often tainted with that insipid gallantry
which I doubt was taken for love even at that time. . . . A
single role, that of Cornelia, is excellent, though still marred
by declaiming." [7]

Admiration for the figure of Cornelia is perhaps the most
tenaciously surviving of the old, favorable views of this play,
but some twentieth-century critics do not share even in this.
Henry Carrington Lancaster points out: "As she appears in
only five scenes and over two-thirds of her role is put in four
long speeches, the effect she produces is oratorical rather than
emotional." This scholar, always conservative in his literary
judgments, would, like Merlet, Hémon, and Petit de Julleville,
assign to *Pompée* a place beside *Rodogune, Sertorius,* and
Attila as next—but greatly—below the five generally acknowl-
edged major tragedies of their author. He challenges Cor-

[3] Pp. 109-110.
[4] *Cours de Littérature, Pompée,* p. 1.
[5] P. ix.
[6] P. 296.
[7] Pp. 153-154.

neille's own defense of the unity of *Pompée,* asking whether "a mere series of events logically connected" is enough to give unity to a play. He ends by saying: "There is . . . too much tendency to description in the play, too much effort to elevate the style to Pompey's dignity, too great a tendency to lengthen the speeches and give statuesque attitudes to the characters." [8]

Auguste Dorchain would appear to have a much higher opinion of some of these dramas of the second rank. He calls *Pompée* "the most magnificent political and historical tableau that has been produced by the hand of Corneille," and maintains that "the sole error of the poet is in not having held with absolute strictness to the program whose heroic austerity would so much better have exhibited his genius,"—in his having thought he should moderate this austerity by "an embellishment even more irritating than it is useless—namely, that gallant love which Caesar, who suddenly becomes a knight errant according to the code of an Amadis, professes for Cleopatra." Dorchain lavishes especial praise on the opening debate between the base King Ptolemy and his infamous counselors, and concludes: "Seek elsewhere in all literature, among the philosophers and moralists as well as among poets, for pages more powerful than these, where words are better employed in the service of ideas or reveal more perspectives in the soul of individuals and of peoples; you will nowhere find them." [9]

Robert Brasillach—a brilliant amateur in this field who is quite unawed by tradition—sees in *la Mort de Pompée* only Corneille's imitation of himself such as a writer with talent but without genius might produce. "The widow of Pompey, compact of insults, is not a character at all, no more than the other dramatis personae (save perhaps the dastardly Ptolemy and little Cleopatra). Drama has disappeared" . . . "this is nowise a tragedy but a chant, eloquent and vacuous, which presents to us a few bewildering pictures . . . in long set-speeches, overpowering and devoid of movement." But he observes that Paul Valéry "ranked this play above all others"! [10]

---

[8] Part II, pp. 500-504.
[9] Pp. 244-250.
[10] Pp. 234-236.

We may note finally Jean Schlumberger, whose task is to call attention to the best in Corneille. He can say only: "In the *Mort de Pompée* we come upon a work that is a strange medley—the most highly colored, the most ornate, of all—one in which his art is most arrogant and adjusts itself least tractably to what it should express; an extravagant, exhausting play, in which we pass continually from enthusiasm to distaste." [11]

I have said elsewhere[12] that Corneille "in depicting character and motivation approaches the complexity of Shakespeare and of life more nearly than any other neo-classical dramatist," though we cannot be sure with him (as we can with Shakespeare except in his very early or very casual work) that any surprising speech or act by a character is a subtlety, not a lapse. We have a striking instance of a possible subtlety even in this play in which Corneille was at times so little possessed by his subject that he could forget that a messenger is not an omniscient narrator and put in Acoreus' mouth a statement of what Pompey's thoughts were when he was falling beneath his murderers' blows. In Act V, Acoreus tells Cleopatra that her brother Ptolemy died heroically, and we are apt to think that this is but another observance of the custom of dramatists in monarchical France to represent a king as cutting a fine figure when he dies, no matter how despicable his life. But if we note the facts which Acoreus tells of Ptolemy's death instead of the way in which they are told, we see that there was nothing heroic about it. On hearing Caesar command the legionaries to take him alive, he is panic-stricken at the thought of what fate may be reserved for him; like a cornered rat he throws himself upon them and does considerable mischief among these foes *who will not strike back;* then, exhausted and espying a possible means of escape, he scuttles away to seek refuge in a boat near by, and so is drowned ignominiously—like the human rat that he consistently has been. But to put a fine face on these sorry details is exactly what any tactful messenger would do who had to recount

[11] P. 97.

[12] First in my Introduction to *The Chief Plays of Corneille,* Princeton, 1952, pp. 47-48.

them to one who was at once Ptolemy's sister and the messenger's mistress and sovereign. Was Corneille aware of all this, or was he merely observing the convention that a king in a play must not die abjectly?

It may seem to us to have been too dangerous a finesse to pretend to observe this convention but really portray with a covertness entirely true to life the inglorious end of an inglorious monarch. But we must remember that Shakespeare once took, quite certainly, a similar and much more serious risk: he ostensibly honored his king's ancestor Banquo with a contrast of his noble loyalty and Macbeth's murderous treachery, but really reveals covertly that Banquo, to further his own ends, concealed his suspicions of Macbeth's guilt, to which he was therefore, in some sense, an accomplice-after-the-fact.

CHARACTERS IN THE PLAY

JULIUS CAESAR.

MARK ANTONY,
LEPIDUS, } *his lieutenants.*

CORNELIA, *Pompey's wife.*

PTOLEMY, *King of Egypt.*

CLEOPATRA, *Ptolemy's sister.*

PHOTINUS, *Ptolemy's chief counselor.*

ACHILLAS, *commander of the Egyptian army.*

SEPTIMIUS, *a Roman soldier, formerly a tribune, now in the service of Ptolemy.*

CHARMIAN, *maid of honor of Cleopatra.*

ACOREUS, *an esquire of Cleopatra.*

PHILIP, *a freedman of Pompey.*

Roman soldiers.

Egyptian soldiers.

The scene represents a room in the palace of Ptolemy, in Alexandria.

The Death of Pompey

ACT I

Ptolemy, Photinus, Achillas, *and* Septimius *are discovered.*

Ptolemy. Fate hath now spoken; we have learned her choice
Between the father-in-law and son-in-law.
When the gods stood aghast and seemed divided,
What they dared not decide, battle decided.
Pharsalia's waters stained with blood and swollen
By that poured forth in this unnatural strife,
The fearsome wreckage of arms, eagles, chariots,
Scattered confusedly on her reeking plains,
Mountains of dead denied their final rites
Whom nature forces to avenge themselves
By the stench wafted from their rotting bodies
Which warreth on the remnant left alive—
These are the signs wherewith, by the sword's verdict,
Caesar is justified, Pompey condemned.
 That hapless leader of the Optimates
Whom Fortune hath abandoned to disaster,
Will be a great example in men's memory
Of how a hero's destiny can change.
He flees now, he who always hitherto
Hath been triumphant and a conqueror
As prosperous as he was noble-souled—
Flees, and within our ports, our walls, our cities,
Seeks a safe refuge from his father-in-law,
Proud in defeat still, in those very places
Where the gods found one erstwhile from the Titans.
He deems that these same climes, in war's despite,
That sheltered deities can shelter men
And when at last involved in his disaster
Can prop the fortunes of a shaken world.
 Yes, Pompey bears here with him his world's fate,
And fain would have our Egypt, land of marvels,
Be liberty's defense or sepulcher
And raise him from his fall or fall with him.
'Tis about this, my friends, we must decide.
He brings us victors' wreaths or heaven's dire bolts.

9

He crowned my father; he puts me in peril.
He gave us Memphis and now makes us hazard
Its loss. We have to welcome him or quickly
Kill him,—follow his leadership or hurl him
Headlong to the abyss. One course seems to me
Little safe and the other little generous.
I dread both being unjust and being ill-fated.
Whatever I may do, cruel destiny
Offers me great risks or great infamy.

    I must needs choose; and ye must needs consider
To what choice your advice had best dispose me.
What as to Pompey? We shall have the glory
Of finishing or foiling Caesar's victory.
I can say finally that no monarch ever
Had to decide problems of such great moment.

PHOTINUS. When matters, sire, are settled by the sword,
Justice and right are naught but empty words;
And whosoe'er would at such times act wisely
Weigheth his power and not what is just.

    Consider, then, thy strength and look on Pompey,
His fortunes broken and his valor fruitless.
He flees not Caesar only, in this plight;
He flees, too, the reproaches and the sight
Of the Senate, more than half of whom now offer
A piteous quarry to Pharsalia's vultures.
He flees Rome brought to ruin, flees all Romans,
That he by his defeat hath put in chains.
He flees the mad despair of lands and princes
That would avenge on him their people's blood,
Their realms depleted of both men and treasure,
Their thrones laid in the dust, their scepters broken.
Source of the woe of all, he is their target
And flees the whole world 'whelmed beneath his fall.

    Wouldst thou defend him 'gainst so many foes?
The sole hope of his safety lay in *him*.
He alone could achieve it; let him perish.
Wouldst thou assume a burden that crushed Rome,—
'Neath which the entire universe succumbed,—
'Neath which great Pompey's strength itself gave way?
When one would aid those whom Fate overwhelms,

One oft is culpable in acting nobly,
And loyal friendship persevered in rashly
Hath brief fame followed by long chastisement,—
Fraught with misfortunes, whose resistless blows,
Though glorious to be borne, are not less grievous.
  Sire, draw no lightnings down upon this land.
On the gods' side and Fortune's take thy stand.
Accuse them not of cruelty or injustice;
'Tis they who make men blest; revere their work.
Whate'er be their decrees, show thou assentest;
And to obey their will destroy the luckless.
Beset on every hand by heaven's wrath,
Pompey comes hither to make some portion of it
Be visited on thee; and, scarcely able
To escape now with his head, which is about
To fall, he seeks a friend to fall with him.
  His flight here really is a crime against thee;
It shows an ill will, not a good will, toward thee.
He here takes refuge only to destroy thee—
And thou canst doubt if he deserves to die!
Thy hopes and expectations he would better
Fulfil were he to come with victory
Hovering above his vessels; then he here
Would have found naught save joy and festal cheer.
But since he is defeated, let him blame
Only the Fates for his reception by us.
I have no quarrel with him, but with his downfall;
I shall in sorrow do what heaven ordaineth,
And with the selfsame dagger meant for Caesar
Shall pierce reluctantly his hapless breast.
  Thou at the cost of *his* head canst from harm
Shield thine,—thus only save it from the storm.
Let his death even be called a heinous crime:
Rectitude is, in statecraft, not a virtue.
To think of whether deeds are right or wrong
Will utterly destroy a sovereign's power.
'Tis a king's duty to be ruthless. Timid
Goodness is fatal to the art of reigning.
One afraid to do wrong must be afraid
Always, and he who wishes to become

Most powerful must dare to violate
All moral laws, to flee as from dishonor
From virtues harmful to him and do promptly
Without qualms evil deeds to serve his interests.
Those are my views. Achillas and Septimius
Will champion, perhaps, different principles.
Each hath his own thoughts; but whatever *theirs* be,
One who spares not the vanquished need not fear
The victor.

ACHILLAS.　　　　Sire, Photinus speaks the truth;
But though we see the fortunes and the valor
Of Pompey fail, his blood is precious blood
Which even at Pharsalia heaven respected.
I in affairs of State censure not crime;
But this where needless should not be committed,
And what need is there now for aught so drastic?
One who aids not the vanquished need not fear
The victor. Neutral thus far, thou canst still be.
Thou mayst e'en worship Caesar if folk do so,
But though thou burnest incense unto him
As unto one divine, this is too great
A victim to be slain upon his altar,
And such a sacrifice to victory's god
Will leave too black a stain upon thy name.
　　To help him not suffices without acting
Against him, nor canst thou be blamed if thou
Behavest in this way. Thou owest him much:
Prompted by him did Rome give back the throne
Of Egypt to the late King Ptolemy;
But gratitude and hospitality
Have limits to their claims upon a monarch.
Whate'er a king owes, were it for his crown,
He owes more to his subjects than to any
And doth not owe aught when the debt is one
Which only at their blood's cost can he pay.
　　If all, though, should be taken into account,
What risk did Pompey run, serving thy father?
He wished thereby to show his power supreme
And gained in glory by restoring him.
He indeed served him, but with voice alone.

The purse of Caesar did more than his speeches.
Without that thousand talents, what Pompey said
Would have been little aid to our return.
Then let him boast no more his small deserts.
What Caesar did wrought more than Pompey's words;
And if these were a boon to be requited,
Thou canst for him speak as he spoke for thee.
Thus canst thou, and thus shouldst thou, recompense him.

To welcome him, is to welcome here a master
Who, though defeated, scorns the name of king
And in thine own land would give orders to thee.
Then close thy ports to him, but spare his life.
Yet if he must be slain, my hand is ready;
I gladly shall obey, and would be envious
If any arm but mine struck the first blow.

SEPTIMIUS. I am a Roman, sire; I know them both.
Pompey needs help; he comes here seeking thine.
Thou canst, being wholly master of his fate,
Aid him, drive him hence, give him up dead or living.
The first of these four courses would be fatal.
Then let me briefly discuss now the others.

To drive him hence, would win thee a great foe
Without obliging much the victor thus,
Since thus thou leavest him the continuation
Of a long, hard war by both land and sea,
Of which they both may equally be weary
And all whose woes they might avenge on thee.

To give him up to Caesar is no different.
He, if he must decide his fate, will spare him
And, with a show of magnanimity,
Against his will, boast a false clemency,
Fortunate to enslave him by thus granting
Life to him, and to please thus Rome enslaved!
But being forced to let his rival live,
He will no less than Pompey wish thee ill.

Thou shouldst relieve him of all crime, all danger,—
Make sure his power and save his good repute,—
By slaying the other faction's mighty leader
Take on thyself the crime and leave its fruit
To him. Those are *my* views; they should be thine.

> Thus thou'lt win one and fear no more the other;
> But if thou followest Achillas' counsel,
> Thou'lt not win either of them but lose them both.

PTOLEMY. Let us no more inquire which course is right
> But yield ourselves to Fate's all-mastering tide.
> I go with the majority, and myself
> Agree and wish to share in this new course.
> Long enough and too long Rome in her pride
> Hath deemed a Roman something more than man.
> Let us end, with her liberty, that pride,
> In Pompey's blood drown all her haughtiness,
> Quench the one hope that feeds such arrogance,
> And give these masters of the world a master.
> Let us help destiny, which in chains would place them,
> And lend aid in avenging all mankind.
> Rome, thou shalt serve; and those kings whom thou floutest,—
> Whom in thine insolence thou dost treat as slaves,—
> Will bow to Caesar with less bitterness
> When he will be thy lord as well as theirs.
> Go, then, Achillas—with Septimius go!
> Immortalize us with this heroic crime.
> Let whether it please the gods be my concern.
> I think they wish his death, since here they lead him.

ACHILLAS. Sire, I deem all meet when a king commands it.

PTOLEMY. Go ye, and hasten to make safe my crown,
> And ne'er forget that in your hands I put
> The fate of Egypt and of the Roman people.
> > (*Exeunt* ACHILLAS *and* SEPTIMIUS.)
> Photinus, either I am quite mistaken
> Or else my sister is. From the arrival
> Of Pompey here she hopes a different outcome.
> Knowing he hath my father's Testament,
> She feels no doubt about her being crowned;
> She thinks herself already sovereign mistress
> Of a shared scepter which his love bequeathed her;
> And, promising herself all from their long
> Affection, she now taketh half my throne
> In fancy, where her pride's rekindled embers
> Already lift new smoke into the air.

PHOTINUS. That is a matter, sire, I did not speak of,

Which ought to speed the death of Pompey. He
Would judge between the brother and the sister
According to the late king thy father's Will,
His host and friend, who chose to seize him of it.
Think what henceforth would be thy wretchedness.
I do not wish, in speaking to thee 'gainst her,
To break the bonds of a fraternal love.
Not from thy heart, but from the throne, I fain
Would banish her; for it is not to reign
When two together rule. A monarch who
Consents that this shall be is a poor statesman.
He quite destroys his power when he shares it,
And the realm's interests . . . But, sire, here she is.

Enter CLEOPATRA.

CLEOPATRA.   Pompey hath come, and thou, my lord, art here!
PTOLEMY.   I wait for that brave warrior in my palace
　　　And have just sent Achillas and Septimius
　　　To meet him.
CLEOPATRA.　　　　　What! Septimius to meet Pompey?
　　　Achillas to meet Pompey?
PTOLEMY.　　　　　　　　If these two
　　　Are not enough, go, follow them.
CLEOPATRA.　　　　　　　　Then 'tis
　　　Too much for thee thyself to welcome him?
PTOLEMY.   I must preserve the dignity of the crown.
CLEOPATRA.   If thou dost wear a crown, remember only
　　　To kiss the hand of him from whom thou hast it,
　　　Pay homage for it at the great man's feet.
PTOLEMY.   After Pharsalia is he still called "great"?
CLEOPATRA.   Had all abandoned him in his misfortune,
　　　He still is Pompey, and he did crown *thee.*
PTOLEMY.   He is that man's ghost, and he crowned my father,
　　　Whose ghost, not I, doth owe him what he hopes for.
　　　He can go, if he wishes, to my father's
　　　Tomb to receive his homage and his thanks.
CLEOPATRA.   After such boons, 'tis thus that he is treated!
PTOLEMY.   I well recall them. I see, too, his defeat.
CLEOPATRA.   Thou indeed seest it—with a scornful eye.
PTOLEMY.   Time orders everything and sets the price

Thereof. Thou, who esteemest him so highly,
Go and pay homage to him; but bear in mind
That he can even in the port find shipwreck.

CLEOPATRA. He can find shipwreck, even in the port—
How now! thou darest prepare him there his death?

PTOLEMY. I do what heaven hath inspired me to,
And what I deem essential for my kingdom.

CLEOPATRA. I see too well Photinus and his like
Have poisoned thee with their dastardly advice—
Those souls that heaven made out of naught but mire . . .

PHOTINUS. 'Tis our advice, yes, madam, and I avow . . .

CLEOPATRA. Photinus, I am speaking to the King.
Make answer for thyself and all thy fellows
When I so far stoop as to speak to thee.

PTOLEMY (*to* PHOTINUS). Her haughty mood must briefly be endured.
I know thy innocence and her hate of thee.
After all, 'tis my sister; hear without
Replying.

CLEOPATRA. Oh, if there yet is time for thee
To repent of what thou doest, free thyself
From them and their vile yoke! Resume anew
The lofty feelings banished by their counsels,
Those noble traits which heaven and royal lineage
Ever implant in all of kingly blood.

PTOLEMY. What! Entertaining futile hopes already,
Thou talkest as queen to me, talking of Pompey;
And thus thy pride with assumed ardor makes
Thy interests speak under the name of virtue.
Confess, my sister: thou'dst hereof be silent
Save for the Will of the late king our father.
Thou knowest Pompey hath it.

CLEOPATRA. And thou knowest
My sense of right alone makes me speak thus;
But if self-interest were my sole concern,
For Caesar would I act, and not for Pompey.
Learn thou a secret I hid formerly,
And do not taunt me e'er again with aught.
When Alexandria's presumptuous rabble
Forced the late king to leave his throne and country,
And he at length in Rome went to the Senate

Begging their pity for the outrage done him,
He brought us both with him to touch their hearts—
Thee still quite young, me old enough already
For this small beauty which the gods have given me
To lend my glance some flash of radiance.
Caesar was caught by it; and I had the honor
Of seeing him openly give me grounds to think so;
But he, finding the Senate hostile to him,
Had Pompey act, and his authority.
The latter served us but at Caesar's prayer,
Which was the earliest proof of their accord.
Thou knowest the result, and it rejoiced thee.
   But this was not enough for him who loved me:
After he used that great man for our aid,
Who won us promptly every voice in Rome,
He fain would second Pompey's efforts and,
Opening his heart to us, opened his purse.
We had because of his yet burgeoning love
The sinews both of war and of all power,
And the one thousand talents we still owe him
Placed in our hands again all our lost realm.
The King, remembering this in his death-hour,
Left to me as to thee his royal station,
And in his Will bound thee by his decree
To give me part of what he held through me.
'Tis because *thou* knowest not whence came our aid
Thou callest "favor" what is only justice,
And darest accuse him of blind doting when
Of all he owed to me he gave me half.
PTOLEMY.   Truly, this tale, my sister, is told shrewdly.
CLEOPATRA.   Caesar will soon come, so his letter saith.
Perhaps thine eyes will on this day be witness
Of what thou hast in fancy least imagined.
I spoke not as a queen without good reason.
I have had only hate and scorn from thee,
And thou who wrongly torest my scepter from me
Hast treated me as a slave more than a sister.
I even have, to avoid a still worse fate,
Had to speak fair thine insolent ministers,
From whom I feared till now dagger or poison.

But Pompey or else Caesar for all this
Will give me ample vengeance, and whatever
Achillas with Photinus does, the hand
Of one or the other will restore to me
My crown! Meanwhile, my pride will leave it to thee
To learn whose interests prompted me to speak.

(*Exit* CLEOPATRA.)

PTOLEMY. What wouldst thou say, friend, of this haughty soul?

PHOTINUS. Sire, her amazing revelations stun me.
I know not what to think, and being o'erwhelmed
By secrets I would never have suspected,
My hesitating, turmoiled mind cannot
In its uncertainty arrive at any
Decision calmly.

PTOLEMY. Shall we now save Pompey?

PHOTINUS. Even had we resolved to save him, we
Would needs now try to bring about his death.
Thy sister hates thee; she is proud, is fair;
And if victorious Caesar feeleth any
Love for her, Pompey's head is the sole gift
Which will suffice thee for protection 'gainst her.

PTOLEMY. She is a dangerous foe, with many wiles.

PHOTINUS. Whose wiles mean little beside such great service.

PTOLEMY. But what if, though 'tis great, her charms enslave him?

PHOTINUS. We must beguile her; but trust not me herein,
And to prevent her from undoing thee
Consult again Achillas and Septimius.

PTOLEMY. Let us go, then, to see their work; yes, let us
Now mount the tower, and, when they come back, make
Plans with their aid about the course to take. (*Exeunt.*)

A C T   I I

CLEOPATRA *and* CHARMIAN *are discovered.*

CLEOPATRA. I love him, but the blaze of love's sweet flames,
However ardent, doth not blind mine eyes,
And though the victor hath my heart, my sense
Of duty tells me what I owe the vanquished.
Besides, one who will love is too high-souled
To bear to be suspected of aught wrong,

And I would be unworthy of him if I
Aspired by any base means to be his.

CHARMIAN. What! thou lov'st Caesar, yet if thou wert heeded,
Egypt, on seeing Pompey, would draw sword,
Defend him, and by instant aid reverse
The tide of Fortune flowing from Pharsalia?
Love certainly hath little power o'er thee.

CLEOPATRA. Sovereigns act thus because of their high birth.
They so are influenced by their royal blood
That in them passions bow to rectitude.
Their innate loftiness of heart makes all things
Subordinate to their fair fame. In them
Naught is ignoble when they trust their instincts;
And if they show a lack of principle,
The advice of others hath corrupted them.
Such evil counsel completes Pompey's ruin.
The King would succor him, but will murder him
Thanks to Photinus; Ptolemy lends ear
To that vile knave and shows himself without
Honor; but if he lent ear to his own
Soul, he would act as doth befit a king.

CHARMIAN. Then, loving Caesar and yet being his foe . . .

CLEOPATRA. I keep for him my love free from all stain,
My heart worthy of him.

CHARMIAN.   Dost thou possess
His?

CLEOPATRA. I believe I do.

CHARMIAN.   But are thou sure?

CLEOPATRA. Know that a princess valuing her fair fame
Is, when she says she loves, sure she is loved,
And that, however keenly her heart loveth,
She dares not risk the shame of being spurned.
    Our stay in Rome lit love's flame in his breast,
I had there the first evidence of his love,
And since then even till now each day his couriers
Have brought me tribute of his vows and laurels.
Everywhere—Italy, all Gaul, and Spain—
Fortune hath followed him and love ne'er left him.
His arm hath overcome no lands nor peoples
Whence he hath not paid homage to my glance,

And the same hand which laid aside his sword
Still reeking with the blood of Pompey's friends
Writes of his longings and with plaintive phrases
Names him my captive on his field of victory.
Yes, 'mid his triumph he wrote me from Pharsalia;
And if his haste is not less than his ardor—
Or rather if the waves impede him not—
Egypt will see him offer me his troth.
   My Charmian, he comes here within our walls
To seek me as his battles' prize,—to lay
All of his glory at my feet and make
Subject to my decree that heart and hand
Which rule great kings; and a rejection by me,
If mingled now with his campaign's success,
Would leave earth's master reft of happiness!

CHARMIAN. I well might dare to take oath that thy charms
Boast of a power which they will not employ,
And mighty Caesar will have naught to vex him
If thy disdain alone can mar his fortunes.
But what dost thou expect, to what aspirest thou,
Since he already is another's husband,—
Since an untroubled marriage with Calpurnia
Holdeth his spirit bound by sacred bonds?

CLEOPATRA. Divorce is common now among the Romans
And can remove for me these obstacles.
Caesar knows well its practice and procedure:
It made room in his own home for Calpurnia.

CHARMIAN. He might in the same way abandon thee.

CLEOPATRA. Good fortune may be mine to hold him better.
My love perhaps will have advantages
By which I somehow can retain his heart.
But let us leave to chance whate'er may come,
And make this marriage if it can be made.
Though it should last for but one day, my glory
Will be unrivaled, for I shall become
At least for one day mistress of the world.
   I have ambition, and be it vice or virtue
My heart will 'neath its load be gladly broken.
I love its fervency and will ever call it
The only passion worthy of a princess.

But I wish honor to incite its ardor
And lead me without shame to lofty greatness;
And I would disavow it, should its madness
Offer to me a throne dishonorably.
Then, Charmian, be no more amazed to see me
Still defend Pompey as my duty bids me.
Able to do naught for him in his error,
I in my heart silently urge his flight,
Wishing some storm would drive his ships afar
And save him from his murderers' hands despite him.
But here is good Acoreus, come back,
From whom I shall learn certain news of him.

(Enter A<small>COREUS</small>.)

   Is it already over? Are our unhappy
Shores stained already with that noble blood?
A<small>COREUS</small>. Madam, I as thou bad'st ran to the beach.
I saw the treachery; I saw all its frenzy.
I saw the greatest of men's life cut short;
I saw him in his hapless fate die bravely;
And since thou'dst have me now recount to thee
The glory of a death that is our shame,
Hear of that death, admire and pity it.
   His three ships in the roadstead lowered their sails;
And, seeing our galleys in the port made ready,
He deemed the King, touched by his great misfortunes
And moved by thoughts of honor and obligation,
With all his Court was coming to receive him;
But when he saw that this ungrateful prince
Was sending but a skiff filled with his minions,
He instantly suspected his bad faith
And was seized briefly with some slight dismay,—
Then, seeing our shores and fleet bristling with arms,
He blamed himself for these unworthy fears
And limited his concern o'er what impended
To risking not Cornelia's life with his.
   "Let us," he said, "expose but this one head
To the reception Egypt hath for me;
And since I, only, need incur this danger,
Prepare for flight in order to avenge me.
King Juba is more truly loyal to me.

2 1

With him thou'lt find my sons and thine own father;
But even should they descend to Pluto's realm,
Do not despair so long as Cato liveth."
   While their love kept them arguing o'er their parting,
Achillas drew his fatal skiff alongside;
Septimius presented himself then,
Stretched out his hand to him, and, hailing him
As *Imperator* in the Roman tongue,
Said as the deputy of the young king:
"Come here, sir; come and get into this boat.
The reefs and sands lying beneath the waves
Make approach difficult for larger vessels."
   The hero saw the ruse and in his heart
Laughed at it, heard his wife's and friends' farewells,
Forbade their following him, and went to death
With the same mien wherewith he gave men kingdoms;
The selfsame majesty of countenance
Showed to his murderers his fearless spirit.
Unalloyed courage led him to his doom.
   His freedman Philip alone went with him.
It is from *him* I learned what I have told thee.
Mine own eyes saw the rest; my heart bleeds at it.
I think that Caesar's self could not refuse
His sighs and tears to such extreme misfortune.

CLEOPATRA. Do not spare mine, Acoreus. Tell the story
   Through of a death I have already wept for.

ACOREUS. They brought him: from the port we saw him come,
   And none among them deigned to talk with him.
   This treatment showed him what he must expect.
   As soon as they reached land he was invited
   To get out of the boat. When he stood up,
   Achillas gave the signal, drawing his cutlass
   Behind the great man, and Septimius
   And three base sons of Rome who were his followers
   Pierced with their eager swords the hero's breast,
   While even Achillas himself, horror-stricken,
   Marveled at the mad fury of the four.

CLEOPATRA. Ye who consign the world to civil discord,
   If ye avenge his death, gods, spare our cities;
   Lay naught to this land; see whose hands are guilty!

The crime in Egypt done was done by Romans.
What did their noble victim do or say?
ACOREUS. He covered with his toga's fold his face,
Accepting without question his cruel fate;
Nor looked he on the heavens which betrayed him,
For fear a glance would seem to beg their aid
'Gainst such an outrage or their vengeance for it.
No groan escaped him as he died, to show him
Weak enough to deserve his doom. Impassive
Midst all, he turned his thoughts to what good things
His life had held, and what will be said of him,
Deeming the treachery enjoined by the King
Too much beneath him to give mind to it.
Beside such crime his virtues seemed the fairer,
And his last sigh, wherewith his great life ended,
Showed to his murderers all of Pompey's grandeur.

His head, which finally lay on the skiff's edge,
Was by Septimius shamefully cut off
And set upon a lance borne by Achillas
As a great trophy after his great career.
They disembarked, and for his foul fate's climax
His body was given to the sea for burial
And henceforth will be tossed upon the billows
As Fortune and the winds and waves may choose.

His poor Cornelia, seeing these fearful deeds,
With long and piercing screams tried to prevent them,
Pleading for her loved lord with voice and eyes,—
Then, every hope gone, lifted to the skies
Her hands and, suddenly o'ercome by grief,
Fell on her galley's deck, swooning or dead.

Her people have, by dint of rowing, got her
Far from shore and regained the open sea;
But their escape is doubtful, for Septimius,
Seeing the survivors of his crime in flight,
Hath taken six vessels from the port to seize them,
Pursuing o'er the brine all that remaineth
Of Pompey still. Meanwhile Achillas bears
His prize of victory unto the King.
Everyone trembles and turns away his face
In general terror that the earth will open

Beneath his feet to avenge this great man's death.
Some await thunderbolts, and they all expect
A sudden cataclysm of all nature;
A crime so monstrous doth unseat their reason
And make them dread its monstrous punishment!
    Philip, however, on the beach displays
A noble spirit in a freedman's bosom
And seeks with watchful eye and anxious care
To find out where the waves will bring ashore
Their precious burden, that he if possible
May give it what is due unto the dead,
In some frail urn place the collected ashes,
And bury 'neath a little dust that man
Who had the loftiest fortunes in the world.
    But as toward Africa they pursue Cornelia,
Caesar is in another quarter spied
Coming from Thessaly; a fleet is seen
Whose numbers one could scarcely count . . .

CLEOPATRA.   'Tis he
Himself, Acoreus; that is beyond doubt.
Quake, quake, ye miscreants; here is heaven's thunder.
Means have I now to grind you into dust!
Caesar comes; I am queen; Pompey hath vengeance;
Tyranny is brought low; Fate's course is changed.
    But let us marvel at great men's destinies,
Pity them, and by them judge what we are.
That general of a senate the world's master,
Whose prosperous lot appeared above disaster,
He whom Rome saw, more feared than bolts of lightning,
Thrice triumph, in three regions of the earth,
And who in his last battles still beheld
Both consuls alike following his banners—
No sooner doth calamity attend him
Than Egypt's monsters can ordain his fate.
One then sees an Achillas, a Septimius,
And a Photinus suddenly become
The sovereign arbiters of his noble fortunes.
A king who from his hands received his crown
Basely abandons him to these Court-vermin.
Thus endeth pompey; and perchance someday

Caesar may meet his end in the same way.
Make false my augury, gods, who see my tears!
Favor my heart's prayers and his conquering spears!
CHARMIAN.   Madam, the King is coming. He may hear thee.

Enter PTOLEMY.

PTOLEMY.   Knowest thou the happiness we are to enjoy,
    My sister?
CLEOPATRA.   Yes, I know: Caesar is here;
    I am no more a prisoner of Photinus.
PTOLEMY.   Wouldst thou hate ever this faithful subject?
CLEOPATRA.   No;
    But I, now being free, laugh at his plans.
PTOLEMY.   What plans had he of which thou couldst complain?
CLEOPATRA.   I suffered much from them,—had more to fear.
    So great a schemer would do anything,
    And thou to all he counseled gavest ear.
PTOLEMY.   If I have followed his advice, I knew
    Its wisdom.
CLEOPATRA.   If I dreaded the results,
    I knew its ruthlessness.
PTOLEMY.   For his realm's welfare,
    Everything that a king may do is just.
CLEOPATRA.   This kind of justice is for me to fear.
    For my share of the scepter and its claims
    Usurped, it cost the life and head of Pompey.
PTOLEMY.   Never was there a stroke of policy
    Better to execute. If we had sought
    To succor him, Caesar would have surprised us.
    Thou seest how swift he is. Egypt, bewildered,
    Would be crushed ere she could defend herself.
    But I can now to this triumphant conqueror
    Safely offer my kingdom and thy heart.
CLEOPATRA.   I can make *my* gifts; see thou but to thine,
    And with thy interests do not confound mine.
PTOLEMY.   Thine are mine own, we being of one blood.
CLEOPATRA.   Thou canst say, too, "We having the same rank,
    Being alike sovereigns"; and yet I think
    There are some differences between our interests.
PTOLEMY.   True, for the realm which satisfies my soul

Hardly extends beyond the Nile's two banks;
But Caesar, placing his heart 'neath thy sway,
Will make thee rule from the Ganges to the Tagus.
CLEOPATRA. I have ambition, but in bounds can keep it.
It fascinates me, but it cannot blind me.
Talk not now of the Tagus nor the Ganges.
I know my measure and follow no false scent.
PTOLEMY. The occasion smiles on thee and thou wilt use it.
CLEOPATRA. If well I do not use it, thou wilt blame me.
PTOLEMY. I hope much from it, with the love that moves him.
CLEOPATRA. Thou dreadest it yet more, but whatsoe'er
Good chance is offered me, have thou no fear;
I wish naught that is not mine. I feel toward thee
No hate nor wrath, and I am a good sister
Though thou hast not been a good brother.
PTOLEMY.   Thou
Revealest, however, some slight trace of scorn.
CLEOPATRA. Time orders everything and sets the price
Thereof.
PTOLEMY.   Thy line of conduct shows it plainly.
CLEOPATRA. Caesar hath come now, and thou hast a master.
PTOLEMY. He is the whole world's master; I make him mine.
CLEOPATRA. Go, pay him homage; I shall await his.
Go; thine is not too much for him to have.
I shall preserve the dignity of the crown.
Photinus comes to help thee welcome him
Aright. Discuss with *him* what is thy duty.
                              (*Exit* CLEOPATRA. *Enter* PHOTINUS.)
PTOLEMY (*to* PHOTINUS). I followed thy advice, but the more I
Spoke her fair, the more arrogant she grew,
So that I finally, angered by her insults,
Was on the point of flying into a passion.
My heart, whose caution her contempt destroyed,
No more had thoughts of Caesar nor his coming,
And despite all his favor would have put her
In such plight that she could complain to Pompey
Of it before she could to him. The haughty
Woman! To hear her, she is queen already;
And if great Caesar hearkens to her pride
And hatred,—if she is, as she hath boasted,

The object of his love,—from being her king
And brother, I shall needs become her subject.
   No, no! let us forestall her; it is weakness
To await the evil which one seeth approaching
And not try to defend oneself against it.
Let us not leave her able to scorn us further;
Let us not leave her able to charm and reign;
Nor let us, after all her vaunting, let
My crown reward her for her glance of love.

PHOTINUS.   Sire, give not Caesar any grounds for binding
Egypt to his triumphal chariot.
With his ambitious heart, which everywhere
Seeks only to bring slavery and war,
Inflamed with victory and the fierce resentment
Which all true lovers feel o'er such a loss,
Though thou didst but accord thyself strict justice,
He will embrace the opportunity
To avenge her whom he loves, and, that he may
Subject thee and thy realm to him, will call
Thy righteous wrath a crime.

PTOLEMY.   If Cleopatra
Lives, and he sees her, she will be our queen.

PHOTINUS.   If Cleopatra dies, thine own destruction
Is certain.

PTOLEMY.   Being unable to save myself,
I shall destroy that one who would destroy me.

PHOTINUS.   To destroy her with any joy in doing so,
Thou must safeguard thyself.

PTOLEMY.   What! to behold
My crown upon her head? If it must be,
O scepter, that my hand relinquish thee,
Pass—rather, pass—into a conqueror's grasp!

PHOTINUS.   More easily canst thou wrest it from thy sister's.
Whatever love he showeth at first for her,
He soon will go and thou wilt here be master.
In men like him love never hath an ardor
Which doth not yield to cares born of their greatness.
He seeth Africa and Spain still held
By Juba, Scipio, and the sons of Pompey;
Nor will the world accept his sway while yet

Survive these remnants of the opposing party.
After Pharsalia so great a captain
Would know his trade but ill if he allowed them
To get their breath or gave such valiant hearts
Time to recover from the blow that stunned them.
If he o'ercomes them and attains the goal
Of his desires, he needs must go to Rome
To found his empire and enjoy the fruits
Of his good fortune and his crime of State
And change the form of government to suit him.
Judge what thou then canst do.

                           My lord, meet Caesar.
Constrain thyself to please him; and, conceding
Everything to him, vouchsafe to remember
That what now takes place will decide the future.
Put in his hands crown, scepter, throne; without
A murmur, let him make disposal of them.
He doubtless will believe it right to ordain
According to the late king's hest and Will.
The value, also, of thy recent service
Forbids thy fearing complete injustice from him.
What'er he does, feign to consent to it,
Praise his good judgment, suffer him to depart;
Then, when the proper time for vengeance comes,
We shall have both the power and skill to take it.
Until that time, restrain those violent passions
Thy sister's scornful insults roused in thee.
Boasts, after all, are only empty talk,
And one who planneth deeds cares not for words.

PTOLEMY.   Ah, thou restorest to me both life and crown!
A wise adviser is a king's greatest blessing.
Dear mainstay of my throne, let us forthwith
Offer to Caesar all, to gain back all.
Let us go welcome him with my whole fleet;
This victor will find such vain honors sweet.   (*Exeunt.*)

A C T   I I I

CHARMIAN *and* ACOREUS *are discovered.*

CHARMIAN. Yes, while the King himself is going in person

    To lay his crown before the feet of Caesar,
    Cleopatra shuts herself in her apartments
    And, without stirring thence, awaits his homage.
    What name wouldst thou give such a haughty temper?
ACOREUS. A proper, noble pride, worthy of a queen
    Who spiritedly and with lofty soul
    Maintains the honor of her birth and station.
    Might I speak with her?
CHARMIAN.   No, but she sends me
    To learn at once what joy Caesar displayed,
    How he received the dainty present given him,
    Whether he seemed well pleased by it or loathed it,
    Whether he dealt mildly or masterfully,
    And what he found to say unto the murderers.
ACOREUS. The sight of Pompey's head produced in him
    Effects not very satisfactory to them.
    I know not whether Caesar chose to feign,
    But thus far I have cause to fear for them.
    If they love Ptolemy, they ill have served him.
      Thou sawest him go forth; I followed him.
    His ships, ranged in good order, left the city
    But only went one mile ere they met Caesar.
    He came under full sail; and if in war
    He always hath by Mars been wholly favored,
    His fleet, which Neptune vied in favoring,
    Had the wind with them as they bore his fortunes.
    From the first sight of him our king, confounded,
    No more remembered that he wore a crown.
    His fear was plain 'neath his false show of pleasure;
    All that he did smacked of servility.
    I myself blushed for him and inly murmured
    At seeing there Ptolemy but not a king;
    And Caesar, reading in his face his terror,
    In pity spoke him fair to give him heart.
      He in a faint voice, offering the fell gift
    To Caesar, said: "Sir, thou hast no more rival.
    As the gods could not do in Thessaly,
    I shall give Pompey and Cornelia to thee.
    One is already here; the other flees,
    But with six ships one of my men pursues her."

Achillas at these words disclosed the head.
It looked as though 'twere trying to speak again,—
As though at this new shame some spark of life
Breathed forth its misery in wordless gasps;
Its mouth, still open, and its vacant stare
Recalled the mighty soul now sundered from it;
And Pompey's dying wrath made a last effort
To reproach heaven for his defeat and death.
    Caesar at this sight, as if thunderstruck
And knowing not what to think or what to do,
Motionless, with his eyes fixed on that object,
A long while kept his feelings hid from all;
But I would say, if I might dare to guess,
That by an impulse natural to mankind
A certain perverse joy woke in his breast,
Of which his honorable, indignant heart
Was barely conscious. The delight of seeing
The whole world now submissive to his power
Flattered, despite him, being unexpected,
His soul, but this, though tempted by its sweetness,
Resumed nobility with little effort.
If he loves greatness, he loathes perfidy.
He judged himself like others, probed and studied
His feelings, weighed his weal and woe in secret,
Made his decision, let his tears flow freely,
And forcing himself still to cleave to virtue,
Showed himself noble by this touch of weakness.
He ordered the gift taken from his sight,
Lifted his hands and eyes to heaven, let fall
Two or three words against its ruthlessness,
And thereon, sad and thoughtful, remained silent
And deigned to answer even his Romans only
With distraught glances or with heavy sighs.
Then, having come ashore with thirty cohorts,
He seized the harbor, seized the gates, put guards
Everywhere, and by giving secret orders
Showed his distrust and his regret. Of Egypt
He speaks as master, and of his adversary
Not as a foe but as his son-in-law.
That is what I beheld.

CHARMIAN. 'Tis what the Queen
Expected,—prayed for to the just Osiris.
I shall delight her ears with this good news.
Do thou continue faithfully to serve her.
ACOREUS. Let her ne'er doubt I shall. But Caesar cometh.
Go, paint to her our people pale and anxious.
As for me, sweet or dreadful be the upshot,
I shall come tell her when I have seen the rest.

Exit CHARMIAN. *Enter* CAESAR, PTOLEMY, LEPIDUS, PHOTINUS, *Roman soldiers, and Egyptian soldiers.*

PTOLEMY (*to* CAESAR). Good my lord, mount the throne and govern
here.
CAESAR. Dost thou know Caesar, to suggest this to him?
What worse could hostile fortune offer me—
Me, who regard a throne as infamy?
Certainly if I took it Rome could boast
Of having had good reason to persecute me—
She who alike confers thrones and disdains them,
Who sees in kings naught that she loves or fears,
Who in our breasts puts with our blood and soul
Hate of the name of king, scorn for the rank.
That is what Pompey could have taught you. Had
He loved the offer, he still would have refused it;
And throne and king would both have been ennobled
By aiding him who re-established them.
Ye might have fallen, but such a fall would be
More glorious than the greatest victory;
And had your destiny not saved you from it,
Caesar would gladly have again upraised you.
Thou wert not capable of such generous conduct,
But what right hadst thou to slay this famed hero?
What right to stain thy hands with his brave blood—
Thou, who dost owe respect to the humblest Roman?
Was it for thee I conquered at Pharsalia,
And by a triumph too fatal to the vanquished
Did I that day acquire such absolute
Power for *thee* over his life or death?
Would I, who never could let Pompey have it
O'er others, let thee have it over him

Or let thee so misuse my arms' success
As to do more than I would e'er have dared?
  By what name, really, thinkest thou I shall call
This deed by which thou hast cut short the days
Of Rome's first citizen, and which, wrought on him
Alone, is more of an affront to her
Than that one which the King of Pontus wrought
On many thousands? Thinkest thou that I know not,
Or that I shall feign not to know, that thou
Wouldst have had no more scruples as to me,
And that, had I been vanquished, thou wouldst blandly
Have made him a like present of *my* head?
Thanks to my victory, homage is now paid me
Where, as a fugitive, I would have suffered
All kinds of wrongs. 'Tis to the conqueror,
Not to me, thou accordest all these honors.
If I enjoy them, 'tis through my success.
O deadly friendship, formidably zealous,
By Fortune governed and changing sides with her!
But speak! thou art too long stunned and dumbfounded.

PTOLEMY. I am, 'tis true I am, if e'er I was;
And thou'lt confess I have good cause to be.
I, born a sovereign, behold here my master;
Here, I say, where my Court trembles before me,
Where I have ne'er done aught save as a ruler,
I see a new Court 'neath a different sway
And can no longer act save to obey.
At thy mere sight I found myself bewildered.
Judge if thy words have reassured my mind.
Judge how I can escape from my confusion,
Born of respect and doubled then by fear,
And what a prince dismayed can say to thee
On seeing such anger and such majesty.
  In the amazement that hath seized my soul
At finding now in thee Pompey's avenger,
I still recall that if he was our helper,
We owed thee not less but e'en more than him.
Thy favor was the first displayed for us;
All he did later was at thy request;
He moved the Senate to assist wronged kings

As without that request he would not have,
But that great Senate's pious ordinance
Would have been little help without thy gold.
Thereby the flames of our revolt were quenched,
And to speak truly we owe all to thee.
We honored thy good friend, thy son-in-law,
Until he dared to pit himself 'gainst thee;
But seeing him, jealous of thy great achievements,
Become a tyrant and take arms against thee . . .

CAESAR.   Hold; let thy hate be satisfied with his blood.
Touch not his honor; to take his life sufficed.
Say nothing now which Rome can contradict.
Defend thyself without thus slandering him.

PTOLEMY.   I leave it, then, to heaven to judge his thoughts
And shall but say that in thy wars just ended,
Into which thou wert driven by many wrongs,
All of our prayers have been for thy good fortune;
That since he treated thee as a mortal foe,
I thought his death a necessary evil;
That his unrighteous hate, increasing daily,
Would seek for aid till he was in the grave,
Or else, were he to fall into thy hands,
We for thy sake must fear thy clemency—
Fear lest the feelings of a heart too generous
Would make thee use thy rights ill, and undo thee.
I deemed, then, that in view of this great danger
We ought to serve thy interests, sir, despite thee;
And not awaiting orders this time from thee,
I in my zeal gave them—the worse for me.

Thou disavowest my deed, call'st it a crime,
But naught is illegitimate that serves Caesar.
I stained my hands with it, to keep thine stainless;
Thou profitest thereby, while thou condemn'st it;
And the more foul it is, the more have I
Done for thee, since I have so much the more
Sacrificed my good name for thee, and since
That sacrifice, offered to thee in duty,
Assures thee of *thy* good name and thy power.

CAESAR.   Thou findest, Ptolemy, with too great cunning
Sorry pretexts and coldly-reasoned excuses.

Thy zeal for me was false if it could dread
What the whole world desired whole-heartedly,
And if it gave thee such o'er-subtle fears
That leave me no fruit of our civil wars
Into which honor drove me and to end which
I wish but that of vanquishing and pardoning,—
In which my deadliest and most dangerous foemen
As soon as they are beaten are my brothers
And my ambition is but to constrain them,
Hate gone, to live and clasp me to their breasts.
    Oh, how great happiness a war so tragic
Would throughout all the world have left if Rome
Could have seen ride together in one chariot
Pompey and Caesar, conquerors of their discord!
That is the great misfortune thy zeal feared!
O fear no less ridiculous than wicked!
Thou fearedst my clemency! Fear it no more.
Desire it, rather; thou hast need of it.
If I regarded naught but laws of justice
I would appease Rome by thy punishment;
Nor all thy deference, nor thy repentance,
Nor yet thy royal dignity, could save thee;
Thy throne itself would be the stage for it;
But wishing to spare Cleopatra's brother,
I ascribe all the treachery to thy flatterers
And I would see how thou'lt make reparation
For it to me. According to the feelings
Of which thou'lt show that thou art capable
I can adjudge thee innocent or guilty.
    Meanwhile, raise altars unto Pompey. Pay him
Those honors which are paid to the immortals.
Atone with instant sacrifice for thy crimes,
And above all choose heedfully thy victims.
Go, give commands for this, and leave me here
To talk with mine own men of other matters.
    (*Exeunt* PTOLEMY *and* PHOTINUS. ANTONY *has entered while*
        CAESAR *was speaking.*)
Antony, hast thou seen that lovely queen?
ANTONY. I saw her, sir. She is beyond compare.
    Heaven ne'er linked before in such sweet concord

So many virtues with such grace and beauty.
A gentle majesty lends to her face
An aspect to enslave the noblest heart.
Her eyes entrance, her converse is enchanting,
And were I Caesar I would gladly love her.

CAESAR. How did she take the proffer of my love?

ANTONY. As though at once not daring to believe it
Yet really in her heart believing it.
She with a modest and alluring protest
Says she deserves it not, but thinks she does.

CAESAR. Might she in turn love me?

ANTONY.   To doubt she loves thee,—
She, who from thee alone expects her crown,
Whose sole hope lies in thee! To doubt her fervor—
Thou, who canst lift her to earth's pinnacle!
Let thy heart fearlessly aspire to hers.
To Pompey's conqueror she must needs surrender,
And thou wilt find it so. She fears, however,
The scorn which Rome is wont to have for sovereigns,
And above all she fears Calpurnia's love.
But when both fears are banished by thy sight,
Thou'lt cause a hope full sweet to take their place
When for thyself thou'lt come to speak with her.

CAESAR. Let us then go and free her from these needless
Fears, showing her how deep are my heart's wounds.
Come, let us wait no longer.

ANTONY.   Ere thou seest her,
Know that Cornelia now is in thy power.
Septimius brings her here, proud of his crime,
And thinks to win a place high in thy favor.
When they appeared, thy captains, as thou badest,
Giving no hint of aught, have led them hither.

CAESAR. Let them come in. Oh, irksome, vexing news!
How cruel it seems to my impatient soul!
Ah gods! and could I not give to my love,
Unhindered, what remaineth of this day!

Enter SEPTIMIUS *and* CORNELIA.

SEPTIMIUS. Sir . . .

CAESAR.   Go, Septimius; go unto thy master.

Caesar cannot endure the sight of traitors,
Romans base enough to serve 'neath a king,
Having served once 'neath Pompey and 'neath me.

(*Exit* SEPTIMIUS.)

CORNELIA.   Caesar—for Fate, which in thy chains I brave,
Makes me thy prisoner and not thy slave,
And thou expectest not 'twill so abase me
That I shall pay thee homage and say "my lord"—
However cruel the blows that it hath dealt me
As widow of young Crassus and of Pompey,
Daughter of Scipio, and (to say yet more)
A Roman woman, I am still high-souled;
And midst all storms its cruelty hath brought on me
Naught makes me blush except the shame of living.
I have seen Pompey die and have not followed him;
And though the means of death were snatched from me—
Though a compassion cruel to my deep grief
Hath taken from me all help of waves or dagger—
Rightly I blush still, after such disaster,
That I could not die from excess of woe.
Death would mean honor, and Fate robs me of it,
To increase my misery making me thy captive.
I should indeed, however, thank the gods
That I on my arrival find thee here,—
That Caesar rules here, and not Ptolemy.
Alas, O heaven, 'neath what star was I born
If I owe thanks to thee for letting me
Encounter here my greatest enemies
And fall into their hands and not a monarch's
Who to my husband owed his throne and realm!
Caesar, heed less the outcry o'er thy victory.
Thou wonnest it through the bad luck that attends me,
My dowry both for Pompey and for Crassus.
Twice have I brought to ruin the whole world;
Twice hath a marriage ill-contracted with me
Driven all gods from the more righteous cause.
Blessed were my misfortunes, had those fatal
Nuptials, for Rome's good, given me to Caesar,
And had I borne with me, into his house,
The cureless poison of a malignant fate!

For do not think that I shall curb my hate.
I told thee, Caesar, I am a Roman woman;
And though thy prisoner, one with heart like mine
Asks naught of thee lest she forget her duty.
Do thy will; only hope not I shall tremble
Or bow; remember that I am Cornelia.

CAESAR. O noble, worthy mate of an illustrious
Husband, whose courage astounds, whose fate arouses
Pity, thy sentiments indeed show plainly
Who gave thee life and who a hand in marriage;
And one sees easily, from the heart thou hast,
Whence thou wert born and to whose home thou wentest.
The soul of Pompey and of the younger Crassus,
Whose valor was alike betrayed by Fortune,
The blood of the Scipios, our gods' defenders—
All these speak through thy mouth and light thine eyes;
And Rome hath in her walls no family
More honored by a wife or by a daughter.
    Would to great Jupiter,—would to those gods
Whom Hannibal, but for thine ancestors,
Could have defied,—that this belovèd hero
Whom heaven hath sundered from thee had not known
The Court so badly of a barbarous king,
Nor had preferred to put faith in that monarch's
Uncertain loyalty rather than in the old
Friendship he would have found in me; that he
Had not refused to let my arms' success
End his suspicions and dispel his fears;
And that, in short, he had awaited me
Without further distrust and thus had given
To me a chance to vindicate myself!
Then, trampling under foot discord and envy,
I would have begged him to vouchsafe to live,
Forget my victory, and love a rival
Glad to have conquered but to be his equal;
Then would I have won back his heart and so
Well satisfied him that I would have made him
Pardon the gods for his defeat, and he
Would in his turn, in giving me back his heart,
Have made Rome pardon the conqueror for his conquest.

But since Fate by his death, which ne'er will be
Paralleled, robbed the world of this delight,
Caesar will try to acquit himself toward thee
Of what he hoped to render to thy great
Husband. Enjoy, then, complete freedom here.
Only for two days be my prisoner,
To witness how, after our differences,
I cherish his memory and avenge his death,
And to be able to tell Italy
With what new pride Pharsalia filleth me.
   I leave thee to thyself, and go hence briefly.
Lepidus, choose for her a fit apartment.
Let her be honored—as a Roman lady;
That is, a little more than the Queen is honored.
    (*To* CORNELIA) Command, and all here will obey thee
     straight.
CORNELIA.   Ah heaven, what virtues thou dost make me hate!

A C T   I V

PTOLEMY, ACHILLAS, *and* PHOTINUS *are discovered.*

PTOLEMY.   What! with the same hand and the same sword
    Wherewith he had just slaughtered hapless Pompey,
    Septimius, driven forth in disgrace by Caesar,
    Hath passed beyond our ken in his despair?
ACHILLAS.   Yes, my liege; and his death can show thee what
    Shame he foresaw and thou must needs expect.
    Judge Caesar's nature by his wrath's slow kindling.
    A moment stirs and ends a violent passion;
    But indignation born of due reflection
    Mounteth with time and launcheth fiercer blows.
    Hence do not hope to see it moderate.
    He shrewdly becomes angered only after
    Assuring himself of his position; then,
    His power established, he hath heed of honor.
    He pursued Pompey, but holds dear his memory,
    Wishing to have, with well-feigned rage, the credit
    For avenging him, with profit by his death.
PTOLEMY.   Ah, had I heeded *thee,* I would have no master.
    I would be on the throne which heaven meant for me.

But kings quite often indiscreetly hear
Too much advice and make a wrong choice from it.
Fate blinds them while they tread a chasm's brink,
Or if some light does seep into their souls,
Its false illumination, dazzling them,
Plunges them into an abyss, then fails them.

PHOTINUS. Ill I knew Caesar, but since in his judgment
So great a service is a monstrous crime,
He in his body hath what will wash guilt from us;
There lies our pardon, and we there must find it.
No more I urge thee to submit, unmurmuring,—
To await his going hence to avenge thy wrongs.
Better can I adapt the cure to the evil.
Let us on him make good his rival's death,
And when our hands are equally dyed red
With blood of Pompey and with blood of Caesar,
Rome, viewing them alike, will deem herself
By thee alone delivered from two tyrants.

PTOLEMY. Yes, only thus my ruin can be avoided.
'Tis too much to fear him I made supreme.
Let us show that his fortune is our work.
Twice in one day let us decide Rome's fate,
And give her freedom as we gave her slavery.
Caesar, no more let thy deeds make thee vain;
Consider mine, whereof thine eyes are witness.
Pompey was mortal, and thou art no less so.
He had more power than thou; thou enviedst him;
Thou hast, like him, only one life, one soul;
And his end, which thou pitiest, should tell thee
Thy heart is vulnerable and can be pierced.
Thunder thy fill, and make thy justice dreaded;
It is for me to appease Rome by thy death;
It is for me to punish thy cruel lenience
Which spares in me only my sister's brother.
No longer will I leave my life and power
At the mercy of her hate or thy caprice.
Think not that thou canst e'er at such a price
Reward her love or punish her disdain.
I shall employ against thee nobler maxims.
Thou badest me just now make choice of victims,—

To choose them heedfully. I obey, and see
That I can choose none worthier than thou—
None whose blood's offering, whose pyre's smoke and ashes,
Can so content thy son-in-law's vexed ghost.
    But it is not enough, friends, to be angry.
We must discover how we can take action.
All of our fierce resolves perhaps are futile.
The tyrant's troops are masters of the city.
What can we do against them? To defeat them
What moment must we seize, what plan pursue?

ACHILLAS. We can do anything, as matters stand.
Against two thousand men thou hast six thousand,
Whom lately I, fearing disturbances,
Have kept prepared for all emergences.
Whatever Caesar's care, he feels safe wrongly.
The city hath a secret subterranean
Passage, by which one can with ease this night
Silently bring them here into the palace.
To go with open force 'gainst Fortune's darling
Would be to rush, thyself, to thy destruction.
We must surprise him midway through the banquet,
Drunk with the sweet joys of both love and wine.
The populace are ours. During his entry
Just now, I marked the aversion they displayed
When they beheld the pomp wherewith his fasces
Were arrogantly challenging our banners;
And at the insulting sight of such an outrage
Their savage glances were ablaze with fury;
I saw their anger scarce could be restrained,
And with the slightest urging 'twill burst forth.
But above all, the Romans whom Septimius
Had led, beset now with the terror which
His death inspired in them, seek only vengeance
By gallant blows for the disdain the haughty
Conqueror hath shown for them in their commander.

PTOLEMY. But who among us could come near his person
If at the feast his guards stand all around him?

PHOTINUS. Cornelia's household, among whom your Romans
Already have found brothers and near kindred
Whose bitter sorrow hath shown them their desire

To sacrifice this tyrant to their master.
These pledge their word and better can, than we,
Launch the first blows against the breast of Caesar.
His cunning clemency, or his folly rather,
Which thinks to win Rome o'er to him by treating
Cornelia well, will doubtless give to them
Free enough access to him to assure
The consummation of this great design.
  But here is Cleopatra now. Dissemble,
Sire; display naught but weakness, naught but fear.
We shall take leave of thee as odious objects
Whose sight would be offensive to her eyes.
PTOLEMY. I shall rejoin you. Go.

  Exeunt ACHILLAS *and* PHOTINUS. *Enter* CLEOPATRA, ACOREUS,
  and CHARMIAN.

CLEOPATRA.   I have seen Caesar,
 My brother, and striven my best against his anger.
PTOLEMY. Thou art most generous, and I had expected
 This sisterly act of service thou hast done me.
 But thy illustrious lover left thee soon.
CLEOPATRA. About some discord broken out in the city.
 He wished himself to allay an altercation
 Of certain soldiers with our citizens;
 And I, I wished to say again to thee
 That thou needst fear naught for thy life or throne,
 And that the mighty Caesar blames thy actions
 With less wrath than compassion. He pities thee
 For hearkening to those base politicians
 Who inspire kings only to play the tyrant.
 Their nature is ignoble, like their birth.
 Vainly one elevates them to rule lands;
 Those born to serve know ill how one commands;
 Power o'erwhelms one when it is too great;
 And his weak hand, which crime in vain makes dreaded,
 Lets fall the burden that it cannot bear.
PTOLEMY. Thou speakest truly, and the evil results
 Show me my fault in choice of ministers.
 If I had hearkened to more noble counsels,
 I would now live with fair fame, like my peers.

I better would deserve the sweet affection
Which blood-ties give thee for an unworthy brother,
Caesar would in this palace embrace Pompey,
And Egypt would have restored peace on earth
And would have seen her king, still so-called rightly,
Their friend, perhaps the arbiter between them.
But since the past is quite irrevocable,
Let me, I pray, open my heart to thee.
    Ill have I treated thee, and thou art so good
That thou preservest for me my life and crown.
Conquer thy feelings wholly; by magnanimous
Aid, save from death Achillas and Photinus.
It is indeed their due; they sinned against thee;
But in their fate my honor is involved.
If Caesar punishes them for their king's crimes
The ignominy will recoil on me.
Their punishment is mine—my penalty.
Do violence for my sake to thy just hate.
How could the base, vile blood of these two wretches
Bring satisfaction to a soul so lofty?
Let me owe all to thee. Caesar adores thee,
And thou canst with one word disarm his wrath.

CLEOPATRA.   If I had in my hands their life or death,
Too much would I despise them to take vengeance;
But I have little influence with great Caesar
When Pompey's blood opposeth my desires.
I boast not of the power to bend him. I
Have spoken hereof already, but he would not
Listen; he turned our talk to other subjects
And neither heeded nor refused my prayers.
I wish, however, still to try again.
My efforts, when redoubled, might fare better;
And I dare think . . .

PTOLEMY.   He comes. Let me avoid him.
I fear my presence with thee might incense him,
His anger at my sight be made yet fiercer.
Thou canst act more effectually alone.

Exit PTOLEMY. *Enter* CAESAR, ANTONY, *and* LEPIDUS, *with Roman soldiers.*

CAESAR. Queen, all is peaceful; and the city, quieted,
Which but a small disturbance had alarmed,
No longer dreadeth the intestine strife
Of insolent soldiers with an unruly people.
But alas, gods! This moment that I left thee
Hath shaken my soul with a much worse disturbance,
And these vexatious cares that tore me from thee
Kindle my wrath against my very greatness.
I cursed it for so cruelly thwarting me
By having made my presence needed elsewhere;
But I forgave it at the simple thought
Of the good fortune my love owes to it.
'Tis through it that I have the soaring hopes
Which flatter my desires with wondrous prospects
And which make Caesar deem he can breathe vows,
That he is not unworthy of thy love,
And that he can aspire to win thy heart,
Having only the gods above him now.
    Yes, Queen, if anyone in the whole wide world
Could proudly bear thy love's chains higher still,—
Were there some throne whereon thou couldst appear
More worthily seated as its master's conqueror,—
I would go there—there—less to take it from him
Than to dispute with him the right to serve thee,
And would aspire unto thy favor's bliss
Only when I had worsted such a mighty
Rival. 'Twas to acquire a right so precious
That my ambitious arm strove everywhere,
And even at Pharsalia I drew sword
More to preserve that right than vanquish Pompey.
    Queen, I o'ercame him; and the god of battles
Aided me less than thy divine charms did:
They guided all my blows; they fired my heart;
This complete victory is their final work,
The outcome of those longings they bred in me;
And thy fair eyes, which roused my love that thou
Shouldst gloriously respond to it, have made me

The foremost man in Rome and in the world.
'Tis this proud title, now indeed mine, which
I come to make more glorious by adding
Unto it that of thy love's captive—happy
If my heart can so far prevail on thine
Thou'dst prize the first and let me have the second.

CLEOPATRA.   I know what thanks I owe the great good fortune
Wherewith such honor crowns me and o'erwhelms me.
I shall not keep my feelings hidden from thee.
I know what I am, and I know what thou art.
Thou deignedst to love me from my tenderest years;
The scepter which I have is one of thy
Gifts; thou hast twice given back my crown to me.
After this, I confess, sir, that I love thee
And that my heart is not proof 'gainst the shafts
Of so great virtues and of so great boons.
But this high rank, alas! this royal birth,
This realm anew made subject to my sway,
This scepter by thy hands restored to mine,
Are all alike foes to my maiden love.
They breed against me a relentless hatred,
They make me one to be disdained when they
Make me a queen, and if Rome hath the same
Mind as of old, the throne whereon I sit
Degrades me in exalting me, and these
Tokens of honor, like marks of infamy,
Make me forever unworthy of thy love.
   Yet I still dare, when I behold thy power,
To let my heart's desires hope loftily.
I know so great a man, so oft victorious,
By rights should triumph over Rome's caprices,
And the blind horror she hath always had
Of kings can yield by thy command to laws
More reasonable. I know thou canst o'ercome
All other obstacles. Such was thy promise
To me, and I await these miracles.
Thine arm wrought others greater at Pharsalia,
And I shall ask them of no god but thee.

CAESAR.   All miracles are easy for my love.
I need but hie me unto Africa

4 4

And show my banners to the trembling remnant
Of that unhappy faction which assailed me.
Rome, having no more foes to give me then,
Will in her impotence try to do my pleasure,
And thou wilt see her with a glorious welcome
Give up for thee her hatred and her pride.
One victory more, and I would have this ingrate
In Alexandria beg thee to espouse me,
And with a proper respect governing him,
Implore thy love to bring to birth new Caesars.
    That is the only happiness I aspire to,
The sole fruit of the laurels that await me,
Blest if my destiny had been even sweeter
And let me wear them without parting from thee.
But oh, to my love's grief my love incites me:
If I would e'er be thine, I needs must leave thee,—
Wherever my foes flee, must hasten thither,—
To consummate my triumph and win thee!
Permit me now, from these dear moments with thee,
To gain new mettle and new strength to make
Affrighted peoples still say that to come
And see and conquer are for me all one.

CLEOPATRA.   'Tis too much, sir, too much. But let me trespass
Upon thy kindness. Thy love prompteth me
To do so and is my excuse.
                    Thou giv'st me
The scepter taken from me, and perhaps life;
But if I may abuse thy too-great love,
I shall adjure thee, by its sweetest charms,
By the good fortune which attends thine arms,
By all I hope for and thou waitest for,
Not to befoul with blood what thou dost give me!
Be merciful or suffer me to be so,
And thus show all I have regained my place.
Achillas and Photinus are beneath
Our vengeance. 'Tis enough they see me reign,
And their guilt . . .

CAESAR.   Nay, give other proofs that thou
Art queen. Thou rulest supreme over my wishes;
But if my sentiments may have a hearing,

Choose subjects who deserve thy graciousness,
And assume o'er me only a just power
Nor make me a compounder of their crime.
'Tis much that for thy sake I spare the King;
And were my love not . . .

Enter CORNELIA.

CORNELIA.   Caesar, be on thy guard.
Thy death has been resolved on, sworn, arranged for.
They wish to add thy head to that of Pompey.
Look well to it, Caesar, or thy blood, poured forth,
Will soon be seen mingled with his. My slaves
Are in the plot. I turn them o'er to thee.
Learn from their testimony who conceived
The crime, its plan, and who are parties to it.

CAESAR.   O truly Roman heart, one worthy of
The hero who gave thee his hand and love!
His spirit that from on high beheld the mood
Wherewith my soul prepared to avenge his wrongs,
Laying aside all hate, saves me today
Through his dear other half left us on earth.
He lives, still lives, in her he loved. He speaks
By her mouth; he acts in and through her heart,
Inspires her, and thwarts this foul crime, thereby
Outdoing me, through her, in nobleness.

CORNELIA.   Thou flatterest thyself, Caesar, in believing
That hate hath given place to gratitude.
Think it no more; my husband's blood hath ended
Forever now all friendliness between us.
I await the freedom thou hast offered me,
To use it wholly to work thy destruction;
And I shall everywhere seek foes for thee
If thou darest keep thy promise unto me.
But I despite my thirst for thy undoing
Would throw myself between a murderer's blow
And thee. Too just are the desires I feel
For me to like to accomplish them by treachery.
Whoever knows of that and doth allow it
Shares in its infamy. If I wish thy death
'Tis as thy rightful enemy. My husband

Had sons; he will have grandsons. When they fight
In combat against thee, 'tis then I wish it,
That someone's worthy hand, inspired by me,
In battle and before thine army's eyes
May immolate thee honorably and fitly
Unto that hero's shade whom thou avengest.
All my activities and all my prayers
Will speed that vengeance; thy death will postpone it,
Thy safety hasten it. Whatever hope
Dares—or can—offer it to me otherwise,
My just impatience would have too much to bear.
When vengeance is deferred, it is half lost,
And when perforce awaited, costs too dear.
I will not go to seek in Africa
The thunderbolt I here see in thy hands.
The head it threatens must be smitten by it.
I could have given thine instead of that one
To Pompey. My hate had the choice. But this
Hate I nurse made between his vanquisher
And his assassin a distinction then
And did not think it right to avenge defeat
Till after punishing a deed so heinous.
  Rome thus would have it. Her belovèd brow
Would rightly redden at the shameful insult
Of seeing in one day her two loftiest heads
Fall 'neath a base sword after all their conquests.
Her mighty heart, which wrongly thou believest
Resigned to thy dominion, would want vengeance
Taken on criminals ere on her foes
And deem no blessing even liberty
If the Nile's crime should set the Tiber free.
As no one but a Roman could enslave her,
None likewise but a Roman should now save her.
Thou wouldst fall here and yet not be *her* victim.
Thy death would be no punishment, but a crime,
And without others like thee quaking at it
The example thou shouldst be would perish with thee.
Avenge Rome for the ill-given aid of Egypt;
And I shall, if I can, avenge Pharsalia.
Go; lose no time; it presseth. Farewell. Thou

Canst boast that I have once prayed for thy safety.

(*Exit* CORNELIA.)

CAESAR.   Her spirit astounds me no less than their daring.
Queen, see for whom thou askedst me for mercy.

CLEOPATRA.   I have no more to say to thee. Go, go, sir.
Avenge upon these miscreants their faith-breaking.
'Tis aimed at me more than thee. 'Tis *my* death
They long for. 'Tis against my power that these
Perfidious men conspire. To overthrow it
They in blind rage attack my prop and stay,
And by thy death seek to proceed to mine.
But I amid my feelings of just anger
Cannot forget their leader is my brother.
Sir, wilt thou think of that? Can I persuade
Thy wrathful heart to vouchsafe to remember?

CAESAR.   Yes, I shall recollect thy generous nature
Wishes to pardon him for his birth's sake.
Farewell. Fear naught. Achillas and Photinus
Are not folk to undo my glorious fortunes.
To rout them and all their accomplices,
I need but to display my preparations
For carrying out death-sentences, and send
Forth as the executioners picked soldiers
Who proudly carry axes for their banners.

(*Exeunt* CAESAR *and the Roman soldiers.*)

CLEOPATRA.   Do not leave Caesar; go thou, good Acoreus.
Help him prevent my death, which hath been vowed;
And when he punishes our enemies,
Make him remember what he promised me.
Watch o'er the King amid the heat of battle;
Save one of mine own blood to spare me tears.

ACOREUS.   Be assured, madam, that death shall not have him
If my painstaking loyalty can save him.   (*Exit* ACOREUS.)

A C T   V

CORNELIA, *holding a small urn in her hand, and* PHILIP *are discovered.*

CORNELIA.   Mine eyes, can I believe you? Is it no dream
Which at my sad wish cheats me with delusions?

I again see thee, Philip? and through thee
My beloved husband hath received a pyre's
Honors? This urn I hold contains his ashes?
   O thou sweet, dreadful object of my sorrow,
Eternal theme for hatred and for pity,
Remains of the great Pompey, hear his wife!
From me look not for tears nor for repinings.
Not thus a great soul dealeth with its woes.
A trivial grief findeth in speech diversion;
He who laments seeks to console himself.
For me, I call the mightiest gods to witness—
Nay, more, I call to witness thine own self,
For over my wracked heart thou hast more power
Than have my vows to gods who ill preserved thee.
I swear by thee, then, piteous remains,
My sole divinity after that dire deed,
By thee, who canst alone here solace me,
Never to lose mine ardor to avenge thee.
Ptolemy hath, O Rome, by base contrivance
Made sacrifice to Caesar of thy Pompey;
And ne'er will I within thy sorrowing walls
Come till that priest, that god, to him are offered.
Let me recall this, and my hate maintain,
O ashes, my sole hope as well as pain;
And, to help me someday destroy his conqueror,
Let all hearts feel all things that my heart feeleth.
   Thou who didst honor him on these vile shores
With a pyre small indeed but reverential,
Say, what good spirit put it in thy power
To give this hero his due funeral rites?

PHILIP. Drenched with his blood and scarce less dead than he,
When I had cursed the crown unnumbered times,
Madam, I turned my steps and, weeping, went
Toward that beach whither the wind drove the billows.
Long did I scour in vain, but I at last
Spied from a rock the body near a sandbar
Whereon the angry waves seemed to take pleasure
In feigning to cast it, then would snatch it back.
I plunged in, seized it, dragged it to the shore,
And having gathered wood from a wrecked ship,

I built for it a pyre in haste and crudely,
Such as I could forthwith and chance permitted.

    Scarce was this burning when a kindlier heaven
Sent me a partner in that pious office.
Cordus, an agèd Roman, lived near by.
Returning from the city, he looked toward us;
And seeing only a headless body there,
He knew by this grim sign that it was Pompey's.
With tears then in his eyes he said: "O thou,
Whoe'er thou art, whom heaven allows to do
A task so noble, thou hast very different
Fortunes from what thou thinkest: thou art afraid
Of being punished; thou wilt be rewarded.
Caesar is now in Egypt and avenging
Thoroughly him to whom thou art so loyal.
Of this work which thou doest, thou canst boast.
Thou canst e'en bring his ashes to his widow.
His conqueror hath received her with a mien
No less respectful than he would a god.
Wait; I shall come back."

                  He went, leaving me,
And soon returned with this urn, which he gave me—
In which his hands and mine collected then
All that the flames had left of the great man.
CORNELIA. Oh, how his piety deserves men's praise!
PHILIP. Reaching the city, I found strange disorders.
I beheld all the populace, in crowds,
Fleeing toward the harbor, where the King is strongest,
'Tis said. The Romans were pursuing them,
And Caesar, there, bathed in this people's blood,
Displayed a fine example of his justice:
Photinus in an executioner's hands.

    On seeing me, he promptly recognized me;
He took from me the ashes of my master,
And said: "Ye ashes of a demigod,
Whose great name will be hard for me to equal
Although I am his conqueror, see punished
The crime of those who have been treacherous to him.
Till altars can be reared to him, accept
These victims. Many more will follow them.

"And thou, go quickly to the palace. Bear
Unto his wife this gift I make to her,
This small alleviation of her grief;
And tell her that I fly to finish taking
Vengeance for him." This great man, at these words,
Left me with sighs, having kissed reverently
The urn, which he restored to me.

CORNELIA.   Oh, sighs!
Oh, reverence! Oh, how easy 'tis to pity
A foe's fate when he need no more be feared!
How hotly, Philip, one flies to avenge him
When one's own danger forceth one to do so
And the concern that one takes for his memory
Makes one safe while increasing one's own glory!
       Caesar appears magnanimous—that I grant him;
But the King seeks to slay him, and his rival
Is dead. His conduct leaves me grounds for doubting
What he would do if Pompey were alive.
Although 'tis noble, his peril cheapens it;
The clouds above him lowering dim its glory.
Love, too, hath part in making him draw sword;
Avenging Pompey, he aids Cleopatra.
So many interests besides my husband's
Hath he that I would hold I owe him nothing
For what he does for us if I did not,
As lofty souls judge others by themselves,
Prefer to judge his virtue by our own
And think he takes up arms for us alone,
Because in his place I would do no less.

Enter CLEOPATRA *and* CHARMIAN.

CLEOPATRA. I come not here to trouble a lament
Too natural to the grief which doth afflict thee.
I come to pay my homage to the ashes
Of a great man whose body hath been rescued
Now by a faithful freedman from the waves,
To mourn him with thee, and to swear to thee
That I would have saved, madam, thy heart's lord
If heaven, which is so cruel to thee, had given me
The power as well as the desire to do so.

Yet if, on seeing what it restores to thee,
Thy sorrow gives place to some little joy
And vengeance hath the power to solace thee,
I would say, too, that thou hast been avenged.
The false Photinus . . . But perhaps thou knowest it?

CORNELIA.   Yes, Queen, I know this traitor hath been punished.

CLEOPATRA.   His death, so prompt, ought to be sweet to thee.

CORNELIA.   If it hath sweetness, that is for thee only.

CLEOPATRA.   All hearts find sweet a thing for which they wish.

CORNELIA.   Our feelings, like our interests, are different.
If Caesar adds Achillas' death to his,
Thou wilt be satisfied, and I shall not.
The shade of Pompey needs another offering;
The victim is too vile, the wrong too great,
And this is no such blood as for atonement
His spirit and my grief would deign to think of.
The flame of vengeance kindled in my soul,
Waiting for Caesar, demands Ptolemy.
Unworthy though he is to live and reign,
Caesar, I know, constrains himself to spare him;
But whatsoe'er his love hath promised thee,
Heaven, more just than he, will not allow it;
And if just heaven can hear all my prayer
They both will die, each by the other's hand!
My heart will at this blessing, if 'tis granted,
Forget its woe and open wide to joy;
But if my great prayer asks too much,—if thou
Wilt slay but one,—O heaven, slay the King!

CLEOPATRA.   Not by our wishes heaven decrees events.

CORNELIA.   Heaven oft decrees the due results of deeds,
Rendering to criminals what they deserve.

CLEOPATRA.   It is not only just, but merciful.

CORNELIA.   Yes, but it makes us deem, from this first death,
That now its justice acts and not its mercy.

CLEOPATRA.   From justice it oft turns to kindliness.

CORNELIA.   My words, Queen, are a widow's, thine a sister's.
Each hath her reason for bitterness or mildness
Which rightly interests her in the King's fate.
Let us find out from the blood spilled by now

To whose prayers heaven hath responded better.
Here thy Acoreus is.   (*Enter* ACOREUS.)
CLEOPATRA.   Alas, his face
Shows to mine eyes naught but an evil presage.
    (*To* ACOREUS) Hide nothing from me; flatter not mine ears.
What must I fear, Acoreus, or regret?
ACOREUS.   As soon as Caesar learned the perfidy . . .
CLEOPATRA.   'Tis not his doings that I wish to hear of.
    I know that he cut off and blocked the passage
    Whereby his foes' troops were to be brought in,
    And sent for all his men to hold the place
    At which Photinus got his crime's reward;
    That, sore dismayed by *his* swift punishment,
    Achillas easily seized the abandoned harbor;
    That the King followed him; that Antony brought
    Ashore the soldiers left on board the ships;
    And that then Caesar joined him—and I doubt not
    That he was able to conquer still and punish
    Achillas.
ACOREUS.   Yes, his wonted success, madam . . .
CLEOPATRA.   Tell me but this: if he hath spared my brother;
    If he hath kept his word to me.
ACOREUS.   Yes, madam;
    He hath left naught undone to keep it to thee.
CLEOPATRA.   That is the sole thing that I wish to know.
    Madam, thou seest the gods have hearkened to *me*.
CORNELIA.   They have deferred, naught else, a death deserved.
CLEOPATRA.   Thou wishedst it at once; they saved him from it.
ACOREUS.   He would have had to second our aims better.
CLEOPATRA.   What saidst thou first, and what do I hear now?
    Explain thy words; I do not understand them.
ACOREUS.   No orders given nor care we took could save him.
    In spite of Caesar and us he wished to die.
    But he hath died, madam, with all the glory
    Which the most worthy monarchs leave behind them.
    His virtues, reacquired, beseemed his rank,
    And his death cost of Roman blood no little.
        He withstood Antony so valiantly
    That he ere long gained some advantage o'er him;
    But Caesar's coming changed the face of Fortune.

Soon did Achillas follow then Photinus;
He died, but died too nobly for a traitor,
Sword in hand, in his lord's defense. The victor
Cried vainly that the King was to be spared.
This filled him not with hope but with affright.
He feared it was a wile meant to reserve him
To suffer ignominious punishment.
He plunged into our ranks, pierced them, and showed
What valor which despair hath armed can do;
And, carried away by his mistake, he sought
Everywhere for that death which all refused him.
Breathless at last, after these mighty efforts,
Nearly surrounded, his best soldiers slain,
He saw some fugitives climbing into a boat.
Thither he rushed; and his men, following him,
In such great numbers thronged aboard this vessel
That the sea swallowed it with all its load.
   His death thus gives to him all honor back,
To thee all Egypt, victory to Caesar.
He now proclaims thee queen; and though no Roman
Hath stained a hand with blood of him thou mournest,
He shows to all of us his sore regret;
He sighs, he groans. But here he is, himself,
Who better than I can will show the sorrow
Wherewith the King's fatal disaster fills him.
              (*Enter* CAESAR, ANTONY, *and* LEPIDUS.)

CORNELIA.   Keep thy word, Caesar; give me back my galleys.
Achillas and Photinus have had payment,
Their king could not enjoy thy softened heart,
And Pompey is avenged as much as here
He can be. Here I can no more see aught
Except a fatal shore that offers me
The dreadful picture of their crime, thy new
Victory, and the loud clamor which at changes
Of sovereigns an inconstant people raiseth;
And midst all these what pains me most is seeing
Always my enemy who is kind to me.
Let me escape from this indignity,
And suffer all my hatred to act freely.
To this prayer I add one request. Thou seest

The urn of Pompey; there his head is lacking.
Withhold it not from me; 'tis the sole favor
That I can still with honor ask of thee.

CAESAR. 'Tis fit; and Caesar is prepared to give thee
This gift which thou hast such good right to wish for.
But 'tis fit, too, that after so much weeping
We should give true peace to his restless shade;
That a pyre lit by my hand and by thine
Should well atone to him for the other's shame,
His ghost should be appeased in seeing our grief,
And an urn worthier of him and thee,
After the flames are quenched and the rites ended,
Should enclose nobly his united ashes.
By the same hands which smote in war against him
Altars shall be erected to his virtues.
Prayers, incense, victims there will be his portion
Without his having aught but rightful honors.
I can perform these proper tasks tomorrow;
Give me till then; refuse not this great favor.
Exercise some restraint on thy impatience;
After that, thou art free—to go apace.
Bear such a precious treasure to our Rome.
Bear . . .

CORNELIA.   No, no, Caesar; not to Rome; not yet.
Thy overthrow and death are necessary
To make Rome ready for these belovèd ashes;
And though she holds them no less dear than I,
They must return there but in triumph o'er *thee*.
To Africa I bear them, where I hope
That Pompey's sons and Cato and my father,
With the assistance of a nobler king,
Will have on their side Fate as well as justice.
There shalt thou see, on land and on the waves,
Pharsalia's remnant arm a whole new world.
There will I go—to speed thy fall—and show
Throughout their ranks these ashes and my tears.
I hope they will make *my* hate their example,—
In battle follow urns instead of eagles,—
And this sad object will keep, living, in them
The will to avenge him and to punish thee.

Thou wouldst accord this great man his high due;
The honor thou doest him redounds to thine.
Thou'dst have me see it; I obey the conqueror.
But do not think thereby to touch my heart.
The loss I have is too irreparable.
My hate's source is too inexhaustible.
Throughout my life-days I shall cherish it.
I wish to live with it, and with it die.

Yet I confess, as a true Roman woman,
That my esteem for thee equals my hatred.
Just are both feelings, and they show the power
In turn of thy worth and my obligation.
One is disinterested, one prejudiced;
And in my heart both are compulsory.
Thou seest thy worth, when plots are made against thee,
Compels me to preserve him I must hate.
Think likewise to what hate my duty binds me:
The widow of Pompey makes Cornelia feel it.
I shall go, do not doubt, on leaving here
To rouse against thee men and gods—those gods
Who smiled on thee; who cheated all my hopes;
Who at Pharsalia served great Pompey ill;
Who, thunderbolts in hand, have seen him murdered;
Who will perceive their error and avenge him.
If they do not, my zeal, spurred by his memory,
Can well, without their aid, wrest victory from thee;
And if my efforts all should be in vain,
What I cannot do, Cleopatra will.
I know what love thou hast, how strong it is,
That thou well knowest the process of divorce,
That thy love blinds thee, and that to espouse her
Rome hath no laws which thou wilt not dare break;
But do thou know that then the youth of Rome
Will deem naught wrong to do 'gainst a queen's husband,
And that thy friends, indignant at this marriage,
Will with thy blood avenge their flouted counsels.
Thy death do I delay by my delaying
Thy kisses now. Farewell. I wait for thee
To keep tomorrow thy pledged word to me.

(*Exit* CORNELIA.)

CLEOPATRA.　Rather than let me, sir, unto these dangers
　　　　Expose thee, end in me the source of them.
　　　　Sacrifice my life to thy life's good fortune.
　　　　Mine will be great enough—and I want none other,
　　　　Being unworthy to be Caesar's wife—
　　　　To live still in thy heart when dead for thee.
CAESAR.　Queen, these vain notions are the one resource
　　　　Which her great soul is in its helplessness
　　　　Permitted to possess by heaven. If she
　　　　Hath little power, she hath many thoughts.
　　　　She would desire less if she could do more.
　　　　The gods will bring to naught her prophecy;
　　　　And not less unalloyed my bliss will be,
　　　　Provided love prevails over thy fears
　　　　And thou for Caesar's sake driest thy tears,
　　　　And hearkening to my prayers, for a true lover
　　　　Vouchsafest to forget a wicked brother.
　　　　　Thou mayest have been told with what regret
　　　　I saw his preference to embrace despair,—
　　　　With how great efforts I then sought to save him
　　　　From the mad panic which had mastered him.
　　　　He to the end put no faith in my kindness,
　　　　And fearing to be killed, was finally killed.
　　　　What shame for Caesar, having so much power,
　　　　So much anxiety to do thy will,
　　　　That he should be unable, as it befell,
　　　　To carry out the first of thy commands!
　　　　Blame that on heaven, whose sublime decrees
　　　　Will punish crimes in spite of all we do.
　　　　Its slaying him makes thy lot the fairer shine,
　　　　For by his death all Egypt will be thine.
CLEOPATRA.　I know that I receive thus a new crown,
　　　　Which can be blamed on heaven and him alone;
　　　　But as it is, sir, life's fatality
　　　　That sorrow mingles with felicity,
　　　　Be not offended if thine arms' success,
　　　　Which gives so much to me, costs me some tears,
　　　　And if, although his treachery caused his death,
　　　　I hearken to blood-ties no less than to reason
　　　　And cannot look on my impending greatness

Without their voice at once reproaching me.
Deep in my heart I hear its murmur yet,
And cannot mount the throne save with regret.

ACOREUS (*to* CAESAR). A host of people, sir, packed in the courtyard,
With clamorous outcries ask to see their queen
And, all impatience, wail to heaven already
That they are given too late this priceless blessing.

CAESAR. Let us refuse them not the boon they crave.
Let us go, Princess; thus begin thy reign.
May righteous heaven, propitious to me, grant
That these long cries of joy may hush thy sighs
And leave within thy mind only the thought
Of how my heart is pierced with thy love's shafts!
Meanwhile my retinue and thy Court shall vie
In preparations for a great day tomorrow,
When they—busy alike with noble tasks—
Will crown the queen and make my peace with Pompey,
Let him have altars, her the throne ascend,
And swear to both a reverence without end.

Héraclius

INTRODUCTION

Strictly speaking, *Héraclius* (1646-1647) has not been a play of mooted excellence like the others translated in this volume. Comparatively little difference of opinion has existed as to its degree of merit. Those who see in *Rodogune* a genuine tragedy, though a tragedy tending toward melodrama, see in *Héraclius* a mere melodrama. Those who regard *Rodogune* as itself a melodrama, regard *Héraclius* as a more extreme one. No important critic has ever ranked it among the very best plays of its author as *Pompée* was ranked in the seventeenth century or as *Suréna* is ranked by some today.

It is included here because there has at least been some difference of opinion as to its merit in comparison with *Rodogune,* and because I myself wish to pose that question as properly a moot point.

The chief defect usually found in *Héraclius* is a bewildering complexity of plot. Corneille himself encouraged the view that this complexity is altogether too great when he wrote: "I believe it has to be seen more than once to be understood completely." Merlet expresses well enough the resulting misconception by saying that its plot is confusing "even to a reader." [1] The fact is that this play would be much clearer to an audience than to a reader; for the confusion lies mainly in the identity of two of the dramatis personae, and in a stage presentation, when they are before one's eyes, such confusion is lessened enormously, as anyone familiar with the theater should know.

Recognizing, then, as true—but minimizing—the difficulty in following the action with a full appreciation of all its nuances, we can find little but praise for Corneille's handling of the subject matter with which he dealt. "It could hardly be presented more clearly and dramatically than Corneille presents it," says Lancaster. "The material of the exposition is not given, as in *Rodogune,* by minor persons, obviously serving only to inform the audience of the situation, but is brought naturally into the conversation of those who are vitally concerned in the events discussed. . . . Confidants are eliminated, unless the son-in-law of Phocas can be considered

[1] P. 138.

one. . . . The style is vigorous, without padding or affectation." [2]

The great Lemaître—not only a great critic but himself a successful playwright, which gives especial value to his pronouncements on drama—wrote in substantial accord: "The situation is strange and poignant; the partial revelations which develop it are graduated with finished art; the denouement is extremely ingenious, and is unexpected although it has been prepared for from the outset." [3] Petit de Julleville called *Héraclius* "one of the most interesting plays in our classical drama," and added: "The especial beauty of this unappreciated play is that all the roles are 'sympathetic,' even that of the tyrant Phocas, whose heart is torn, hard though it be, when he sees these two young men—one of whom is his son, but he does not know which—both disown this name, infamous in their eyes. . . . *Héraclius* is no doubt obscure, but it well deserves an effort to understand it." [4]

N. M. Bernardin was even more appreciative in his estimate of it. "What is marvelous in *Héraclius,*" he points out, "is that not only each act but almost every great scene changes . . . the respective positions of the characters and their state of mind. The construction of this play is altogether masterly. . . . It is a *tour-de-force* without an equal in all our tragic drama. . . . The place which it seems to me worthy of holding is, I do not say beside the *Cid* and *Polyeucte,* but at least beside *Nicomède* and *Rodogune.*" [5]

Much too appreciative, all would feel, when he sets this play beside *Nicomède*—or else not nearly appreciative enough of *Nicomède.* But why not beside *Rodogune,* and why not, perhaps, definitely or even considerably above *Rodogune*?

I have argued (first in the Introduction to my volume of translations, *The Chief Plays of Corneille*) that *Rodogune,*

[2] Part II, pp. 525, 528.

[3] P. 308.

[4] Pp. xii, xiii.

[5] *Les Clefs du Chœur,* Paris, 1914, pp. 81, 83, 88. Bernardin says further (p. 86) that, though *Héraclius* was "completely forgotten" at the time when he wrote, in the long reign of Louis XV it was played in Paris more frequently than any other tragedy of Corneille but the *Cid,* and at Court more than any but *Cinna,* and that it continued to have some vogue during the reign of Louis XVI, the Revolution, and the Empire, and down into the Restoration.

which is included there because of its long renown, is not only a melodrama but a bad melodrama. Its expository scenes are as clumsy and tiresome as those of *Héraclius* are adroit. Critics, down to René Jasinski, have vainly tried to find character-consistency in the figure of Rodogune herself. None of the dramatis personae in *Héraclius* is as impressive as Cleopatre, but they are in the main likable and generally behave as they might be expected to in the given circumstances. The only one who seems to transcend nature is Leontina: her sacrifice of her own son's life to save that of her prince may be accepted as credible in a world that worshipped royalty with fanatical devotion, and the monstrous plan she nurses, to rear the tyrant's son to be an unwitting parricide, is perhaps imaginable as a not unnatural consequence of her having thus done violence to a mother's natural feelings; but to be able to rear him with no lack of the appearance of parental affection, when feeling thus, is indeed melodrama and not life. She is, however, though the very mainspring of the action, not a primary character in the play.

No one in *Héraclius* is a mannered figure, thoroughly irritating today, like Antiochus in *Rodogune*, nor is *Héraclius* similarly marred with "gallantry" to any great extent, and it is almost as well written. It has no scene so theatrically effective as the famous last scene of *Rodogune*, but it is better sustained, with more interest and tension, throughout the earlier acts. Its denouement is not brought about by any of the principal characters, and is thus no logical consequence of the action which precedes it; but this is not of the highest importance in a melodrama, which we must never forget that *Héraclius* is—full of excitement, suspense, sharp turns, and striking situations. It is, I think, the greatest of French-classical melodramas, as *The Revenger's Tragedy* is the greatest of Elizabethan melodramas; and through its pre-eminence among plays of its own type, although this is a tawdry type, it merits a good deal of admiration and no very low rating.

In *Héraclius* an old and wide-spread superstition is curiously introduced: the idea that one instinctively feels an impulse of affection for one's unrecognized kindred when one encounters them. The French have a name for this alleged impulse: *la voix du sang*, "the voice of the blood," heard when the presence of a kindred strain is mysteriously sensed. It has often found a place in cheap, conventionalized literature, but never (at least since ancient times) in the dramas of a master-genius, unless he was working at a further remove from reality than usual, like Shakespeare in *Cymbeline*. Even in the melodrama of *Héraclius* Corneille did not create a world in which it is operative—save fleetingly, perhaps, in Martian at the news of Phocas' death—but he created a world in which people believe in it and, ludicrously, listen for it in vain. Phocas wonders distractedly why the *voix du sang* does not reveal his son to him; Martian argues that he must be the true Heraclius because otherwise he would shrink from killing Phocas; and Heraclius at length doubts his own identity because Phocas shows a love for him which he thinks may be possible only in one's real father. These believers in the *voix du sang* are invariably mistaken whenever it would have guided them if there were any such thing. Phocas finally imagines that Heraclius, being the youth whom he instinctively prefers, must be his son; and he is wrong. Heraclius hopes that his sister will by her instinctive sisterly feelings prove to him that he is her brother; and she is more inclined to believe that Martian is. She explains the love between her and Martian as a misunderstood emotion prompted by the *voix du sang;* and they really are not related. Never has any superstition been so derided elsewhere, save in comedy.

With the belief that it will aid the reader's keeping in mind the tangled identities of Heraclius and Martian, I have departed from Corneille's own practice of designating them, alike as speaker and in stage directions and in the list of the characters in the play. He presents them among the dramatis personae as follows:

> HERACLIUS, *son of the emperor Maurice, [but] supposed to be Martian, son of Phocas* . . .
> MARTIAN, *son of Phocas, [but] supposed to be Leontius, son of Leontina* . . .

and throughout *Héraclius* he similarly designates each as the speaker—and in stage directions—by his real name. I think it will make for clearness to designate each by the name instead which is supposed to be his and by which the other characters call him, until the identity of both is finally established near the end of Act V. It is thus that Corneille does with the name of the long-unidentified hero of his *Don Sanche d'Aragon,* and thus that the great dramatist's brother Thomas Corneille does with the hero of his famous *Timocrate;* and this is in keeping with the way these characters would present themselves to an audience in a performance of the play—at least to all members of the audience who did not have programs listing the dramatis personae. But to remind the reader constantly that these are not the real names of those characters, I enclose them in quotation marks—except, of course, where they occur in the verse lines of the dialogue itself.

CHARACTERS IN THE PLAY

PHOCAS, *Emperor of the Eastern Roman Empire; a usurper.*

"MARTIAN," *so called, supposed to be the son of Phocas. He is really Heraclius, the son of the late, rightful emperor, Maurice. He knows his real identity and that of the supposed Leontius.*

"LEONTIUS," *so called, supposed to be the son of Leontina. He is really Martian, the son of Phocas. He does not know his real identity or that of the supposed Martian.*

PULCHERIA, *daughter of the late emperor, Maurice.*

LEONTINA, *a lady of Constantinople.*

EUDOXIA, *daughter of Leontina.*

CRISPUS, *son-in-law of Phocas.*

EXUPERUS, *a nobleman of Constantinople.*

AMYNTAS, *friend of Exuperus.*

A page of Leontina.

Guards of Phocas.

Citizens of Constantinople.

The scene is laid in Constantinople (called Byzantium in the play); it represents a hall in the imperial palace on which the apartments of Phocas, of Pulcheria, and of Leontina open.

Heraclius

ACT I

PHOCAS *and* CRISPUS *are discovered.*

PHOCAS. Crispus, 'tis but too true: the fairest crown
Is girt round only with false splendors' radiance;
And he whom heaven makes choice of for a scepter
Knows not how heavy it is, until he wields it.
Countless sweet joys seem to be linked to it
Which all alike are bitter at the core.
He who thinks to possess them sees them vanish,
And fear of losing them balks their enjoyment—
Especially for a man who is, like me,
Of humble birth and rises by rebellion
To supreme power; who climbs when a mere soldier
To empire's throne; who wins this, and who keeps it,
Only by crimes. As in his mad ambition
He took lives to attain it, he believes
He sees dire storms about to break above
His head; and as he everywhere aroused
Horror and fear, he hath in the end only
Confusion and dismay.
                               I have aroused them
Very much, and for twenty years my throne
Hath by the death of great, famed folk alone
Been made secure. I brought unto their graves,
That I might reign quite unafraid, all those
Whom I have seen more worthy of it than I.
But vainly hath the blood of the Emperor Maurice
Been spilled, and his five sons were sent to die
Before his eyes, first to confirm it mine,
If they can even yet serve to rob me of it.
  One of them is now made to live again,
Thou tellest me, when those twenty years have passed.
Byzantium to conspiracy lends ear
And the populace, who love whatever harms me,
Welcome this false report with credulous
Eagerness, so impatient they already
Are to allow themselves to be beguiled

By any impostor seeking to destroy me
Who dares take the beloved shape of this phantom
And fain would be the idol of their deluded
Fervor.
    But dost thou know what name is used
In this unfortunate rumor?

CRISPUS.   Heraclius
  Is he whom it brings back to life.

PHOCAS.   Whoever
  Its source is ought to have devised it better.
  The name of Heraclius should cause me little
  Alarm. Too certain is it he is dead,
  And much too notable was his death for me
  To fear great consequences from a tale
  So idle.
     He was only six months old;
  And when his body was pierced through, more milk
  Than blood flowed from it; and this ghastly marvel,
  At which I trembled inwardly, was followed
  Almost immediately by my wife's death.
  I well remember he had for two days
  Been hidden, and would but for Leontina
  Have been long searched for. She betrayed him to me,
  And to reward her I gave unto her
  My infant son to rear, my little Martian,
  Of almost the same age, who had been made
  Motherless in that fateful hour. Herefrom
  See how ridiculous this story is.

CRISPUS. Howe'er ridiculous it is, it pleaseth
  The populace, who are credulous; but before
  They let themselves be carried away by it,
  Thou easily canst prevent their doing so.
   When thou slewest Maurice and his family
  Thou madest an exception of his daughter,
  Resolving then that she should have for husband
  This prince who shall reign after thee. The people
  Still love and reverence in her her father
  Maurice, also her grandfather Tiberius,
  And they will quietly let thee wear the crown
  If they are sure it presently will fall

Into the hands of her who is the last
Survivor of these emperors' line. No longer
Will they come rallying round her brother's phantom
When they behold his sister on the point
Of mounting to her father's throne. But hasten
This marriage. On the fields of Mars the Prince
Exposeth himself every day and every
Moment to countless perils, and had it not
Been for Leontius, in our latest war,
Thy hopes and aims would have been buried with him,
Since but for this young soldier's valor Martian
Would have been left there, either dead or captured.
Before he dies, if he must needs die, let him
Leave thee a grandson who is that of Maurice
Also, and who, uniting your two houses,
Will draw to thee the love left for his name.

PHOCAS. Alas me! What doth this wise plan avail me
If all is adverse to its being followed?
Pulcheria and my son seem in accord
In nothing but their shrinking from this marriage
As though from death. Their mutual aversion
Makes them alike in their rebelliousness.
The Princess quivers at my very sight,
And though she tries to feign respect a little,
Her pride of birth and memories of her family
Impel her ever to defy my power.
Her mother, whom I long desired to spare
And vainly hoped by kindness to win over,
Told her about her people; and the result
Punishes me for having let *her* live.

CRISPUS. Compulsion, sire, is needful with such folk.
To humor them makes obdurate their despite.
When mildness fails, the use of force is right.

PHOCAS. 'Tis thus that I today would curb her hate.
I have sent for her, not that I may cajole her,
But to receive my mandate and obey it.

CRISPUS. Here she is. *(Enter* PULCHERIA.)

PHOCAS. Madam, the time hath come for thee
To yield. The good of the realm forbids my waiting
Longer. It must have Caesars, and I have promised

Myself they shall be soon born to my son
And thee. 'Tis no great recompense for all
My care of thee in childhood, if I wish thee
To deign today, in payment for my kindness,
To accept the gifts I give to thee. They cannot
Bring shame to one of even the highest birth.
He and my crown deserve appreciation.
After thy long refusal of them I still
Offer them to thee; but know this: I shall not
Endure yet more of it. By thy consent
Or else by force I mean to have my will.
Thou needs must either cherish me as thy father
Or fear me as thy master; and if thou
Persist in hating me in thy stubborn pride,
He who cannot be loved can make himself
Obeyed.

PULCHERIA.   I have to this extent requited
The care with which thou boastest thou hast reared me,
That I as long as I have been left free
Have courteously declined to do thy will.
But since thou usest now a tyrant's power,
I see I must in turn explain my stand,
Lay bare my whole heart to thy rage, and speak
To my oppressor as an emperor's daughter.
    I would need no small cleverness to forget
I was Pulcheria and a child of Maurice
If 'twas thine aim to blind mine eyes so well
I would accept thy gifts as precious gifts.
Behold what things they are, which I refuse—
To thy dismay. Thou givest me, thou sayest,
Thy crown, thy son. But what, then, dost thou give me,
Since one of them is rightly mine, and the other
Unworthy of me, being born of thee?
    Thy generosity is hard to see.
Thou talkest of giving me what thou but restorest
To me, and since thou wishest to crown with me
Thy son, thou givest me back what is mine own
To give it to thyself. Thou'dst have this marriage
Thou darest prescribe for me to bring to *thy* house
The right to rule the Empire, and from being

A vile usurper, a cruel tyrant, make thee
A lawful sovereign, the just holder of it.
Taunt, then, no more my outraged soul with having
Spared me alone when thou slewest all my family.
That shadow of affection, that feigned kindness,
Was born of policy, and not of pity.
Thine interests alone made thee make exception
Of me; thou leftest me life, to serve thine ends;
And on thy throne uneasy, fearing the future,
Thou'dst seat me on it but to keep thy place there;
Thou'dst have me mount it, lest thou shouldst fall thence.
Know thou Pulcheria's heart, and cease to ply her.

    Yes, it belongs to me, this throne thou sitt'st on;
Thence I should see the whole world at my feet.
But, being with my father's blood still foul,
Unless washed clean by thine it could not please me;
And thy death, which my prayers attempt to hasten,
Is the sole means by which I wish to gain it.
Thus do I feel, and thus I wish to feel.
Let someone else, then, love thee as a father
Or fear thee as a master; for Pulcheria's
Heart is too lofty and too brave to flatter
Or fear the slayer of her own flesh and blood.

PHOCAS. I have compelled my wrath to accord thee silence
To learn how far thine insolence would go.
I see what makes thee err and flout me so,
And I still love thee enough to disabuse thee.

    Deem not my throne usurped from Maurice, thy father.
Think not thy marriage needful to maintain it.
I have reigned twenty years—reigned without thee—
And every right is mine through being chosen.
The crown I wear is not hereditary;
The army can, for good cause, re-award it.
Their choice entitles me thereto; and such
Our lot is, that a new election dooms us
To die. The one that chose me condemned Maurice
To death. I saw the immolation of him
Regretfully. The public peace required it;
Though loath, I had to allow it; but to restore
The Empire someday to his family,

I did all that I could: I saved his daughter,
And without need of warrant or support
Would share with thee what was no longer his.
PULCHERIA. A mere centurion of the Mysian soldiers,
Whom mutineers set up by their caprice,
Dares to boast arrogantly to me of being
The rightful holder of my heritage!
He, with no claims to the Empire but his crimes—
He, who of all my nearest kin made victims—
Thinks he hath cleansed himself of his black guilt
By saying their murder was for the public peace!
He does yet worse: he thinks I could believe him!
Let *me* now, in *my* turn, disabuse *thee*.
Know that if in uprisings formerly
The throne was usurped sometimes by elections,
With us the right to it is hereditary.
Only as being Tiberius' son-in-law
Did Maurice have it; and my rights beyond him
Go back to Theodosius the Great
And even to Constantine; and could I have
A soul so tame . . .
PHOCAS.   Very well! if thou wishest,
I shall restore it to thee—this high throne—
And consent further that thou shouldst impute
To my remorse what my good will hath prompted.
Say I restore it to thee and am kind
To thee to appease thy family's vengeful ghosts,
And all else that in any other fashion
Can warrant thy hate and give thy grief some solace.
By a last effort I would fain endure
The rage a bloody picture kindles in thee.
    But how hath my son wronged thee? In his cradle
Was he the judge or slayer of those of thine
I put to death? Do not his many virtues,
Which all the world admires, make him deserve
The Empire's throne? Have I had any hopes
Concerning him which he hath not fulfilled?
Is there beneath the skies a prince more faultless?
A heart like thine, so great, so generous . . .
PULCHERIA. His virtues I confuse not with thy crimes.

Yes, since my hate is just and nowise blind,
I see enough in him for the greatest realm,
Daily admire the proofs he gives of them,
Honor his valor, and esteem his person—
Inclined so much the more to wish him well
As he asks nothing, seeing himself unworthy,
As by long unresponsiveness he shows
That he dislikes what is demanded of me
Beyond his due, and as his heart, abashed
And made unhappy by thine aims, approves
Of my refusal of him and does me justice.
This noble son of such a wicked father,
If he were not to reign, could rouse my love.
The very fact thou'dst raise him to such greatness
Is the sole reason for which I reject him.
After thy murder of all my family,—
When thou hast left me neither father, mother,
Nor brother,—shall I make thy son their lawful
Heir? thus assure their murderer of their throne?
No, no, if thou believest my heart so generous
It separates his virtues from thy crimes,
Separate, too, thy gifts and offer me
Only thy son without the throne or else
The throne without thy son. Consider well;
And if thou fearest 'twould be too shameful for thee
To yield the Empire to a woman's hands,
Thou mayest yet see it better filled this day.
Heaven gives me back a brother who escaped
Thy rage. 'Tis said that Heraclius now
Is ready to appear. Descend, vile tyrant,
Then, from the throne and give place to thy master.

PHOCAS.　'Tis this, thou haughty woman—a new phantom
Which a vague rumor calls forth from the tomb—
That gives thee so great confidence and boldness!
Thou deemest e'en now this rumor worthy of credence.
But . . .

PULCHERIA.　　Well I know 'tis false. To assure thy having
This throne, thou in thy blood-lust wert too careful
To take the lives of all my family.
My longings for thy death, though, at this juncture

Cause me to love the author of the fraud.
The name alone of Maurice makes thee tremble;
Calling himself his son, he would be like him;
And this resemblance which his heart aspires to
Makes him deserve the Empire more than thou.
I shall abet the falsehood with my voice,
Declare he is my brother and my emperor,
And draw to his side all the populace,
Convinced by my acknowledgment of him.
    If any remorse gives thy heart just fears,
Quit the throne; let thyself like me be hoodwinked.
Take thou this chance to do that which thou shouldst.

PHOCAS.   Yes, I shall do it soon by putting thee
    To death. My kindness can no longer stay me
    From the right course. My patience is exhausted.
    He who allows himself to be insulted
    Deserves to be, and insolence left unpunished
    Becomes too bold. Rail, threaten, and defy me;
    Put faith in lying rumors; encourage those
    They have beguiled; decree me in thy heart
    What fate thou wilt; but make choice for tomorrow
    Of death or marriage.

PULCHERIA.   That choice is no great task
    For one who loathes the marriage and fears not death.

Enter "MARTIAN."

PHOCAS (*to* PULCHERIA).   Say, if thou wishest, that thy heart desires it.
    (*To* "MARTIAN")   Come hither, Martian, that thou, too,
      mayst hear me.
    This thankless Fury, so long contumelious,
    Still plots thy father's death and his son's death.
    She hath herself spread the report now current
    Of a false Heraclius, whom she will
    Acknowledge as her brother; but whatever
    The fraud that she can foist upon these rebels,
    Tomorrow they shall see her die or wed thee.

"MARTIAN."   Sir . . .

PHOCAS.   Have a care thou drawest not down mine anger
    On thee.

"MARTIAN."   Though I should treat thy love but ill,

I, being who I am, feel obligated
To tell thee, sir, that thus thou puttest thyself
In the wrong, and showest too much unjustified
Distrust in thine ability to reign
Save by alliance with her. My birth, without
A further claim of being married to her,
Sufficeth for me to reign after thee.
I lack not spirit, and would deem the throne
Itself a cause for shame, had I to owe it
To a woman's hand.

PHOCAS.   Well, she will die, and thou
Wilt not need hers.

"MARTIAN."   Deign, sir, to be more careful
Of thine own fortunes. The populace loved Maurice.
To slay his last remaining child would make
Their unrest dangerous in the highest degree.
The name of Heraclius hath half made them
Riot; thou wouldst see her death complete the work.
'Twere better to deprive her of the rank
Which she refuseth, let another reign,
Leave her a subject, and with a lower station
Punish her pride . . .

PHOCAS.   When Maurice in his grave
Can be so powerful, thou speakest of adding
To his supposed son, against whom I must
Defend myself, a genuine son-in-law!

"MARTIAN."   Sir, I have friends with whom she as a wife . . .

PHOCAS.   There is no friend whom a crown's lure can shake not,—
None whom its pomp and splendor will not blind,—
None whom she, after marriage, will not corrupt.
I tell thee, she shall die.

PULCHERIA (*to* "MARTIAN").   Ah, do not keep me
From joining, by a blessed death, my loved ones!
My blood's reek will make heavier the bolt
Which God holds poised to blast him into dust;
And my death, which will be the crowning horror . . .

PHOCAS.   By her thanks, judge her frenzy. I have pronounced
Her sentence, and it must be carried out.
If thou desirest her to live, persuade her
To love thee, or—again I swear, and will

Hear thee no more—her death shall on the morrow
Punish her for refusing.

> (*Exeunt* Phocas *and* Crispus. *Enter* "Leontius.")

"Martian" (*to* Pulcheria).   Wrongly he
    Tells himself that because of this threat I
    Expect to win some place in thine affections.
    Rightly dost thou refuse me, and I know why.
    'Tis not for us twain to unite our two
    Families. A different lot awaits us both.
    My pledged love binds me elsewhere. So doth thine;
    Leontius hath that, and is worthy of it;
    And I am fortunate in having his sister's.
    This valiant soldier loves thee; thou lov'st him.
    I love Eudoxia; she loves me no less.
    Their mother, Leontina, looks with favor
    Upon our troth; and whatsoever effort
    Is made by anyone to break these dear ties,
    The chains of love so perfect are so sweet
    That our captivity should be eternal.

Pulcheria.   Sir, well thou knowest my hapless heart. Leontius
    Hath much power o'er it; thou hast given him to me,
    And thy most noble hand augments the worth
    Of qualities whose distinction pleads his cause
    With me. But I must turn to other thoughts.
    When one must die, 'tis not the time to love,
    And when a soul prepareth to go hence . . .

"Martian."   Dread less the cruelty of a barbarous—nay,
    O'erlook my using that word; trying to help thee,
    I scarce can still consider him my father.
    Resolved to die to save thy life, I feel
    All deference for him fade in this desire.
    I am no more his son if he would kill thee,
    And I with but one thought fly to thy rescue.

Pulcheria.   'Tis rightly, then, that I begin to fear—
    Not my death, not the marriage he would force on me,
    But this dire peril into which, to aid me,
    I see thee, with thy great heart, blindly rush.

"Leontius."   Oh, my prince,—oh, madam,—ye had much better
    Decide to shun his anger's blow by marrying.
    In the name, sir, of thy friendship, and *thy* love,

Madam, have ye some pity for your fate.
Let the son's virtues, so unfeigned and numerous,
Conquer the horror thou feelest for his father,
And for my sake do not, now, both expose . . .

"MARTIAN."   What is this that thou sayest to me, Leontius,
And what is this that thou wouldst have me do?
Thou savedst my life; and could I, to requite thee,
Be willing to rob thee of thy love's reward,
And, as the puppet of a wrathful monarch,
Cover with shame thereby my honored name—
To my friend thankless, false to my beloved,
Cruel to the Princess, odious to myself?
    I know thee better than thou deemest, Leontius.
I know thy worth and what I owe to thee.
    His happiness is mine, madam, and I give thee
Leontius and Martian in one person.
'Tis Martian in him that now seeks to aid thee.
Let us be steadfast in the face of perils.
I go hence to make trial of prayers to Phocas;
And if I win not thy full pardon from him,
Despite the name of son and that of father
I shall become the deadliest of his foes.
Yes, if his cruelty on thy death insisteth,
I shall use open force to prevent that;
And if I stop at anything to save thee,
May a false Heraclius reign in my stead!
Madam, farewell.

PULCHERIA.   Farewell, too noble prince—

                                          (*Exit* "MARTIAN.")

Prince worthy of a throne gained without crime,
Worthy of a different sire! Oh, Phocas, tyrant,
Can Martian really be thy flesh and blood?
    But while admiring his courage, let us go,
Leontius mine, and try to balk the blow,
Ourselves, that threatens us. Thou hast thy friends;
I know some malcontents. The populace
Now are unsettled; let us lose no time.
Honor commands—love urges—us to act.

"LEONTIUS."   This tiger holds, as hostage, in his hands
    Thy life. I dare do nothing, for I fear

He will avenge on thee whatever dread
I cause him.

PULCHERIA.　　　　　Think not of it. The present danger
Bids us run every risk, dare everything.
Naught must be feared when all is to be feared.
Let us go find, this noble task to speed,
The safest means which soonest will succeed.

(Exeunt.)

A C T　I I

LEONTINA *and* EUDOXIA *are discovered.*

LEONTINA.　'Tis what I feared he in his love would do.
EUDOXIA.　Had he concealed his parentage from me,
He would have loved me little.

LEONTINA.　　　　　　　　　He revealed it
Unto thee most imprudently. Thou'rt a girl,
Eudoxia, and thou hast talked. Thou couldst not
Have learned this great fact and not whispered it
To someone false of heart, to someone frivolous
Or jealous of thy happiness, upon whom
As upon thee this secret hath weighed sorely.
'Tis thus that it is known, that we are told
The miracle that Heraclius lives,—
Thus that a tyrant, well informed, not troubled,
About the hidden foe who would have crushed him,
Will add *his* death soon to his former crimes
And for his latest victims immolate
This prince reared in his household as his son,
Thee whom that prince adores, and me who saved him.
Such fate is ours, since thou couldst not keep silent!

EUDOXIA.　I bear respectfully everything from my mother,
Who, if she would at all listen to reason,
No more would charge me with this vile betrayal.
For is not one indeed most worthy of death
Who, knowing such a secret, breathes aught of it?

LEONTINA.　But who today, then, makes it known to all?
Is it the Prince, or I?

EUDOXIA.　　　　　　Not he, nor thou.
Inspect, I pray, this rumor which alarms thee.

'Tis said he is alive; and his mere name
Thrills every heart; but 'tis not told in what
Way thou deceivedst Phocas, giving up
One of thine own sons to be slain in place
Of Heraclius, nor how, when Phocas later
Placed in thy charge his own son, thou by trickery
Still cleverer then madest an exchange
And, taking Martian, leftest to the usurper
This prince in his son's stead,—in consequence
Of which his son here passes for my brother
While Phocas thinks he is the other's father,
Deeming his Martian to be thy Leontius,
Who died, and loving Heraclius as Martian.
All this would now be told, had some imprudence
Made me confide this secret to another;
But the whole news is that 'tis said he lives,
None can tell aught of his life's history,
And as the paths it followed are unknown
To all, 'twould seem to some he must have fallen
Out of the clouds, and I know one who thinks,
In his credulity, that to punish Phocas
God hath brought Heraclius back to life.
But here he is.

Enter "MARTIAN."

"MARTIAN" (*to* LEONTINA). Madam, the time is past
For silence about our dark and perilous secret.
Thy tyrant in alarm at the report,
Which took him by surprise, hath made my fears
Only too just, and all too great the danger.
Not that he guesses aught as to my birth;
He on the contrary thinks the entire rumor
A gross fraud, and so far is he from knowing me
That, to defeat it, he intends to force me
Into the marriage he desires. He fain
Would use me 'gainst my name, which startled him.
I am the son of Maurice, and he wishes
To make him be my father-in-law, acquiring
The rights himself of so beloved a ruler
By giving me my own sister as my wife.

We resist vainly his impatience, she
With blind aversion and I knowing all.
He, ne'er suspecting the eternal barrier
Which nature rears to thwart a tie so criminal,
Threatens Pulcheria, who obstinately
Declines to do his will, and offers her
Tomorrow either marriage with me or death.
I made a fruitless effort to dissuade him;
Only by dying can she avoid this incest.
Judge if 'tis not time to prove who I am,
To cease to be the son of earth's worst man,
Slay him and save my sister in her peril,
And to my father give a fit successor.

LEONTINA.   Since thou dost fear only her death or incest,
I give thanks, sir, to gracious heaven that Fortune
Hath been so kind to us midst all these rumors
That we have nothing yet to fear for thee.
Thy great heart alone gives us grounds for fearing.
Temper thine ardent spirit; I pray thee, curb it;
And seeing suspicion still tells Phocas naught,
Be his son still; do not declare thyself.
As for the tyrant's threatening Pulcheria,
I have too many ways to stay his rage,
Prevent that marriage, or at least postpone it,
Provided thou wilt not expose thyself
To any danger. Assure me of thy safety,
And I will assure thee of hers.

"MARTIAN."   So fair
An opportunity will ne'er again
Be offered us. Thou seest a mighty people
Half risen in revolt, without the source
Of this change in their temper being known.
It seems that God, whose hand is soon to fall
On the usurper, makes himself his foe
And thus would hasten his just punishment,—
That by this great, confused report now spread,
He makes men's hearts ready for a new master
And urgently incites me to stand forth.
It is for us to do what he intends.
Let us show Heraclius to the people

Who are awaiting him. Let us not run
The risk that some impostor may deceive them
And that he, being armed thus with a name
Which I refuse to take, may on the throne
Wrested by virtue of that name from Phocas,
Punish me for too well having kept hidden.
It will then, madam, be no time to bid him
To give me back my name, my birth, my empire,
When he can of that name, already taken,
Avail himself to link me with the tyrant
Whose son I pass for.

LEONTINA.   Without giving thee
Unto the populace, to be their leader,
I can avert that danger, should it threaten;
But let us keep to the end this vital secret.
Put trust in me, not in the fickle throng.
What I have done for thee since thou wert born
Should make me seem, sir, worthy of such trust.
I will not leave my work unfinished; soon
Mine aims will be achieved completely. I
Shall punish Phocas, I shall avenge Maurice,
But none will share in this great act of justice.
I want the whole glory of it; 'tis my due.
Thanks to me thou wilt reign, as thanks to me
Thou livest. Leave thy fortunes in my hands;
Imperil not the fruit of twenty years.

EUDOXIA.   Sir, if thy love can hearken to my tears,
Do not expose thyself to utter ruin.
To slay the usurper, though entirely right,
Would seem, if done by thee, a monstrous crime.
The populace would think that heaven's dire justice
Had chosen his own son to punish him,
And, clinging to this fancy, they would loathe thee
As being a parricide when thus thou tookest
Vengeance for thy real father. Then the truth
Would seem a clever lie to cloak thy guilt,
And everything would be as though it were:
Such a supposed deed would so blacken thee
That 'twould eclipse the brightness of thy fame.
I know thy eagerness to avenge thy parents . . .

"Martian" (*to* Leontina). Thou, too, madam, art one of them,
and I
Give in. I say no more; 'tis past my power
To struggle 'gainst both love and gratitude.
Thine is this secret, and I were an ingrate
If without thy consent I dared to tell it;
And all my story, if not confirmed by thee,
Would needs be thought a fraud or a delusion.
I shall say, too: the Empire is more thine
Than mine, since to Leontius' death I owe it.
It cost his blood; and I, to pay my debt,
Will give his sister what he gave to me—
Not that 'twas duty which inclined me toward her:
Through his death I saw her who charmed my heart;
Through it was I fuel for the flames she lit here;
And her divine eyes with a single look
Made me do everything that was my duty.
    My heart, beloved Eudoxia, sought the throne
Only to see thee rule, ere long, the Empire;
And I desire to hazard all my fortunes
Only because I crave to share them with thee.
That is my single object. To shun incest
I need do naught save quit these fateful climes;
But if I take flight from that throne so due thee,
'Twill be through me alone that thou wilt lose it;
I alone will keep from thee what I owe thee.
Decide thou when and how I shall acquire it;
When thou desirest to reign, bid me to seize it;
But as I with good cause fear for my sister,
Extricate her today from her dire peril
Or I tomorrow will take counsel only
With myself.

Leontina.   Trust in me as to her fortunes.
Fear not her death, sir, nor thy marriage with her.

                        (*Exit* "Martian.")
(*To* Eudoxia). I need dissimulate with thee no longer.
His love empowers me to hide naught from thee.
Thou knowest mine aims in all that I have done,
And thou couldst help me hasten their achievement.
    The real Martian adores the Princess.

Let us both urge him on to serve his loved one,
And make his love avenge us upon Phocas—
Yes, arm the tyrant's own son's hand against him.
If I have reared him,—if I let him live,—
If I have brought death to Leontius
And did not make him follow him,—'twas solely
Because I hoped that someday, through ambition,
He might grow bold enough to take full vengeance
For me. I have preserved him only that
He thus may commit parricide.

EUDOXIA.   Oh, madam!

LEONTINA.   The very word itself e'en now dismays thee.
'Tis to such hands that we must have recourse;
'Tis thus that a usurper ought to perish;
And heaven's wrath, to rid the world of him,
Owes us a parricide when its lightning strikes not.
The task is ours to make its dread bolt fall;
Phocas will kill his son if not killed by him;
And we shall offer to thy brother's blood
Either the sire slain by the son or else
The son slain by the sire. The plan is well
Worthy of us; the crime beseemeth them.
Let us save Heraclius from them both.

EUDOXIA.   'Tis true that such a father does deserve
To die by his son's hand; but is it needful
That such a son should be a parricide?
And, knowing his noble nature, canst thou justly
So take advantage of his ignorance?

LEONTINA.   The odious origin of a tyrant's son
Makes him deserve to incur through a mistake
Foul guilt, and, though he hath won great renown,
Stain his soul thus with crime he knows not of.

Enter a page.

THE PAGE.   Madam, Exuperus is here and asks
For thee.

LEONTINA.   Exuperus! to hear his name,
How great is my surprise! Bid him to enter.

                                        (*Exit the page.*)
What purpose bringeth him to speak with us—

Him, whom I never see and scarcely know?
He hates Phocas at heart, who slew his father,
And his now coming here bespeaks some mystery.
I told thee that thy tongue would ruin us.

Enter EXUPERUS.

EXUPERUS. Good madam, Heraclius hath been found.
LEONTINA. Indeed?
EUDOXIA.   If . . .
LEONTINA (*to* EUDOXIA). Be thou silent!
                    (*To* EXUPERUS) When?
EXUPERUS.   Just now.
LEONTINA. And the Emperor hath ordered him to be slain?
EXUPERUS. The tyrant hath no knowledge at all of him.
LEONTINA. How so?
EXUPERUS.   Fear nothing, madam. Look, behold him.
                    (*Enter* "LEONTIUS.")

LEONTINA. I see none but Leontius.
EXUPERUS.   Nay, stop feigning.
"LEONTIUS." Madam, shall I think this Maurice's letter?
        See if the hand be his, or counterfeited.
        Tell me if what it says be false or true,—
        If I am *thy* son, or was he my father.
        Thou shouldst remember his handwriting still.
LEONTINA (*taking the letter, which* EXUPERUS *gives her, and reading it
        aloud*).
        "By Leontina Phocas was deceived.
        She gave him her own son, whom he believed
        My son, to slay, and saved him who should reign
        O'er the realm after me. Ye who remain
            Yet loyal to me, honor her and give
        Your aid to what she plans. Under the name
            Of Leontius doth Heraclius live.
                            "MAURICE."

        (*She gives back the letter to* EXUPERUS *and continues.*)
        It tells the truth, sir: thou wert in my care
        When to the world's worst man Byzantium's gates
        Were opened. Maurice honored me with his trust,
        And I was faithful to it beyond his dreams.
        Seeing him taken with his four other sons,

I for some days hid the one left with me;
But when he was about to be discovered,
My zealous loyalty turned death aside
From thee to mine own flesh and blood. I chose
To save thee by surrendering thee to Phocas,
But 'twas in name I gave thee, not in person.
My ardent zealousness made me, as a faithful
Subject, cruel to myself to save my prince.
My son was given up, as the Emperor's son,
To die. I thus hoodwinked the tyrant,—cheated
His fell rage. In thy stead Leontius
Served as his victim.   (*She heaves a sigh.*)
                         Ah, forgive that sigh,
I pray thee. It escaped me innocently.
I took his life for thee and let him have
One sigh. 'Tis not too much, sir, for such memories.
When duty forced this signal act upon me,
I curbed but did not quench my natural feelings.
    Phocas, ravished with joy by his illusions,
O'erwhelmed me with his favors, and his hand
Gave us the lofty fortunes which I need not
Weary thee by recounting. This is what
I carefully have left thee ignorant of;
And I was waiting, sir, to tell thee of it
Till thy rare valor and thy mighty exploits
Could make the world believe what birth was thine
And till some such occasion as that furnished
By this great rumor could give promise to us
Of some advantage from the revelation;
For since I did not know that our late emperor
Knew anything, or left any proof, of it
I doubted that a secret known to none
But me could find under so cruel a tyrant
The slightest credence.

EXUPERUS.   When his cruelty
Forced Maurice to behold, for a worse torture,
The slaughter of his sons, that emperor
Observed the exchange and wanted to prevent it;
But the executioner was more swift than he.
Thy son's death put an end to his intentions

One moment ere he could refuse to accept
That sacrifice.

              Maurice, who let some hopes
Solace him then, opened his heart concerning
All this to Felix—who came to visit him—
And found the means to give his visitor
This proof, which might someday bear ample witness
About thee. Felix died not long ago,
Madam, and ere his death gave it to me,
His nearest kinsman, and having told me all,
      "Take it," he said, "Exuperus;
Serve thy prince and avenge thy father thus."

   Armed, sir, with that great secret, I desired
To learn what it could do among the people.
I, without making *thee* known, spread this rumor
And, finding that all wanted thee for master,
United the usurper's unguessed foes,
But told them naught more than 'twas right to tell them.
They love thy name, knowing beyond it nothing,
And this one happiness fires their hearts without
Any, except the two that spoke with thee
Out there, e'er knowing, of all that she had done,
Aught more than Phocas. Now hast thou just heard
What thou hadst wished from her. It is for thee
To repay suitably her great-hearted zeal.
The populace revolt, our friends are gathered,
The tyrant quakes, his counselors are bewildered.
Approve as emperor his death now plotted,
Nor fail to order us to take his life.

"Leontius."   Astounded by this new turn of events,
I stand before you tongue-tied with amazement.

   I know my debt to thee for thy great service,
Madam, by which thou savedst the heir of Maurice.
I thought I owed thee everything as thy son,
But more I owe thee when I am less thine.
Yet to express all of my gratitude
To thee, my spirit is too disturbed and shaken.

   I loved, thou knowest, and my burning heart
Now finds in my beloved one mine own sister.
I gain a throne and lose my soul's dear mistress.

At this my love doth murmur and my breast
Sigheth; my mind, seething with countless thoughts,
Is overwhelmed, confounded. Now 'tis time
To leave this trance, so honor doth command,
And give a leader to your noble band.
Go, brave Exuperus, go; and I will join you.
Let me speak briefly with her privately.
Meanwhile prepare thy friends to bear themselves
Well. Above all, let us in slaying Phocas
Preserve his son's life. He had with the usurper
Nothing at all in common but a little
Bad blood, of which the last war drained his body.

EXUPERUS.　We shall accord thee, sir, entire obedience,
And shall await thee most impatiently.

(Exit EXUPERUS.)

"LEONTIUS" *(to* LEONTINA).　Madam, to leave the glory of thy supreme
Act of heroic sacrifice unimpaired,
I shall believe the reasons thou hast given me
Were all that made thee keep this secret from me
So many years. Other folk might suspect
That when thou sawest whom Prince Martian loved,
Some small spark of ambition made thee wish
To see him raise thy daughter to the throne
And leave the Empire in their children's hands,
Letting me find this outcome meet and good
Since I should ne'er know I am not thy son.
But I would deem it wicked to think thus.
I complain only of my insensate passion,—
Of the detestable love which thou didst kindle
Thyself within my heart for mine own sister.
What aim hadst thou through our unwitting incest?

LEONTINA.　I would have told thee all before your marriage;
And this I feared but little, being too sure
The tyrant, with his plans, would not allow it;
And I had hopes, sir, that a love so great
Would fire thy soul to manhood worthy of it,
And that, when by thy worth thou hadst deserved her,
Phocas' refusal of her to thee could better
Rouse thee. Thou hast not proved these hopes were vain;
I saw thy love a fertile source of hate;

And I dare still say that an arm so famous
Perhaps would have wrought less hadst thou not loved.
Then go on, sir, and since Pulcheria
Must fear the wicked violence which blind fury . . .

"LEONTIUS." Perhaps 'twere best I should myself persuade her
To do what the usurper shows he wishes.
Her love for me, which made her brave his anger,
Will not resist him if I am her brother.
How could I find for her a nobler husband?

LEONTINA. What wouldst thou do, sir? What is this thou sayest?

"LEONTIUS." That to prevent so suitable a marriage
Perhaps 'twere wrong to risk my life and fortunes,
And make of Heraclius the ring-leader
Among conspirators whose plans are still
But ill concerted. None of them hath access
Unto the tyrant's person, and although
Their efforts may succeed, perhaps 'tis shameful
For me to gain the crown by a vile murder.
Better should I as leader of an army
Let all my deeds' fame speak in my behalf
And find a glorious pathway to the throne
To avenge my parents with a conqueror's arm.
I go now to decide this with the Princess,
To whom no longer love but kinship binds me.
Thou, with thine own Eudoxia . . .

LEONTINA.   Ah, sir, hear me!

"LEONTIUS." Much need have I of counsel in this crisis;
And, to be frank, thou hast too many interests
Besides mine own for me to listen to thee.
I doubt not thy good will nor loyalty,
But want advice only from one with heart
All mine. Farewell!   (*Exit* "LEONTIUS.")

LEONTINA.   Everything that hath happened
Confounds me; everything is going wrong.
I have accomplished nothing, just when I
Thought to accomplish all things; and when chance
Flattered me beyond reason, my whole purpose
Is thwarted on the threshold of success!
'Twould seem as though some demon hostile to it
Hath spoiled the outcome of the best beginnings.

This letter by which Martian is deceived
Does more to aid my schemes than I dare do;
It arms now the son's hand against the father;
But when he lifts that hand as I have hoped,
Ere he can strike I see to my dismay
That nature's tie, unknown, barreth his way.
The truth misleads him, will not let him sin.
He by his qualms spares him whom he intends
The better to destroy; he hesitates;
And by the course to which I see him tending
Will abet incest, thinking to avoid it.

EUDOXIA.   Madam, at least thou knowest now the author
Of the report, and mine own innocence.
But I am much amazed to see the rights
Of the prince Heraclius thus surrendered
Together with his name. This letter, which
Thy testimony hath confirmed, will be
A mighty help in mounting to the throne.
If Martian doth attain this by its warrant,
Thinkest thou that he will let thee undeceive him
Easily, and that on thy first retraction
He will restore the crown to his true master?

LEONTINA.   Thou art too curious, and wouldst know too much.
Have I not said I could provide 'gainst that?
Let us go seek Exuperus, without more
Delay, for counsel in this troubled hour.

(*Exeunt.*)

A C T   I I I

"LEONTIUS" *and* PULCHERIA *are discovered.*

"LEONTIUS."   I shall confess it, madam—for my soul
Still finds it hard to call thee now my sister—
When, as I laid my fortunes at thy feet,
I dared to lift my dreams even to thee,
Filled more with wonder than with fear I often
Would ask my heart how it could be so bold,
And by its impulses, a secret answer,
I knew that I was more than mere Leontius—
One whose imperious will, despite all reason,

Drove him to hopes that matched not with his station.
PULCHERIA.   I myself have felt often in my heart
My pride of birth reproach me for my love;
But 'twas the empress who gave birth to me
That innocently made this love be born.
I was not quite fifteen years old when she,
Poisoned for having opposed the unworthy marriage
Planned for me, spoke these words with her last breath:
"The tyrant would by trickery or force
Make thy desires conform with his, my daughter,
Fiercely resolved that thou shalt wed his son;
But take from Leontina's hands thy husband.
She guards a treasure that will be dear to thee."
These words disposed me greatly in her favor,
So that instead of hating her for having
Given my brother up to be slain, I deemed
That story false, and became fond of her.
Confounding the two words, "treasure" and "husband,"
I thought my mother by both meant, clearly, thee.
Hence to my royal pride I would oppose
Precepts of filial obedience,
And even blamed myself for vanity
In finding thine estate too far beneath me.
Leontius being of patrician stock,
His brilliant merits made him quite my equal,
And I would tell myself in my fond error,
" 'Tis of such heroes emperors are made.
Thou canst without shame love a noble being
To whom the whole world justly can pay homage."
I did not scorn to heed this inward sanction;
I deemed love spoke, when it was kindred blood;
And love's sweet simulation in my breast
Fed upon what was due to nature's tie.
"LEONTIUS."   Ah, sister!—since 'tis thus my destiny,
Revealed at last, requireth me to call thee—
How easily affection leads to love!
That is a path so sweet that without effort
'Tis entered on, but when love must be changed
Into affection, how well worthy of pity
Anyone is who so constrains himself!

How piteous is the heart which, while it dares not
Refuse to do this, needs must suffer tortures
Before complying! Thus, then, nature's bond
Makes horror take the place of dearest hopes—
Horror of being thine! That which I am
Robs me of all that I desire to be.
Oh, that I might but know not who I am!
How preferable were such fond ignorance
To the cruel truth that opens now mine eyes!

PULCHERIA.　Too much I loved thee, not to know love's power.
I know the bitterness of being thus sundered,
And hate would, to my mind, make easier
The rupture than necessity of loving
Still, but of loving in a different way.
I have, like thee, felt a pang keen indeed
In breaking the sweeet chains that held me captive,
But I would blame my dearest memory of them
Were it to cost my soul more than a sigh.
This great blow hath surprised me but not stunned me;
My heart hath suffered it, but is not crushed;
And as my love's flames were in naught unholy,
Honor lighted them, duty quenches them.
I see no more my lover in the man
In whom I find a brother; as a lover
He cannot move me now, nor as a brother
Can he displease me; and I shall regard
As boundless my good fortune if the tyrant
Is punished and my loved ones are avenged.
　　　Thou whom thy birth will raise unto the throne,
Rule thine own heart before thou rulest the Empire,
And, like me, curbing thy insurgent feelings,
Begin to measure up to thy great fortunes.

"LEONTIUS."　Ah, thou wert always the *renowned* Pulcheria,
Reared from thy cradle as an Emperor's daughter,
And easily this noble name hath taught thee
That thou must needs maintain self-mastery.
But as for me, who in mine other guise
Have taken some semblance of a soul less lofty,
It is no marvel if what I deemed I was
Hath mingled in the heart of Heraclius

Some little portion of Leontius.
Be less harsh, then, toward my confused regrets.
In them Leontius speaks and not thy brother.
But if the one speaks ill, right well the other
Will act, and neither of them will make thee blush.
I go to share the plot of the conspirers
Now that a soul so royal bids me strike:
I reckon that to shed such wicked blood
Murder is noble and befits my rank.
May I, however, ask one thing of thee?

PULCHERIA.   Assume complete authority o'er me.

"LEONTIUS."   Since thy dear lover can no more be thine
Nor place the scepter in thy husband's hands,
Wed Martian as it were my second self.
If thou canst not be mine, be his I love.

PULCHERIA.   Since I cannot be thine, I naturally
Would fain be no one's, fleeing all other suitors;
But thus to set my heart might seem to show
A spark still smouldering of incestuous love.
Then, that I may accord all to thy choice,
Be thou my emperor and command it of me.
Martian is great in worth, and I am fond
Of him; but rid him of his father's crimes
And make of the usurper's son, to be
One I can fitly love, thy foremost subject.

"LEONTIUS."   Thou seest me fly to do so, but if haply
The outcome of my efforts should be luckless
Or slow in happening, *thy* death is assured;
And furthermore, our partisans will wish
To add to the usurpers' death his son's.
Save from such perils both his life and thine;
Protect each other by this blessed marriage;
Safeguard my sister from the wrath of Phocas,
My friend from following to the grave his father.
Compel Exuperus and his associates
To spare my brother-in-law today despite
His hated blood, and grant to the usurper,
Who will not have long to rejoice, some brief
Moments of joy in order to beguile him.

PULCHERIA.   But in those moments, made one of his family,

I shall become his daughter, he my father.
I shall owe him respect, love, loyalty.
My hate no longer will be vehement.
My prayers for thee will all be weak and timid
When prayers 'gainst him must needs be parricidal.
    Besides, success is still uncertain; ye
May be betrayed; he may defeat your efforts.
If ye are worsted by him, could I say
I have not given him good claims to the throne?
How much these moments thou cajolest me for
Would then decree me of unending torture!
Thy hate sees not 'tis wrong to think of friendships.
As it hath just been born, 'tis still but weak.
Mine is far stronger, and mine eyes are clearer;
And though I should destroy the whole world with me,
Not for one instant, do whate'er one might,
Could the usurper ever have the right
To act as if he were my father. I
Refuse not to the son my heart or troth-plight.
Thou lovest him; I esteem him; he is worthy
Of me. His one crime is to have the sire
Unto whom blood-ties bind him, whom his losing
Will leave him without blemish, and whose death
Will help to form the bond thou wishest, by cleansing
Him of all stain, and justify my love.
    Go to prepare, then, for this glad event,
And with the tyrant's blood sanction that marriage.
But by what evil spirit is he brought to us?
"Leontius." I am betrayed. Exuperus comes with him.

    Enter Phocas, Exuperus, Amyntas, *and* Crispus.

Phocas (*to* "Leontius"). What is it that thou talkest of with this
    princess?
    The marriage I wish of her?
"Leontius."   I urge her to it.
Phocas. Hast thou persuaded her to wed my son?
"Leontius." He is to be her husband, she hath promised.
Phocas. That is much to obtain from so rebellious
    A heart. But when?
"Leontius."   "When" is a secret which

She hath not told me.

PHOCAS.   Thou canst tell me one
I am more anxious to find out. 'Tis said
Thou knowest Heraclius well. If thou
Lovest my son, let me know who he is.

"LEONTIUS." Too well thou knowest, for I see this traitor.

EXUPERUS. I serve my emperor, and I know my duty.

"LEONTIUS." All will concede thou dost. Thou showest it plainly.

PHOCAS. Please, tell me what I ask thee to. This letter
Indeed half tells me something, but not much,
Leontius, unless thou confirmest it.

"LEONTIUS." Nay, call me by my true name, since thou knowest it.
Say "Heraclius." There is no Leontius
Now, and I know my doom ere 'tis pronounced.

PHOCAS. Prepare thyself for it, after thy vain effort
To snatch the crown from me and work my death.

"LEONTIUS." I did my duty. To live 'neath thy sway
Would have been to belie my name and birth
And nowise hearken to my parents' blood,
Which cries out in me for the usurper's death.
Whoe'er hath had the glory to be born
To rule the Empire, doth renounce that honor
If he can tolerate a master o'er him.
All but his throne or grave must he disdain—
Vile if he dares not either die or reign.

I know my doom, then, ere it is pronounced;
And Heraclius will die as lived Leontius,
First a good subject, now a better prince—
My life and death worthy of either lot.

Death has naught dreadful to a lofty soul.
For thy sake I a hundred times have faced it,
And my last exploit against thy foes
Hath been to stay the sword raised o'er thy son.

PHOCAS. Thou triest a poor trick to touch my heart.
No part had Heraclius in this service
Done me. I have repaid Leontius
For it, to whom alone was due the honor
Supreme of having rendered it to me;
But with his different, conflicting names
He who preserved the son would slay the father,

And, disavowing what in his ignorance
He did, as soon as he knows who he is,
He seeks my death. I owed a life to him,
And I owe justice to myself. Leontius
Is done away with by the son of Maurice.
Naught countervails his treasonable aims,
And I can punish as well as recompense.

"Leontius." I know too well a tyrant is without
Gratitude, to have formed a craven hope
Of thy now feeling any, and am too much
Above aught so unworthy, to desire
To awaken generosity in thee.
What would it serve me, shouldst thou let me live,
If life without the throne is shameful for me?
Would Heraclius live to dance attendance
On thee? Restore, restore his scepter to him,
Or take life from him. Be, in thine own interests,
An incorruptible judge. Thou and I both
Cannot continue living. Such a foe
Is not to be won over; and wert thou
To spare me, I would punish thee for that.
    If I reminded thee of thy son's rescue,
It was to show the mettle of Leontius
That thou, in seeing it, shouldst doubt no longer
To what point that of Heraclius would go.
I hold it happier to die a monarch
Than live in splendor but unknown to be one;
And since I have, to enjoy a fate so glorious,
Only the moment destined for my death,
I shall make that so fair, so worthy of envy,
That 'twill surpass the most illustrious life.
Let me, then, reach it; make thy power secure;
And rid mine eyes of the loathed sight of thee.

Phocas.   We shall make trial of this proud spirit's manhood.
Have him withdraw into the neighboring chamber,
Crispus, and guard him there until I choose
His punishment and give thee further orders.

"Leontius" (*to* Pulcheria).   Farewell, madam, farewell! I cannot do
Aught more. My death will leave thee still in bondage.

May heaven send other hands to set thee free!

(*Exeunt* "Leontius" *and* Crispus.)

Phocas (*to* Pulcheria). And thou, hope not henceforth to move
me. I
  Hold Heraclius, and no more have aught
  To dread, or reason to speak thee fair, or reason
  To put constraint upon myself. Thy brother
  And all thy hopes shall go down to the grave.
  His head and thy pride at one blow shall fall.
  But choke not back all utterance of thy woe.
  Let thy sighs find a vent; let thy tears flow.

Pulcheria. I, weep? I, wail, tyrant? I would have wept
  If any cowardice had dishonored him,
  If he had not kept his fair fame untarnished,
  If he had made me blush by the least prayer,
  Or if by some base hope of being spared
  He had deserved the death which thou wilt give him.
  His manhood to the end hath never weakened.
  He hath not taken heaven nor Fate to task,
  Nor railed at him who dealt the treacherous blow,
  Nor deigned to waste a righteous wrath upon him.
  He hath not called thee ingrate, nor him traitor,
  But proves he is superior to you both
  And master of himself; and although taken
  Thus by surprise, he can unfalteringly
  Go to the death he seeth must needs be his.
  I have this joy despite his luckless end:
  I loved him as my lover, and I love him
  Now as my brother, and I proudly see him
  In his misfortune show himself well worthy
  To be my brother or to be my lover.

Phocas. Nay, better, better speak thine inmost thoughts,
  And, without more parade of a strained courage,
  To appease me give thy heart unto my son
  And try to purchase thus thy brother's life.

Pulcheria. Think'st thou that, trusting thy false promises,
  My soul would ever stoop to be so base?
  Take *my* life, to buy his; but if my heart
  Must be the price of that, let Heraclius
  Perish with his sad sister!

PHOCAS.   Very well!
     Then he shall perish; to this thou art the accomplice.
PULCHERIA.   And I shall soon see heaven punish thee.
     God, to reserve thee for his own dread hands,
     Aborts deliberately all human vengeance.
     He wills to deal the blow without our aid.
     If thou receivedst Leontius as my brother,
     To thy deluded eyes the other four
     May falsely have, like him, seemed to be Caesars.
     The realm, which in their death beheld its ruin,
     Had loyal subjects besides Leontina.
     These hoodwinked easily a raging savage
     Who ne'er had seen the Emperor or the Court.
     Tremble, still tremble, tyrant: all my other
     Four brothers one by one may yet appear,
     And despite all thy efforts, all thy care,
     Thou'lt know them not till at their hands thou diest!
     I myself, in their lack, will be the prize
     Of whosoe'er will bring to me thy head.
     The vilest slave imaginable will be
     Worthy to wed me if he murders thee.
      Go and kill Heraclius, and stop thinking
     That I make boast of a pretended courage.
     Urge me no more to yield to thy desires;
     If thou wouldst reign, make way with both of us.
                             (*Exit* PULCHERIA.)
PHOCAS.   I hear with pleasure these thine empty threats.
     I laugh at a despair armed but with words;
     And howsoe'er thou darest to insult me,
     The blood of Heraclius will avenge it.
      Ye, my true friends, who rid me of anxiety,—
     Ye whose love, when I feared men's hate, ye show,—
     Ye who betrayed to me my hidden foe,—
     Do not by halves be faithful unto me!
     Help me decide upon the way to kill him.
     Shall it be secretly or openly—
     The surest way or the most notable?
EXUPERUS.   Sire, doubt not this: the surest way is best;
     But the way surest for thee is by a death
     In all men's sight, or else the populace,

Not knowing of it, still may nurse false hopes,
Await this prince, and have some grounds to rally
Blindly to anyone who may take his name.

PHOCAS.   To rid the populace of all doubt, then,
Let us display his head in the public square.

EXUPERUS.   But if thou strikest it off inside the palace,
These stubborn rebels will not believe it his;
Not one of them will turn from his wrong course;
They all will say Leontius was given
A name not his and made a phantom prince
To hoodwink them. They will be ready always
To follow anyone claiming to be him.

PHOCAS.   Then we can show this letter of Maurice to them.

EXUPERUS.   They will not think it genuine, but forged.
Sire, after twenty years thou vainly hopest
That they could recognize the handwriting in it.
If 'tis thy wish to make this tempest end,
His head must be cut off before them all
And he must tell the affrighted throng in dying,
"Doubt not, O people, I am Heraclius!"

PHOCAS.   He must, I see; and I already destine
For the same scaffold the vile Leontina.
But what if these bold rebels snatch him from us?

EXUPERUS.   Who would dare do it?

PHOCAS.   This rabble whom I fear.

EXUPERUS.   Nay, recall better into what confusion
Their first dismay throws men without a leader.
The mere news of this prince's being arrested
Here in the palace, will disperse forthwith
All who supported him. The most audacious
Of them will fear thy justice, and the rest
Will trembling go to view his punishment.
But do not give them, by too long delaying
The execution, time to pluck up heart
And gather again. Put guards at all street-corners
And seize the Hippodrome and its approaches,
With special strength in every public place.
As for us, whom his death so much concerns,
For fear that any others might be corrupted,
Leave it to us to lead him to the scaffold.

We have too many friends not to succeed.
I stake my head on it, and will see to all things.
PHOCAS. Thou sayest enough, Exuperus. Go; I
Yield to the loyal counsel that thou giv'st me.
'Tis the one way in which to tame these rebels
And end forever this intestine strife.
I go at once to give to all my captains
The orders requisite in this great business.
Do ye, to carry out what ye have promised,
Go, on your part, to assemble all your friends;
And know that next to me, until I die,
Ye shall be, ye and they, the Empire's masters.

(Exit PHOCAS.)

EXUPERUS *(to* AMYNTAS). We are in favor, friend; all things are ours.
Our prospering fortunes will make many jealous.
AMYNTAS. Whate'er joy thou mayst now display, dost thou
Find sweet the name of a perfidious traitor?
EXUPERUS. To gallant hearts, I know, 'tis horrible;
It sore offendeth mine ears, pierceth my soul.
But soon, with the results we can expect,
We shall be able nevermore to hear it.
Come; for the moment it must be endured.
Let us not lose the good to be secured.

(Exeunt.)

A C T   I V

"MARTIAN" *and* EUDOXIA *are discovered.*

"MARTIAN." Thou hast good reason to feel apprehensive.
Phocas will deem her the worst sort of criminal;
And ill I know him, or, if he can find her,
There is no human means by which to save her.
I pity thee, dear Eudoxia, not thy mother.
Exuperus treated her as she deserved.
He betrayed one who sought to play me false.
EUDOXIA. Thou thinkest her to this extent thy foe—
Her, who for thee did violence to her natural
Feelings?
"MARTIAN." How, then, wouldst *thou* view her deceit?
To stay my hand and by a lying statement

9 9

Ascribe to Martian my own name and rank,—
To use amiss a letter which chance gave her,
Assign thereby my heritage to him,
Put him in such plight he would in good faith
Reign in my place or perish in my stead—
Madam, was this to render me true service?

EUDOXIA. Was she to contradict Maurice's letter?
And was she able to, unless she revealed
That which above all had to be concealed?
Even had Martian then not known his father,
She would have made thy life depend upon
The loyalty of Exuperus; she felt doubts
Of that, and by what followed thou canst see
That in her zealous care she rightly did so.
Confident that she had, herself, the means
Of giving the Empire back to thee, whereof
She ne'er was willing to tell even thee,
To Martian she diverted the dread risk
Of putting to the proof a heart she knew
But ill. Where wouldst thou be, sir, but for this
New service she did thee?

"MARTIAN."   What matters it
Which of us two hath been condemned to die?
What matters it, Martian, in view of what
I owe thee, who—Exuperus or I—
Betrayeth my identity? If he does not
Disclose it, I must needs expose myself,
And both are in the end the same, except
That if betrayed I would die miserably,
But if I give my life for thee, die nobly?

EUDOXIA. What! undeceive the blindness of the tyrant,
Frustrate thy destiny and give thy life?

"MARTIAN." Thou art more blinded by thy love. Shall one
To whom I owe my life die in my place?
When 'neath my name he goeth to meet death,
Shall I 'neath his keep hidden and be safe?
If 'twere a question now of making him
Emperor, I well might leave him with my name
In his mistake, but basely to connive
In my being robbed of that name while his father

Before mine eyes kills him in *my* stead,—let him
Expose himself to *my* lot's bitter portion,—
Live by his sacrifice and reign by his death!

EUDOXIA.   Ah, 'tis not that, sir, which I ask of thee.
Such cowardice hath too great infamy.
Appear and save this brave man from his doom,
But in thy might appear; court not destruction.
Resume that boldness against which my mother
Protested, save the son by slaying the father,
And taking a heroic path to empire,
Show Heraclius to the waiting people.

"MARTIAN."   It is too late; another hath my place.
His seizure chilled with fear the populace.
Engrossed now in a different Heraclius,
In their dismay they will believe me not,
Deem me a false son, and shrink horrified
From following a would-be parricide.
But even if they would aid me in my purpose,
Martian already is a prisoner.
If I should come with open force, the tyrant
Enraged by my insurgency, would speed
His death, and fancy that by robbing me
Of the hope of saving him, he took from me
The motive force that fired me to revolt.
   Say nothing more; in vain thy love would stay me.
The fate of Heraclius is my affair.
Whether I am to reign or perish, I
Shall to the tomb or throne alike now fly.
But here is the usurper, and the traitor
Exuperus.

Enter PHOCAS, EXUPERUS, *and guards.*

PHOCAS (*pointing to* EUDOXIA).   Let her be held securely
While we await her mother.

"MARTIAN."   What hath she . . .

PHOCAS.   We shall learn at more leisure. In the meantime
'Tis well to have her seized.

EUDOXIA (*to* PHOCAS, *as she is led out*).   Sir, believe nothing
Of what he now will say.

PHOCAS.   I shall believe

What serves the Empire's weal.

> (*Exit* EUDOXIA, *guarded.*)

(*To* "MARTIAN")   Was she imploring
With tears thy pity for that guilty man?

"MARTIAN."   Sir . . .

PHOCAS.   I know what was thine affection for him
But I would have thee, weighing well his crime,
Regard thy love as wrong, and his death proper.

(*To his guards*) Let him be brought. To force him to confess
There will be need of neither steel nor flame.
Far from repenting, he is proudly boastful.

(*Again to* "MARTIAN") But what wilt thou tell me that I should not
Believe? Eudoxia begs me not to. She
Surprised me. Hast thou learned of some yet greater
Crime?

"MARTIAN."   Yes. Her mother has done more against thee
Than Maurice witnessed or Exuperus knows of.

PHOCAS.   The faithless woman! This day shall be her last.
Speak.

"MARTIAN."   I shall finish in the prisoner's presence.
Believe 'tis best that I tell such a secret,
Since thou hast bidden me tell it, before him.

PHOCAS.   Here he is. But above all, plead not for him.

> (*Enter guards with* "LEONTIUS.")

"MARTIAN."   I know my prayers would give him little aid,
And, far from putting myself to fruitless trouble,
All that I beg thee in thy natural anger
Is that such crimes should not be left unpunished.
Slay Heraclius and preserve thy son.
That is my sole desire and my one prayer.
Wilt thou refuse it me?

PHOCAS.   'Twill all be granted.
Thy life indeed is risked unless he dies.

"LEONTIUS."   Ah, Prince, I went to meet death without protest.
Fate's unjust cruelty is not what now moves me.
But from thy lips to hear my doom decreed!
I ill have known thee till the day I die!

"MARTIAN."   And at this moment thou still dost not know me.
Hear, blinded father, and thou, credulous prince,

What honor now forbids me to keep hidden.
   Know thy child, Phocas, and thy real foe. *I*
   Am Heraclius; Leontius is thy son.
"Leontius." What sayst thou, sir?
"Martian."   What I can hide no longer:
   That Leontina twice deceived thy father
   And, causing all to know not our true names,
   Made a false Martian of the babe Heraclius.
Phocas.   Maurice gives thee the lie, base youth. Thou hast
   Only to read his words: "Under the name
   Of Leontius doth Heraclius live."
   After that, thou devisest such tales vainly.
"Martian."   Sir, if those words were true, they now are not.
   I was Leontius then; and when I ceased
   To be so, Maurice, murdered, knew naught of it.
   If he left written what he had beheld,
   What followed his demise was past his knowledge.
   Thou carriedst war forthwith, then, into Persia,
   Where for three years' space thou hadst varying fortunes,
   And meanwhile Leontina, in the palace,
   Presiding o'er our fates and o'er our cradles,
   To give me back the rank thou heldest, took
   Martian as hers and put me in his place.
   Her zeal in my behalf was so successful
   That thou on thy return suspectedst nothing;
   And those yet unshaped features children have
   At six months' age having shown little difference
   Between us, thy faint recollection of them
   Was lost in three years and thou readily
   Tookest as thine the child she gave to thee.
   Each of us lived under the other's name.
   He passed for her son, and I passed for thine,
   Nor did I deem it wicked by this path
   To reach my father's throne with no blood spilled.
   But seeing the error which would cost his life
   Save for whom mine would have been lost already,
   I should regard my guilt as beyond measure,
   Sir, if I still let this mistake continue.
   I come to take a name back which is all
   His crime. Cease not to hate, but change thy victim.

I ask for naught but what was promised me:
Slay Heraclius and preserve thy son.

"Leontius" (*to* Phocas).   Marvel at him, the son whom heaven hath
given thee;
Marvel at what his noble heart hath done,
Tyrant, and do not take to be the truth
The tale he generously invents to save me.

(*To* "Martian")   'Tis too much, Prince, too much for
that small service
Which my good fortune granted to mine arm.
I saved thy life, but did not lose mine own;
And thou for me seekest thy certain death.
Ah, if thou owest me any gratitude,
Rob me not of the honor of my birth!
To have such pity for a lot so glorious,
For fear of being ungrateful, is to wrong me.

Phocas.   In what perplexity this dispute leaves me!
To what new trials it exposeth me!
Which is to be believed, which not believed?
Am I misled now, or now undeceived?
If true this letter, true the rest may be.

Exuperus.   But who knows if the rest *is* false or true?

Phocas.   Leontina could have hoodwinked Phocas twice.

Exuperus.   Could have exchanged the babes, or not exchanged them;
And more than thou, sire, in our plight I see
Only confusion and uncertainty.

"Martian" (*to* Phocas).   'Tis not today I first knew who I am.
Thou knowest the consequences of my knowledge.
For more than four years thou hast seen how I
Tactfully refused marriage with the Princess,
To which my heart might easily have consented
If Leontina had not warned me 'gainst it.

"Leontius."   Leontina?

"Martian."   She herself.

"Leontius."   Ye heavens, her guile!
See: Martian loved Eudoxia, and her mother
Deceived him. By his horror of a marriage
Which he believed incestuous, she made it
Certain the Prince would plight troth with her daughter;
And her ambition, artful to delude him,

Immersed him in an error, whence she expected
To gain the Empire's throne, and that is why
Only today have I learned who I am;
But from my ignorance she hoped this fruit,
And would have kept the truth still hidden from me
Had not this letter just now dragged it from her.

PHOCAS (*to* EXUPERUS). She foully hoodwinked him as well as me.

EXUPERUS. She may have hoodwinked him, and she may not have.

PHOCAS. Her daughter shared, thou seest, in her ruse.

EXUPERUS. And yet her mother may have deceived her, too.

PHOCAS. How many possibilities! How many
    Varying anxieties!

EXUPERUS.   I shall relieve thee
    Soon of them, sire.

PHOCAS.   Tell me, is everything
    Made ready for the execution?

EXUPERUS   Yes,
    If we knew which is the real son of Maurice.

"MARTIAN." Can ye have doubts, after what I have told you?

"LEONTIUS." Do ye accord his error still some credence?

"MARTIAN" (*to* "LEONTIUS"). Friend, give me back my name. 'Tis
    no great favor.
    Only to die do I request it of thee.
    Take back from me the hapless life thou savedst,
    Or give me back the honor of which thou'dst rob me.

"LEONTIUS." Why, as this tyrant's willing victim, throw
    Thy life away to blacken me with crime?
    Whoe'er I am, I have conspired to kill him,
    And these names give my purpose different aspects.
    In Heraclius it is truly glorious,
    And by it Martian becomes parricidal.
    Since I must die illustrious or a villain,
    Covered with praise or with eternal opprobrium,
    Smirch not my death nor wish to make the Emperor's
    Avenger his own father's would-be murderer.

"MARTIAN." My name alone is guilty, and without
    Further contention, to be innocent
    Thou needest but to give it up. *It* hath
    Alone conspired; thou art not its accomplice.
    'Tis only Heraclius whom Phocas sends

To death. Be *his* son. Live.

"LEONTIUS" (*to* PHOCAS).   Had I been that, sir,
Vainly this traitor would have come to me;
For had he made me attempt aught against thee
Nature's tie secretly would have restrained me.

"MARTIAN." Learn, then, that secretly my will outstripped thee.
I wanted to conspire but was held back;
For, fearful of my peril, Leontina . . .

"LEONTIUS." Could not let Martian be a parricide.

"MARTIAN." Thou, whom she led to love Pulcheria,
Judge, under either name, thy plot and love.
She hath made one or the other dreadful for thee—
For Martian one would be foul parricide,
For Heraclius the other would be incest—
And would not have left me a great crime's horror
Since she devised that this should be thy portion.
But she prevented me from hazarding
My head, and hoped I by thine arm should triumph.
The avowal in thy favor that beguiled thee
Placed thee in danger to give me its fruit,
And it was thy success which she awaited
To let the people know my birth—or not.

PHOCAS. Alas, I cannot tell which is my son,
But I perceive that they are, both, my foes!
In this sad plight, what counsel should I follow?
I feared an enemy; good luck hath given him
Into my hands; I know that he is helpless;
I know I see him; yet I cannot find him.
My natural instincts, fearful, vague, bewildered,
Shroud his identity in a darkling cloud;
The assassin in its gloom escapes my wrath,
And though before mine eyes, hides in my heart.
Martian!—to that name neither will respond,
And a sire's love serves only to confuse me.
Too many a Heraclius is in my hands;
I hold my foe, but now I have no son.
What wouldst thou, then, my heart? What wilt thou do?
If I have no son, can I be a father?
What saith thy too-uncertain murmur to me?
Say naught to me at all, or speak out clearly.

Whichever of these twain is mine own son,
Cause me to know him, or else let me slay him.
   O thou, whiche'er thou art, unnatural child,
Who art most worthy of the doom thou choosest,
Is death less shameful than my throne to thee?
O hapless Phocas! Fortune-favored Maurice!
Thou has two more sons to die after thee;
I cannot find one to reign after me!
How must I envy thee thy death's proud honor
Since mine own son prefers it to his life!

Enter CRISPUS *with* LEONTINA.

CRISPUS. Sire, my diligence hath at last succeeded.
   I have found Leontina. Here she is.
PHOCAS (*to* LEONTINA). Come hither, wretched woman.
"MARTIAN" (*to* LEONTINA).   Confess
   all, madam.
   I have told everything.
LEONTINA (*to* "MARTIAN").   What, sir?
PHOCAS.   Dost thou know not,
   Vile miscreant! Which of these two is my son?
LEONTINA. What makes thee now feel doubts of that?
"MARTIAN" (*to* LEONTINA).   The name
   Of Heraclius, which his son would claim.
   He trusts this letter and thy testimony;
   But leave him not in error any longer.
PHOCAS (*to* LEONTINA). Wait not till thou art tortured. Tell no lies.
   Didst thou give *thy* son to me to be slain?
   Didst thou exchange mine and the child thus saved?
LEONTINA. I gave thee my son, and I glory in it.
   If I say more, wilt thou dare trust my words?
   What guarantees thee that for Heraclius
   I who so tricked thee will not trick thee further?
PHOCAS. No matter! Tell us what wise prudence caused thee
   To make, so far apart, disclosures to them—
   Four years ago to one, today to the other.
LEONTINA (*indicating each of the two young men in turn*).
   That secret is not known to him, or him;
   Nor shalt thou more know the real reason for it.
   Divine the truth, if thou art able to;

And make a choice between them, if thou darest.
  One of them is thy son; one is thine emperor.
Tremble thou in thy love and in thy rage.
I want to see thee, whatsoe'er thy frenzy,
Fear thy foe always in thine own flesh and blood,
And always love thy son in thy foe's person,
Not being, save by halves, tyrant nor father.
While as to these two thou wilt vainly ponder,
I shall rejoice at thy anxiety,—
Shall laugh at thy distress; or, if thou slayest me,
The secret of thy son will die with me.

PHOCAS.   What if I slay them both, without my knowing
Who they are—one for being Heraclius,
And the other one for wishing to be him?

LEONTINA.   I would console myself with seeing Phocas
Think to make firm his throne by cutting off
His own arm and for Heraclius take,
By his own orders, given at the same time,
Vengeance upon his only son.

PHOCAS.   Thou ingrate,
How thou repayest me for the boons I lavished
On thee and thine, for having entrusted to thee
This son thou hidest from me, for having placed
In thy care him whose heart thou tookest from me,
And made my Court bow down to thee and love thee!
Give me my son back, ingrate!

LEONTINA.   He would not
Accept my statement he is thine. That son,
Whoe'er he be, whom thou canst never know,
Is far too noble to wish to be thy son.
Admire his manhood, which destroys thy peace.
I made this hero of a tyrant's offspring:
'Tis the good rearing he received that quelled
The evil instincts given him by his blood.
It is a full repayment of thy boons
To disengage thy son from thy misdeeds.
Corrupted docilely by thy example,
He had been like thee, had he known his birth,—
Been like thee impious, cruel, and cowardly,—

And thus thou owest me more than I owe thee.

EXUPERUS (*to* PHOCAS). Effrontery and pride attend imposture.
Expose thyself no more to all these insults,
Which only make thee angrier and give thee
But little light on what thou seekest to learn.
Leave me to guard her, sire, for a short time.
Since I began all this, the rest concerns me.
Despite the mystery veiling her deception,
I hope to unravel the whole tangled skein.
Thou knowest how great my interest in the matter.

PHOCAS. Attain thine end, by force or cleverness,
And be assured I shall owe all to thee,
Exuperus, if thy zeal can reach its goal.
I meanwhile shall take each of them aside,
And presently perhaps shall find my son.
I leave her with thee. Do thy part. Constrain,
Cajole, entrap her. Follow me, ye others.

(*Exeunt all but* EXUPERUS *and* LEONTINA.)

EXUPERUS. No one can hear us. It is proper, madam,
I should at last lay bare to thee my heart.
I have too long passed for a traitor with thee.
Thou hatest Phocas; we all hate him . . .

LEONTINA.   Yes,
Well dost thou show to him thy hate and wrath,
Who sellest to him thy prince and thy sire's blood.

EXUPERUS. Appearances deceive thee; I am really . . .

LEONTINA. The vilest man whom nature hath produced.

EXUPERUS. That which to *thine* eyes seemeth treachery . . .

LEONTINA. Oh, yes, conceals a brave and noble purpose!

EXUPERUS. How canst thou judge it when thou knowest it not?
Think of the plight of all of our conspirers.
There is not one of them to whom Phocas' fury
Hath not afforded grounds for righteous vengeance;
And hence assured we hate him in our hearts,
The tyrant keepeth us far from his palace.
One must gain entrance there by some great service.

LEONTINA. And dost thou think thou by these words canst blind me?

EXUPERUS. Madam, learn all. I have risked naught. Thou knowest
By how great numbers he is always guarded.
Could we surprise him or break through the cohorts

Which day and night are holding every door?
How could we quietly come near him better?
Thou seest on what footing I am here:
He talks to me, hearkens to me, and trusts me;
Puts himself in my hands, furthers my schemes.
'Tis solely by my counsel that he wishes
To execute Prince Heraclius in public,
And that his troops, posted at all street-corners,
Have left the palace almost undefended.
I in a flash can be the stronger here.
My friends are ready: 'tis done, and he is dead;
And I shall use so well the access given me
That I shall lay at Heraclius' feet
His crown. But since my plans are fully told thee,
I pray thee, let me know whom I must serve,
And hide him not, still, from this heart that seeketh
Only to make him now the Empire's master.

LEONTINA.   Base, brutish creature, what stupidity
Makes thee conclude I am so credulous?
Go; such a gross snare is set vainly for me,
Traitor, and if thou hast no subtler ruse . . .

EXUPERUS.   I spoke sincerely, and I shall tell thee further . . .

LEONTINA.   Concoct not now for me such futile stories.
Thy deeds forbid all credence to thy words.

EXUPERUS.   So be it! persist, then, in distrusting me.
I ask no more and tell thee nothing more.
Guard well thy secret; well shall I guard mine.
Since thou still deemest me one who would delude thee,
Come to the prison where I am to bring thee.
If thou dost not believe me, fear my power.
Thou'lt know me better, ere this day's last hour.

(Exeunt.)

ACT V

"MARTIAN" *is discovered, alone.*

"MARTIAN."

What confusion great and strange
Comes from two princely babes' exchange
That makes two friends not be at one!

A father knows not which to choose;
And the more they both alike refuse
The shameful title of his son,
The more those secrets but confuse
Them both, which were to them made known.

Leontina by her wiles
So favors me or my hopes beguiles
She leaves dark all our destiny.
What I have learned thereof from her
Made me defy an emperor
Who will not credit my futile plea;
But doubts of my birth begin to stir
In my heart when death is refused to me.

This proud tyrant's mercy shown me
And his affection lavished on me
Make me in my soul afraid.
When he unto me appeals,
Such great love 'twould seem he feels
That I know not if 'tis bred
By the instinct which reveals
Blood-ties, or by long wont instead.

I have in this uncertainty
Transports of hate for him which I
Cannot succeed in holding to.
That he should wish to be so kind
To me, confounds my vengeful mind,
And naught dare I resolve to do
When a father's care and love I find
In him who mine own father slew.

Shade of great Maurice, pluck me back
From that sheer brink of a chasm black
Which in my doubts I stand upon;
And help me that I may all convince
That in thy son God brought no prince
So weak to birth—or that I am one
Who at least deserved to be a prince
If I indeed am not thy son.

Preserve my hate, now given pause,
And strengthening two-fold in thy cause
That noble eagerness to die,
Show . . . But my prayer is heard; help comes.

(*Enter* PULCHERIA.)

O sky

Above! What blessed angel sends thee to me,
Madam?

PULCHERIA. Thy tyrant, who would have me see thee.
He tries all means to bring the truth to light.

"MARTIAN." Through thee in this confusion he expects
Success?

PULCHERIA. Yes, he expects it, sir, and hopes—
The beast—rather himself to find a son
Than me a brother, as if I were a daughter
To hide naught from him of all that which kinship
Might reveal to me.

"MARTIAN." May it, with truth's ray,
Reveal this to thee more than it doth to me!
In the meantime, help me, madam, to repress
The unworthy fears by which I am beset.

PULCHERIA. Ah, Prince, there is no better proof than this.
If thou dost fear death, thou art not my brother.
These shameful fears too well identify thee.

"MARTIAN." I, fear death, madam? I asked for it. Let him
Be tyrant, let him send me to my doom:
I—*I*—am Heraclius, son of Maurice.
I under these proud names rush to destruction,
Dismayed so little that I make him blench.
But he behaves toward me as would a father,
Utters endearments, clasps me in his arms.
I cannot wring from him a single threat.
I vainly act and speak to anger him.
He pays it such small heed that I am forced
To feel doubts. He always, in spite of me,
Looks on me as his son. Instead of being
In prison, I do not have even one guard.
I know not who I am, and I dread knowing.
I want to do my duty; I seek to learn it.
I fear to hate him if I owe him life;

I pity him for loving me if I owe
Vengeance upon him to myself. My heart,
Shocked by such kindly feelings toward him, quivers
With fury at them, and with pity trembles.
My soul distrusteth all its impulses;
It instantly condemns all that it sanctions.
Anger and love and hatred and respect
Suggest naught to me I do not suspect.
I fear all, flee from all; and in my plight
I listen vainly for the voice of kinship.
Help, then, in this perplexity, thy brother.

PULCHERIA.   Nay, thou art not that, since thou doubtest of it.
He who like thee aspireth to this honor
With stouter heart feels what he ought to feel.
Plied as thou art with blandishments, he yields not.
Naught moveth him enough to give him doubts;
And kinship's voice with inward promptings speaketh
In thee for Phocas and in him for Maurice.

"MARTIAN."   By these signs recognize thou him as Martian.
The tyrant's son, he hath the harder heart.
Fineness of nature comes with royal blood;
Pity accompanies it, and gratitude.
A true prince with this loftiness of soul
Is sensitive even to an enemy's dole.
The hate that he should feel cannot prevent him
From being touched, on seeing himself loved;
And he quite often finds what he should do
Impeded by his natural impulses
Of kindliness. A virtue that beseemeth
One of the highest birth ought not to impugn,
Madam, my lot. I doubt; and if such doubt
Is at all wrong of me, I have sufficient
Punishment for it if thou doubtest like me;
And my heart, which without cease pleads my cause,
Seeks to be reassured and not unmanned.
I implore help for my bewildered wits,
And not the mortal, murderous blow thou dealest me.

PULCHERIA.   The eye with clearest vision in such matters
Can mistake false light on them for true light,
And as our sex is very quick to venture

To follow its original impressions,
Perhaps my hate of Phocas hath too much
Persuaded me in favor of my first thought.
For thee his love is a most virulent poison;
And although pity shows a generous nature,
That which one feels for him corrupteth one.
Thou oughtest to hate him—yes, were he thy father;
That fact is doubtful but his crime is not.
Let him show kindness to thee or destroy thee,
In favoring thee he is not less a tyrant,
For 'tis thy heart itself he tyrannizes
Over, then, and in this way thwarting best
Thy duty, he may harm thy character.
Doubt on, but hate him; and, do what he may,
I shall doubt whose the name is which another
Disputes with thee. To doubt thus when thou seekest
Some aid in me, if 'tis too little for thee,
Is all that I can do for thee 'gainst *him*.
One of you is my brother, and the other
Can hope he is. With both of you so noble,
My choice may be mistaken, but I cannot
Fail, in your dubious fortunes, to love both
Of you and pity both. But I still have hope.
Murmurs there are, and threats; 'tis said an uproar
Hath risen in the Square. Exuperus
Hath gone to fall upon the rioters,
And on that fray our fate perhaps dependeth.
But here is Phocas.

Enter PHOCAS, "LEONTIUS," *and guards.*

PHOCAS. (*to* PULCHERIA). Well, will he give in, madam?
PULCHERIA. However hard I try to read his heart,
    I see there only what I had expected:
    Too much my brother and thy son too little.
PHOCAS. Thus heaven wills to enrich thee with my loss.
PULCHERIA. It favors me by keeping their birth hidden.
    The brother it restores to me already
    Would be dead were he not confused with thy
    Son.
PHOCAS.   This confusion may destroy them both.

I for the sake of mine own flesh and blood
Will show thine mercy, but I wish to know him,
And I shall grant him *his* life at this price
Only, that he will give me back my son.
    (*To* "MARTIAN")   For the last time, thou ingrate, I adjure
    thee;
For 'tis toward thee my natural instincts lean,
And not for him do I have those sweet feelings
Which move unerringly in a father's heart.
Mine is drawn to thee by a resistless spell.
Wilt not believe my sighs, believe my tears?
Think with what loving care I brought thee up.
Think how his valiant arm hath saved thy life.
Thy debt to us is two-fold.
"MARTIAN."   And to pay it
    I shall give thee thy son, him his true lineage.
PHOCAS.   Thou robbest me of my son, and lettest him die.
"MARTIAN."   I die to give him to thee, and to save him.
PHOCAS.   Thou robbest me of him, refusing to be him.
"MARTIAN."   I give him to thee in telling who he is.
PHOCAS.   Thou robbest me of him in supposing *him* mine.
"MARTIAN."   I give him to thee when I undeceive thee.
PHOCAS.   Leave me mine error, since 'tis dear to me.
    I take thee as my son; take me as father.
    Give Heraclius life one way or the other.
    For me, for thee, for him, make this small effort.
"MARTIAN."   Ah, that is too much; mine offended honor
    Throws off the old respect I forced upon it.
    Into what ignominy wouldst thou lure me?
    Whene'er, usurper, one accepts adoption,
    One wants a house illustrious and beloved;
    One seeks for honor and not infamy;
    And what a horrible monstrosity
    The son of Maurice in thy realm would be
    As the adopted son of Phocas!
PHOCAS.   Go!
    Hope not to have the death which thou deservest.
    Thou angerest me only against *him;*
    And vainly, wretch, wouldst thou claim thou art not
    My son. I am to blame for this, and spare

My flesh and blood. Since thou, in thine affection
For him, so far distrustest my pledged word,
That thou assumest his name to save his life,
Soldiers, without delay let him be slain
Before our eyes, and then, when he is dead,
Be thou my son if thou art willing to.

"MARTIAN."   Hold, traitors!

"LEONTIUS."   Nay, what thinkest thou, Prince, to do?

"MARTIAN."   Save a son from the frenzy of his father.

"LEONTIUS."   Preserve a son he seeks in thee alone,
Nor mar a lot which seems so dear to him.
Happy enough doth Heraclius die
When 'tis unto thy hands his realm will fall.
May heaven vouchsafe to bless thy life and reign!

PHOCAS.   We lose too much time listening to this talk.
     (*To a guard*) Make end, Octavian!

"MARTIAN."   Commit no such crime,
Thou savage! I am . . .

PHOCAS.   Come, acknowledge it.

"MARTIAN."   I tremble, my mind reeleth, and my heart . . .

PHOCAS.   Thou canst take thought about it at thy leisure.
     (*To the guard*) Strike!

"MARTIAN."   Stay! I am . . . Can I pronounce the
     words?

PHOCAS.   Go on, or . . .

"MARTIAN."   Then I am, if I must say it,
That which I needs must be to save his life.
     I owe enough to him, let come what may,
To give to thee for him the love he owes thee.
I promise thee that mine will be whole-hearted,
Constant, sincere, and such as Heraclius
Would give to his real father. For *his* sake
I will accept his parents as mine own.
But know that *thy* life will be answerable
For his; thou'lt guarantee it to me against
War's hazards, secret foes, and lightning's bolts;
No matter in what fashion heaven's wrath
Deprives me of a friend so precious to me,
I will avenge on thee—wert thou my father—
That which its unjust anger does to him.

PHOCAS.   Fear naught: my power shall on you both be based.
          The love he hath for thee assures me of him.
          With gladness I grow faint, and I aspire
          Only to associate both of you with me
          In ruling. I have found again my son;
          But be this thoroughly, and give proof thereof
          By overt act. No more leave room for fraud.
          To make my joy complete, marry Pulcheria.
"MARTIAN."   My lord, she is my sister.
PHOCAS.   Thou art not
          My son, then, since already thou so vilely
          Dost contradict thyself?
PULCHERIA.   What gives thee, tyrant,
          A hope so vain? Thou thinkest that *his* surrender
          Would stifle *my* hate? That by bending *him*
          Thou makest *me* change? That I would have a heart
          So heedless as to bear such shame? That I
          Would wed either thy son or mine own brother?

                    Enter CRISPUS.

CRISPUS.   Thou owest all, sire, to the noble Exuperus.
          He is sole author of our fairer fortunes.
          He with his friends hath quelled the rioters,
          Capturing their leaders, whom he brings to thee.
PHOCAS.   Tell him to guard them in the adjoining hall.
          I go to learn from them about their plots.
                (CRISPUS *withdraws and* PHOCAS *turns to* "MARTIAN.")
          Thou, ingrate, be my son now if thou wilt.
          As things stand, I no more have reason to feign.
          The rebels are subdued. I cease to fear.
          I leave all three of you.
                (*To* PULCHERIA) Use well the moment
          That I shall spend in punishing these people;
          And if thou wouldst not both the twain should die,
          Find or choose one to be my son and wed him
          Straightway; or else, if their identity
          Is doubtful still, I swear they both shall perish
          On my return. I do not want a son
          Who deems, in his implacable hate, my name
          An insult, my love irksome. As for thee . . .

                    1 1 7

PULCHERIA.   Threaten me not. I am prepared to die.

PHOCAS.   To die! Thou thinkest I would be so indulgent
　　　To thee? Hope not for that great favor from me.
　　　Expect . . .

PULCHERIA.　　　What, tyrant?

PHOCAS.　　　　　　　To wed me myself
　　　Amidst their blood, flowing about thy feet.

PULCHERIA.   Oh, what a doom!

PHOCAS.　　　　　　'Tis harsh, but thou deserv'st it.
　　　Thy scorn of death too much defied mine anger.
　　　It lies with thee to kill or save thy brother;
　　　And howsoe'er I wrongly was disturbed,
　　　At least I have found a way to make thee tremble.

　　　　　　　　　　　　　　　(*Exit* PHOCAS.)

PULCHERIA.   The coward! When his heart feared, he fawned on you!
　　　This infamy is natural in a tyrant:
　　　He ne'er is kind save when constrained to be.
　　　If he is not afraid, he doth oppress;
　　　If he doth not oppress, he is afraid.
　　　In either circumstance he showeth his baseness,
　　　In one case arrogant, in the other abject.
　　　Scarce hath he got free of his craven terrors
　　　Than he hath found for me a crowning horror.
　　　　My brothers—for ye fain would both be such—
　　　If as your sister ye do love me, prove it.

"MARTIAN."   How can we, when our lives will be cut short?

PULCHERIA.   In noble counsel there is mighty aid.

"LEONTIUS."   There is no counsel which can aid thee aught,
　　　Except to wed the son to escape the father.
　　　Dread of a worse fate should persuade thee to it.

PULCHERIA.   And which is he, if I consent to wed him?
　　　And in this marriage fatal to mine honor,
　　　Who is to guarantee me against incest?

"LEONTIUS."   I see its danger is too great to risk it;
　　　But, madam, one can take the empty name
　　　Of husband to deceive a raging tyrant
　　　And in feigned marriage live as with his sister.

PULCHERIA.   Feign? Stoop to aught so dastardly?

"MARTIAN."　　　　　　　　To hoodwink
　　　A tyrant, 'tis a noble act. It puts,

To aid a brother whom it gives to thee,
Two secret enemies near that tyrant's person,
Who, fired by righteous hate and steadfast in it,
Can choose their time to slay their common foe
And with his death ere long end all deception.

PULCHERIA. To save your lives and shield me, let us feign.
Ye so desire, and I resist in vain.
Up, then! which one of you will lend his hand?
Which will feign with me? which be mine accomplice?

"MARTIAN." Thou, Prince, whom heaven inspired to plan this
ruse.

"LEONTIUS." Thou, whom the tyrant stubbornly wants for son.

"MARTIAN." Thou, who for four years wert in love with her.

"LEONTIUS." Thou, who canst win his love better than I.

"MARTIAN." Thou, who canst better play the part of husband.

"LEONTIUS." Thou, who just now agreedst to be his son.

PULCHERIA. Ah, Princes, ye cannot belie your nature;
And ye are, both, too noble, too high-souled,
To accept guilt's semblance, even, without shrinking.
Too well I knew you, to think otherwise
Either of your advice or of its outcome,
And I deferred to it to see you revoke it.
Imposture shames those born to govern. Let us
Await whate'er comes, but consent to nothing.

"MARTIAN." Yet marvel at what hapless fate is mine.
The hidden truth to which my blood will bear
Witness cannot confer on me the exalted
Name which hath doomed me. No one will believe
The testimony of my death about it;
And that death will be wasted, since in dying
I cannot rescue it to be mine own.

"LEONTIUS." See, on the other hand, what is my portion,
Madam: I in the course of one same day
Am Heraclius, Leontius, and Martian—
An emperor's son, a tribune's, and a tyrant's.
Of all three this confusion makes me born
In one day, finally to make me die
Without my ever knowing which I am.

PULCHERIA. Yield, both of you, yield place to my fate's cruelty.
It makes a mighty effort to outdo yours.

Your plight is dire, but whatsoe'er comes of it,
The death refused to me will be its cure.
But I . . . What doth this false wretch want?

Enter AMYNTAS.

AMYNTAS.   My hand
Hath just washed out that name in Phocas' blood.
"MARTIAN." What sayst thou?
AMYNTAS.   That thou wrongly takest us
For traitors; that the tyrant is no more;
That ye are masters now.
"MARTIAN."   Of what?
AMYNTAS.   Of all
The Empire.
"LEONTIUS."   And by *thy* work?
AMYNTAS.   Nay, my lord.
That glory is another's; but I shared
In the honor of it.
"MARTIAN."   And what blest deliverer
Ended our misery?
AMYNTAS.   Princes, would ye
Have e'er believed it? 'Twas Exuperus.
"LEONTIUS." He who betrayed me?
AMYNTAS.   Thus can I astound thee;
For he betrayed thee thus only to crown thee.
"MARTIAN." Did he not quell the fury of the rebels?
AMYNTAS. His orders alone roused them to rebel.
"LEONTIUS." And yet he captured the ring-leaders?
AMYNTAS.   Marvel
How these same prisoners conspiring with him
Sped to their vengeance under this pretense.
All of us being united 'gainst the monster,
We freely went, followed by many friends,
Across the palace to his own apartments.
The guard was small there, and without suspicions.
Crispus himself to Phocas bore our message.
He came; the prisoners were made to kneel;
These for a signal drew their daggers first.
The rest, impatient in their generous wrath,
Closed round the victim—when Exuperus

Suddenly cried: "Stay! the first blow is mine.
It will restore mine honor almost lost."
He struck, and the usurper fell forthwith,
Lifeless, so many blows followed his own.
A mighty tumult rose, from all whose voices
Could be heard only "Long live Heraclius!"
We seized the doors; the guards straightway surrendered;
The same cry spread forthwith on every side;
And of the many soldiers that maintained
His power, Phocas had after his death
None loyal.

PULCHERIA.   What a course Exuperus took
To slay him!

AMYNTAS.   Here he comes, with Leontina.

(*Enter* LEONTINA, EUDOXIA, EXUPERUS, *and many others.*)

"MARTIAN" (*to* LEONTINA). Is it true, madam? Are our fortunes now
Changed? Did Amyntas tell us all aright?

LEONTINA. Sir, such an outcome scarce can be believed in.
The wondrous carrying-out of this great plan . . .

"MARTIAN" (*to* EXUPERUS). High-souled betrayer, come straight to embrace
Two princes powerless to recompense thee.

EXUPERUS. I need forgiveness, sir, by one of them.
If I avenged thy father, I slew his.

"LEONTIUS." Whiche'er it be, he must find consolation
That 'twas a tyrant died who wished to kill him.
Yet somehow in my heart I feel compassion.

"MARTIAN." Perhaps thereby are ties of blood revealed.
Yet, Prince, thy fortunes will not be less happy.
If mine the Empire, thou wilt have Pulcheria.
The father dead, the son is worthy of her.
     (*To* LEONTINA) Then, madam, put an end to our contention.

LEONTINA. My single testimony will decide it?

"LEONTIUS." What other evidence could we require?

LEONTINA. Then I am not suspected still of trickery.
But no; believe not me; believe the Empress.
     (*To* PULCHERIA, *giving her a letter*) Thou knowest her
          hand, madam; 'tis to thee
That I consign a brother's and a husband's

Fortunes. Read this which, ere she died, thy mother
Left me.

PULCHERIA.   I kiss, with sighs, her sacred writing.

LEONTINA.   Learn from it, Princes, who gave life to you.

"MARTIAN" (*to* EUDOXIA).   Whoe'er I be, to thee do I belong.

PULCHERIA (*reading the Empress Constantina's letter*).
"My single blessing 'mid such bale is strange.
When she had given up her son to save
Mine, Leontina by a new exchange
My son in place of his to Phocas gave.

"Ye who knew naught of her great sacrifice,
Know this: she hoodwinked the usurper twice.
Leontius is Martian; and that one
Called Martian now, is Maurice's real son.
                                  "CONSTANTINA."

(*To* "MARTIAN," *now known to be* HERACLIUS). Ah, thou'rt
my brother!

HERACLIUS (*hitherto called* "MARTIAN").   Yes, and fortunately
The truth disclosed restores thee to thy lover.

LEONTINA (*to* HERACLIUS).   Thou knewest it well enough to avoid
incest
And not to make the secret fatal to thee.
(*To* MARTIAN, *hitherto called* "LEONTIUS") But, sir, forgive
my single-souled devotion—
What I have tried to do and another did.

MARTIAN.   Nowise would I oppose the common joy;
But suffer me to grieve as blood-ties bid me.
Though Phocas never deserved any love,
A son cannot accord less to his father.
One does not instantly renounce that title.

HERACLIUS.   Then, to forget him, be again Leontius.
Under that glorious name love thou his foes.
Let of a tyrant even his son's name perish.
(*To* EUDOXIA) Madam, do thou accept my hand and empire,
And give to me a heart for which mine yearns.

EUDOXIA.   My lord, thou actest as a noble prince.

HERACLIUS (*to* EXUPERUS *and* AMYNTAS). And ye, whose brave hearts
       rendered me such service,
  Await the evidence of my gratitude;
  And let us, friends, give thanks to heaven's power,
  Worship it, and with glad soul show the face
  Of Heraclius to the populace.

Don Sanche d'Aragon

(DON SANCHO OF ARAGON)

INTRODUCTION

For two reasons *Don Sanche d'Aragon* (1649), which failed because some exalted personage found offense in it, may be regarded as still open to question. As we shall presently see, there are certain misconceptions, generally current, about it. Moreover, it is the first example, so Corneille declares, of a new type of play, intermediate between comedy and tragedy and called by him "heroic comedy," which critics have been so engrossed in defining, analyzing, and relating to the previous tragi-comedy, to eighteenth-century *drame,* and to the romantic tragedy of Hugo and the elder Dumas, that they have devoted little time to discussing the merits and defects of *Don Sanche* as a drama.

About the relative potentialities of this new dramatic type —or of tragi-comedy, or of French romantic drama—and tragedy there ought to be no difference of opinion. Merlet, in his pages on *Don Sanche,* has stated it well:

"In falsifying the conditions of life, one condemns oneself to artificial feelings which awaken in the imagination a taste for idle fancies, for mere day-dreaming, for a scorn of reality. That is the reef on which this type of play splits. The great genius who originated it has nowise avoided that danger." [1]

It is entirely possible, however, that a flawless or little-flawed play of an inferior type may be a better—even greatly better —play than some badly-flawed play of a higher type. A failure to realize this fact is a reef on which critics are in danger of splitting.

Don Sanche d'Aragon is far from being flawless. Recognition is general that this play does not fulfil the promise of its first act. This act, says Lemaître, "smacks of Hugo at his best. Its heroic flourish [*panache*] is amazing; and nothing is more Castilian, and nothing is more romantic." [2] Similarly Dorchain: "If the subsequent acts were as good as the first, *Don Sanche* would be yet another masterpiece." [3]

Such disparity appears to Lanson an inevitable consequence of Corneille's mental bent. "When the romanticism of the

[1] P. 151.
[2] P. 310.
[3] P. 320.

first act has beguiled the reader, and he admires the great Corneille for having written a cloak-and-sword drama, let him read the rest: he will see very soon that there is nothing but pyschology in what follows, a development often subtle and searching—always moral, always within the mind, and wholly put in words—of the data of the first act. This romanticism of *Don Sanche* is only a brilliant, Spanish-flavored expository introduction; it is not the real play, which is as severely classical as *Cinna*." [4]

It is doubtful, however, if anyone else would agree with the last clause of this quotation. Petit de Julleville had a higher opinion of the type to which *Don Sanche* belongs: "In reality it had existed for seventy years under the name of tragi-comedy —an attractive and varied genre, nearer to us, more human, more animated than tragedy is; it might have produced some masterpieces, but had not the good fortune to do so." He went on to say: "*Don Sanche* comes very close to being such a masterpiece; it lacks an indefinable something, a better sustained action, a livelier development—not good verses, which are plentiful, vigorously fashioned, sonorous, and stately." [5]

Schlumberger also thinks that the in-his-opinion "entirely original genre" which Corneille "creates this time," did not "have the good fortune which it deserved." But he finds the change in the tone of *Don Sanche* at a later point and not for the worse. "The play is ingenious, charming, in half-tints for three acts; then it comes to life, and the action becomes closely knit and is resolved in a final act which is very moving." He believes that today "a revival of *Don Sanche* might be a success." [6]

The misconceptions to which I alluded at outset would, I think, militate against it on the stage now, as they doubtless have hindered a just appraisal of it by readers. We are disappointed and dissatisfied when the claims of personal merit, ability, and achievement, regardless of one's lowly birth, which are asserted by Carlos, cease to be an issue upon the discovery that he is a king's son. Of course, no other denouement would

---

[4] *Corneille,* 5th ed., Paris, 1919, p. 131.
[5] P. xiv.
[6] Pp. 155, 159.

have been tolerated in seventeenth-century France; but we feel, because of our own convictions on this subject, that the issue ought not to have been raised and then shirked. The truth is, however, that this issue never bulked large in Corneille's mind when he wrote *Don Sanche*. The task which he here proposed to himself from the first was, instead, to demonstrate that "blood will tell." He sought to show that one who was a king's son would always, though believing himself of the humblest origin, behave in the noblest manner; and the plot is shaped to exhibit him doing this in various trying circumstances. Thus viewed, the play will be seen to have been devised with no little cleverness.

In *Don Sanche* the *voix du sang* is again made ridiculous, but this time by representing it as a genuine phenomenon with grotesque consequences. The hero loves the young queen of Castile, but is equally devoted to the Aragonian princess Elvira; and Elvira appears to be in love with him and with the nobleman Don Alvar, both at the same time. These strange acrobatics of the heart are finally accounted for by the discovery that he is Sancho, the rightful king of Aragon; the *voix du sang* has aroused mutual love in him and Elvira, and as they never dreamed they were brother and sister, they mistook their affection for being in love with each other, although each was conscious of being in love with someone else!

It seems impossible that Corneille did not realize that such nonsense was nonsense. He had put nothing like it into any of his tragedies. Its effect helps to give this play—no tragedy, but a *"comédie héroïque,"* a new type, according to its author himself—an atmosphere of make-believe not unlike, in some degree, that of a modern musical comedy. We can accept in a slightly unreal, slightly conventionalized stage-world Isabella's outburst of jealousy about Carlos and Elvira, surely excessive in its virulence even by French-classical standards; we can smile at it as a part of the convention, whereas if regarded soberly it would render despicable an otherwise attractive heroine. Thus taken not too seriously, *Don Sanche* seems to me one of the very best of Corneille's lesser plays.

I shall conclude by quoting two especially appreciative estimates of it, one written some fifty, the other only some

twenty, years ago—the first by a great and famous critic, the
second by a brilliant modern non-conformist in criticism. The
first is by Faguet:

"*Don Sanche d'Aragon* is a romanesque comedy which is
altogether charming. . . . The true Corneillian hero reappears
in it, or rather the true hero of Corneille's youth, Roderick,
chivalrous, ready to fight at the drop of a hat, magnanimous,
a swordsman, a duelist, whose religion is honor. Only he does
not incur very great perils, and that is why this drama is a
comedy. It is full of romantic eloquence, of challenges, of
bravado, and of rhetorical speeches which have a heroic
flourish; and it often seems as though it were written by that
poet of the school of 1630 [*sic;* but is not this a misprint for
1830, meaning the advent of French romantic drama with
Hugo's *Hernani?*] who came a little late, Edmond Rostand." [7]

The other quotation is from Brasillach. "Beyond doubt,"
he says, "we shall not find again in this action-packed comedy
the feverish fire of youth, the vital and marvelous accents of
the *Cid;* but we shall find again the same color, the same
sword-thrusts and sunlight, the glowing love, and a certain
pride which here is strangely transformed into a plebeian
pride . . . All this without overstressing at any time the tone
of romantic comedy, rather than of melodrama, that char-
acterizes this play—which is nearer to Lope de Vega than to
Shakespeare, nearer also to the elder Dumas, but has a charming spriteliness, a gaiety which seems to make sport of even the
theatrical devices used by it, and which Corneille will henceforth recapture but rarely. . . . Thus he has given us a blithe,
proud poem which best of all brings back to the stage the
spirit of the *Cid.* That he has taken, as he says, some elements
from the *Palacio Confuso* of Lope de Vega or from the story
of Don Pelago detracts nothing from his romantic and graceful
inventiveness or from the exquisite charm of his work. . . .
Pierre Corneille returns once more to the Spain of all fairy-
lands and of all enchantment, and without any note that seems
new, or any strained invention, he delights us simply with a
smoothly flowing, romantic tale." [8]

[7] P. 170.
[8] Pp. 269, 272-273.

CHARACTERS IN THE PLAY

ISABELLA, *Queen of Castile.*

LEONORE, *Queen of Aragon.*

ELVIRA, *Princess of Aragon.*

CARLOS, *a young soldier of unknown origin.*

DON RAIMUNDO DE MONCADE, *favorite of the late King of Aragon.*

DON LOPE DE GUZMAN
DON MANRIQUE DE LARRA } *great Castilian nobles.*
DON ALVAR DE LUNA

BLANCA, *lady-in-waiting of the Queen of Castile.*

Nobles and guards.

The scene is laid in Valladolid, in a room in the palace of Queen Isabella.

Don Sancho of Aragon

ACT I

QUEEN LEONORE *and the Princess* ELVIRA *are discovered.*

LEONORE. After so much misfortune, propitious heaven
      Has now resolved, daughter, to give us justice.
      Our Aragon, uprisen in our favor,
      Takes from our enemies what they took from us,
      Breaks the vile fetters of their wicked rule,
      Accepts our governance and hails its queens.
      Its emissaries, who are today expected,
      Will proudly bring us home from our long exile.
        Like us, Castile hath waited for this day,
      Which will arrange the marriage of its queen.
      We are to see her here select a husband.
      Would I could say the same for thee, my daughter!
      We go to lands where twenty years of absence
      Leave thee a power that is weak and doubtful.
      Confusion reigneth where thou art to reign.
      The people have recalled thee, and can flout thee
      If in returning from Castile thou bring'st them
      Only a mother's counsels and thy name.
      The arm and mandates of a valiant husband
      Would better far than we make thy realm stable
      And by his lordly, great, and glorious deeds
      Quell insurrection and put down rebellion.
      Thou lackest not lovers who are worthy of thee.
      They love thy crown; they love thee, and the Count
      Don Alvar, most of all, with his rare virtues,
      Loved thee in exile and midst thy misfortunes.
      One who thus loved and aided thee is truly,
      When thou regainest thy throne, well worthy of it.
ELVIRA. The Count is noble and has proved it to me;
      Such heaven hath wished to acknowledge him to me;
      For the Castilians name him one of three
      From whom they ask their great queen to make choice,
      And since his rivals are of lesser merit,
      A sweeter hope solicits him at present.
      Without us, he will reign. But, after all,

Knowest thou if Aragon hath not some preference
And what new turmoil I may there awaken
If I bring thither a stranger for its master?
Let us, please, mount the throne, and we much better
Can from its height look down to choose a husband.

LEONORE.   Thou "lookest down" too much; thy love in secret
Already hath, despite me, made its choice.
The dazzling valor of the unknown stranger
Carlos hath closed thy heart to others' worth.
Noble is he in all things, I confess;
But his descent, which is from common clay,
And which he stubbornly conceals with care . . .

ELVIRA.   Thou mightest judge more favorably of him.
His lineage, though unknown, may be unblemished.
Thou hast presumed it base because he hides it;
But oft have princes in disguise been seen
Showing their prowess under assumed names,
Subduing lands, and winning crowns without
Anyone's knowing them—or their knowing themselves!

LEONORE.   What! those, then, are the fancies that beguile thee?

ELVIRA.   I love and prize in Carlos his great merits.
There is no lofty soul wherein such valor
Doth not rouse such esteem and kindly feelings,
And the innocent tribute paid by these emotions,
And owed by everyone to heroic deeds,
Is naught which can dishonor a young princess.
He being such, I both love and cherish him.
He being such, his assiduous attentions
Render me the respect my birth makes proper.
He pays court to me as any other can.
He is of too high character to be forward,
But if his vows should ever reach mine ear
I well know who I am and what befits me.

LEONORE.   May heaven vouchsafe to give thy heart the courage
To recall that and act accordingly!

ELVIRA.   What thou commandest will always rule my heart.

LEONORE.   But is this Carlos to accompany thee?
Is he to come even to the lands thou'lt govern,
Render thee that respect thy birth makes proper,
And simply pay court there to thee as here?

ELVIRA.   War is for men like him the one true sphere.
　　　　　Wont to proceed from victory to victory,
　　　　　They everywhere seek dangers and fresh glory.
　　　　　The capture of Seville and the defeat
　　　　　Of the Moors hath left Castile in utter peace;
　　　　　And as he finds himself without employment
　　　　　Here, his great soul is restless, and he would fain
　　　　　Make complete Don Garcia's overthrow
　　　　　And 'gainst the efforts of the remaining rebels
　　　　　Hasten with all his valor our good fortune.
LEONORE.   But when he makes firm on the throne thy seat
　　　　　And casts thy strongest foes down at thy feet,
　　　　　Will he go thence forthwith to alien climes
　　　　　To seek anew for glory and for dangers?
ELVIRA.   The Queen is entering.
　　　　　　　　　　　　　　(*Enter* QUEEN ISABELLA *and* BLANCA.)
LEONORE (*to* ISABELLA).　　　Today, then, madam,
　　　　　Thou art to make some hero's love most happy
　　　　　And with one word fulfil the fervent prayers
　　　　　Thy faithful subjects have addressed to heaven.
ISABELLA.   Say, rather say, that I today, great queens,
　　　　　Impose upon myself before your eyes
　　　　　The sorest constraint, do outrage to my feelings,
　　　　　And sacrifice myself to the realm's good.
　　　　　How sad and grievous is the fate of queens,
　　　　　Who cannot reign save 'neath another's sway!
　　　　　How heavy for them is the scepter thought
　　　　　To be, to need a husband to sustain it!
　　　　　　Scarce had I worn the diadem two months
　　　　　When I was told on all sides I was loved—
　　　　　If I without sin and without being indignant
　　　　　Can speak of eagerness to reign as "love."
　　　　　The ambition of those nobles who aspire thus
　　　　　Seems ready to undo me to obtain me,
　　　　　And, to cut short the course of their dissensions,
　　　　　I needs must shut the door upon their hopes.
　　　　　I must choose one of them, they themselves urge it;
　　　　　My people beg me to, my realm implores it,
　　　　　And by my own command three are proposed
　　　　　From whom they wish me to make a worthy choice.

Don Lope de Guzman, Don Manrique de Larra,
And Don Alvar de Luna have great merit;
But what serves me this choice to be made from them
If none of them is really my heart's choice?

LEONORE.   They have been named but not prescribed to thee.
Whome'er thy wish selects, 'twill be obeyed.
Thou, if thy heart hath chosen, canst make a king.

ISABELLA.   I am queen, madam, and must rule o'er my feelings.
The rank we hold, jealous for our fair fame,
Often forbids us to believe our judgment
In such a choice, to an imperious yoke
Bends our desires, and disregards the counsel
Both of our hearts and of our eyes.
                    (*Calling out*) Throw open
The doors!
(*To herself*) Just heaven, behold my pain. Inspire me
As to what I should do, what I should say.
        (*The doors are opened. Enter* DON LOPE, DON MANRIQUE,
            DON ALVAR, CARLOS, *and other notables.*)
    Before I choose, I ask your oath, Counts, that
My choice will be agreed to without question,
And that the two, or perhaps three, rejected
Will from my hands accept, whoe'er it be,
A master. For I, after all, am free
To make disposal of myself. The choice
Made by the realm is not a mandate for me.
It rids me of a too importunate throng
And turns my thoughts from all of them to you three,
But without binding me to look no further.
I am glad thus to know ye are preferred
Above all others; ye are hence the dearer
And the more valued in my sight. I see
Herein the honorable proofs of your
Great worth. I see herein the high esteem
In which your mighty deeds are held. But though
I mean now to confine my choice to you,
Heaven sometimes instructs us in an instant.
I wish, in choosing thus, to be able not to,
And ask you to agree that to be king
Whoe'er may please me needs but my decision.

DON LOPE. Yes, thy authority remains wholly thine.
   The realm can only make requests of thee,
   And it hath shown thee its opinion of us
   Only in obedience to thy commands.
   'Tis not at all its choice or the distinction
   Of my descent which makes me hope this honor,
   Great queen, is to be mine; I look for it solely
   From thine own graciousness as one expecteth
   A blessing which he hath not merited,
   And which without regard to birth or service
   Thou canst dispense to the lowliest in Castile.
   It is for us to obey, and not to murmur;
   But thou'lt permit us to believe that thou
   Wilt let this sign of favor, the good fortune
   Of being thine, fall on the least unworthy
   And that thy noble heart will make thee see
   That 'tis not best to use all of thy power.
   Those are my sentiments.

ISABELLA.   Speak thou, Don Manrique.

DON MANRIQUE. Madam, since I must needs declare before thee
   My feelings, though thy words have told us things
   Which might awaken in us just suspicions,
   I none the less shall say to thee as my sovereign
   That thou, to make a true king, needs must act
   In the capacity of a queen. To let
   Thy power be limited is thyself to weaken
   The dignity of the rank which should exalt it,
   And if thou deemest the choice given thee binding,
   The king thou makest will owe little to thee;
   For he will be a monarch and thy husband
   As much through the realm's choice as through thine own.
    As for me, who have loved thee without scepter
   Or crown and ne'er had eyes save for thy person,—
   Whom the late king deigned so far to consider
   As to permit my love and give me hope,—
   I dare to anticipate a happy fate
   From four years' service and thy brother's sanction;
   But if I must of that sweet hope be cheated,
   Since thou desirest this, I swear to obey.

ISABELLA. Thus should one love me. And Don Alvar de Luna?

DON ALVAR.   I shall not tire thee with a lengthy speech.
Choose outside of us three; let thy will rule us;
I swear to obey, madam, implicitly.

ISABELLA.   Beneath the deep respect such deference showeth,
Thou perhaps hidest from us some indifference;
And as thy heart doth not lack other love,
Thou knowest how to pay thy court to both.

DON ALVAR.   Madam . . .

ISABELLA.   Enough! Let all now take their places.
                *(Each of the three queens seats herself in an armchair, and
                after them the three counts and the rest of the nobility
                present on the settles reserved for them.* CARLOS, *seeing an
                empty place, goes to sit there, and* DON MANRIQUE *stays
                him.)*

DON MANRIQUE.   Not so fast, Carlos, not so fast! Whence art thou
So bold? What right entitles thee to this seat?

CARLOS.   I saw it vacant and thought I well might take it.

DON MANRIQUE.   Well that a soldier take a noble's seat?

CARLOS.   Sir, what I am gives me no shame at all.
For more than six years there was never combat
In which I earned not that great name of soldier.
                (To ISABELLA*)* I had for witness the late king, thy brother,
Madam, and three times . . .

DON MANRIQUE.   We have seen thy deeds
And know better than thou dost thine arm's might.

ISABELLA.   Ye are informed about that; I am not.
Let him tell *me* hereof. 'Tis well for rulers
Who wish to reward manhood worthily
To learn to recognize it and to know
Among their subjects those they ought to honor.

DON MANRIQUE.   I deemed not I was here to listen to *him*.

ISABELLA.   Again I say, Count, let him tell his story.
We shall have time for everything. Speak, Carlos.

CARLOS.   I shall say who I am in few words, madam.
I was called "soldier." I am proud of being one.
I proved myself one thrice to the late king.
The standard of Castile, seized and borne off
Before his eyes, was saved by me alone
From the foe's hands. This single act retrieved
The battle, drove the Moors back to their walls;

It restored courage to the faintest hearts,
Mustered the vanquished, routed the victorious.
    The same king saw me once in Andalusia
Rescue his person at my own life's hazard,
When, pierced with blows, upon a heap of dead,
I made my body serve as a shield for him
So long that finally his troops rallied round him,
Those who had hemmed him in were all cut down,
And the same squadron that had succored him
Brought him home victor and me almost dead.
    I mounted first the ramparts of Seville
And held the breach there open for Castile.
    I shall say naught of numerous other exploits,
Which were not witnessed by my sovereign's eyes.
Witnesses see and hear me and still scorn me
Who but for me would groan in Moorish prisons.

DON MANRIQUE. Of me and of Don Lope speakest thou, Carlos?

CARLOS. I speak alone of what the King hath seen, sir.
    Let him who wishes speak as conscience bids him.
    For these deeds the King promised to reward me,
But death o'ertook him even as he so resolved.

ISABELLA. He would have paid in full the debt he owed thee;
    And I, inheriting his crown and scepter—
I take on me his debt, and I will pay it.
    Be seated; have done with these petty quarrels.

DON LOPE. Vouchsafe that he shall name his parents, first.
    We question not the greatness of his prowess,
Madam; and if it needs our recognition
We both will testify, in the last battle
Both of us, but for him, would have been captured.
    Yet still his valor, without noble race,
Gives him no right to occupy this place.

CARLOS. Let him who will make boast of his high birth.
    Nowhere would I show aught but mine own worth.
    I would owe nothing to mine ancestors
And am enough known without making *them* known.
    But in some fashion to obey thy hest,
Sir, as my parents I shall name my deeds.
    My valor is my race, mine arm my father.

DON LOPE. Thou seest, madam: the proof is evident;

He certainly is not a nobleman.

ISABELLA. Well then, I make him one, whate'er may be
His lineage, and whoe'er may be his father.
Let it no more be questioned.

DON MANRIQUE.   One word further,
Please.

ISABELLA.   Don Manrique, this is too presumptuous.
Can I not, without thy consent, confer
Nobility on him?

DON MANRIQUE.   Yes, but this place
Is meant for none but those of highest rank.
One not a marquess or a count profanes it.

ISABELLA (*to* CARLOS). Well, sit down, then, Marquess of Santillana,
Count of Peñafiel, Governor of Burgos.
Is this enough, Don Manrique, to let Carlos
Be seated, or dost thou still doubt 'tis proper?
(DON MANRIQUE *and* DON LOPE *rise, and* CARLOS *seats
    himself.*)

DON MANRIQUE. Go on, go on, madam, and make him king.
To lift him to our level by these honors
Is less to equate him with us than to bring him
Near thee. This clever preface had its meaning,
And these oaths we were asked to take just now
Showed well what choice thou hadst at heart intended.
Thou finally canst make it; we have sworn.
I shall submit and, far from arguing 'gainst it,
I leave thee and thy kingdom in his hands.
I shall go ere thou choosest him, not that I
Am jealous, but from fear of blushing for thee.

ISABELLA. Stay, insolent man! thy queen forgives thy ill-judged
Suspicion which unworthy doubts bred in thee,
And to confute it, wishes to assure thee
That she would choose from those her realm suggested,
That thou still holdest the same place in her heart,
That she regards thy outburst as inspired
By an excess of love, and that instead
Of punishing its offensive violence
She shuts her eyes to crimes of such a nature.

DON MANRIQUE. Madam, then pardon me if some repugnance . . .

ISABELLA. Make no display now of false moderation.

I have seen thy pride too plainly to absolve thee,
And well I know the way to humble it.
    Whether I do love Carlos or I simply
Pay, through esteem, fit tribute to his virtues,
Ye must respect, whatever be my purpose,
My heart's decision or my hands' creation.
I have made him your equal, and howe'er
That be resented, know, my favor destines
Yet more for him. I wish that he this day
May have more power than I. I made a marquess
Of him; I wish him to make someone king.
If he has such worth as ye say yourselves,
He well knows what is yours; he knows your merits,
And can decide among you with more judgment
Than I, who know only your fame and lineage.
    Take my ring, Marquess. Give it as a token
To the worthiest of the three, that I may make him
A monarch. I shall give thee, to consider
Thy choice, all that remaineth of this day.
    Rivals, ambitious men, pay court to him.
Whoe'er shall bring to me the ring I gave him
Shall that same moment have my hand and crown.
Let us go, Queens—go and let them determine
On what side love was able to enlist me.
                 (Exeunt all but the three counts and CARLOS.)

DON LOPE.   Well, my lord Marquess, wilt thou tell us, prithee,
What, to gain thy support, one has to do?
Thou art our judge; one needs must mollify thee.

CARLOS.   Thou mightest not succeed in doing so.
Have done with such ill-timed and mirthless jesting.

DON MANRIQUE.   It *is* ill-timed, when we must beg thy favor.

CARLOS.   Let us not jest nor beg, but remain friends.
I realize what the Queen left in my hands,
And well shall use it. Ye have naught to fear.
Not one of you will find grounds for complaint.
    I shall not undertake to judge among you
Which of you best deserves to be her husband.
That would be rash. I feel myself unable,
And some might hold me blamable, to do so.
I hence decline, that I may give to you

A judge whom none can doubt without discredit.
'Twill be for each his sword and his own arm.
Counts, on this ring depends the diadem.
'Tis well worth fighting for; ye all have courage;
I hold it . . .

DON LOPE.　　　　For whom, Carlos?

CARLOS.　　　　　　　　　For my vanquisher.
He who can take it from me shall go with it
Unto the Queen. This will be certain proof
Of who is worthiest. Decide among you
The time and place of combat. I shall go there
At once, and shall await you. Fare ye well.　　(*Exit* CARLOS.)

DON LOPE.　Ye see his arrogance.

DON ALVAR.　　　　　　　　Thus lofty natures
Find noble ways in which to answer insults.

DON MANRIQUE.　He is mistaken if he thinks that we
Would deign to measure swords with such as he.

DON ALVAR.　Decline a combat?

DON MANRIQUE.　　　　　　　A commanding general
Who for his honor and renown is jealous
Does not expose himself 'gainst an adventurer.

DON ALVAR.　Rate not so low a warrior so valiant.
Though he be what thy hate would fain believe him,
He must for us be what the Queen hath wished.

DON LOPE.　The Queen, who flouts us, who recks naught of lineage,
And sullies thus the luster of our rank!

DON ALVAR.　Monarchs cannot be censured for their favor.
They at will make and unmake men like us.

DON MANRIQUE.　Thou art indeed discreet as regards sovereigns.
But seest thou not that secretly she loves him?

DON ALVAR.　Say, if thou wouldst, that they are leagued together,—
That she hath such great confidence in his prowess
She hopes by it to make her choice approved
And wed with pride the conqueror of all three of us,—
That she hates us as much as she loves him:
We needs must honor one whom the Queen honors.

DON MANRIQUE.　Deeply dost thou respect her; but dost thou
Desire to win her? It is said the Princess
Of Aragon hath charms so sweet . . .

DON ALVAR.　　　　　　　　No matter

If they be sweet to me or not, I think
It would be criminal to disavow
The high regard in which my country held me.
Since it hath deemed me fit to be its king,
I ever will uphold the estimate
It voiced of me.

                Therefore I go—and nothing
Shall stay me—to dispute now with the Marquess
Don Carlos the possession of this ring
He keeps for us; and if I can prevail
Against his valor, I shall await whichever
Of you twain wishes to deprive me of it.
The field will then be open to you.

Don Lope.   Good!
With thee we can dispute it without shame.
We shall face gladly such a worthy rival.
But this thy marquess—let him seek his equals!

A C T   I I

QUEEN ISABELLA *and* BLANCA *are discovered.*

Isabella. Blanca, hast thou known aught like my misfortune?
Thou seest all my desires condemned to silence,
My heart choose without daring to accept
Its choice, and cherish a sweet love without daring
To hearken to it. Thereby see what it meaneth
To be a queen: I am accountable
Unto myself to act as doth befit
The name of sovereign; I am subject always
To the demands of that throne whereupon
I sit; I can do everything for others
And nothing for myself!

                O royal scepters,
If it be true that all is possible
For you, why can ye not make hearts devoid
Of feeling? why do ye permit that there
Should be charms other than your own, or that
One should have eyes and be unable to trust them?

Blanca. I thought just now thou wert about to trust them,
And more than once for thy fair fame I trembled.

The oath thou madest thy three suitors take
Seemed to prepare thy way to choose Don Carlos.
I was myself pronouncing his name for thee,
But in the outcome I at length discovered
My fears were fortunately false. Thou provedst
Able to keep love's impulses in bounds.
Thou honoredst him without dishonoring
Thyself, and satisfiedst at once, deceiving
My expectations, the greatness of a queen
And the ardor of a loving woman.

ISABELLA.   Rather
Say that to honor his great-heartedness
My love hath played with my authority,
And that it made, against thy expectations,
The Queen's power serve the loving woman's anger.
   By my first words, which seemed to thee suspect,
I wished but to make trial of their respect,
To uphold—throughout—the dignity of queen,
And, as this choice indeed caused me distress,
To consume time and choose a little later.
Yet I did mean to choose—to choose at random—
But then thou knowest what arrogance the counts
Displayed, the affronts he suffered, and my shame.
It of a truth is hard for one who reigns
To show esteem and see its object scorned.
In seeking to avenge its slighted greatness,
Love easily was inclined to show him favors.
Being bound up at the outset with concern
Now for my throne's prerogatives, it acted
So much the more as it believed 'twas hidden,
And dared imagine that it revealed nothing
Which my ennobling him would let men fathom.
   I then made Carlos marquess, count, and governor;
He to those jealous of him owes all these
Titles of honor. In their wish to make me
Sparing of them, they made me lavish of them.
The torrent swelled, encountering a dam.
Less would I favor him than punish them.
Love spoke to me too loudly, and I sought
To give it play; by such extremes I thought

To satisfy it and, on having done so,
To oblige it to be silent. But, alas!
It in my heart had such support that I
Was never able to choose any other
And put the giving of the throne in *his* hands
Only to force him to debar himself.
Thus my rejection of him, to prevent
The murmurs of the Court, seems favor shown him;
And covering o'er this secret slight with honors,
Lest I should make him king I made him more.
Besides, as I was to all three indifferent,
I hoped that I would love the one he chose,—
That even the least of them, himself exceptional,
Might prove, when by him given me, lovable.
    That Blanca, is my plight—is what I did.
Those were the real motives for my actions;
For, although hard beset, I could not for him
Have let my soul have an unworthy thought;
And I would die e'en yet sooner than do
What my heart secretly dares ask me to.
    But now I see that it was a mistake
To leave all in the hands of one who weareth
A sword and findeth herein a chance to avenge
The scorn with which his high worth has been treated.
My choice was to have ended countless quarrels,
And the command I gave to him breeds new ones
And among these great men who are in love
With my estate makes bloodshed necessary.
But I can deal with that.

BLANCA.   'Tis a hard task
To prevent duels which custom authorizes,
Which have their rules, and which the kings thy forebears
Often vouchsafed to grace with their own presence.
One cannot unsay aught without some shame,
And great hearts value more than life fair fame.

ISABELLA.   I know all this, and I shall not give orders
Impetuously which they would think disgraced them.
Whene'er dishonor sullieth obedience,
Rulers may well doubt their almighty power.
One who then risks that, knows not how to use it;

One who would fain be able to do all things
Ought not to dare all things. I shall break up
This duel by feigning to allow it, and I
Shall deem it broken up if I can postpone it.
The queens of Aragon themselves can help me.
Here, now, is Carlos, whom I had just sent for.
Remain, and thou shalt see how perfectly
Honor is always mistress of my heart.

(*Enter* CARLOS.)

  Well hast thou served us, Marquess, and till now
Thine arms have brought us notable success.
I think thy services have been well rewarded
Also.
   Despite those envious of thee,
And their bad offices, I have done much for thee,
And all I did hath cost thee but the wishing.
Yet if this recompense is still too small
To match thy merit,—if there still remaineth
Something else for thee to desire,—speak out
And show me how I may discharge my debt.

CARLOS. After so many favors heaped upon me
Of which my heart would not have dared to dream,
Taken by surprise, confused, o'erwhelmed with blessings,
How should I dare conceive yet more desires?

ISABELLA. Thou'rt then content. *I* have cause to complain.

CARLOS. Of me?

ISABELLA.   Yes, of thee, Marquess. I speak frankly.
Hearken. Thine arm hath served the realm right well
So long as thou hadst but the name of "soldier."
Then, when I made thee great, when I gave to thee
The power to dispose of mine own person, straightway
That arm prepared to trouble the realm's peace,
As though the Marquess were no longer Carlos
Or this thy greatness but supplied the means
By which thy valor would achieve its ruin.
The three counts are its stoutest props and stays;
In them thou strikest at its supports and mine;
Its purest blood is this which thou wouldst shed;
And thou canst judge what great respect is owed them,
Since this land, when it asks of me a king,

Deemeth these three to be the worthiest of me.
    Pride may have put it in thy head that thou
Hadst a good pretext by which to avenge
Their scorn; thou hast obeyed thy first, fierce impulse;
But did their scorn extend unto thy valor?
To that did they not testify before me?
They think but poorly of thine unknown lineage.
They have their doubts about those origins
Thou strivest to conceal. When such quite natural
Misgivings must have stung thee, I took pains
Myself to punish them for thee. To place
In thy hands the bestowal of the crown
Was not to avenge thee by half-measures, Marquess.
I have made thee their judge, and not their foe;
And if I would subject them to thy choice,
It is to honor thee, not destroy them.
'Tis but thy counsel, not their blood, I want;
And ill thou understandest me when thou drawest
Thy sword against them.
                              Mayst thou not have told
Thyself that if thou with thy mighty prowess
Wert to prevail against all three of them,
It would be said the realm, seeking for me
A husband, found none to compare to thee?
Oh, if I thought thou wert so vain, presumptuous . . .

CARLOS.   Madam, curb thy just anger. I am guilty
Enough, and have too greatly dared, without
Thy choosing an imagined crime to undo me.
    I struggle not against the love for thee
Felt by thy lowliest subjects blamelessly.
When I behold in thee the heavenly union
Of all thy graces, both of mind and body,
I can, with heart enraptured by such charms,
Envy the happiness of thy future husband.
I can, in secret, murmur against Fate
For not being born a king, able to hope;
Then, suddenly dazzled by thy matchless radiance,
I lower mine eyes and am myself again.
But to allow my heart to go so far
As to feel toward thee an ambitious love,

With absurd hopes and criminal desires! . . .
   I love thee, madam, and honor thee as queen;
But if my love were one thou shouldst detest
And thou wert thawed by its vile flames and couldst
So far forget thyself as to endure
My wooing,—if by some fatality,
Which I cannot imagine, I should see thee
Stoop from thy throne even to me,—that instant
Would I begin to esteem thee less, and then
I beyond doubt would also cease to love thee.
   The love I feel for thee is to thine honor.
Nowise do I aspire unto thy hand
As my reward if I should be victorious.
I shall engage thy suitors with no aim
To gain aught save the happiness of showing
Which is the worthiest of them, and thus dying;
And I would deem that I deserved men's envy
If I might show this at my life's expense.
Would I requite thy favors adequately
By letting this choice hang on my sole judgment?
It gives Castile a master, thee a husband.
I might judge ill; I ill may know these men.
'Tis true, the genius that presides o'er combats
May likewise give thee and thy realm to him
Who hath the smallest worth, but if the uncertain
Issue of arms should with my death result
In faulty guidance, I shall at least escape
Shame and regret thereat; and verily
If thy heart loves one of the three in secret,
And this bad choice accords not well with thine,
I shall not see thee, in another's arms,
Reproaching Carlos with mute sighs for being
The single author of thy every woe.
ISABELLA.   Seek not excuse in doubts as to my feelings.
I can love; I am, after all, a woman.
But if I love, thou payest court to me badly
When thou exposest to death him whom I love;
And all thine ardency would be abated
Hadst thou amid thy doubts respected me
Enough. I wish to clarify them now,

And better to enlighten thee, in order
To teach thee to respect me properly.

    I shall not hide it: I love someone, Carlos,—
Yes, I love someone,—but I love my country
More than myself, and seek, instead of him
Who is the dearest to mine eyes, the hero
Who is the worthiest to rule these lands;
And fearing lest love might beguile me, I
Wished in this matter to rely on thee
To instruct me. But I think it is sufficient
That he I love should lose the throne and me,
Not lose his life too; and my heart, wherefrom
He will be banished, suffers enough fears
Without his death requiring of me tears.

CARLOS. Ah, had but heaven just now deigned to let me
    Know whom I should revere as thy blest lover,
    By what a quick and easy victory . . .

ISABELLA.   Think
    But to defend thyself and thy repute.
    Whoe'er he be, if thy respect should spare him
    Thou'dst give him thus a prize he could not win;
    And, bowing to my love more than his prowess,
    Thou'dst make its judgment, which I shunned, prevail.

    I nowise shall abuse my sovereign power
Now by forbidding the agreed-on combat.
Thus would I wound the honor of all four.
The law permits your duels, and I shall watch you.
It is my place, as queen, to name the victor.
Tell me, though: who hath shown the bravest spirit?
Which of the three will try his fortune first?

CARLOS. Don Alvar.

ISABELLA.   What! Don Alvar?

CARLOS.   Yes, Don Alvar
    De Luna.

ISABELLA.   It is said he loves another.

CARLOS. So 'tis said; but as yet 'tis he alone
    Who would make trial of this high destiny.

ISABELLA. I almost surely know what interest sways him,
    And we shall see what courage he hath tomorrow.

CARLOS. Thou gav'st me but this one day for the choice.

ISABELLA. I would prefer to accord thee three days for it.

CARLOS. Madam, his challenge specifies today.

ISABELLA. What matters that, unless I give consent?
> Let him be brought hither to see the time
> Postponed. I go to make all preparations
> About your duel. Farewell. Bear thou in mind,
> Above all, that thou must defend me from him.
> Tomorrow I shall favor you with my presence.

>>> (*Exeunt* ISABELLA *and* BLANCA.)

CARLOS (*alone*). Canst thou consent, honor, to this delay?
> Canst thou consent to it? Is there in this mandate
> Naught which attaints my manhood? Have I no
> Reason to blush at my obedience, bought
> From me by being given leave to fight?
> Thou murmurest, doth it seem? Then state thy case.
> Hath the Queen any right to lay down laws
> For me? I am not her subject. Aragon
> Beheld my birth. . . . Ah heaven! I remember
> That, and I dare be seen here still; I can
> Under the names of Count and Marquess know
> Myself the son of a poor fisherman!
>   Ignoble origin, which alone dismays me!
> Vile portion, which alone renders me piteous!
> The more I climb thence, all the more I dread
> Returning thither and think that I escaped thee
> Only again to find thee. The cruel memory
> Of thee without cease hounds me; from the station
> To which I have risen it shows me how I well
> Might fall. Henceforth no longer make me tremble.
> I seek for honor; come not to confound me.
> Let me be unembarrassed in the presence
> Of royalty, and rob me not of more
> Than thou canst give me. Now I owe thee naught.
> War hath drained from me all that lowly blood
> With which thou gavest me life. I have abandoned
> Everything but the name I owe to thee,
> And cannot . . . But lo, here is my true queen.

>>> *Enter the Princess* ELVIRA.

ELVIRA. Ah, Carlos—for 'tis hard to call thee "Marquess";

Not that thou hast not well earned that fair title,—
Not that it is not rightly given thee,—
But it comes to thee from another's hand,
And I had fancied 'twould be solely mine
To exalt thee to the glorious rank now thine.
Yet I would joyfully be reconciled
To favors showered on thee by heaven without me,
And without jealousy would see a hero
Exalted, if the Marquess would adhere
To all that Carlos promised me,—if he
Would like him have an arm prepared to serve me.
I was going to the Queen to ask for justice
Of her; but since I have encountered thee,
Thou'lt give me satisfaction in this matter.
   I then accuse thee, not of being false—
That crime is too black for a noble heart—
But only of some little lack of memory.

CARLOS.   In me, madam?

ELVIRA.   Hear quietly my complaint.
It is against the Marquess, not 'gainst Carlos.
Carlos would keep whole-heartedly his word
To me, but that which he hath given me
The Marquess now takes back. 'Tis he alone
Who thus makes free with what belongs to others
And wastes his arm's might when 'tis his no longer.
Carlos would have recalled that his great prowess
Was to make Don Garcia become my subject;
He was to seat me firmly on my throne;
He was, perhaps, to accompany me tomorrow.
But Carlos is no more, and in his place
There is the Marquess now, whom other cravings
For glory—other loyalties—possess,
And who with the same arm he pledged to serve me
Undertakes now three duels for someone else.
Oh, if those honors which the Queen heaps on thee
Reduce my expectations to vain hopes,—
If the new purposes which thou conceivest
Make thee forget what thou shouldst do for me,—
Give back those honors to her, which are sullied
By such forgetfulness; give back to her

Peñafiel, Burgos, and Santillana.
Aragon has wherewith to recompense thee
For spurning them and give thee more besides.

CARLOS. Both Carlos and the Marquess are thine, madam.
My change in rank hath nowise changed my heart.
But thou'lt approve that by these three duels Carlos
Should try to pay the debt the Marquess oweth.
To reserve for thee an arm disgraced by baseness
Would draw down Fortune's enmity on thee
And would expose thee by such infamy
To the just punishment I would deserve.
When to a lofty soul two tasks for valor
Present themselves, honor engages him
Eagerly in the one nearer to hand,
And without rendering him unfaithful makes him
Prefer that one which offers itself to him
Rather than that one which is waiting for him.
Yet it is not that he forgets aught, madam.
But though I must slay Don Garcia for thee,
I have seen disrespect shown to the Queen,
Her heart suspected of an unworthy love;
I have seen her, for honoring me, insulted,
And I cannot be quits till I avenge her.

ELVIRA. I understand, in the excuse thou offerest,
Just this: her service is preferable to mine,
And thou, ere following me, shouldst die for her
And, being her subject, shouldst to me be faithless.

CARLOS. Not as her subject rush I to the combat.
I was perhaps born in some other country.
But with the same whole-hearted loyalty
I undertake to serve both her and thee,
Nor do the greatest perils involve aught
That I would not dare face for either of you.
I stand engaged to fight for her tomorrow;
Yet were there need to avenge thee in some matter
Today, all that I owe her would not keep me
From baring my breast for thee in more than three
Duels. Would that I could satisfy you both—
Thee without failing in aught toward her, and her
Without displeasing thee—but I can nowise

Serve either her or thee without arousing
The anger thus of one or the other of you.
   I would feel pity for a lover who
Suffered my pain,—who, placed 'twixt two fair ladies
As I am 'twixt two queens, found himself torn
With equal love for both, like mine own reverence
For both of you in paying court to both.
The soul of such a lover, wavering
Wretchedly, sees its feelings fluctuate
With endless travail, and not being able
To choose to which to limit its attentions
Dares win naught and dares give up naught. His love
Is always troubled; his glance is always anxious;
Whate'er he doeth affords cause for complaint;
His homage is seen ever in false colors;
And in the eyes of one his greatest service
Done for the other appeareth a great crime.

ELVIRA.   And this is love's first rule, that to divide
One's heart is of all crimes the very worst.
A heart which two share doth belong to no one.
Its vows are taken back as soon as uttered.
What loyalty it hath, too timorous
To make a choice, renders it constantly
Perfidious to one or to the other;
And as there really is no scorn nor harshness
That is not such a heart's deserved reward,
It cannot merit from any eyes that charm it
One glance in serving or one tear in death.

CARLOS.   Thou'dst be indeed severe toward such a lover.

ELVIRA.   Let us go find out if the Queen would act
Differently,—if he could expect a kinder
Treatment from her. Howe'er that be, Don Alvar
Will enter the field first; and well thou knowest
What great love he hath always shown for me.

CARLOS.   I know what power thou hast over him.

ELVIRA.   When thou shalt fight with him, think of my wishes
And be as careful of *his* life as thine own.

CARLOS.   What! Thou wouldst have me make him now a king?

ELVIRA.   I bid thee only this: to think of me.

A C T   I I I

The Princess ELVIRA *and* DON ALVAR *are discovered.*

ELVIRA. Thou canst, then, love me and in thy right mind
Canst take part in a duel to win the Queen?
What star can rule thee so inexorably
As to compel thine arm to thwart thy wishes?
Honor, thou sayst, acquits thee toward thy love.
Either thou knowest not what are honor's claims
Or whom thou lovest; and in this dilemma
I cannot grasp the nature of such honor
Or of such love. A lover's honor lies
In being constant; and if *thou* lov'st *me,*
To what dost thou aspire regarding her?
And if thou winnest her, what wouldst thou of me?
Wouldst thou have then a right to be unfaithful
To her? Wouldst thou disdain her, having won her?
DON ALVAR. I, who was born her subject, e'er disdain her?
ELVIRA. What wouldst thou, then, of me? Beaten by Don Carlos,
Couldst thou have charms to trouble my heart's peace?
Wouldst thou be worthier? and by his victory
Would he shed rays upon thee of his glory?
DON ALVAR. How, if defeated, could I dare come near thee?
ELVIRA. What, then, doth thine ambitious heart wish of me?
DON ALVAR. That thou'dst take pity on the woeful plight
To which thy long rejecting me hath brought me.
   A favorable hearing of my suit
Could happily have saved me from the honor
That hath been done me, and the realm would not
Have by its choice e'er given me this dilemma
Of failing in duty or winning my queen's hand.
Thou hast involved me, by refusing me,
In the sore task of fighting in a combat
Where the result must be adverse to me.
I equally fear either outcome of it.
How, indeed, could I desire either one?
Not as the vanquished man or as the victor
Can I be thine: if vanquished, I shall be
Unworthy of thee; and if victorious,

Her husband;—and thus Fate so cruelly wrongs me
That I would find the greatest success torture.
So, when in duty I dare fight for her,
I wish to win her merely to deserve *thee,*—
Merely to show that 'tis thyself I love
And that I could elsewhere obtain a crown.
May heaven grant this, either that I may die
Or may deserve her only to win thee!

ELVIRA.   Vainly thy prayers ask for a miracle
When honor gives thee unsurmountable
Obstacles and the Queen, in place of me,
Can well reward thee for the time which thou
Usest amiss because thou lovest me little.
My crown is ill assured, hers firmly 'stablished.
The advantage in thy change robs it of baseness.
Go, and lose not thine opportunity;
Seize it without embarrassment or shame.
Inconstancy itself where such strong claims
Of honor bind thee is less inconstancy
Than loftiness of spirit, but beware
Lest Carlos shall avenge me now on thee.

DON ALVAR.   Ah, let me love this anger of thine, madam.
I thought till now my combat would seem noble,
But I am happy if 'tis judged a crime
And if, when honor bids me serve another
Thou prizest me enough to be resentful.
Howe'er thou punishest this crime against thee,
At least it gives me more than all my service
Of thee, for by displeasing thee it makes me
Know that thou deignest to take some interest in me.

ELVIRA.   The crime thou seest anger me, Don Alvar,
Is that thou plaguest me after turning from me;
And, to say more to thee, it vexes me
To hear thee blame me for refusing thy suit.
   I am a queen uncrowned, queen but in name.
Power should be mine; time will decide the outcome.
If thou hast served me as a devoted lover
When heaven hath treated me so harshly, I
Have tried to show thee all the appreciation
That one with heart so noble could expect.

Could I, while still an exile, do aught more?
I want no husband whom I cannot make
A king, nor is my soul abject and vulgar
Enough for me to take one who might be
In my misfortune of some help to me.
'Tis in my realm, 'mid pomp and circumstance,
That I must choose one for my land's best interests.
Thou hadst needs torn my scepter from the rebels,
And given it to me, to receive it from me.
Then might I have been able to pay heed
To thee more than my wretched fate hath let me.
But a more brilliant opportunity
Hath first been offered to thy wavering love;
And be it that thou foundest this to thy liking
Or that my long refusal of thee hath left thee
Open to its solicitings, I blame thee
Nowise for having seized it: some more constant
Than thou might well have hearkened unto it.
Whate'er thy motive or thy woe may be,
Thou couldst have acted with less eagerness,
Fought last, and by some outward show suggested
That honor had constrained thee; such pretence
Would have forced me to pity thee, and to lose thee
Regretfully—but to rush forward first
Of all, and to be willing to show plainly
That thou art glad that thy vows did not win me!

DON ALVAR.   Thou wishest, then, that the honor of being chosen
Should prove thy lover the least brave of the three,—
That glory should have few attractions for him
Until his adversary's strength is spent,—
That ...

ELVIRA.   Thou wilt triumph on issuing from the combat
With Carlos if thou'rt in a state to do so.
Here thy two rivals are; with them I leave thee,
And I will say tomorrow whom I favor.   (*Exit* ELVIRA.)

DON ALVAR.   Alas! to know this I can see too clearly!

Enter DON MANRIQUE *and* DON LOPE.

DON MANRIQUE (*to* DON ALVAR).   Which treats thee better, love or
   fortune? Do

The Queen's charms approach those of Doña Elvira?
DON ALVAR. If I bear off the ring, I needs must tell thee.
DON LOPE. Carlos stands in thy way at every turn—
    At least 'tis thought so.
DON ALVAR.   He makes more than one
    Jealous of him—at least it so appears.
DON LOPE. He out of pity ought to let thee have
    One or the other.
DON ALVAR.   In thy concern for my
    Interests, forget not thine.
DON MANRIQUE.   There is in sooth
    Much ado as to which will make him king.
DON ALVAR. I greatly pity both of you if he
    Slays me.
DON MANRIQUE. But if thou o'ercom'st him, should we
    Be greatly pitied?
DON ALVAR.   If I do o'ercome him,
    Ye will have reason to fear.
DON LOPE.   Yes, that thou wilt
    Long be disabled and cannot fight with us.
DON ALVAR. I shall have faced the hardest blows already.
DON MANRIQUE. We are most eager to make test of that.
DON ALVAR. Ye can be cured of your impatience.
DON LOPE.   Prithee,
    Arrange it, then, that this may soon be done.

Enter QUEEN ISABELLA.

ISABELLA. Let me, Don Alvar, speak to them a moment.
    I shall do nothing prejudicial to thee.
    My aim is only to be fair to thee—
    Only to favor thee more than thou wishest.
DON ALVAR. I, when thou speakest, know but to obey.
                      (*Exit* DON ALVAR.)
ISABELLA. Counts, I no more would give cause for complaint
    That choosing through someone else becomes me ill;
    And since the choice will be more prized if mine,
    I wish to take my ring back and myself
    Choose. I shall do more for you: from the three
    Proposed for me, I shall exclude Don Alvar.
    Ye know why: I would not constrain a heart

That loves another; I rid you of a rival
To let him to his own desires return.
One who woos only by compulsion fain
Would be rejected, so I accord to him
At least as great a favor as to you.
   Ye two are all, then, that I shall consider;
But ere I dare to risk a choice between you,
I wish from you some sure proof that in me
'Tis I ye love and not my rank of queen.
Love is a marriage, it is said, of minds,
And I should deem him the more taken with me
Who favors all I favor and despises
Only all I despise,—who would acquire
In loving me the same heart, the same eyes.
If ye have understood me not, I shall
Better explain my meaning.
                     I have seemed
To reward generously the deeds of Carlos.
I wish to see a like esteem of him
In you twain, that ye may accord the same
Honor and the same justice unto him.
For think not I intend to take a husband
To expose myself to this shame: that a king
My hands have made will soon undo my work.
Then hope not, either one, unless some fitting
Act by you follows what I did for him,
And I may thus feel sure that whatsoever
Seemed good to me shall be perpetuated.

DON MANRIQUE. 'Tis always Carlos, madam, and our hearts
And thine always depend on his advancement.
But since 'tis thus that we must please thee, tell us
Thyself what we must do. We both believe him
One of the bravest soldiers unto whom
War ever hath brought laurels. Our own freedom
Is due to his great valor; and though he
Displayed just now some insolence which should have
Been galling to the eminence of our station,
Thou hast made up for his obscure extraction.
Worthy is he to be what thou desirest him.
We owe him much, and this we meant to acknowledge,

To honor him as a soldier and requite him;
But we can do naught more after thy favors.
He who could do for Carlos anything
Can for a count do nothing; there is nothing
We have which he could without shame accept,
And thou hast taken pains to reward him for us.

ISABELLA.   Ye in your power have precious gifts wherewith
To clear your names of all ingratitude
And rid me of all cares concerning him.
He could be their recipient without shame.
In short, each of you hath alike a sister,
And I would have the king I choose to make,
When wedding me, make him his brother-in-law,
That thus his fortunes may be established firmly
And he may find no enemy in my husband.
  'Tis not, though, that I fear your hate for him.
I know that in this realm I shall be always
Queen, and that such a king, whate'er his purpose,
Shall ne'er be anything but my foremost subject.
But I would constrain nobody, and least
Of all a heart to which I gave mine own.
Then tell me, both of you: do ye not consent?

DON MANRIQUE.   Yes, madam—to the slowest, cruelest death
Rather than ever by such nuptials see
The honored luster of a thousand years
Dimmed in one moment. Seek not thus that marriage
Of minds. Thy scepter, madam, is at this price
Too dear; and never . . .

ISABELLA.   Is it thus ye tell me
That what I did was worthy to be done
And I can rectify an obscure lineage?

DON MANRIQUE.   Thou canst exalt him even to our station.
A monarch never oweth an accounting
To anyone for the titles that he gives,
The dignities that he confers. If he
Createth or supporteth unworthy fortunes,
He alone does it, the shame is wholly his.
But give in marriage one of mine own blood
Which I received unsullied, and thus taint it—
Sooner than that, I would shed all of mine!

I am answerable for it to my forefathers,
To all their offspring, to posterity.
ISABELLA.   And I, Manrique, am answerable to no one
For it; I shall alone dispose of it,
And mine shall be the shame. But what fantastic
Logic can tell thee that I would when giving
Myself to thee dishonor thee, and that
My scepter in thy hands would bring disgrace?
If I to that extent am mine own foe,
In what capacity—subject or suitor—
Darest thou set forth to me thy lofty feelings?
Ah, if thou learn'st not to speak differently . . .
DON LOPE.   Pardon the fervor, madam, which transports him.
He ought more tactfully to ask to be
Excused.
          We each have, it is true, a sister;
But if I may hereof dare to speak frankly,
They both are pledged to others than the Marquess.
ISABELLA.   To whom, Don Lope?
DON MANRIQUE.   His to me.
ISABELLA (*to* DON MANRIQUE).   And thine?
DON LOPE.   To me.
ISABELLA.   Then I was wrong to try to make
One of you king. Go, blissful lovers, go
To your heart's mistresses, and 'mid the sweetness
Of your caresses, do not fail to tell them
That ye have nobly scorned a throne for them.
I have already said I constrain no one.
I thank the realm for those proposed to me.
DON LOPE.   Hear us, please.
ISABELLA.   What, then, will ye say to me?
That constancy is deemed by all a virtue?
That no prospective greatness should o'ercome it?
Others than ye can best instruct me in it.
If one should not do violence to it,
Perhaps I can in my turn practice it.
DON LOPE.   Practice it, madam, and suffer us to explain.
Thou knowest at least Don Lope and Don Manrique
And that the real love they both have for thee—
Since one could not be happy without making

The other jealous—leads them to avoid
The quarrels so natural between two great rivals.
They hence have bound themselves unto each other
By these ties which will for the luckless one
Alone be joined. He will owe me his sister
If it must be thou choosest him; and if I
Am chosen by thee, I shall owe him mine.
He who must lose thee will thus still, despite
His loss, try to be somewhat nearer to thee;
Thus, to console whichever hath ill fortune,
The sister of one of us shall wed, she only;
We know not which 'twill be, and thou shalt choose her,
For 'tis the sister of him thou choosest for king.
    Judge, then, if Carlos can be brother-in-law
To him, and if thou shouldst prevent a union
So beneficial and thus jeopardize
The sweet peace of thy realm, which harmony
Between us will ensure beneath thy sway.

ISABELLA.   And know ye not that, being who ye are,—
Your sisters like you being my foremost subjects,—
To give their hand without my leave, and even
Against it, is to dare in mine own realm
To dictate to me?

DON MANRIQUE.   Then act thou indeed
In thy capacity of sovereign, madam,
And suffer one to decline, or else command him
As queen; we shall obey, though 'gainst our will.
But to speak all our minds ere going hence:
Carlos is noble-souled; he knoweth his birth;
Let him, in his own heart, judge with that knowledge,
And if he deemeth his blood meet for such honor,
Let him come; we shall gladly be allied
With him; let him choose either of the two
Ladies, and wed her, if he dares to do so.
    We have no more aught left to say to thee.
To take this risk in choosing them a husband
Is as far, madam, as we can go for thee;
But, I repeat, Carlos should well consider
To just what perils this marriage would expose him.

ISABELLA.   Yourselves beware, of scorning him too much,

Lest I then show you I know how to rule.

                   (*Exeunt* Don Lope *and* Don Manrique.)

(*To herself*) What is it that makes both of them rebellious
When by obedience they can win a throne?
Is it pride? is it envy? is it enmity,
Mistrust, disdain, or lofty-mindedness?
Does this mean heaven permits unwillingly
The union of a subject with a queen
And raises obstacles at once to plans
Which let my scepter fall into such hands?
Feel I no horror that when I must stoop
To wed, I stoop to love so far beneath me?
What fate opposeth my love to my fair fame,—
Opposeth my royal state to my heart's flame?
If I can only thus defend myself,
Heaven, let me give for husband to another
Him whom I dare not take as mine; and since
Thou hast provided me no king, allow me
The least unworthy choice among my subjects.   .

                      (*Enter* Blanca.)

      Blanca, I have but wasted time.

Blanca.   I likewise.

Isabella.   At such a price the counts want not the crown.

Blanca.   And Carlos wants not greatness at that price.

Isabella.   Pays he back hate for hate and scorn for scorn?

Blanca.   Nay, on the contrary, he thinks these ladies
      Worthy of the noblest hearts and truest love.

Isabella.   Then why doth he not love and choose one of them?

Blanca.   Some secret obstacle checks his desire.
      His praise of them goes not beyond esteem.
      Fair though they are, he deems it wrong to love them.
      He gives not the excuse of lowlier birth;
      Rather he seems to fear being false to someone,
      And his confused, obscure words showed to me,
      Despite him, something like a horror of changing,—
      Like a distaste which could have had for basis
      Only the bonds of other, secret love.

Isabella.   *He* love another!

Blanca.   Yes, if I mistake not,

One higher placed than those whom he refuses,
And if I did not fear thy just wrath, madam,
I would make bold to guess that it is thou.

ISABELLA.　Ah, it is not for me he is so rash.
His recent words have shown me this too plainly.
If my crown's splendor could have charmed his soul
He ne'er would have forbidden me to love him.
If he loves one so great, 'tis Doña Elvira.
He was to accompany her back to her kingdom
And gave my suitors his heroic challenge
Not to win me but to take vengeance on them.
　I have exalted him to see him vanish,
And for a queen, ungrateful as this recreant,
To rob me, after twenty years' asylum,
Of what in all my realm was dearest to me.
Nay, I too carefully shielded his life.
Let him fight, let him die, it will delight me.
I shall know by his death whom to accept,—
Shall of those three love him who can avenge me.

BLANCA.　How can his love or going hence offend thee
Since thou desirest but to see him lose thee?
I know not if he loveth her or thee
Yet cannot understand thy jealous spirit.

ISABELLA.　Thou understandest it not! This doth amaze me.
I wish to make disposal of his heart,
Not see his heart's love make disposal of *him*.
I wish his reverence for me to keep him
From loving me, not the love's flames another
Was better able to kindle in his breast.
I wish yet more, that really he should love me
And that a fitting silence should do like
Violence to our hearts, which love alike;
That the great difference in our estate
Should cause him the same grief; that he should suffer
As much on my account as I on his;
That with the sole aim to enhance his fortunes,
And not because of love, he should e'er wed;
That but by my command should he form ties;
That it should be to obey me, not forsake me;
And, since my love was prone to honor him,

That he should save me from it but not shame me.
For he hath seen it, and too well knows of it;
But he desires a throne, and 'tis not mine,
Prefers to me another, and this preference
Creates a false show of respect for me—
Respect which flouts me and would reign without me!

BLANCA.   He is not yet a king, through loving Doña
Elvira.

ISABELLA.   She is queen and hath complete
Power over her mother.

BLANCA.   If 'tis not
Mere rumor, heaven gives her back a brother.
'Tis said Don Sancho is not dead, but comes
With the expected deputies from Aragon.
That is what, reaching here, their servants gave us
To understand.

ISABELLA.   Blanca, if this be true,
What great good fortune I must look for from it!
Heaven's injustice, in the lack of others
To wed me, made me turn unto my subjects
Because I saw no prince in birth my equal
Not married already, nor Moorish, nor a child.
But if it gives her back a brother, heaven
Sends me a husband.

                         Counts, I have eyes no longer
For Carlos or for you; and in becoming
My rival's queen thus, I shall have the right
To keep her from dishonoring herself
And will not let her have more happiness
Than these cruel laws of honor allowed *me*.

BLANCA.   An opportunity which thy jealousy,
Though based on mere conjecture, promptly seizes!

ISABELLA.   Let us go find out more about this story
And see what it is reasonable to hope.   (*Exeunt.*)

A C T   I V

QUEEN LEONORE, DON MANRIQUE, *and* DON LOPE *are discovered.*

DON MANRIQUE.   Although a throne and a queen's love once hoped for

Are blessings never easy to give up,—
Although she promised to wed one of us,—
We cease to aspire when we behold a king.
Midst our ambition we know what we are;
And, blessing heaven which gives us such a master,
We shall be found, by this prince it at last
Restores to thee, his subjects, not his rivals—
Happy if Aragon, joined with Castile,
Shall make one family of two royal lines.
　　We swear this to thee, far from being jealous,
As we both seek our land's good more than ours.
Impatient each to see its strength, united,
O'erthrow the tyranny of the Moors, our neighbors,
We without shame renounce our glorious lot,
Which made a great queen look too far beneath her.

LEONORE.　The magnanimity of your deference, Counts,
Flatters too soon my new hopes. From reports
So questionable, I expect but little,
And all this talk perhaps is only talk.
But judge ye of it, both of you, and tell me
What I may reasonably expect from it.
　　Well known to you are Aragon's dissensions.
I oft have spoken with both of you about them
And shall not again tell you what long troubles
Drove from his fathers' throne King Ferdinand.
He had already seen his foes ascend it—
This hapless monarch—when I brought to birth
A son. He named him Sancho, and to hide him
From the fell rage of the traitor Don Garcia
Scarce had I time to bid farewell to him
Before he had him borne off without saying
Where to me, and I knew but a few signs
By which to recognize this heir of kings.
Too vain precautions against evil fate!
He himself, after a year, told me the child
Was dead. He four years later died and left me
A daughter, to bear whom I by his orders
Came to Castile. Ever do I remember
His words as in mine arms he breathed his last:
　　"I die, and leave thee in a woeful plight.

May heaven be kindlier to thee someday! Don
Raimundo hath important secrets for thee,
And thou wilt learn them when the time is come.
Flee to Castile."
               With these words he expired,
And never hath Don Raimundo told me aught.
I went forth with no light on those dark sayings;
But seeing him come here with these deputies
And knowing that 'tis among their retinue
That this great rumor first was noised (observe
How easily one believes what would be welcome!)
I deemed the time had come for him to tell me
That secret, and it was about Don Sancho,
And he was bringing him to meet his mother.
Alas, how vainly did my love hope this!
The rumor is explained, to my confusion:
Far from bringing him, they seek him here.
Judge what is likely, and if this domain
Hath ever heard that luckless prince's name.

DON LOPE.   If thy belief is in the name, thou wilt
        Believe him dead,—believe men seek Don Sancho
        Where there is no Don Sancho. But if thou
        Wishest to believe the public voice about it,
        Know that our judgment is expressed thereby;
        Heaven hath taken him forever from thee,
        Or else this noble prince is our brave Carlos.
        We both will say it, though we are suspected
        Of envy: his career is utterly
        Miraculous. His lofty, manly nature
        That charms so many, his high-spirited
        Gallantry that defies our slights, his bearing
        Majestic, which when he is quite unknown
        Lets him come nearer than we can to the throne,
        The fact two queens vie in esteem for him
        And find it, perhaps, difficult not to love him,
        The prompt voice of the people, who adore him—
        After all this, madam, I say again:
        Heaven hath taken thy son already from thee
        Or else this noble prince is our brave Carlos.
        We have disdained him for his unknown birth

But with this ray of light naught seems the same,
And we would with regret now find we must
Renounce our hopes to anyone but him.
LEONORE.   He has the worth but not the birth, and he
Himself gives proof enough hereof when *he*
Renounces thus the Queen to choose among you
For her a husband, and for Castile a king.
DON MANRIQUE.   And seest thou not he plans to worst all three
Of us by his own valor's might? Hast thou
Forgot already that he said before thee
He would owe naught to his ancestral name?
He nobly wishes to divest himself
Of this advantage and to be indebted
To nothing but his prowess for his greatness.
In a Court full of beauty and of charm
Hast thou observed him loving anyone
Of less than royal rank?
LEONORE.   Here he is. Let us
See what he thinks himself of this report.

Enter CARLOS.

CARLOS.   Madam, protect me from an injurious glory.
The people seek to rob me of my name
And stubbornly insist I am Don Sancho
And Prince of Aragon. Since this false rumor
Will die when he arrives, while we await him
Must I be for an hour a phantom prince?
Or if it is not true that he is coming,
Wilt thou permit this wrong to thee and me?
LEONORE.   Whate'er thou thinkest of the people's judgment,
Heaven oft lends it secret light to guide it.
Thou learnest at least what all wish to be true
And what opinion they all have of thee.
DON LOPE.   Prince, try to hide no more what heaven discloseth,
Nor seal our eyes when its hand opens them.
Thou shouldst grow tired of causing us to err.
We know not what thou thinkest to gain thereby,
But we both have for thee an esteem too high
For us to be compelled to treat thee wrongly;
And when in blindness honor sets us 'gainst thee,

We should be pitied and hence disabused.
Our pride did not reject thee in thyself
Nor can forget the reverence owed a crown;
And if our glance pierced not a king's disguise,—
If the unknown stranger Carlos was scorned by us,—
We shall revere Don Sancho and accept him
As master when he to the Queen reveals
Who he is, and he doubtless in his heart
Will say we have done right. Hasten this union,
Good my lord, of her scepter and thine own;
And laying aside the feigned role of a soldier,
Receive as king our homage first of all.

CARLOS.   Your sham respect, Counts, which I looked not for,
Is more offensive even than your disdain.
Methinks I have made my name much too renowned
For it to stand in need of being given
A spurious luster. Take your deference back,
To which I have no claim. I had ascribed
This false report to mad chance, and I thought not
That any could be bold enough to fashion
A comedy of Carlos as a king.
But since this is a toy for your amusement,
Know that brave men pay honor unto manhood
And that your peers would all feel certain scruples
At making mine a thing for ridicule.
If your intent is thus to mock me here,
Ye can jest better when ye have vanquished me.
The time to jest is after victory.
One does it then with grace as well as glory.
But ye are over-hasty. The Queen's ring
Is in my hands still, and the unknown stranger
Carlos, without naming his ancestry,
Still stands between you and Castile's fair throne.
This arm, which saved you from captivity,
Remains an obstacle to your ambition.

DON MANRIQUE.   To be but Carlos, thou dost speak in lordly
Fashion and playest the Prince well while denying
That thou art he. If we have to the utmost
Defended just a while ago the honor
We felt was due our station, we can still

Defend it to the utmost; but whatever
We owe thee, we shall gladly give to thee.
　Whether thou or another be Don Sancho,
We both shall render him that which we owe him.
As for thy new-made marquess, though his pride
Takes umbrage, let him know that he is honored
As much as he deserves, but that to fight
With us 'tis necessary that gentle blood
Second in some degree his native worth
To justify his rank. Let him in no wise
Expect to face us till he says who he is.
Not that we ask that he should be a Guzman
Or Larra; let him be a nobleman—
That will suffice, to treat us as an equal.
We both will see in him a worthy rival,
And if Don Sancho be but a vain hope,
We will contend with him for the Queen's ring.
But he, though a brave warrior, must bear it
That our sword scorns a mere adventurer.
　We leave thee, madam, to solve this mystery.
Birth has its secrets best known by a mother;
And in our differences with him, we fear
We might somewise forget thy presence here.
(Exeunt DON MANRIQUE and DON LOPE.)

CARLOS.　Madam, thou seest how in their pride they treat me.
To accord me honor, they would have me buy it.
But if its price to me must be the secret
That I have kept for twenty years, this ring
Will long be in my hands.
LEONORE.　　　　　　　Let us stop talking
About your duel, and talk about Don Sancho.
Rumor swells loud thou'rt he; all the Court thinks so.
Tell me, I pray thee, knowest thou who thou art?
CARLOS.　Would to God I knew nothing of my birth!
If I had been some child spared by the tempests,
Left in a desert to the wild beasts' mercy,
Exposed because of hate or being feared,
By chance discovered and in pity reared,
My heart would in this rumor find some hope
From thy uncertainty and my ignorance.

1 6 9

I would imagine mine those wondrous fortunes
Whence fabled heroes rise from nothingness,—
Would weave about myself the splendid fancies
Our fathers idly fashioned as to them.
For I am most presumptuous, and I cannot
Scan my ambition without growing indignant.
I cannot think of diadem or scepter
Without my soul soaring beyond all bounds.
Vain fervor of an impetuous flight, impelled
By an aspiring heart to climb the heavens,
Sustained on high by certain deeds in war,
And by one probing glance brought swift to earth!
    I know my parents, and I am not Don Sancho.
Rumor in vain gives me a name which I
Give back to thee. Reserve it for this prince.
Perhaps thou in an hour or two wilt find him
Among the deputies. Leave me, though, in that
Obscurity which alone befits my rashness.

LEONORE.   Have I beguiled myself? Is what I so
Love to believe, then, only a delusion
Created in me by thy glorious exploits?
My heart gainsays thee; a mysterious impulse
Inclines it toward thee and doth contradict thee
In spite of me. But I know not the source
Of this—not whether it be the voice of kinship
Or whether it be admiration for thee,—
Whether 'tis natural instinct or my wish,—
Whether my heart knows thee or chooses thee.
Yet I would silence willingly its murmur
As falsely prompted by thy worth, and censure,
To please thee, a report so sweet to me;
But where, then, is my son if he lives not
In thee? It is insisted he is here;
But *I* see no trace of him, and save thee
I know of no one worthy to be him,
And the true scion of kings, oppressed by Fate,
Can hide his birth but not his native worth.
He wears upon his brow a shining token
Which tells despite him what he will not tell,
And that which heaven hath placed on thine could, aided

By naught else, have misled me, hadst thou let it.
Then thou art not he, since thou tellest me so.
But thou, with such great merit, must be feared.
Permit me to remain hereof in darkness.
I blame thee not for thy temerity;
My esteem for thee, on the contrary,
Is so great that on thee alone depends
My heart's acceptance of thee. Thou hast only
To state thy parentage to me, and I
Will after that give thee the right to hope.
But if thou e'en yet wilt conceal thy lineage,
At least refuse me not another favor:
Prepare no more to accompany us. No longer
Now do we need thine aid to reign. The death
Of Don Garcia hath punished all his crimes
And restored Aragon to its rightful sovereigns.
Seek glory there no more, and whomsoever
Thou lovest, constrain me not against my will.
There must be limits to the reward of valor,
And I do fear thee, who hast such great merit.
I have said enough. Adieu. Think well upon it,
And make thyself known, or aspire to nothing.

Enter BLANCA. *Exit* LEONORE.

BLANCA (*who has heard* LEONORE'S *last words*). Who will not fear
    thee if the queens thus fear thee?
CARLOS. They are right when they scorn me.
BLANCA.   Scorn a hero
    Who is hailed king?
CARLOS.   Assist not envy, Blanca,
    To make sport of me. If 'tis pleasing to thee
    To aid its malice, at least respect in me
    Thy queen's work.
BLANCA.   Even the Queen now sees in thee
    Naught but a prince heaven shows to us despite him.
    But thou too long dost keep her in suspense.
    Thy silence argues thee ungrateful to her.
    What she hath generously done for Carlos
    Makes her deserve the courtesy of Don Sancho.
CARLOS. Ah, fatal name for me, how thou dost hound me!

For what dread downfall thou preparest my soul!

(Enter QUEEN ISABELLA.*)*

(To ISABELLA*)* Madam, command that I be left in peace,
And that Don Sancho be confused no more
With Carlos. 'Tis to wrong a prince's name
Too long. I want that only of thy servant;
And if a jealous Fate, which now appears
To flatter me, wishes to lift me higher
To hurl me down thence, suffer me to go
To some remote place and there hide my head
From the cruel doom thy wrath will visit on me.
I see it from too far away to await it.
Let me escape it now by bidding thee
Farewell. Let . . .

ISABELLA.　　　　　What! this great soul fears a crown?
When thought a king, he trembles—is confounded!
He fain would flee this glory, and takes alarm
At what his lofty qualities make us deem him!

CARLOS.　Ah, dost thou not see that this wide-spread error
Is but a treacherous turn of my good fortune,
Whereby my secrets are half-bared already?
My parentage and country I have vainly
Concealed,—have vainly taken a false name
To cause what I was born to be forgotten.
My true name and my country are discovered.
　　Madam, I am Sancho, born in Aragon;
And I foresee already Fate's grim malice
Destroying all thy work by making known
The rest and showing, to my utter shame,
Who this count is—this marquess—whom thy favor
Created.

ISABELLA.　　　Could I, then, lack power and courage
To prevent Fate's bringing to naught my work?
Take not from me that which Fate cannot tarnish;
And what my hand hath wrought, it can sustain.
But thou devisest a phantom threat to thee
To have a pretext for thy going hence.
I ask no longer why thou wert unwilling
When I desired to arrange a marriage for thee.
Follow thy princess into Aragon,

But at least go there without feigning weakness,
And since thy lordly heart yields to her charms
Show that in following her thou art not fleeing.

CARLOS.   Ah, madam, learn instead all my misdeeds.
My head is thine to strike off, if thou wishest it.
    All worthless that I am, I must confess
That although I lament my fate, I have
Cause to rejoice at it. If in my birth
It gave me disadvantages, it has still
Given me the name and spirit of a king;
And ever since my heart was capable
Of loving, it could love none but a queen.
    That is my first crime, and I cannot tell thee
Whether it is to thee or Doña Elvira
I am unfaithful. But I know my heart,
Pledged to you both, giving itself to both,
In no wise loves by halves, for I am always
Ready to embrace her service or thine,—always
Ready to die for one or for the other.
To love but one of you, I would have to choose,
And in that choice would be involved at least
Some desire, some outrageous hope to be
Better received by that one, and I deem it
Less heinous to appear to be inconstant.
He who aspires to naught can love two women—
Expend on more than one his sighs and longings.
    That is my second crime, and though I never
Have let my fond love hope for anything,
I cannot without dying of my jealous
Despair see either thee or Doña Elvira
In any other man's arms. Realizing
That this choice thou wouldst make would bring to me
Such martyrdom, I wished to absent myself
Therefrom by following hence Doña Elvira
And linger in her Court, waiting till Fate
Should, by her likewise marrying, cause my death.
    Later, the opportunity thou gav'st me
Made me abandon all thought of thus fleeing.
The strife engendered hath beguiled my grief.
I hoped by these duels to defer my misery.

The blow of losing thee appeared less cruel
When I now found the time 'twould fall uncertain
And I could see to it that my death would give thee
Someone more valiant than I am for husband.
    But there no more is any duel to fight.
I see Don Sancho is the right husband for thee—
For 'tis not love makes marriages for queens.
Reasons of State always decide their choice.
The inexorable claims of their high station
Never permit them to stoop lower when
They see at hand a prince who is their equal;
And since the consecrated bond that makes him
Thy husband will keep Doña Elvira here
With thee, she being his sister,—since I cannot
See her without seeing also what will kill me,—
Vouchsafe that I may shun that fatal sight
And may elsewhere carry, with criminal sighs,
The woeful remnant left me of my life.

ISABELLA.   Enough thou tellest me to deserve my hate
If I gave scope to a queen's proper feelings.
They are confounded by an inward turmoil.
Go; I consent; trouble my heart no more.
But nay: before thou fleest Don Sancho, wait
Till he appears. This rumor may be false
And I again be happy. What am I
Saying! Go, Marquess; I consent anew;
But ere thou goest give my ring to him—
That is, if this is not too great a favor
Which a queen asks of thee for her many favors.

CARLOS.   Thou wishest me to die; I must obey,
Even though obedience should to the worst
Betray me. I would deem so just a death
But merciful, if it could end the threat
Of what I dread and thus forestall Fate's malice
And allow Carlos, giving up this ring,
To carry his assumed name and his honor
To the tomb with him. That is now the only
Blessing to which this guilty heart aspires.

ISABELLA.   Why art thou not Don Sancho! . . . What have I said!

Farewell. Believe not my impulsive outcry.

CARLOS.   It tells me enough for me to die content.

A C T   V

The Princess ELVIRA *and* DON ALVAR *are discovered.*

DON ALVAR.   Freed from a plight so adverse to my wishes
    At last, I can thank heaven, which restores
    Thy brother to thee. Since he is to be
    The husband of our queen, their blessed union
    Leaves me entirely thine. I find myself
    Released from duty's tyranny,—from the yoke
    My country's good opinion imposed on me,—
    From her selection, which was making me
    Seek to be king. I have to fight no longer
    Against my love, to fear no longer winning
    The prize of a sad triumph,—and my honor,
    Which made me false to thee, consents that I,
    Released now from its dictates, bring back to thee
    A lover who, though recreant, ne'er hath changed.

ELVIRA.   Thy heart is noble, but in its impatience
    Has too much confidence in an uncertain story,
    And this prompt eagerness to be mine again
    Too soon consoles me for a throne I lose.
    My loss of it is still but a vague rumor
    Which, despite Carlos, makes free with his name;
    And thou knowest not, to speak the truth to thee,
    What prospect and what vows could e'er console me.
    More than thou thinkest, the crown is dear to me,
    And my loss more if Carlos is my brother.
    Wait thou and see what comes of these reports.
    Wait till I know for certain what I am:
    If heaven takes the throne from me, or not,—
    If thou must ask of me or of my brother
    My hand,—if I must be thine through another
    Or I have but mine own heart to consult.

DON ALVAR.   'Tis from that heart alone I ask for thee,
    Madam; 'tis it alone I wish to hear me,
    And my success would with dismay o'erwhelm me
    If only by another's will I won thee.

Could I desire thy brother's aid to obtain thee
Solely through thy obedience to his power,
And by the abuse of his authority
Tyrannize basely over thine own will?
ELVIRA.　Thou fearest with little reason 'twill turn out
That he has wishes that I cannot follow.
Those of a king's blood see but with his eyes,
And his first subjects are the most obedient.
But thou behavest strangely with this deference
Whereby with seeming humbleness thou seekest
Assurances; thou dost not fear to act
Against my wishes save to make me say
That I accept thy suit, and obstinately
Thou wouldst persist in showing me extreme
Respect to force me to declare, "I love thee."
Those words are somewhat bold on women's lips.
Let me find seemlier ways to explain my feelings;
Much can I say and yet say naught directly.
　　I know how long it is that thou hast loved me.
I know what I should do and what I can do.
But let us, I repeat, learn who I am,
And if thou to my heart alone aspirest,
Attempt to solve the present vital mystery.
Carlos hath such good cause to value thee
That, should he prove my king, thou well mayst hope.
DON ALVAR. Madam . . .
ELVIRA.　　　　　　　For my sake undertake this task,
And let me now, I pray, talk with the Queen.
DON ALVAR.　I gladly shall obey and do my best
To tell thee soon whatever can be learned.

Enter QUEEN LEONORE. *Exit* DON ALVAR.

LEONORE.　Don Alvar flees me?
ELVIRA.　　　　　　　　Madam, at my request
He goes to seek some truth in all these rumors.
I feared, on seeing thee, that thou wouldst second
His love, and I might ill defend my heart
Against you both.
LEONORE.　　　　　Can thy heart ne'er be won?
ELVIRA.　He can obtain all, having thy support.

LEONORE. Can I, then, promise him thy hand at last?

ELVIRA. Yes, if thou gainest for him the new king's favor.

LEONORE. And if the news is false and thou'rt still queen?

ELVIRA. What can I answer, in such uncertain plight?

LEONORE. One can have hope, e'en in uncertainty.

ELVIRA. One can expect, too, some debate hereon.
> One does not act the same when power supreme ...

Enter QUEEN ISABELLA.

ISABELLA (*to* LEONORE). I break in on your private conversation,
> But I myself would take part in it, having
> Such great concern to hear of thy son, madam,
> That I shall ask thee what is known of him.

LEONORE. Thou seest me no wiser than thyself.

ISABELLA. Who told thee of the death of Don Garcia?
> In the whole month in which the deputies
> Have come, we heard but of a revolt against him.

LEONORE. On that point I can easily satisfy thee.
> People now with them have made it clear to me.
> When they left, Don Garcia and his son
> Were still being besieged in their last stronghold.
> Soon afterwards, it was taken, whereon Don
> Raimundo, there held prisoner, gained his freedom,
> Saw they were both dead, and proclaimed to all
> We had a king of our true line of kings,
> Saying Don Sancho lived—then went in haste
> To bring the blessing of his sovereign's presence
> To Aragon. He joined our deputies
> Yesterday, as that day came to a close,
> And told them that this prince was at thy Court.
> That is all I could gather from a servant.
> Besides, with such folk little is explained,
> Ill do they understand aught, and their story
> Is generally confused; but Don Raimundo
> Will tell the rest to thee.
> > Now what would Blanca
> With us? She seems dismayed.

Enter BLANCA.

BLANCA. Ah, madam!

ISABELLA.   What

    Is it?

BLANCA.   Oh, hapless day! Thy Carlos . . .

ISABELLA.   Yes?

BLANCA.   His father hath come here, and is only . . .

ISABELLA.   What?

BLANCA.   Only a fisherman.

ISABELLA.   Who told thee so?

BLANCA.   Mine eyes.

ISABELLA.   Thine eyes?

BLANCA.   Yes, mine own eyes.

ISABELLA.   How hard

    I find it to believe them!

LEONORE (*to* ISABELLA).   Wouldst thou, madam,

    Not wish to hear in full what hath occurred?

ELVIRA.   Oh, how unjust is heaven!

ISABELLA.   It is, and shows us

    By this disclosure its almighty power,

    Since from the basest blood it can produce

    A soul so lofty and create a hero

    Made glorious only by his noble manhood.

    Speak, Blanca! tell us how he takes this blow.

BLANCA.   With very great shame and still greater courage.

    I saw him starting to descend a staircase.

    Vainly he sought to silence the false rumor;

    The Court, all round him, stubbornly bent upon

    Changing his name, was whispering, "Don Sancho

    Of Aragon," when a lowly old man seized him

    And clasped him in his arms; and *he,* who saw

    Who it was, quivered at his humiliation—

    Then, giving filial piety free rein,

    Reciprocated fondly his embrace.

    His tears flowed with the old man's tears of pride.

    We heard but sighs: "Ah, my son!"—"Ah, my father!"—

    "Oh, day thrice blest! moment too long awaited!

    Thou givest me back my life!"—"Thou hast destroyed me!"

      Strange was it: at these cries of joy and grief

    A mighty throng of people, who came flocking,

    Wanted none to believe them, were self-blinded;

    And this poor fisherman, in spite of all

Carlos could do, was reckoned an impostor.
In his son's arms he suffered countless insults:
He was a vile fraud, by the Counts suborned.
These did themselves—admire their generous natures—
Attempt to increase the disbelief in him.
Not that they took upon themselves such treachery,
But they would lay it on someone in their service
Who thought to please them and unfortunately
Instructed this poor wretch to humiliate Carlos.
That story was accepted eagerly,
All held it true as soon as it was heard,
And to gain greater credence for the idea
That there had been such foul play, the two counts
Then had the old man dragged away to prison.
Carlos in vain bore witness 'gainst himself,
The truth he spoke could not defeat their purpose,
And now in the disgrace that overwhelmed him
Those who had been most jealous of him saved him
From it in spite of him. He stormed, he threatened,
And, hot with rage, cried at the top of his lungs,
Demanding that his father be restored
To him. All trembled at him, but none believed
What he in anger said; and naught . . . But here
He now is, coming to complain to thee.

    Enter Carlos, Don Manrique, *and* Don Lope.

Carlos (*to* Isabella). Well, madam, finally my birth is known.
That is the consequence of my obedience.
I foresaw this calamity and would have
Shunned it, had thy commands not stayed me here.
They have brought on me this disastrous moment,
And the one thing left me still is now torn from me.
My father is torn from me, is held a criminal.
His name is given an eternal odium.
    I am a fisherman's son, but not a vile one's.
Baseness of blood extends not to the soul.
I can renounce the names of count and marquess
More honorably than the feelings of a son.
Naught can make that relationship not sacred.
Command, I pray thee, that my father may be

Restored to me. It ought to be enough
For those who hate me to know who I am
Without o'erwhelming me by further trials.

DON MANRIQUE.   Compel this hero to safeguard his honor,
Madam, and let him not believe himself.
We could not suffer one who hath so often
Made the Moors tremble and our king win victories
To incur thus through his birth undying shame:
Such manhood well deserves a seemlier source.
Abet, like us, the people's self-deception.
They love their error; vouchsafe to authorize it.
Do justice to so many glorious exploits;
Confirm what we in pity have devised.

CARLOS.   I am most hapless if I rouse your pity.
Resume your arrogance and hostility.
With envy surfeited by my misfortune,
Ye can with ease pity my origin;
And, thinking me forever crushed thereby,
Not hard ye find it to show noble virtues.
Perhaps ye only set a snare for mine.
The honor of my name is worth preserving,
But all its luster would be bought too dearly
If at the cost of doing something base.
My birth, though humble, is without dishonor;
And since ye know it, I would have all know it.
   Sancho, the son of a fisherman but not
Of an impostor, saved two counts from capture.
Sancho, the son of a fisherman, made uneasy
Of late two lordly rivals as to whom
Their queen would choose. Sancho, the son of a fisherman,
Holds in his hand still that which will determine
Soon all the fortunes of a sovereign. Sancho
Finally, despite himself, hath in this country,
Although a fisherman's son, been thought a prince.
   That, that is what one who must count as naught
The name of his forefathers hath been able
To do, and did, before your very eyes.
The glory that remains his after this
Humiliation is still great enough
To honor his whole family, and 'twill seem

Greater to all who rightly realize
That he, like heaven, hath made much out of nothing.

DON LOPE. This noble pride belieth such a father,
And by its contradictory testimony
Again obscures what seemed to be revealed.
Nay, nay, a fisherman's son does not talk thus,
And thou appearest of such noble mould
That I can credit more than I can thee
That false report which I have circulated.
I maintain, Carlos, thou art not his son;
Just heaven never could have let thee be.
Thy filial affection hath misled thee,
And I gainsay for thee the voice of nature.
(*To* ISABELLA)   Do not regret thy giving him those titles
Wherewith it pleased thee to reward his worth.
Never did nobler hand do nobler work,
Madam; his lofty spirit does them honor;
And thou couldst find none to sustain them better,
For even to Fate itself he is superior.

ISABELLA. The magnanimity I admire in all
Three of you leaves me nothing I can add,
And when such strange things have just come to pass,
Hath led you to anticipate my feelings.
  They do not need expression, Counts, to impel you
To accord him the respect his deeds deserve
And not disdain the illustrious man whose mighty
Valor appears in one of humble lineage.
Ye take the lead herein so openly,
I am as much surprised as by the fisherman.
  And thou, who here remainedst at my command,
Sancho, since by that name we now must know thee,
Miraculous hero, who for honor's sake
Now wilt not take advantage of the mistake
Of a deluded populace: amidst
The unhappiness that hath come to thee, can I
Console thee for a fate thou dost defy?
Need I ask of thee what I see thee do?
I reckon thee unfortunate to be born
Of such a father, but I reckon thee
At the same time most highly enviable

That, born of such a father, thou dost not blench
Thereat, and that thy noble heart, when set
In the other scale, so outweighs such a birth.

Enter DON ALVAR.

DON ALVAR.   Queens, marvel at a prisoner's stubborn pride
Whom people in his son's behalf defame.
This wretched fisherman could not be induced,
By fear or promises, to confirm our story.
I sought to talk with him, but accomplished nothing.
I tried in vain to make him comprehend
How his ill-timed, disastrous presence here
Ruined the fortunes of his gallant son,
And would, unless he should confess his coming
Was a vile trick which someone made him play,
Deprive that son of honor. I have even
Added threats to these arguments. Naught can shake him:
Sancho is still his son; and as to loss
Of honor and high estate, he says he has
Something wherewith to make him a great lord,
And that his wife has told him countless times
(This is how credulous and simple-hearted
He is) that when the Queen of Aragon
Saw the gift which he put into my hands,
She to great eminence would raise his son.
(*To* QUEEN LEONORE)   If thou receivest it, madam, with
      such joy
As this old man showed when he sent it to thee
Through me, thou'lt surely give this noble son
Of his a rank even above that of marquess.
The old man's whole heart seemed to be o'erflowing.
      (DON ALVAR *gives to* QUEEN LEONORE *a little casket which
      can be opened without a key, by means of a secret spring.*)
ISABELLA.   Madam, on seeing this thou appearest moved.
LEONORE.   I have good reason to be when I am given
This gift. 'Twill tell me whether my son lives
Or not. The late king, when concealing his birth,
Placed there the precious secret of his fate.
Let me, before I open it, first tell thee
What it contains. Ah, Sancho, if through it

I can now find him, thou mayst rest assured
That thou'lt lack nothing in those lands which heaven
Appointed as our portion, and that after
Thou hast restored this treasure unto me
Thou wilt receive the reward rightly thine.
But to these sweet emotions I already
Give myself up too much. Let us discover
Grounds for our happiness ere we promise thine.
    This casket, then, contains a lock of hair
Which Ferdinand had as earnest of my troth,
His picture and mine, two of the rarest gems
Which the sun fashions in barbaric climes,
And—evidence more certain still—a letter
Which he himself wrote with his own hand.

Enter a guard.

THE GUARD (*to* QUEEN LEONORE).   Don
    Raimundo, madam, craves an audience of thee.
LEONORE.   Let him come in.   (*Exit the guard.*)
    (*To* ISABELLA)   Pardon thou my impatience,
    If in my eagerness to see and hear him
    I have presumed, without thy leave, to have him
    Enter.
ISABELLA.   Thou canst command throughout Castile.
    Henceforth I see thee with a daughter's eyes.
                  (*Enter* DON RAIMUNDO.)
LEONORE.   Say nothing, Don Raimundo, of the usurper's
    Death; only give Don Sancho back to us.
    Is he alive? Can he uphold our royal
    Fortunes?
DON RAIMUNDO.   On leaving prison after more
    Than six years, madam, I have sought for him
    Where, to uphold them better, by the orders
    Of the late king I had him reared with such
    Great secrecy that even his second father,
    Who thought him his own son, knew not the truth.
    As in thy Court, he had his true name, Sancho;
    Only the title "Don" was taken from it.
    I learned that when he was sixteen years old
    His lordly heart revolted against following

The occupation of his supposed father,
And that, already chafing at a lot
So lowly, he had stolen away and, changing
His name and telling nothing of his family,
He had wrought marvels for Castile in war,
Wherein some former neighbor of his, thence lately
Returned, had seen him crowned with fame and much
Favored at Court, which with his name's renown
Was full, and said that he was even known
And cherished by the Queen—so greatly so
That the old fisherman, wildly delighted,
Had flown to seek this son so boasted of.

LEONORE.   If, Don Raimundo, thou couldst recognize him . . .

DON RAIMUNDO (*espying* CARLOS).   Yes, there I see him! Ah, sire! Ah,
    my master!

DON LOPE.   We had judged well. Great prince, confess thou'rt he.
    The truth appears. Yield to the prayers of all.

LEONORE.   Wilt thou alone, Don Sancho, not believe it?

CARLOS.   I still fear to be made ridiculous
    By some new stroke of Fate; but, madam, see
    Whether the letter of the King confirms
    What Don Raimundo tells thee about me.

LEONORE (*opening the casket, taking a letter from it, and reading this
    aloud*).
    "To deceive a tyrant, thee, too, I deceive.
    Thou'lt yet see him for whom I let thee grieve.
    Thine error will someday give him the throne.
    To assure this best, I hide from thee thy son.

    "If my deceit toward thee seems wrong, forgive
    Thou me the woe in which I make thee live
    For fear a mother's love, that knows no bound,
    Would by its fond care cause him to be found.

    "Nuño, a fisherman, thinks him his own son.
    His wife, when he was absent, bore him one
    Born dead, took thine, and told him naught of this.
    Neither he nor the child knows who it is.

    "She herself knows not; she knows this alone:
    The boy is not of such blood as her own.

She deems this casket by some miracle,
If given thee, will his name and rank reveal.

"Then recognize him by this proof someday.
May Aragon, then, again beneath your sway,
Learn too from me that Sancho is indeed,
Though supposed Nuño's son, her kings' true seed.
                        "FERDINAND OF ARAGON."

> (*Having finished reading the letter*) Ah, my son, if thou
>   needest still further proof
> Trust thy great prowess and thy mighty heart.

CARLOS (*to* LEONORE). To wish still to refuse these royal honors
Would be to appreciate ill my great good fortune.
(*To* ISABELLA) But I shall declare Nuño is my father
Again, unless thou lettest me hope to win thee.

ISABELLA. To hope is not enough when all is thine.
I did thee wrong in making thee a marquess,
And thou wilt not be able to complain
Henceforth of the delay that I constrained thee
To make in going hence. And as for me,
Whom heaven hath destined for a king well worthy
Of me, well worthy also of Castile,
I placed my ring in hands most fit to give it
Unto Don Sancho and unite our crowns.

CARLOS. No more I marvel at my heart's presumption
By which I, without feeling the less fondness
For either, have supposed I loved two women.
In the obscurity of our situation
I confused love and brotherly affection.

ELVIRA. The voice of nature wakened this affection
Between us without shame to royal rank.
Mine gave thee what was owed to kindred blood.

CARLOS. If thou still lovest me and as thy brother
Honorest me, would a husband given thee
By me displease thee?

ELVIRA.   If he is Don Alvar
De Luna, he is worthier in my sight
Than anyone but thee.

CARLOS.   He honored in me
My naked worth.

(*To* Don Manrique *and* Don Lope)   And ye, Counts, who
    disdained me
For being of unknown birth, but in the end
Were those who first judged rightly in my favor,
Your scorn was just, as well as his esteem.
'Tis the same virtue in a different aspect.

Don Raimundo (*to* Isabella).   Let him now show himself to Aragon,
    Madam. Our deputies, eager to enter . . .

Isabella.   'Tis best to give them public audience
    That all eyes may behold this miracle.
      Come; but meanwhile let that old man whom such
    Good fortune sent us be set free and brought
    Hither, far luckier than he dreams he is,
    To be repaid for all his services.

Sertorius

INTRODUCTION

Of Corneille's *Sertorius* (1662), Lancaster says "the material is skillfully presented, with few lines devoted to the exposition or to events that take place off the stage and an equable distribution of material, so that there are at least two striking scenes in each act." Further on, he says that it "is, perhaps, the only one of his later plays that would not have seemed out of place, if it had been composed in the midst of his earlier period." He had already said: "No other play written in the later period of Corneille's life recalls so markedly his earlier work, especially such tragedies as *Cinna* and *Nicomède*." [1]

That had been, throughout nearly all of the eighteenth and nineteenth centuries, the generally accepted estimate of this drama, quite in line with its very notable success on the stage when first produced and for many decades afterwards. Like *Pompée* and *Rodogune*, it is therefore still included in the *Classiques Larrouse* school texts of Corneille. In his *Théâtre de Pierre Corneille*, Hémon had dubbed it "the finest of the tragedies that belong to what has been called Corneille's decadence," but added that it has two parts, "the historical, which is definitely first-rate, and the invented, weaker or at least of more debatable quality." [2] Merlet had said a little earlier: "*Sertorius* . . . might have made one believe in the rejuvenation, as it were miraculously, of the genius

> that drew
> Great Pompey's soul and that of Cinna, too.

There is the same vigor, but passion is lacking." [3]

With some critics, however, admiration for this tragedy was limited to its style and a portion of Act III. Thus Petit de Julleville: "*Sertorius* is still kept half alive by a fine scene between the rebel general and Pompey, and by the many beautiful verses with which the play is filled. But the tremendous success which it achieved on its first appearance somewhat amazes us today." [4] The great Lemaître was even less favorable in his criticism, speaking of the "glacial compli-

[1] Part III, pp. 474, 859.
[2] Vol. iv, p. 387.
[3] Pp. 172-173.
[4] P. xiv.

1 8 9

cations" in the midst of which "we suddenly come upon the interview between Sertorius and Pompey, an oratorical joust which leads nowhere but is very fine in itself." [5]

And the great Faguet is severest of all: "The play is exceedingly poor because, however hard one tries, one cannot, I think, be interested in anybody in it." [6]

From this extreme there seems to have been a considerable reaction. Brasillach goes to the opposite extreme; he regards *Sertorius* as one of Corneille's "most carefully wrought and beautiful achievements, superior at all events to *Cinna* and to *Horace*," tragedies which he rates much lower than other critics do. He maintains that "the whole play is dominated by the figure of the soldier in love, almost naive but possessed of inner depths and greatly suffering, to whom death alone, welcomed perhaps with a strange relief, can bring the solution of so many riddles. Whatever Corneille's opinion, it is indeed love, and not affairs of State, that is the center of interest in *Sertorius*—or rather this question: what to do about love during a war which upsets so many notions and so many lives; what to do about one's personal happiness in the midst of the world's unhappiness?" [7]

Of the three tragedies, *Sertorius, Sophonisbe,* and *Othon,* which appeared in immediate succession and constitute a little group to themselves in the work of Corneille, "only *Sertorius,*" says Schlumberger, "has been able to endure, and it could still find favor by virtue of its vigorous and delicately shaded portrait of a great leader. . . . Contrary to all his principles, Corneille has pictured not a crisis but a man." [8]

I am told that "many" authorities today would prefer this play to *Cinna*. For my own part, I am quite in agreement with Faguet about *Sertorius*. I cannot be interested in dramatis personae whom I find contemptible when sympathy for them is essential to securing the intended—or any proper—dramatic effect.

A certain degree of ineptness and irresolution is of course

[5] P. 330.
[6] P. 196.
[7] Pp. 379-381.
[8] Pp. 201, 206.

not unnatural in a veteran soldier who loves a beautiful young woman and is constantly aware of his own physical unattractiveness. Such a man might indeed suppose that he could disregard his feelings and resign her to a friend for reasons of policy, and then might find his act of renunciation far more difficult than he had anticipated. But a Sertorius worthy of the name would never talk of dying if he should lose to a rival the woman he loves, as Corneille makes him talk in his scene with Viriate in the fourth act, one moment unable to control himself and the very next thinking of expediency again,[9] continually failing to keep his true goal in mind, and proposing to behave in bad faith towards Perpenna and the friends of Aristia, and not meeting the issue when Viriate would have him leave his own Roman followers in the lurch. It is hard to conceive that she would not realize that it would be utterly dishonorable for him thus to be false to his soldiers who were his countrymen, and harder still to have any sympathy for her when she urges him to commit this perfidy, if she does realize it—and equally hard to have any for her if she cannot realize it. In either case, a man of real honor, self-respect, and manhood would have faced such an issue squarely by declaring that what he was urged to do was dishonorable, and that he would not do it. Sertorius can evoke no healthy sympathies after this scene.

Aristia also forfeits all sympathy. Though she discovers that Pompey still adores her, she refuses to wait for him even for the brief interval till the end of Sulla's regime will permit

[9] Is it really true to life that he would so recur to thoughts of expediency when he had once cast off all restraint in his speech beginning "Let me, after these words, die at thy feet"? His behavior can perhaps be accounted for, however, by Viriate's answering speech, in which she takes pains to explain to him that *she* does *not* love *him*, nor anyone else, and that she is actuated solely by ambition. But this speech, besides being somewhat at variance with what she has told her confidante about her feelings towards him, is itself doubtfully true to life. Would she thus have risked chilling his ardor just when she was now finally able to wed him, as she desired? Sertorius' vacillation persists throughout his scene with Perpenna which immediately follows. After he has appealed to Perpenna to give up Viriate for the sake of their great common cause as he himself had done earlier, and Perpenna has consented to do so but then speaks of how hard such renunciation is, Sertorius (incredibly?) says at once: "Do not constrain thyself."

him to return to her; unless he will break with the Dictator forthwith, she will marry Sertorius—so much greater is her pride in the figure she cuts than her love, or than her concern for her country's best interests! And Pompey, who has made such sacrifices for what he believes to be the good of Rome, thereupon declares that he will abandon all attempts to conciliate the insurgent faction, and will break the truce between the two armies and wage war to the death (necessarily at the cost of thousands of lives) for his own personal ends! Even in his famous scene earlier with Sertorius, after all his lofty talk of patriotism, he has finally refused to join forces with him on the unworthy ground that in such an alliance he himself would be the lesser in power.

One excellence (unmentioned by any critic, so far as I can recall) I do find in this play. Its last scenes, following the murder of Sertorius, are very good indeed.

CHARACTERS IN THE PLAY

SERTORIUS, *leader in Spain of the party of Marius.*
PERPENNA, *Sertorius' lieutenant.*
AUFIDIUS, *tribune in the army of Sertorius.*
POMPEY, *commander of the army of Sulla in Spain.*
ARISTIA, *Pompey's former wife.*
VIRIATE, *Queen of Lusitania.*
THAMYRAS, *maid of honor of Viriate.*
CELSUS, *a tribune in the army of Pompey.*
ARCAS, *a freedman of Aristia's brother, Aristius.*
Soldiers.

The scene represents a room in the palace of Viriate, in the town of Nertóbriga.

The names "Sertorius," "Perpenna," "Aufidius," and "Aristia" are accented on the second syllable, "Thamyras" on the first syllable. "Viriate" is to be pronounced as a four-syllable word, accented on the third syllable; the accent would seem more properly to fall on the second syllable, but in that case the sound of the name would be too much like "variety."

Sertorius

ACT I

PERPENNA *and* AUFIDIUS *are discovered.*

PERPENNA. Aufidius, whence comes this perturbation?
    What means it that my heart controls its feelings
    So ill? The horror wherewith treachery fills me,
    Despite myself, makes me revolt against
    All that I hoped for, and the dreadful picture
    Of greatness based on crime, the thought of which
    Hath until now beguiled me, at the moment
    When I must act, no longer finds mine arm
    Ready. In vain the ambition which assails
    My breast bedecks its foul task with false semblance
    Of honor. Vainly hath my soul, to bend
    My efforts to such baseness, shaken off
    Unnumbered seizures of remorse. This soul,
    Renouncing its own wishes, hath again
    Bowed 'neath the yoke, not broken yet, of conscience;
    And thus Sertorius' great good fortune stays
    My hand, that was about to pierce his heart.
AUFIDIUS. What ill-timed qualms of squeamish virtue thwart
    The fair fruition of thy cherished hopes?
    And since when hath a man who would stand foremost
    Yet feared to shed a little human blood?
    Hast thou forgotten the great truth, my lord,
    That civil war meaneth the reign of crime,—
    Forgotten that where crime doth rightly reign
    Innocence deserves nothing but disdain?
    "Honor" and "virtue" are ridiculous words.
    Marius and Carbo had no scruples; never
    Did either Sulla nor . . .
PERPENNA.   Sulla and Marius
    Never spared the blood of those they vanquished.
    Each in turn, in the mad rage of his victory,
    Has carried anger to sheer savagery.
    Each in turn has with slaughter and proscriptions
    Made all Rome suffer in their ferocious quarrels;
    But that fierce strife, which gave us masters, made them

Murderers alone; it did not make them traitors.
They in their greatest frenzy ne'er consented
To shed the blood of one of their own party,
And none in either faction would have dared
To assassinate his leader to supplant him.

AUFIDIUS. Wilt thou renounce thy hopes, then, and no more
Be loath to follow the banners of a captain
Less great than thou? Ah, if we must obey
Someone, let us no longer strive, but wear
The same yoke that the whole world hath accepted.
Why all these dangers? Why so many battles?
If we are minded to be subjects, Sulla
Will welcome us with open arms. 'Tis ill
For Romans e'er to live 'neath one man's sway;
But with a tyrant there or here, 'tis better
To live in Rome.

PERPENNA.   See plainer what thou sayest
When thou speak'st thus. Here freedom still draws breath
At least. The noblest part of our Republic,
Destroyed at Rome, here flourishes anew;
And this asylum, open to those proscribed,
Harbors the precious remnant of the Senate.
Through it Sertorius rules these provinces,
Imposes tribute on them, and controls
Their princes, leaving independent all
The rest of Spain, but as all parts of it
Require a leader, the success beyond
Men's hopes which everywhere attends his efforts,
The name he now has with the Spanish peoples . . .

AUFIDIUS. Ah, 'tis that name, won by good luck too largely,
Which mars thy fortunes, robbing thee of honors.
Thou canst not doubt this, howso little thou
Recallest the day thy army went and joined him,
When . . .

PERPENNA.   Poison not the wounds of my remembrance
That the command should have belonged to me.
I had more troops and higher birth than he;
Without my aid he would have been destroyed;
But he no sooner had appeared than I
Saw in a twinkling all my men desert me

To swell the numbers of his own. I saw
My eagles, taken from me by my soldiers,
Borne to his trenches to be ranged 'neath him;
And to make worse the shame of that defection
The same mad impulse seized me and I took
My place there, too, like them.
                The bitterness
Of the keen jealousy with which my soul
Was thenceforth filled hath day by day grown greater
'Neath the compulsion of a passion even
More overmastering than ambition is.
I adore Viriate, and this great queen,
The noble ruler of the Lusitanians,
Could, if she wedded me, give me the power
O'er *his* troops that he took from me o'er mine.
But she herself, alas, charmed by the spell
Of his great name, doth cherish that legend of him
Which his renown creates, whence he, unmoved
By all her beauty, robs me of her heart,
Which he does not desire. His star is so
Adverse to mine that he at every turn
Takes something from me without knowing it;
And all the while that he thus takes from me
What should be mine, his name does everything
For him without his being aware of this.
I realize he may love her and conceal
His love from us; but I intend to open
My heart to him regarding Viriate,
And if he can give up to me this throne
Which I aspire to, I shall lay aside
My hatred in return for his thus crowning
My love's desires; and I no more will envy
His station, which he took from me, if he
Will promise me as high a one among
This barbarous people whom we diligently
Have moulded, and taught patiently, until
They 'neath our discipline have become Romans.
AUFIDIUS. When one hath formed such great plans, can love's in-
        terests
        Be weighed in the same scale? and if the interests

Of love are still so dear to thee, when he
Is dead, will Viriate not be thine?
PERPENNA.   Yes; but what else will then ensue I know not.
    Would I, besides his place, have his success?
    Will those whose confidence and support he won
    Obey me quite as willingly as him?
    And to avenge his life's being wrongfully
    Cut short thus, will they not raise Pompey's banner?
AUFIDIUS.   Too late are such fears, and too great: thine orders
    Are given to slay him at thy feast this evening.
    The truce hath caused our army to disperse
    Over the countryside, and thou commandest
    Those who are with us still. The occasion smileth
    Upon us in pursuance of our great purpose;
    But only till the morrow are there hands
    To serve thee. If thou stayest the blow, prevent
    Anyone's knowing it was intended. Kill
    Sertorius or else thine accomplices.
    Fear what should be feared. There are those among us
    Who well might feel the same remorse as thou.
    If thou deferrest . . . But here the tyrant is.
    Try to obtain from him her who enthralls thee,
    And I shall pray the gods that thou mayst be
    So fortunate as to gain naught from your meeting.

Enter SERTORIUS. *Exit* AUFIDIUS.

SERTORIUS (*to* PERPENNA).   Let me inform thee of surprising news.
    Pompey will be here in an hour or two.
    He wishes to discuss our differences
    With me and takes my word for his safe-conduct.
PERPENNA.   One's word sufficeth between noble natures.
    From such a man as thou 'tis better than
    A hundred hostages, and I am not
    Surprised thereover; but what does surprise me
    Is to see Pompey, who is called "the Great,"
    Defer entirely to thee and not seek
    To hold this conference in a neutral spot.
    'Tis no small thing to have made the pride of Sulla's
    Most valiant heroes stoop to this extent.
SERTORIUS.   If he be stronger, it is not in Spain,

Where we have forced them to break off the war
And to entrench themselves in doubtful power
Which with regret one or two lands permit him
But which he fears I shall deprive his shattered
Fortunes of, when next spring the truce will end.
　　It is thine eagles' union with mine own
That makes my efforts constantly successful.
It is to thee I owe the power I have.
Expect no limit to my gratitude.
　　To speak again of Pompey, I think I fathom
The motives that thus bring him unto us.
As he can here lay little claim to glory,—
Far from attacking, scarce can hold us off,—
He would like some arrangement, advantageous
Or not, which could release him from a task
Wherein the brightness of his fame is tarnished;
And, moved by flattering hopes of better fortune
In a campaign 'gainst Mithridates, he
Now longs to be in Rome, that he may have
Orders and troops for it given him by the master
To whom he bows.

PERPENNA.　　　　　　　I would have thought the presence
Here of Aristia, whom that master forced him
To put away, would bring him, through the love
Which he still feels for her, here under pretext
Of other reasons, to say farewell to her;
For his dear tyrant was so unkind that they
Were not permitted even a leave-taking.

SERTORIUS.　That may be true; they loved each other fondly;
But he may learn that there has been a change.
So greatly hath the outrage done her stung
Aristia's proud heart that, with its love
Now turned to hate, she seeks here less a place
Of refuge than a more illustrious husband.
'Tis thus she talks, and offers me the aid
Of people of importance still in Rome,
Who—some her kinsmen, and her friends the others—
Have promised to me everything if I wed her.
Their letters, which she gave me, guarantee it.
Think at thy leisure what I can hope from them;

I gladly will abide by thine impression.

PERPENNA.   Couldst thou indeed, sir, hesitate a moment
Unless some secret, strong antipathy
Would make Aristia's marriage to thee torture?
Seeing what dowry Rome would give with her,
Thou hast no reason to look any further.

SERTORIUS.   I must needs, then, confide in thee, Perpenna,
As to both what I fear and what I think.
I love another. 'Tis so unbecoming
To love at my age that I hide my love
Even from her who hath enthralled my heart.
But being what I am, I yet am loved,
Or, rather, Queen Viriate fain would wed me.
She would have this choice, prompted by ambition,
Begin the union of her subjects with us,
Whereby a thousand other marriages
Then emulating ours and binding our
Two nations to each other, would so well
Mingle alike our blood and common interests
That they would soon make the two peoples one.
This is her aim as worthy recompense
For having helped us with a constancy
Which hath not spared her subjects' blood or treasure
To aid us in our noble efforts here.
Not that she told me this, nor others for her;
But every day I see sure signs 'tis so,
And as I feel no doubt about her wishes,
Only deliberately can I not heed them.
I fear, then, that if I should wed Aristia
'Twould anger her, and that the greater part
Of those she ruleth would, to avenge the slight
And serve her wrath, now turn their arms against us.
Beside such a misfortune, which would be
Irreparable for us, what hath been promised
On the other hand is scarce to be considered,
And to accept that new help, with false hopes
Of strengthening our cause, would make us weaker.
That is what keeps my mind thus undecided.
I do not feel repugnance for Aristia,
And the Queen hath not so enthralled my heart

That I would not still act to serve our common
Interests.
PERPENNA.   This fear with which thy soul is troubled
Should not delay the marriage for one instant.
Viriate, it is true, might be much moved,
But what does wrath avail when one is powerless?
Whate'er her jealousy and empty threats,
Art thou not in possession of her strongholds?
Are any of her subjects, whose resentment
Thou dreadest so, commanders in thine army?
Dost thou not hold as hostages in Osca
The sons of those highest in birth and bravest?
Their officers are Roman; their own soldiers,
Scattered among our ranks, have shared such combats
That the long comradeship which binds them to us
Hath made them love our rule and want none other.
Why fear them, then, so much and why refuse . . .
SERTORIUS.   And thou, Perpenna—why dost thou dissemble?
What I have heard, I see is true: thou lovest
Queen Viriate; and the love thou hidest
Is manifested in thy reasoning.
But logic here is needless. Only say
Thou lovest her, and I no longer love her.
Speak out! So much I owe thee that 'twould shame me
To hesitate one instant to requite thee.
PERPENNA.   'Tis so sweet to confess as thou dost wish me
That I shall venture . . .
SERTORIUS.   Enough! I will speak for thee.
PERPENNA.   Oh, sir! thou art too kind, and . . .
SERTORIUS.   Say no more.
All my desires are turned now towards Aristia,
And I shall wed her if on this same day
The Queen consenteth to reward thy love.
For, despite what thou sayest, I must dread
Her hate, and would not at that price espouse
This noble Roman lady. . . . Here *she* is.
Let me prepare and sound her mind, and meanwhile
Do thou see what things have been written to me.
          (He gives PFRPENNA *some letters. Exit* PERPENNA.*)*

Enter ARISTIA.

ARISTIA.　Be not offended if in my misfortune
　　　　　My weakness makes me be importunate.
　　　　　Not for our marriage; that step's consequences
　　　　　Make it deserve more than a moment's thought;
　　　　　But thou canst add, sir, to my hopes some further
　　　　　Assurances 'gainst a new threat. I learn
　　　　　Now that the false man formerly my husband
　　　　　Will come within these walls for conference with thee.
　　　　　His tyrant master and his still-felt love
　　　　　May grudge to me the honor I would have here.
　　　　　The one foresees its sequel, and the other
　　　　　Dreads its effulgence, and both have against it
　　　　　Reasons of State. I ask complete protection
　　　　　By thee, against both violence and entreaties,
　　　　　If this man would by either take possession
　　　　　Of me, whom he would see wed with displeasure.
SERTORIUS.　He would have grounds to, madam; such a treasure
　　　　　Seems still more precious when one is compelled
　　　　　To give it up, but safety here 'gainst all things
　　　　　Is thine if thou canst find it 'gainst thyself
　　　　　And canst defend thyself against an ingrate
　　　　　Who once so loved thee, when he speaks to thee.
　　　　　'Tis hard to hate one who hath been much loved,
　　　　　And fire not yet quite out is soon rekindled.
ARISTIA.　He, by divorcing me to wed Emilia,
　　　　　Made me a woman scorned in all Italy.
　　　　　Thou knowest how grievously my heart is wounded,
　　　　　But if he disavowed a deed forced on him,
　　　　　Cast off Emilia, and gave me back my place,
　　　　　It would be hard for me not to forgive him.
　　　　　So long as I am mine own mistress still,
　　　　　I owe him all if he returns to me.
SERTORIUS.　Vainly I hope, then; vainly I dare, madam,
　　　　　To promise myself some place in thy heart.
　　　　　Pompey still reigneth as sole monarch in it.
　　　　　All that thou feelest offers but thy hand;
　　　　　And when I might aspire, through his rejection
　　　　　Of thee, unto thy heart, this, always his,

Does not wish to be mine.

ARISTIA.   Of what importance
Is my heart, if I know my wifely duty
And if my marriage to thee swells thy power?
Wouldst thou descend so low as to require
Signs of affection from this heart, and wouldst
Thou prefer these to the attempt it makes
To flout the tyrant and redeem my fortunes?
Let us leave, let us leave to petty souls
The ignoble traffic in love's sighs and flames.
Let us unite only to champion better
The liberty which in Rome is almost dead.
Let us unite my vengeance and thy statecraft
To save in its last shift the whole Republic.
Marriage, and naught else, can combine our interests.
I know how high an honor I aspire to,
But even in this cruel exile which the tyrant
Imposes on me, Pompey's cast-off wife
Is someone still, and I have too much pride
To wed save with the greatest living Roman.

SERTORIUS.   This title I do not deserve; I am . . .

ARISTIA.   That which thou seemest to all the world, and art, sir.
But even if this name seems too great for thee,
At least my faithless husband stands below thee.
He serves on *his* side, thou commandest on thine;
Thou art a leader, he is but a subject;
And really the divorce that tore him from me
Makes him a victim more than I of Sulla
If marrying thee lifts me to heights supreme
While his new marriage abases him to slavery.
    But I am carried away, sir, and such great
Good fortune makes me speak too fervently.
All this good fortune still remains uncertain;
I can have only anxious hopes of it;
And I must ever fear to have aspired
Too highly till thou reassurest those hopes.
With one word thou canst do so or confound me.

SERTORIUS.   But, madam, after all, what can I answer,
Of what assure thee, when thou speakest thyself
Without yet being sure of what thou wishest?

    I know the advantages of marriage with thee;
I like to have thereby as hostages
Such great names, and I see that their assistance
Could strengthen us and soon crush tyranny.
But such a hope could find itself defeated
If thy hand's offer is withheld for Pompey
And here parades the greatness of its gift
Only to promise all and give me nothing.

ARISTIA. If thou didst ask my hand because thou lov'dst me,
    Sir, I would say to thee: "Take it; 'tis thine.
Whatever Pompey's wish, he is too late."
But since love hath no least part in our marriage,
Which is a thing of policy alone,
Let me say this to thee, to be explicit,
That if I had a million swords for dowry
Thou wouldst gain yet more by not wedding me.
    If I cause Pompey to cast off Emilia,
Can he, while Sulla rules, e'er turn his eyes
To Italy? Will he go there to surrender
To Sulla, naturally incensed? No, no!
If I regain him, he must come to thee.
Thus, if I wed thee, thou canst be assured
That thousands of true Romans will side with thee;
But if I break our pact and re-espouse him,
Thou'lt have those Romans and besides them Pompey.
Thou'lt have his friends after his new divorce;
Thou'lt have the principal army of the tyrant—
That army or at least its bravest soldiers,
Who would elect to follow their commander.
Ye twain would march on Rome 'neath common banners.
    Then is the time, Sulla, for thee to fear me.
Tremble, and look to see thy pride soon totter
If I take from thee what thou took'st from me.
To make my Pompey thy wife's son-in-law
Thou'st made him perjured, infamous, ignoble;
But if I still have o'er his heart some power,
He will return to sworn faith, manhood, honor.
To be again mine, he will break thy chains,

And we shall crush thee 'neath our common hate.
(*Turning to* SERTORIUS *again*) I take up too much of thy
   precious time.
So matters stand; it is for thee to choose.
If sudden love makes thee wish all concluded,
My hand, I say, is ready to be thine.
Thou canst reflect on 't. Most of all, remember:
My honor requires here a husband for me;
It cannot bear to have my flight here make me
A prisoner of war, subject to being exchanged,
But seeks a great man to plight faith with me
And deems none meet for me but thee and Pompey;
And . . .

SERTORIUS.   Thou wilt see him and wilt learn his thoughts.
ARISTIA.   Farewell. They are of most concern to me,
   And I shall use what power I can to sway them.
SERTORIUS.   I shall give orders to receive him well.

                          (*Exit* ARISTIA.)

   Gods, let me bare, in turn, my soul to you!
How cruel a fate it is to have to love
As policy requireth; and what strange
Misfortunes its needs are, if they compel us
To give the hand when 'tis without the heart!

ACT II

VIRIATE *and* THAMYRAS *are discovered.*

VIRIATE.   Thamyras, he must speak; our situation
   Demands it. Rome e'en here sends me a mistress,
   And midst her woes Aristia, in her exile,
   Threatens to win him despite all I am.
   Vainly my glances, eloquent of meaning,
   Left naught undone to lay bare my heart's feelings;
   Vainly by my disdain of all our kings
   I thought to show I proudly chose another.
   The one man whom I tried to make perceive it
   Either does not dare understand or cares not,
   And leaves me thus confused and shamed, with thinking
   Myself rejected, which my pride denieth.
   Spare me that shame, and see thou tellest him,

This hero dear . . . Thou, Thamyras, understandest.
How could my throne find elsewhere firm support,
And for whom else would I scorn all our kings?
Sertorius, alone worthy of Viriate,
Deserves that my whole heart be given to him.
Let him, oh, let him know my glorious purpose
To make my throne secure by wedding him.
Tell him . . . But I would wrongly try to instruct thee—
I, who well know thy zeal to serve thy princess.

THAMYRAS. All in this hero, madam, is great and noble;
But, to be frank, thy love surpriseth me.
'Tis a new thing for someone of his age
To have such power to charm a youthful heart,
And for a yellowing, deep-wrinkled face
To find a secret way to stir the senses.

VIRIATE. 'Tis not the senses that my heart consults.
It loathes tumultuous impulses of passion,
And its love's flame, which I make serve my interests,
Disdains all trace of such insensate fervor.
I love Sertorius for that skill in war
By which an exile holds the world at bay;
I love him for his head with laurels crowned,
His mien, which makes the bravest warriors tremble,
His arm, which victory ever doth accompany.
A love of true worth takes no reck of age;
Merit hath always dazzling charms for it;
And whosoever can accomplish all things
Is ever worthy to be loved.

THAMYRAS.   But, madam,
Our kings, whose love offends thee—has not one,
Among them all, true worth or power or merits?
And can it be that none of these, thine allies,
Hath signalized his name by glorious exploits?
Would the Turdetan or the Celtiberian
King guard so ill the scepter of thy fathers?

VIRIATE. 'Gainst sovereigns like themselves their aid would please me,
But 'gainst the Romans all their power is nothing.
Only a Roman can resist Rome now.
If we are to defy her, she must lend us
A man, that one of her own sons, defending

Our soil, may equalize the scales and make
The gods take different sides. Since she hath deigned
To give protection to our land, and honor
Our princes with her friendship, our own rulers,
Humiliated by support so mighty,
Have been but subjects falsely called allies,
And all attempts to end their servitude
Have made its yoke but firmer and more galling.

What hath Mandonius done, what hath Indibilis,
But abase further still their humbled thrones
And see the proud ship of their power and glory
Broken upon the rocks of one defeat?

Mine own forefather, the great Viriatus,
Though favored more by Fate, had a like end.
Three praetors he had beaten, won ten battles,
And oft hurled back assaults upon walled towns,
But the ascendant star of their Servilius
Undid at one blow his amazing fortunes.
That great king was thus vanquished; thus he died,
And would have left his realm enslaved forever
Had Rome not sent this noble refugee
To break the chains of our subjected people.

Since he hath ruled our destinies, good fortune
So constantly attends our arms that twice
Five years of war have made our land secure
Against those masters of so many sovereigns
And left them only, after these ten years,
The slopes of the Pyrenees to shield them from us.

Our kings without him, jealous of each other,
Would always see their valor brought to naught.
Ne'er would they choose among themselves a leader.
THAMYRAS. Will they accept a Roman as their leader?
VIRIATE. That name he takes not, treating them as equals,
But none the less he is their general.
They fight 'neath him, unite 'neath his command,
And all these nominal kings really obey him,
While with vain pride of rank they plume themselves
Upon an empty, false equality.
THAMYRAS. I dare not say aught to thee, after this,
And would like thee pay to his age a tribute;

But verily this hero, laden with years,
Too long hath triumphed, still to triumph long.
His death . . .
VIRIATE.   Let us enjoy, despite all envy,
The glorious remainder of his life.
His death will leave to me, for my protection,
His noble memory and his mighty name.
My crown, secure with these two stout supports,
Will dread no hostile power, for they will more
Avail me than a hundred kings. But we
Shall speak hereof again some other time.
I see him now at hand.

Enter SERTORIUS.

SERTORIUS.   What sayst thou, madam,
Of the bold project I now entertain?
Is it not to forget the honor owed thee
To wish to see into thine inmost heart?
VIRIATE.   That heart is so revealed that everyone
Can read there more, perhaps, than I can tell thee.
To see what passes in it, needs but eyes.
SERTORIUS.   Yet I find need thou shouldst explain it better.
All thy kings seek thee eagerly in marriage;
And as our destiny hangs on thy fortunes,
I in those fortunes' name presume to beg thee
To think of us in making this great choice.
If thou shouldst wed a prince inconstant, faithless,
Or with too little ardor for our cause,
Judge in what plight we soon should find ourselves.
If I am long as powerful as now,—
If mine arm . . .
VIRIATE.   Thou conceivest strange misgivings.
I have put all my lands so 'neath thy sway
That when I wish to make choice of a husband
Whatever I decide depends on thee.
To rid thee better of such needless fears,
Choose one for me, thyself, and tell me frankly
Which of these kings thou viewest without suspicion,—
Which of them thou canst trust if I should wed him.
SERTORIUS.   I would fain choose one who might please thee, also;

But judging by thy cold reception of them,
I deem that for them all with no least interest . . .

VIRIATE. Perhaps 'tis true I fancy none of them,
And that the empty splendor of their rank
Fades at the merest glimpse of Roman greatness.

SERTORIUS. Then if I were to give thee, for thy husband,
A Roman . . .

VIRIATE.   How could I refuse a gift
Of thine?

SERTORIUS.   After thou sayst this, I make bold
To offer thee a man worthy to be
Not disavowed even by the Rome of old.
He hath high birth, he hath a noble heart,
He hath great glory, he is full of courage,
Hath won the deep respect of all thy Spain,
Is generous, dauntless, courteous, and magnanimous—
It is, in short, Perpenna whom thy spell . . .

VIRIATE. After all this, I was expecting *thy* name.
The eulogies with which thou didst begin
Permitted me to hope for nothing less.
But certainly the one I heard surprised me.
Thou givest a queen for husband thy lieutenant!
If thus ye Romans choose to woo and wed,
Your merest tribunes must have princesses.

SERTORIUS. Madam . . .

VIRIATE.   Let us talk plainly as to my
Choice of a husband. Art thou too great for me?
For thee am I too lowly? To speak thus,
I well know, is to offer myself to thee,
And these words may offend the ear; but such
Love well befits those of my rank, and I
Would rather, sir, it should be known henceforward
That I have eyes that see just what I do.
I speak, then, plainly—to be understood:
I want a Roman, but he must command;
Nor would I for our kings have felt disdain,
Were it not they better can obey than reign.
Yet if they leave thee master over them,
They in their weakness keep at least their title.
Thus doth my lofty pride, which prefers thee

To any of them, prefer the least among them
To anyone but thee; for, after all,
I should in keeping with my royal birth
Wed one who is a king in name and power
Alike, but as there is no longer such
A one, I think my husband must have either
The power without the name, or else the name
Without the power, of one.

SERTORIUS.   I love thy queenly
Heart, which pays what it owes to the illustrious
Ancestors whom thou art descended from.
Its pride would, if it stooped to thoughts less noble,
Not well sustain the heritage they left thee;
But since, to satisfy thy royal nature,
Thy lofty birth required for thee an equal,
Perpenna is the only one of us
Whose blood would not becloud thy blood's pure tincture.
From our kings and Etruria's is he
Descended. As for me, of birth less high,
I cannot by my small fame be so blinded
As to dishonor with my vows thy throne.
Cease to esteem me to the shame thereof.
I desire only to be called thy servant.
I would be glad to have that glorious name.
It made me triumph, in my wish to aid thee;
And howsoever humbly I was born . . .

VIRIATE. If thou tak'st *that* name, act not as my master,
Or at least show me by what logic, sir,
Thou darest dispose of me but not accept me.
Reconcile the respect thou showest my crown
With this indignity done to my person.
To see all my regard for thee, and use it
Thus ill, is one which art cannot disguise.
Honor me then no longer to insult me.
Since thou so wishest, be indeed my servant,
And let me as a queen command thy vows.
Make them to me because it is my will.
    As for this thy Perpenna, whose high birth
Still doth not free him from obeying thee,
Promise him not the honor of my choice

Were he from gods as well as kings descended.
Rome limits not to noblemen distinction.
Great Marius was of lowly origin,
Yet he is the sole man the Roman people
Have chosen seven times to be their ruler.
Hence, to weigh everyone in his own fashion,
I would select a Spaniard for his lineage,
But in the Romans I pay little heed
To blood when I see native worth attain
The highest rank among them. If thou hatest,
As do the rest of you, the name of queen,
Sir, look upon me as a Roman lady.
The citizenship conferred upon our people
Doth lose, in a crowned head, none of its value.
As an adopted citizen, being like you,
I think myself fully as good as any
Subject of mine; and if a Roman woman
Hath been the cause of thy refusing me,
I am whate'er she is, and queen besides.
Perhaps thy pity for her great misfortunes . . .

SERTORIUS.   I understand thee and, to speak quite freely,
I shall confess Aristia . . .

VIRIATE.   She hath told us
Everything. I know what it is she hopes
And what was written thee. Without losing time
Over that, tell me what thy thoughts are.

SERTORIUS.   She
Is only with the welfare of our cause
Concerned. But since, to rid Spain of the oppressors,
We do not take—thou and I—the same path,
Weigh carefully, I pray, our common interests
And decide what a noble heart should do.
    I would be false to both thy realm and thee,
Madam, to see such aid and not accept it;
But that same aid would ruin us if it robbed us
Of the assistance of that hand which thou
Hast offered to me, and if Fate, averse
To what we both desire, should give that hand
Into bad keeping. I deem Sulla lost
If thou wilt let thy Lusitania join

Its army with the powerful reinforcement
Now promised us. But that may well depend
On who shall be thy husband, and Perpenna
Alone can make me certain of thine aid.
See all that he hath done; so much I owe him
That my prayer rightly seconding his love . . .

VIRIATE.   If much thou owest *him,* dost owe *me* nothing?
And must thou pay thy debt to him through me?
After my power hath guaranteed your safety,
Do I deserve no part in all thy conquests?
Have I thus served thee but to serve thee always,
By mine own aid to thee become thy vassal?
Let this be clear to thee: if Perpenna weds me
I shall be jealous of thy sovereign power
And make him be, himself, too enterprising
For thee to have a king for thy lieutenant.
I shall say more to thee: whome'er I wed,
I shall seek proudly to exalt my throne;
And this it is that turned my thoughts to thee,
The fear of losing all if we are sundered.
I see thou only 'twixt the seas and mountains
Canst under the same flag unite all Spain;
But what I have proposed is the sole means
Of bringing that about, and whatsoever
Thy beloved fellow-countryman hath done
For thee, if he hath helped thee 'gainst the tyrant,
He is well paid for it by his life's being saved.
Your party's evil fortunes so pursued him
That ruin faced him if he had not joined thee;
And the fact is, if I should trust reports,
His troops despite him came to swell thy forces.
    Rome offers great help; so, at least, someone writes thee;
But even if she as one man took up arms
In favor of an exile now proscribed,
When we are on the verge of complete victory
What need have we to share the glory of it?
One more campaign, and our troops can unaided
Drive Sulla's eagles back across the mountains.
Shall these late-comers have the right to tell us
That they established in this land our sway?

Nay, let us both be jealous of that honor,
And where we need no help, owe naught to any.

SERTORIUS.   Even those with the best grounds for hope can never
Have too great strength. The fairest-seeming fortunes
May suddenly be rent by quarrels. Fate loves
To punish over-confidence, and nothing
Should be neglected in our noble efforts.
Ought we to leave uncertain thus the escape
Of Rome from slavery and of us from bondage,
For fear that we would share with other Romans
An honor heaven may wish for them to have?
The glory would, 'tis true, be ours alone
If we unaided set free all the world;
But if misfortune now should overtake us
After so many battles crowned with victory,
How cruelly would we not reproach ourselves?
Besides, remember that Perpenna loves thee,
That he is worthy of a crown or thinks
He is, that he hath here great power, that
'Tis always found the best of governments
Is certain to create some malcontents,
That, angered by rejection, he may dare . . .

VIRIATE.   Say no more. I have made thee, sir, my master;
And I, whate'er I feel, must do thy bidding.
That is what all thy reasoning amounts to.
    Bring, bring this great man here of such importance,
That I may give my first proof of obedience;
And if thou fearest him, fear at least as much
Long, vain regrets for having taken such pains . . .

SERTORIUS.   Wouldst thou think, madam . . .

VIRIATE.   These words should suf-
fice thee.
I understand what thou hast said and wishest
To tell me. Go, yield place to him, and do not
Presume . . .

SERTORIUS.   I speak for another, and yet, alas,
If thou but knewest . . .

VIRIATE.   What ought I to know?
What is the secret which that sigh conceals
From me?

SERTORIUS.   This sigh, again . . .

VIRIATE.   Say no more. Go.
    I shall obey thee better than thou wishest.

(Exit SERTORIUS.*)*

THAMYRAS.   His unresponsiveness amazes me,
    And I cannot . . .

VIRIATE.   Appearances deceive thee.
    He loves me from the bottom of his heart.

THAMYRAS.   What! when he for a rival's sake persists
    In his refusal . . .

VIRIATE.   He wants me to beguile him
    And nothing more.

THAMYRAS.   Thou seest indications
    Hereof which I have not the cleverness . . .

VIRIATE.   Let us talk with this rival. Here he is.

(Enter PERPENNA *and* AUFIDIUS.*)*

        Thou lovest me, Perpenna; so Sertorius
    Tells me. I trust his statements, and I owe him
    My complete confidence. I know thou lov'st me,
    Then; but relieve me of anxiety.
    How hopest thou to deserve to wed a queen?
    Whence be attractive to her? by what magic
    Force her to give thee, for thy love, a crown?

PERPENNA.   By honest vows, by unremitting service,
    By great respect, by willing sacrifices.
    And if by any act I can show proof . . .

VIRIATE.   Well, what art thou prepared to offer to me?

PERPENNA.   All my toil, all my blood, my heart, my life.

VIRIATE.   Wouldst serve me in a matter that involves
    My jealousy?

PERPENNA.   Ah, madam!

VIRIATE.   At that word
    Thy heart throbs needlessly. 'Tis not a matter
    Of love, but only of State policy.
        I have ambition, and in my pride, as queen,
    Cannot unvexed behold another sovereign,
    Who makes my throne a stepping-stone before me
    And takes in mine own realm precedence o'er me.
    Sertorius rules there, and throughout my kingdom
    Administers the laws which I have sanctioned.

Of this do I repent not; he hath used
His power well. I render thanks to heaven
Which hath so favored him, but—now to tell thee
What I indeed am jealous of—what power
Can still be mine beside that of his wife?
Aristia wishes to be that. The offer
That she doth make, or that is made for her,
Assures her will's achievement. Rid our climes
Of this stray woman, who in her exile brings
Disorder to another world than hers.
Without ado, make her grace other regions
With her illustrious presence that offends me.
Quite enough lands will grant asylum to her.

PERPENNA.   Whate'er thou dost command I shall find easy.
But if Sertorius doth not wed *her,*
Thy plight would be the same with any marriage
Of his. What is the difference to thee whether
'Tis with Aristia or with someone else
If . . .

VIRIATE.   Let us bring to naught this plan, Perpenna—
This plan. Yes, let us deal now with the present,
And as regards the future let us do
As seems advisable on each occasion.
Time is a monarch who ordaineth well.
Enough that I am jealous and have told thee
Of what. Is it thy wish to serve me?

PERPENNA.   Is it?
I fly to do so, madam, and already
Am dying to devote my life to thee.
But may I hope that my small services
Will win for me some favoring glance from thee,
And that thy heart, made softer, then will . . .

VIRIATE.   Hold!
Too far thou carriest thy o'erhasty prayers.
Such service would beyond doubt please me greatly,
But let me, pray, decide its fit reward.
I am no ingrate; I know what I owe thee.
This is enough to say to thee at the outset.
Farewell.   (*Exeunt* VIRIATE *and* THAMYRAS.)

AUFIDIUS.   Thou seest, sir, how she plays with thee.

2 1 5

She loves thee not; Sertorius admits it
And is thy rival though he feigns to aid thee,
While the Queen . . .

PERPENNA.   Nay, nay, do not judge her wrongly.
She offers me the means to do her service
Which all my heart embraces with great joy.

AUFIDIUS.   Dost thou not see, then, that her jealous soul
Seeks but to use thee against *thy* heart's interests,
And that thou, in frustrating his new love,
Compellest thy rival to return to her?

PERPENNA.   No matter! I shall serve her and deserve
Her love. Power and revenge will in their turn
Act on her. Let us stake some days upon
The hope that flatters me, though the whole result
Should only be to prove she is ungrateful.

AUFIDIUS.   But, sir . . .

PERPENNA.   Let us have done with useless talk,
Debate no further, but plan how to serve her.
This one concern engrosseth all my mind.
But Pompey hath been seen now from our walls.
Thou knowest what I was told; let us go meet him,
Since it was I Sertorius bade to greet him.

                                   (*Exeunt.*)

A C T   I I I

SERTORIUS, POMPEY, *and their retinues are discovered.*

SERTORIUS (*addressing* POMPEY).   What mortal, sir, would ever have
     dared think
That to such heights the truce would lift my glory,—
Yes, that my name, which war hath made quite famous,
Would gain new stature on the eve of peace?
I still ask if mine eyes have not deceived me
When I within these walls behold great Pompey,
And if it please him, I would fain learn why
Good fortune brings me such a crowning honor.

POMPEY.   'Tis for two reasons. But let all withdraw, sir,
That I may freely tell thee what they are.
                    (*Exeunt all but* SERTORIUS *and* POMPEY.)
The enmity which reigns between our factions

Does not extinguish all the claims of deference.
As genuine worth has its prerogatives
That rise superior to the bitterest hate,
Respect and admiration are just tributes
Which manly virtue claims from one's worst foes;
And this it is that gives me, for the sake
Of thy great genius wherewith I have been
Only too well acquainted, the desire
To see so famed a hero face to face
With neither spear nor javelins in his hand
And brow divested of that dreadful mien
That launched his conquering might against our legions.
    I am, though young, a soldier who hath been
So oft victorious that my too extreme
Good fortune might have swelled my heart with pride;
But I—this frank confession well beseemeth
A generous nature—have learned more 'gainst thee
From my discomfitures than the fairest triumphs
That I have won elsewhere have ever taught me.
Observing thee, I see the way one should
Conduct assaults, clever retreats, and sieges,
How best to make a camp, to choose for each man
His proper task—I study thy example.
Oh, if I might restore thee to the Republic,
How rare a gift I thus, methinks, would give her!
And with what happiness I would go to Rome—
Since the truce yields me leisure now to do so—
If I could bring there with me even some hope
Of reaching so momentous an accord!
Can I do naught with fortune-favored Sulla
For thee? Can I do naught with thee for Rome?

SERTORIUS.   Thou couldst undoubtedly spare me some pains
If thou wouldst have a truly Roman heart.
But ere we enter into these hard problems
Let me make answer to thy courteous words.
    The great esteem they show for me ascribes
Naught to me which thou hast not in the highest
Degree already. The victories which attended
Thy earliest exploits, and a triumph ere thou
Wert of an age at which our laws allow one

Or of a rank which lets one be aspired to,
Prove in what deep respect the entire world holds thee.
If I was able this once to make use better
Of the nature of the land and my position,—
If my experience took advantage of them,—
War's noble art sometimes awaiteth age.
Time teacheth much of it, and if thou wert pleased
To learn some lessons from me, my example
Will someday be in thy turn set by thee,
What I have taught thee thou wilt teach to others,
And those who when I die shall take my place
Will learn 'gainst thee what thou hast learned 'gainst me.
    As for the fortune-favored Sulla, I
Have naught to say unto thee. I have shown thee
How I can sap his power, and if I ever
Can join thereto instruction suitable
To show thee how one can re-cross the mountains,
Closely enough shall I come on the heels
Of thy withdrawal to treat with him without
The aid of any intermediary,
And, pike in hand, on Tiber's banks require him
To pay for the wrongs done the Roman people.

POMPEY. A lesson so ambitious, sir, is arduous
And well might cost thee unavailing pains
If thou intendest to make it known to me
So well that I shall learn to carry it out.

SERTORIUS. Thou alone couldst thyself spare me such pains
If thou wouldst have a truly Roman heart.
I have said that ere now.

POMPEY.   Its repetition
Would weary one of stern and sensitive virtue;
But as for me, who honor thee so much
That I compel myself determinedly
To avoid all themes of which I might complain,
I do not wish to fathom thy vague words.

SERTORIUS. I know one does not love to hear such truths;
But as we are alone, sir, I speak frankly.
Banning all witnesses, thou lettest me do so,
And I use in thy presence the same freedom
As if thy Sulla never had existed.

Can one be truly Roman when commanding
An army which attempts to hold in chains
The masters of the world? That name would still
Be rightly due us, but for him and thee.
'Tis through him, 'tis through thee, that we have lost it.
'Tis ye who 'neath the yoke bow men so brave,
Once more than kings, now lower than a slave.
The glory which attends thy greatest deeds
Only reveals the depth of *their* misfortune.
Their misery is the fruit of thy best toil—
And thou thinkest thine a truly Roman heart!
Thou hast inherited from thy forefathers
The name of Roman, but if it were precious
Unto thee thou wouldst live up to it better.

POMPEY.   I think I live up to it well when all
My heart is being devoted to the task
Of presently restoring the Republic.
But thou, sir, judgest by the arm the soul,
And often one seems what the other is not.
      When two great factions disunite a people
Each man does, by pure chance, the worse or better
According to the opportunity
Or the necessity which leadeth him
To take one course or another. In one's choosing
The better party, which is hard to judge,
One hath full freedom to select a master;
But when one's choice is made, one doth not change it.
I have served under Sulla from the time
Of Marius, and will still serve under him
So long as e'er a fatal destiny
Keepeth alive some remnant of our strife.
As I see not into his heart's depths, I
Know not what plans he in his triumph layeth.
If they go too far, I myself shall blame him:
My arm I lend him, but my soul I bind not.
I yield myself to his good fortune's current
While all my wishes are for liberty;
And this it is that makes me keep an office
Which by some wicked and audacious man
Would but for me be seized, in order that

When Sulla dies this dangerous power may fall
To none who doth not realize his duty.
In short, I know my path, as thou knowest thine.

SERTORIUS.　But meanwhile, sir, thou servest like any other;
And we,—who judge on our eyes' evidence
And leave it to the gods to read the soul,—
Fear thine example, and we wonder whether
It doth not teach the Roman populace
To obey the mandates of one man, and whether
Thy valor, now subservient to another,
Sows not for thee even while it acts for him.
　　As I esteem thee, I can easily
Believe that thou wouldst glory in Rome's freedom,—
That all thy prayers are for it secretly,—
But if I would believe less trustful spirits,
Thou helpest the Romans learn to accept a master
Because thou hopest thou'lt someday be theirs.
The hand of the oppressor whom thou aidest
Inures them to the yoke to which thou'lt bend them;
And not being certain they will endure slavery,
At Sulla's risk thou testest their hearts' courage.

POMPEY.　Time will teach those the truth that now talk thus.
But will it justify what here we see?
Let me in turn speak frankly; thine example
Instructs and authorizes me to do so.
I judge, like thee, on mine eyes' evidence
And leave it to the gods to read the soul.
　　Do not all here live 'neath one man's command?
And dost thou not rule here as Sulla rules
In Rome? What mattereth the name—dictator
Or general—if the power of both is equal?
The difference in titles meaneth naught.
Thy laws dost thou impose as he doth his;
And if 'tis dangerous to incur his hate,
'Twould not be safe to disobey thee here.
　　For me, if I am someday what thou art,
I shall perhaps then use my power like thee.
Till then . . .

SERTORIUS.　　　　Till then thou mightest feel more doubts
And make me somewhat less resemble Sulla.

2 2 0

If I command, our senate bids me to.
No one hath yet been murdered by my orders.
My foes are, all, foes of the common weal,
And I fight fairly 'gainst them—proscribe none.
My supreme power offers to all a refuge,
And I am but obeyed as I am loved.

POMPEY.   And thy dominion all the more is dangerous
As it makes people love thee for thy virtues,
As in subjecting them thou canst win hearts,
As in thy chains one is a willing slave,
And as hence liberty would try in vain
To overthrow one's power whom love makes reign.
    Sir, this is what less trusting souls will say;
But let us not weigh these unpleasant questions—
Nor whether a group of banished men, collected
In this asylum which thou offerest them,
Is a real senate. Is there any way—
Once more I ask thee—by which I can bring
To Rome some gladness? It would be extreme
If I could find the means to give so great
A man back to his fellow-citizens.
'Tis sweet to see one's native walls again.
Rome by my voice, sir, begs this boon of thee.
She . . .

SERTORIUS.   The abode of your cruel potentate
Whose passion's frenzy alone rules the State?
I call no longer Rome that walled enclosure
Which his proscriptions fill with obsequies.
Those walls whose destiny once seemed so fair
Are but Rome's prison now—or, rather, tomb.
But to live elsewhere in her pristine vigor,
She hath renounced completely all false Romans,
And as about me all the true ones rally,
Rome is no more in Rome, but where I am.
    Let us speak, though, of concord. I know only
One way to give us honorably this joy.
Let us join forces, and the tyrant falls.
This great result will Rome with open arms
Welcome. Thus shall we show that love of country
Which noble hearts push to idolatry,

And we shall save those streams of Roman blood
That every year thy sword and mine are shedding.
POMPEY. Would this plan, which for thee shines bright with glory,
Involve for me naught blackened by dishonor?
I, who command—can I serve under thee?
SERTORIUS. I cling not to my power as commander.
I hold it but in trust; to thee I yield it—
Not to the point of serving in thy ranks;
That scarce contents me; but in our alliance
Wouldst thou begrudge my being thy lieutenant?
POMPEY. Only in semblance such lieutenants have
Superiors. Their name retains for them
The power they surrender. They give up
Merely the form thereof, nor will a soldier
Obey or follow others but as it suits him.
I have another plan, nobler and surer.
Sulla, if thou so wishest, will resign
From his dictatorship; he would himself
Already have relinquished it if he
Had seen he here had no more enemies.
Lay down your arms; I answer for the sequel;
I give my word therefor when I have thine.
If thou'rt a Roman, seize the opportunity.
SERTORIUS. Mine eyes are dazzled not by this proposal.
I know the tyrant, and I see his ruse.
Whate'er he seems to promise, he ne'er changes.
Thee hath he sacrificed to his mistrust
To the point of forcing thee to be related . . .
POMPEY. Alas! the mention of this kills my heart.
I shall say frankly to thee, 'tis the sole
Ground he hath given me to complain of him.
I loved Aristia, and he tore me from her.
My heart still quivers with my self-reproach,
It ceaselessly remembers my lost treasure,
And I a thousand times, sir, thank thee for her—
Thee, whose great soul vouchsafed compassionately
To honor her with thy protection here.
SERTORIUS. To protect stoutly virtue in misfortune
Is the least duty of magnanimous natures.
Hence I do more: I give to her a husband.

POMPEY.   A husband! Gods! What news! Who is he?

SERTORIUS.   I.

POMPEY.   Thou! Sir, her whole heart hath been mine since childhood.
　　　　　Be not like Sulla in this violence.
　　　　　My woe is great enough without my having
　　　　　To see my loved one in another's arms.

SERTORIUS.   All is yet thine to have.
　　　　　　　　　(*Raising his voice*) Come, madam, come!
　　　　　Show him whether I have usurped his place
　　　　　Within thy heart; and show to all mankind,
　　　　　If thou canst do so, whether thou hast felt
　　　　　Constrained to give thy hand to me in marriage.
　　　　　　　　　　　　　　　　　　　(*Enter* ARISTIA.)

POMPEY.   'Tis she herself, ah heaven!

SERTORIUS.   I leave thee with her,
　　　　　Knowing her whole heart is still faithful to thee.
　　　　　Take back thy treasure; or complain no more, sir,
　　　　　If I am made rich by what thou rejectest.
　　　　　　　　　　　　　　　　　　　(*Exit* SERTORIUS.)

POMPEY.   Is this true, madam? would it be possible . . .

ARISTIA.   Yes, it is true my heart, sir, is responsive:
　　　　　I love or hate as I am loved or hated,
　　　　　And pride doth keep alive my hate or love.
　　　　　But even if pride reigns sovereign o'er my love,
　　　　　It does not always regulate my hatred.
　　　　　Not I myself do that, and I hate sometimes
　　　　　Less than I should and less than I fain would.

POMPEY.   Thy hate of me is given full scope, madam,
　　　　　And pity nowise holds it in abeyance
　　　　　Nor magnanimity can temper it.

ARISTIA.   Thou seest not, then, it scarcely can continue?
　　　　　My love's flame, quenched only because it should be,
　　　　　In spite of me seeks thine to be reborn;
　　　　　And I, when with thee, feel my wavering anger
　　　　　Sink, lose its force, and die while I am speaking.
　　　　　Mightest thou love me still, sir?

POMPEY.   Do I love thee!
　　　　　Ask if I live, or if I am myself.
　　　　　Thy love is life to me; my life is thine.

ARISTIA.   Ye jealous feelings, from my breast begone—

Black brood of my chagrin, foes of my honor,
Resentful instincts, I henceforth wish not
To heed you. I was wronged, but 'tis forgot.
No more new marriage! no more Sertorius!
I belong to great Pompey, and since still
He loves me,—since he gives me back his heart,—
I again worship him: no more Sertorius!
But speak to me, sir. Let that heart find utterance
Which thou at last restorest to me. No more
Sertorius! . . . Alas, whate'er I say, sir,
Thou dost not say to me, "No more Emilia!"
    Return unto my breast, ye jealous feelings,
Proud offspring of my honor, noble transports!
'Tis ye I fain would heed, and faithless Pompey
No longer can permit my hate to waver;
He hath confirmed me in it. Come, Sertorius;
This mute rejection of me makes me thine.
Let us have this great witness at our marriage.
Wholly another's, he will feel no anguish.
Without pain he will see it; and his indifference
Will pass with Sulla for high-mindedness.

POMPEY.   That which wrongs thee does me an equal wrong.
I indeed love thee, but can do naught more.
If e'er my love meant anything to thee,
Rail, hate thy fill, but give thyself to none.
Remain always my wife in feeling. Keep
Unto the grave dominion o'er my soul.
Sulla hath but his life's span. He is old
And worn; his rule will end, if 'tis not ended
Already. His great power weighs upon him;
He is preparing to relinquish it.
I tell thee this, as I have told Sertorius.
Then rush not, madam, into another's arms.
Rail, hate thy fill, but give thyself to none.
If thou desirest my hand, plight not thine own.

ARISTIA.   How now! Art thou not in another's arms?

POMPEY.   No. Since I must confide to thee this secret,
Emilia obeyed Sulla with regret.
In tearing her from her first husband's clasp
He did not break the tie between their hearts.

    She bears their love's fruit now within her body,
    Which soon she at my home will bring to birth,
    And in her sad plight she whose hand he gave me
    Hath hoodwinked him by a pretense of marriage,—
    While she remaineth her dear Glabrio's only,
    Appears my wife and is so but in name.

ARISTIA.   That name alone is everything for one
    Like me. Give back to me, sir, that great name
    She bears. I used to prize thy tenderness
    And ardor, but am now above such fondness;
    And I would be quite happy if the cutting
    Short of my life's thread would to my forefathers
    Join me as Pompey's wife, and if that noble
    Title engraven upon my tomb would show
    To all the future that I have preserved it.
    I find therein my whole delight and pride.
    One moment of its loss is torture to me.
    Avenge me upon Sulla, who deprives me
    Of it today, or let me be avenged
    By someone upon him and upon thee,
    Another marriage give to me a title
    No less impressive and again exalt me
    As much as Sulla hath abased me—not
    That I could love anyone else as I
    Do thee, but I must to avenge mine honor
    Have now a husband, as I must have one
    Who is illustrious and whose renown . . .

POMPEY.   Oh, weary not of loving and being loved!
    We may be drawing near that longed-for moment
    Which can again unite those who were parted.
    Be more courageous and not so impatient.
    Let Sulla die or lay aside his power . . .

ARISTIA.   Shall I await his death or his repentance
    For thee to vouchsafe to consent to give me
    Back my lost honor, and shall I always see
    Thy heart ice-cold, the oppressor left unpunished,
    My rival in my place, till he renounceth
    His supreme power after having kept it
    As long as he desired it?

POMPEY.   But while he

Is still all-powerful, what can I do?

ARISTIA. Cleave to thy wife in exile everywhere,
Bring her back with thy legions to her home,
And end in blessed peace all factional discord.
What canst thou not do when thou hast an army
Which everywhere except in Spain hath triumphed?
And when Sertorius shall be joined with thee
What can the tyrant do, howe'er enraged?

POMPEY. One is not freed by seeming so for a moment,
Nor doth one break one's yoke by changing masters.
Sertorius is a strong support for thee;
But if I make him mine, I put myself
Under his leadership. To unite our banners
Is to increase his power. Perpenna, who
Joined forces with him, can tell thee as to that.
I serve now, but serve one so far away
That ere his orders reach me they are needless;
And, paying him only some small show of deference,
I, jealous of real power, serve but in seeming.
Methinks I need serve e'en thus very briefly—
And now when Sulla for this happy change
Prepareth, canst thou order *me* to banish
Myself from Rome and bow her 'neath the yoke
And mandates of another man—me, me,
Who cling to my authority but to give her
Back someday all her liberty. No, no!
If thou dost love me as I like to think
Thou dost, thou canst bring into harmony
Thy love and my fair fame, wait prudently
For the approaching hour of change, and not
Undo me trying to avenge thyself.

ARISTIA. If thou hast loved me and rememberest it,
Thou'lt find thy fair fame in restoring mine.
But now 'tis time to end this argument
With one word. Dost thou want me, sir, or not?
Speak; let thy choice decree my destiny.
Do I belong still to the husband given me?
Or do I to Sertorius belong?
There hath been quite enough debate. Give back
My wedlock's bonds to me, or total freedom . . .

POMPEY. Madam, I see that we must end the truce—
To break up as a conqueror this marriage,
If 'tis to be; for thou so little knowest
How to serve thine own interests that to teach thee
To do so, I must conquer thee.

ARISTIA.   Sertorius
Knows how to conquer and defend his conquest.

POMPEY. Thine will cost not a few lives to defend.
As it will slam the door against all concord,
Naught save my death will ever make it sure.
Yes, to the gods I swear, if he must win thee,
Naught can prevent his death except mine own;
And we may both, each by the other pierced,
Make thee perceive to what thou drivest us.

ARISTIA. Sir, I am not of such importance. Other
Cares will soon quench this ardor for revenge.
Thoughts of aggrandizement will bear thee elsewhere,
So thou canst find some fairer destiny.
In serving Sulla, loving his Emilia,
Winning the admiration of all Italy,
Restoring to thy Rome someday her freedom,
Thou'lt turn thy steps unto another path.
Above all else the right of lofty souls
To change their wives or husbands at their pleasure
Deserves to be displayed to earth's last bounds
To set the example in unnumbered climes.

POMPEY. Oh, this is too much, madam, and I swear
Anew . . .

ARISTIA.   Sir, does the truth wrong anyone?

POMPEY. Too soon dost thou forget I am thy husband.

ARISTIA. If that name pleases thee, I still am thine.
Here is my hand, sir.

POMPEY.   Guard it for me, madam.

ARISTIA. The while thou hast in Rome another wife?
The while thou shamest me with another marriage?
May the gods whom thou sworest by punish me
If, when this moment ends and I go hence,
I keep with thee a faith which thou hast broken!

POMPEY. What wilt thou do? Alas!

ARISTIA.   What thou hast taught me.

POMPEY. Stifle such love?

ARISTIA.   Thou thyself stiflest it.

POMPEY. Victory could rightly make it live again.

ARISTIA. If now too weak my hate, that will increase it.

POMPEY. Couldst thou hate me?

ARISTIA.   'Twill be my one endeavor.

POMPEY. Farewell for a few days.

ARISTIA.   Farewell forever!

A C T   I V

SERTORIUS *and* THAMYRAS *are discovered.*

SERTORIUS. Might I speak with the Queen?

THAMYRAS.   While thou awaitest
　　Her coming, she hath bidden me to entertain thee.
　　She fain would be alone for a brief time.

SERTORIUS. Wilt thou not tell me how incline her feelings,
　　And how much hope Perpenna ought to have?

THAMYRAS. She takes me not into her confidence,
　　But I presume that since thou speakest for him
　　He will not find it hard to o'ercome her coldness.
　　Thy power o'er her is limitless.

SERTORIUS.   Nay, I
　　Can there do little, if I am so luckless
　　As to dispose her ever to accept him;
　　Or, to speak of it with more accuracy,
　　I have there too great power and too small.

THAMYRAS. She thinks that she will please thee very much
　　In countenancing his love.

SERTORIUS.   Will please me?

THAMYRAS.   Yes.
　　But whence, sir, cometh this surprise, and wherefore
　　Is a heart troubled that disdaineth her?

SERTORIUS. Call not "disdain" a reverence which her sight
　　Makes govern ruthlessly my dearest wishes.

THAMYRAS. Few feel a reverence that resembles thine,
　　Which can find only arguments for another,
　　And I would like some small outburst of passion
　　Better than such humility's sad homage.

SERTORIUS. I have said nothing which could injure me

That any sighs I let escape my lips
Should not have unsaid promptly; but the Queen,
Responsive to new wishes, understood
My arguments and did not heed my sighs.

THAMYRAS. Sir, when a Roman—when a hero—sigheth
We understand not well what his sighs mean,
And I would serve as thy interpreter
Better if thou'dst explain thyself more clearly.
I know that in this clime, which ye call "barbarous,"
Love by a sigh sometimes declareth itself;
But honor, the sole source of all your passions,
Lifts you too far above such feelings, such
Desires too low for the great hearts of Romans . . .

SERTORIUS. By being Roman I am not less a man.
I love, perhaps more than one ever loved;
Despite my age and me, my heart is all
Aflame. I thought I could o'ercome my feelings,
And all my ingenuity in my greatest
Efforts hath made me see my helplessness.
These, prompted by State policy and friendship,
Have put me in a plight to make me pitied.
The thought of it will kill me, and my life
Depends on my faint hopes placed in the Queen.
Yet if . . .

THAMYRAS.   Sir, she is kindly, but I see
Her heart is greatly vexed; and if thou biddest me
To speak to thee without dissimulation,
Thou well mayst hope but hast good grounds for fear.
Lose no time with her, and neglect thou nothing.
Hers is perhaps a purpose not yet fixed.
Here she is. Profit by the counsel given thee,
And above all take care she knows naught of it.

Enter VIRIATE.

VIRIATE. I hear Aristia failed in her intention
And Pompey fled from that illustrious lady.
Might this be true, sir?

SERTORIUS.   It is all too true;
But though he leaves her, he at heart adores her,
And will tomorrow end the truce, he tells me,

If it is seen she is about to wed me.

VIRIATE.   Art thou but little moved by such a threat?

SERTORIUS.   It is not this that gives me most concern.
But thou—about Perpenna what decidest thou?

VIRIATE.   To obey at once thy sovereign power's mandate;
And if, enthralled still by a tenuous offer,
Thou wishest indeed to marry Pompey's leavings,
It but on thee depends whether tomorrow
Ties shall be sealed in our respective weddings,
Though thus the truce should end and jealousy
Should carry its frenzy to the last extreme.

SERTORIUS.   Thou couldst tomorrow . . .

VIRIATE.   Or this very moment.
To obey tardily is not to obey,
And when obedience is scrupulous
One takes pride in its promptness.

SERTORIUS.   My requests
Could tolerate some refusal.

VIRIATE.   I would always
Deem them peremptory orders. He who can
Do what he will, commands when he requests.
Besides, Perpenna idolizes me.
Such love, his ancestry of many kings,
The sovereign power which sustains his fortunes,
All combined, are well worth a fictive throne
Which can exist only by pleasing thee.

SERTORIUS.   I then need but to die to speed this choice.
My doom hath been decreed by thine own voice—
A positive order which 'tis time I heeded.
To love a Roman thou wouldst have him rule;
And as without my death Perpenna cannot,
To fill thy throne he must have all my lot.
To give him thy hand, madam, is to bid me
To yield my place to him both in the camp
And in thy breast. 'Tis just, most just, that he,
After his great good fortune, should acquire it
In the army even as in thy bosom. I
Obey unmurmuringly, and desire my life . . .

VIRIATE.   Before 'tis by my order ravished from thee
May I complain to thee of an about-face

Which makes thee seem his friend less than his rival?
Thou findest my consent too prompt, too thorough!
The marriage I prepare for gives thee pain!
Thou speakest of it to me as if thou lovedst me!

SERTORIUS.   Let me, after these words, die at thy feet.
I would fain sacrifice there all my welfare
To thine most readily, but I cannot bear
To see thee in another's arms. I thus
Show thee to what extremity my love,
To which I did not hearken, hath reduced me.
   Though such a wondrous being was my excuse,
I deemed it shameful to love anyone
When I no more am one who could be loved.
To avoid doing so, I have remembered
My grizzled hair; and long did I feel certain
Of thy disdain, but I have lately noted
Different ideas in thy mind, whereon
I based hopes instantly, and to myself
Promised more than to all your kings when I
Saw love could not decide thy choice of husband.
Aristia's offer then kept me from speaking—
Not that this aught abated my heart's passion,
But I felt sure that one, if noble, would
Sacrifice everything for the common good.
Perpenna's love for thee to these reflections
Added yet others. Thou has seen what followed
And my forced logic. I had told myself
That such unhappiness as I would feel
Could cost me only a few sighs, and I
Envisaged, to console myself, the fame
That would be mine as a magnanimous leader
And generous friend. But at the crucial moment
My anguish told me that I had resolved
To do more than I can. I cease to struggle,
Then, madam. Of my life make thou disposal.
I once again offer it up to thee.
Lov'st thou Perpenna?

VIRIATE.   I know how to obey thee,
But know not what it is to love or loathe.
The place thou heretofore hadst in my heart

Was given thee by my pride, not by my love.
I have no love for him, had none for thee.
I do not want love, but I want a husband.
I want a great man who, by wedding me,
Can so exalt the throne which I inherit
That he can be the prop and stay of Spain
And leave her true kings of his blood and mine.
    In thee I would have found him, but abjectly
Thou settest thy dear rival's interests higher,
And when I to a hundred kings preferred thee,
Thou chosest, still abject, a cast-off woman.
    But I will forget all, and show thee favor.
Dost thou love me?

SERTORIUS.   Dare I yet have such boldness?

VIRIATE.   Have it—with my consent, sir; and tomorrow
    Give me thy hand in marriage, not Perpenna's.

SERTORIUS.   How happy a less honest love would be
    Which had no goal but its own satisfaction
    And which, absorbed in its felicity,
    Would think not of thy royal dignity!
    But though thou hast forgot what I have told thee,
    Can I forget that I must make thy kingdom
    Great? that thy chief concern is that of reigning?

VIRIATE.   Will doing thyself a favor turn me from it?

SERTORIUS.   Is now a time to do myself this favor?

VIRIATE.   That thou shouldst do it, is Viriate's aim.

SERTORIUS.   We by such haste will ruin everything.
    Perpenna's love will lead him to rebel.
    Allow a little time to deal with him
    That he may see and love some other fair one.
    Let us secure Aristia's friends' aid
    By promises joined ever with postponements.
    To quench now all the hope which animates them
    Is to lose them and end the anxieties
    Of that perturbèd, jealous spirit who must not
    Be cured of fancies which could win him for us.
    After such losses, could we avenge Rome?
    Could we release her from her miseries?
    And such forthright indifference to her interests . . .

VIRIATE.   What matters it to me whether Rome suffers?

Though I should make her woes and shame all end,
I would, for my reward, be called her friend—
Would see thee bring me her commands as consul,
Would bow before her as do other sovereigns!
Sir, if thou lovest me, our seas and mountains
Must give thy wishes bounds, as they do Spain;
Here can we find us fortunes fair enough
And seek no glory 'neath the Aventine.
Set free the Tagus, and forget the Tiber.
Freedom is naught when all the world is free.
'Tis sweet to have it and see all men groan
Beneath the yoke and in their chains make moan.
'Tis sweet to show one's freedom to the eyes
Of those enslaved along the Rhone or captive
In Rome, and see envied by humbled peoples
That deep respect which is the valiant's portion.
    As for the great Perpenna, if thou fearest him,
Leave me the task to make him manageable.
I know how to keep noble hearts from erring.

SERTORIUS.   What good result thinkest thou thus will follow?
I know him no less well and see what storms
This unexpected step will gather o'er us.
Let us not seek to make insurgents, madam,
Nor set kind destiny at variance with us.
Rome without that will cause us enough trouble
Ere countenancing a marriage with a queen,
And we shall ne'er o'ercome her loathing of it
Unless she owes to us glory and freedom.

VIRIATE.   I shall say more, sir: far from countenancing
This marriage, she will feel because of it
A hate toward thee which I desire, an anger
Implacable, an obdurate arrogance;
And thence it is I hope to keep thee here.
What role have I in Rome? and why, I pray thee . . .

SERTORIUS.   But all our Romans, madam, love their country,
And their dear, single hope in all their labors
Is this: to conquer soon and again see her.

VIRIATE.   To bind them all unto the Tagus' banks
We need but leave Rome in her slavery.
Gladly will they live 'neath thy sway and mine

When they must have a king or else a tyrant.

SERTORIUS.   They hold these both alike in equal hate
Nor will obey the husband of a queen.

VIRIATE.   Then let them go and seek what climes they will
Where governments have neither kings nor tyrants.
Our Spaniards, taught your armies' art of war,
Will do, without them, what is left to do.
    Sulla's destruction is not what I seek.
Rome is still less the goal of my ambition.
The marriage I desire can find no charms
Amid a city where divorces flourish,
And from my throne's height I see few attractions
Where one is king for one year and then nothing.
Finally, I have done more for thee than Rome has:
She banished thee and I espoused thy cause;
I saved the life she sought to rob thee of.
Take thou my crown and let her be a slave.
'Tis noble to attempt unheard-of things
Even if the result defeats one's hopes.
For my part, I would fain make a great king
Of a great Roman. Do thou, if 'tis needful
To perish, perish with me; to destroy
Oneself in serving one's beloved is glorious.

SERTORIUS.   But thus forthwith to rush to such extremes,
Madam, and needlessly breed disaffection!
Let us be happy later but much longer.
A victory or two, combined with skillful . . .

VIRIATE.   Thou knowest that love, sir, is not what impels me;
But after all, I must confess, such prudence
Begins to weary me. I am a queen,
And anyone who knows how to wear a crown,
Having decided, likes not argument.
I shall look to my interests. Look to thine.

SERTORIUS.   Ah, if thou hearkenest to thine unjust anger . . .

VIRIATE.   I have none, sir; but my disquieted soul
Wishes no more suspense as to my fate.
Tomorrow thou wilt tell me what it is.
I leave thee with one meanwhile to consult with.

Enter PERPENNA *and* AUFIDIUS. *Exeunt* VIRIATE *and* THAMYRAS.

PERPENNA (*to* AUFIDIUS). Gods! What can cause the Queen to vanish
thus?

AUFIDIUS (*to* PERPENNA). He himself hath a heart much torn by
something,
Sir; and our entrance quite confuses him.

SERTORIUS (*addressing* PERPENNA). Knowest thou what is said of
Pompey here?
Didst thou go with him far beyond the gates?

PERPENNA. Since he had left his escort near the walls,
I spared myself from going farther with him.
But I have great need, sir, of thine assistance.
His whole face showed such haughty arrogance . . .

SERTORIUS. We have concluded naught, but 'tis not *my* fault;
And well thou knowest . . .

PERPENNA. I know that with such issues . . .

SERTORIUS. I do not think we should give up our fight.
'Tis not yet time.

PERPENNA. Say on, I beg of thee.
'Tis not yet time for friendship to grow weary.

SERTORIUS. Thy interests give me pause, as well as mine.
If I thus fared but ill, 'twould not be well
For thee.

PERPENNA. Without thine aid I should be pitied,
Truly; but I see naught for thee to fear.

SERTORIUS. 'Tis I who would be jealousy's first victim,
But then my fate might befall thee. The tyrant
Fears thee next to me above anyone,
And my head's toppling would endanger thine.
We both would do well to wait one year longer.

PERPENNA. What art thou saying, sir, of heads and tyrants?

SERTORIUS. I speak of Sulla, thou shouldst know.

PERPENNA. And I
Spoke of the love enkindled by the Queen.

SERTORIUS. Our wits were equally astray, then. Mine
Were wholly bent upon the perils involved
In making peace, and I was asking thee
What talk the fruitless conference between
Pompey and me gave rise to in the city.
Aufidius, dost thou know?

AUFIDIUS. To hide naught from thee,

    Sir, those in Pompey's escort have contrived
    To turn it to our harm. I fear therefrom
    Presumptuous mutterings among the people.
    Sulla, they say, ends his dictatorship,
    And thou alone wilt not accept the joys
    Of peace and wouldst have war go on forever.
    Our soldiers, with their minds thus biased, already
    Talk too enthusiastically of Pompey,
    And if their views spread to our garrisons,
    Error might there distil a dangerous poison.

SERTORIUS. We shall end that drift ere it groweth greater,
    And by our efforts bring the ruse to naught.
    Heaven hath protected me from much worse perils.

PERPENNA. Is it not best to accept the offered terms,
    Sir? Dost thou find them shameful or unsafe?

SERTORIUS. Sulla may give up his dictatorship,
    But he can still have consuls of his choosing,
    Slaves in the purple who will do his bidding;
    And when we fear no longer his grim mandates,
    We shall be slain by those of his base minions.
    Believe me, for such folk as ye and I,
    Naught is so dangerous as too much good faith.
    Sulla, through policy, hath taken this course
    To show our soldiers their sure way to safety;
    But as for Cinna, Carbo, and young Marius,
    He sought their heads and he hath killed them all.
    For my part, though my whole camp at this rumor
    Forsake me,—though on my side there remain
    Only myself alone,—rather would I
    Disappear in some savage clime than go,
    While Sulla lives, to seek the consulship.
    Thou . . .

PERPENNA.   That is not what keepeth me unhappy.
    Barred from the consulship by marrying
    A queen (if through thy kindness I obtain
    That blessing) I expect from Rome no longer
    Honors of any sort; and being exiled
    In Lusitania forever, I
    Think my remaining days will there be safe.

SERTORIUS. Yes, but I see no safety, sir, in what

    Thou and I planned. Thou knowest that the Queen
    Is of so proud a nature . . . But perhaps
    Time will yet render her less proud. Adieu.
    Spare me from further speech concerning this.
PERPENNA.   Nay, speak, sir! Is my suit so ill received?
    Is it in vain I love, I long for her?
SERTORIUS.   Her going hence told more than I can tell thee.
PERPENNA.   It told me much; but tell me all the rest, sir,
    And hide not from me what thou knowest hereof.
    Canst thou have filled me only with false hopes?
SERTORIUS.   No, I relinquished her to thee, and I
    Will keep my word. I love her, and I still
    Give her to thee despite my love; but I
    Fear that this gift will never have her sanction,—
    That it will draw relentless hate upon us.
    What shall I say, then? Spain has other queens,
    And thou couldst find a destiny far sweeter
    If thou'dst for me do what I did for thee.
    The Ilergetes' princess, or the Vaccaei's,
    Would much more promptly satisfy thy wishes.
    The Queen would zealously help thee with either.
PERPENNA.   Thou didst promise me her, and thou wilt take her
    From me!
SERTORIUS.   What serves it that I promise her
    Or give her unto thee, when her ambition
    Bindeth her unto me? Thou knowest the reasons
    For that bond; I have lately told thee of them
    Without reserve, and thus I still speak frankly
    To thee. Do some small violence to thy feelings.
    I overcame mine; I would do it yet;
    But if we should observe our party's interests
    Can we drive to extremes an obstinate queen
    Who would herself choose and decide her course,
    And whose aid, more than ten years now, hath better
    Upheld our cause than all of its adherents?
PERPENNA.   Is she in a position, sir, to do thee
    Much harm?
SERTORIUS.   She cannot utterly destroy us;
    But if thou holdest me to what I promised,
    She will negotiate with our foes tomorrow.

Their camp is much too near us; here all murmur.
Judge what is to be feared, as matters stand.
Think what prompt remedy there is for them,
And what will come of using compulsion on her.

PERPENNA.   I needs must conquer love; so reason bids me.
But in so great a task all my heart, shuddering . . .

SERTORIUS.   Do not constrain thyself. Though at my life's
Cost, I will keep my pledge, despite my love.

PERPENNA.   If thy pledge hath not Viriate's sanction . . .

SERTORIUS.   I can say naught from her to give thee hope.

PERPENNA.   I must constrain myself, then, and I will.
Yes, I will rule my heart's desires completely.
I wish to be this day, like thee, their master.
Despite my love, which I let grow too great,
Tell thou the Queen . . .

SERTORIUS.   Well, then, what shall I tell her?

PERPENNA.   Naught, sir; naught yet. Tomorrow I shall think on 't . . .
The wrath, however, unto which she gives way,
Might on this very night begin some intrigue.
Thou, sir, shalt tell her anything thou wishest,
And I will follow the course thou settest for me.

SERTORIUS.   I pity and admire thee.

PERPENNA.   My heart is crushed!

SERTORIUS.   I share the woes wherewith thy cup is full.
Farewell; I briefly go to pacify her,
And will return in time to dine with thee.

                              (*Exit* SERTORIUS.)

AUFIDIUS.   This master thou so lovest does marvels for thee;
Thy love hath favors from him without equal!
His name alone, despite him, steals all from thee,
And when he speaks, the Queen forthwith is his.
What services must thou with fond hopes do her
To merit the love she waits to bestow on thee?
When wilt thou rid this place, sir, of that noble
Lady whose presence irks her? She is not
Ungrateful, and when she imposeth tasks
To make herself supreme, promises little;
Yet one has but to leave to her the choice
Of his reward, and rush, by doubts untroubled,
To do her bidding. Thou sayest nothing, sir?

Tell me, I pray, what thou desirest to happen
Now at the banquet? Wilt thou feign to take
No heed of this bad faith? What wouldst thou care . . .

PERPENNA. Let us go to my house and decide there.

(*Exeunt.*)

A C T   V

ARISTIA *and* VIRIATE *are discovered.*

ARISTIA. Yes, madam, I, as thou art, am their foe.
Thou lovest greatness, and I hate abasement.
I seek revenge; thou seekest to establish
Firmly thy power. But thou canst undo me
And I can weaken thee, unless our hearts
By being more frankly bared can reconcile
My vengeance and thy power's establishment.
 I have been robbed of Pompey, and to flout
That ingrate who dared not be true to me
I seek another husband who is greater
Than he or quite his equal; but I have
No wish to be thy rival, and I nowise
Could have foreseen either that to a Roman
A queen would ever deign to give her hand
Or that a hero who appeared to have
A soul so truly Roman would belie
That noble name by marriage with a queen.
I had assumed in *his* birth and *thy* station
Mutual antipathy and contrarious pride.
Yet I am told that he consents to wed thee
And vainly doth oppose the choice of when,
For if he will not share thy crown tomorrow
Thy realm no longer will support his cause.
 As my one goal was to augment his forces,
'Twould grieve me sorely to disrupt your concord
And thus serve Sulla better than all his friends
When everywhere I fain would give him foes.
Speak, then; whatever thou hast seen me hope for,
If thou desirest it I shall cease to do so.
A dream still left me, sweeter and more lawful,
Can see Sertorius thine without chagrin.

Always my heart would fain give up for Pompey
All anger o'er another's usurpation
Of my place as his wife; and since, because
He loved me, he unwillingly was faithless,
I wished to avenge myself but could not hate him.
Hide naught from me, as I have hidden naught.

VIRIATE.　Viriate, in her turn, owes thee like frankness,
Madam; and thou besides wert told too much
To hide from thee aught that is in my mind.
　　　I had Sertorius come from Africa
To save my realm from tyranny's oppression.
The subjugation of my neighbors taught me
That without him our kings were but a futile
Aid against Sulla. With a single ship
This mighty hero landed. He began
The war with but my subjects. In his hands
I placed my ports and strongholds, and entrusted
My sovereignty and wealth to him. He conquered
From the first, and I saw victory increase
His power and glory day by day. Our kings,
Tired of the yoke, and Roman refugees
Joined him so eagerly on every side
That his triumphant arms have finally driven
Your legions to the foot of the Pyrenees.
But after I have set him where he is,
I can see none but him worthy of me;
And viewing thus his greatness as my work,
I would die sooner than see another share it.
My subjects well deserve that I should give them
Kings of a blood which knoweth how to govern,
How to withstand your nation, the world's tyrants,
And crown our Spain with such prolific laurels
That someday yet the Po will dread her power
And even the Tiber tremble on its shores.

ARISTIA.　Thine aims are great, but whatsoe'er they are . . .
VIRIATE.　*He* hath told me the things thou wishest to tell me.
I know 'twere best to say naught and defer
The glorious marriage that he hath roused my hopes of;
But the peace offered now to this great man
Opens too many roads and doors to Rome.

I see if he returns there he is lost
To me; and I would fain exile him thence
By giving him my nuptial troth. If I
Risk much by telling thee my intentions, I
Prefer this danger to my certain ruin;
And if your proscribed Romans all desert us,
Without them our good fortune can sustain us.
My troops, though hardened by your discipline,
Will ne'er have Rome's desire to dominate,
And it is Romans whose sole thought it is
To fight, to conquer, and to triumph here.
While we yet have this hero at our head
We shall go fearlessly from victory
To victory. His example, worthily
Supported, can . . .
                What would this unknown Roman
With us?   (*Enter* ARCAS.)

ARISTIA.   'Tis Arcas, madam, my brother's freedman.
His coming here must cloak some secret.
                               Speak,
Arcas, and tell us . . .

ARCAS.   Better than I these letters
Will tell thee what I scarce can yet believe.

ARISTIA (*reading a letter which he gives her*) .
    "Dear sister, it is time that thou shouldst know,
        With joy, our woes and thine at last are ended.
    Sulla doth now without his lictors go,
        Ready for all he did to be amended.

    "Before the assembled Senate he resigned
        His power. If Pompey's heart doth still abide
    True to thee, heaven hath his new ties untwined,
        For poor Emilia hath in childbirth died.

    "Sulla himself desires, to quench all hate,
        That love so dear again should crown a home
    And marriage restore thee to thy former state,
        Now he gives back her liberty to Rome.
                      "QUINTUS ARISTIUS."

So heaven tires of being pitiless

To me! This happiness seems incredible
To me, like thee. Fly to the camp of Pompey,
Good Arcas, and inform him . . .

ARCAS.   He hath learned
The news, and is retracing his steps hither.
Enjoined by Sulla to convey to him
A similar letter about these great changes,
I came upon him some two miles from here.

ARISTIA.   What love, what joy did he vouchsafe to show?
What said he? what did he do?

ARCAS.   By thine own feelings
Thou canst judge best what his impatience is.
But though called to thee by love's ecstasies,
Which do not let him go back to his camp,
The orders that such weighty news makes needful
Stay him to send them ere he comes to thee.
He will soon follow me, and bade me precede him
To tell thee of this miracle undreamed of.

ARISTIA (*to* VIRIATE).   Thou hast good reason to feel no less gladness,
Madam; this leaves thee with no fears nor rival.

VIRIATE.   I have none now in thee—that, I can doubt not—
But I still have another, more to be dreaded:
Rome, which this hero loves more than himself,
And would prefer beyond doubt to my crown,
If 'gainst that love . . .

Enter THAMYRAS.

THAMYRAS.   Oh, madam!

VIRIATE.   What is it,
Thamyras? Why hast thou that stricken look?
What do thy tears tell us?

THAMYRAS.   That thou'rt undone;
That the renowned arm which defended thee . . .

VIRIATE.   Sertorius?

THAMYRAS.   Alas! the great Sertorius . . .

VIRIATE.   Wilt thou ne'er finish?

THAMYRAS.   Madam, he lives no more.

VIRIATE.   He lives no more? Ah heaven! Who told thee so?

THAMYRAS.   His murderers themselves proudly declare it.
These tigers, whose fell rage there at the banquet

Cut short his life's thread by a traitor's orders,
All covered with his blood, rush through the town
To rouse the soldiery and the feckless rabble,
And by their hailing Perpenna as their general
Show thee too well who launched the fatal blow.

VIRIATE.   That shows me both the source and cause of it.
'Tis I of whom this crime makes disposition;
'Tis I, my throne, whose conquest is intended;
And 'tis my just choice solely that destroyed him.
(*To* ARISTIA) Madam, after his loss, amid my fears,
Expect not of me either sighs or tears.
They are diversions which the promptly-roused
Noble pride of keen feelings can dispense with.
To weep but weakens these; to sigh exhausts them.
More strength is needful in a royal soul;
And my grief, bent upon avenging him . . .

ARISTIA.   Thou art self-blinded in the midst of danger.
Think of flight, rather.

THAMYRAS (*to* VIRIATE).   The time is past for that.
Aufidius, who hath for the traitor seized
The palace doors, making this place thy prison,
Hath been enjoined to guard thee for him. He
Now cometh. Try to hide thy righteous wrath,
And till there is a time more favorable
For thee, remember that thou art a captive.

VIRIATE.   I well know what I am—and shall be always
Had I but heaven and myself to help me.

Enter PERPENNA.

PERPENNA (*to* VIRIATE).   Sertorius is dead; cease to be jealous
Of the high place his wife would have held, madam,
And fear no more, as when he was alive,
That in thine own domains she might outrank thee.
If thy fond hopes clashed with Aristia's
I can assure thee 'gainst her and all others.
This well-struck blow doth guarantee thy station
Both for the present and throughout the future.
He was a great soldier, but one who neither
In birth nor age was a fit husband for thee;
And what despite these defects pleased thee in him,

His power, he used o'er thee tyrannically.
The name of general made him lovable;
Thou hence preferredst him to your kings, or me;
Thou wert bedazzled by his power and title;
And now I come to offer both to thee
In me, with qualities which thy haughty soul
Will find are better worthy of a queen.
A Roman who commands and is descended
From kings (I speak not of my age and his)
Can hope to be acceptable, especially
When my love hath avenged affronts to thee
And my arm hath from a base choice preserved thee.

ARISTIA.　When thou hast slain in thine own house thy general—
Thou, who didst quake at such a rival's shadow—
Coward, thou comest to swagger before women,
Insolently to boast thine odious love,
To seize upon a queen in her own palace,
And claim her hand as thy foul crimes' reward!
Fear the gods, miscreant; fear the gods, or Pompey—
Their wrath or his arm, their bolts or his sword—
And howsoe'er a heinous pride may blind thee,
Know that he loves me still, and begin trembling.
Thou'lt see him, caitiff, sooner than thou thinkest;
Expect from him, from him, thy due requital.

PERPENNA.　If he doth heed thy rage, my death is certain,
But perhaps, madam, he will heed it not;
And when he sees me now command an army
That hath so often been victorious o'er him,
He readily will agree unto a peace
Which can fulfil soon his most fervent wishes.
I even have a hostage good enough
To gain me terms quite advantageous to me.
Meanwhile thou canst, for thy best ease and mine,
Not rail at one so who says naught to thee.
These empty threats put thee to too much trouble.
After what I have done, let the Queen speak;
And without blaming vows not offered thee
Think how to win again thy husband's heart.

VIRIATE.　Yes, madam, 'tis indeed for me to answer,
And my ungracious silence should be censured.

This gallant deed, these noble sentiments,
Deserve warm thanks from me; and to defer them
Yet longer, is to do him an injustice.
   Yes, he hath done me a distinguished service,
But still he knows not half how great it is.
Sertorius was his devoted friend.
Learn, learn, my lord—for I am well persuaded
We owe this title to thy new estate,
And for the brief time that thou canst retain it
'Twill cost me little to show this deference to thee—
Learn, I say, that for thee he dared offend me,
This hero; that he dared deserve mine anger;
That despite *his* love, that despite my wrath,
He did all he could do to give me to thee;
And that unless thou'dst freed him from his promise,
All *I* sought would have been but vainly wished for:
He stubbornly for thy sake refused my hand.

ARISTIA.   And thou couldst plunge a dagger in his breast!
And thy arm . . .

VIRIATE.   Let me, madam, estimate
The greatness of his love by his crime's greatness.
   In his own home, at table, while they dined,
To be the murderer of a friend so loyal,
To sacrifice the life of his own general,
Whose friendship so unselfishly had served him,
To renounce honor, to accept forever
The hate and infamy won by monstrous deeds,
To carry his violence even to my apartments
And hold me helpless there to gain my hand—
All this shows all the more how much I owe
To that great love he deigns to feel for me;
It shows a heart wholly infatuated.
He, if he loved me less, would be less guilty;
And as ingratitude is foreign to me,
I shall advise him not to wed with me.
Else, he would put into his bed his foe
To have his life at all times in her hands,
And I would seize on this great privilege
To choose the hour to stab him through the heart.
   That, my lord, manifests my appreciation.

As for the rest, my person is in thy power.
Thou art the master here; command, ordain,
And in short wed me if thou darest to do so.

PERPENNA. I? If I dare? Thy lofty-minded counsel
Might waste less art, picturing my crimes to me.
Better than thou I know their heinousness;
And since I know it, they have cost me dearly.
Not without keen remorse one stains one's soul
With so much perfidy and ingratitude.
For thee I quelled it, stifled it for thee.
I have the shame and the reward thereof.
Threaten me for my monstrous crimes, proscribe me;
Of these same monstrous crimes thou'lt be the prize;
And could my whole bliss last for but two days,
Thou hast tomorrow only to make ready.
I shall accept thy hate; I have deserved it;
I have foreseen its outcome, known its scope.
My triumph . . .

Enter AUFIDIUS, *bleeding.*

AUFIDIUS. Pompey hath arrived, my lord.
Our soldiers mutiny, the people riot.
The gate flew open at his name, his shadow.
We have no friends who do not yield to numbers.
Antonius and Manlius, torn to pieces,
Lie dead, but still men hack their mangled bodies.
All their accomplices are hunted fiercely;
Pompey designs for them a similar fate.
I tried to hold my post; he promptly forced it,
And now thou seest me pierced by his own sword.
Here complete master, he hath changed the guard.
Look to thyself, I die. Thou shalt be next.

(AUFIDIUS *staggers out.*)

ARISTIA (*to* PERPENNA). Sir, for what hour must preparations be
made
For that rare happiness he will guarantee thee?
Hast thou indeed a hostage good enough
To gain thee very advantageous terms?

PERPENNA. Thou feelest too much anxiety for me,
Madam; I have here means to win them from him.

(*Enter* POMPEY, *with* CELSUS *and other soldiers.*)

(*To* POMPEY). Sir, thou must needs have heard what I have
    done.
I have for thee slain the sole foe of peace,
The wooer of thy wife, the illustrious rival
Who in all things opposed what thou desirest.
I have restored Aristia to thee,
Ending those fears which thou hast shown preyed on thee
And freeing thee from thy heart's jealous dread
That thou mightest see her in another's arms.
    I now do more: I unto thee deliver
A bitter enemy in all her pride,
And Lusitania thus; I make thee master
Of them and all those Romans who forthwith
Are fortunate in being in thy hands.
As in a great step which requires prompt action
One does not announce publicly one's purpose,
I had not thought I should proclaim to all
Mine of surrendering to thee tomorrow;
But I have in my hands sure proof thereof.
These letters will of my good faith convince thee,
And thou wilt learn from their perfidious contents
How many secret foes thou hast in Rome,
Who, fiercely eager to avenge Aristia,
All were intriguing with Sertorius. Read . . .
    (*He gives* POMPEY *the letters which* ARISTIA *had brought
    from Rome to* SERTORIUS.)

ARISTIA. What, villain! What! thou darest? darest thou really . . .
PERPENNA. Madam, he is thy master here, and mine.
Some self-restraint is needful in his presence;
And if I now oblige thee to make any
Rejoinder, do not make it spitefully
Nor mingle insults with it, and forget not
Before whom thou art speaking.
                Sir, thou seest
Two noble rivals here, whom the great loss
Which they have suffered fires with equal hate.
They have insulted me in every way,
But 'tis enough revenge that I behold thee.

2 4 7

I view thee as my guardian deity,
And cannot . . . But, O gods, sir! what art thou
About to do?

POMPEY (*burning the letters without reading them*). Show what I
    wish to know
Of such a secret. Hadst thou understood
At all my nature, thou couldst have foreseen it.
    Rome, far too long divided by two factions,
Shall not for me be plunged in strife again,
Nor when restored to honor and good fortune
By Sulla, have fresh carnage and fresh horror
Through me.
    (*To* CELSUS) Hark, Celsus.
    (*After whispering in his ear*) Above all, prevent him
From naming any of the foes she made me
In Rome.
    (*To* PERPENNA) Do thou follow this tribune. I
Have matters which call now for private talk.

PERPENNA. Sir, can it be that after such great service . . .

POMPEY. I know its worth, and will reward thee justly.
    Go.

PERPENNA. But meanwhile their hate . . .

POMPEY.   That is enough.
I spoke. I here am master. Go; obey.
        (*Exit* CELSUS *with* PERPENNA *and guards.*)
    (*To* VIRIATE) Take no offense at hearing me speak as master,
Great queen; 'twas but to punish a false villain.
    As I had wronged thee, listening too long
To the insolence which he in his foul baseness
Dared utter, I believed it was my duty
To exercise my power at his expense,
To acquit myself ere saying aught to thee.
But I do not deceive myself by thinking
That I so easily can win favor with thee,
And I have never owed success to guile.
    However great the aid his crime snatched from thee,
I offer peace to thee, and will not break
The truce; and all those Romans who are with you
Can dwell here still without fear of my anger.

If I have shielded thee from any danger,
I for my whole reward want but Aristia,
To whom, again my heart's queen, I before thee
Give back with joy my hand and plighted troth.
I say naught of my love—'twas always hers.

ARISTIA.   Mine will requite thee with an equal fervor,
And, better to receive this gift re-given me,
Sir, will forget that thou wert ere torn from me.

VIRIATE.   I shall accept the peace thou offerest me.
'Tis all that I can do, after my loss.
That is irreparable; and as I see
None worthy of thy sword nor of my hand,
I shall renounce both war and marriage. But I
Still have the honor of the throne bequeathed me.
I can hold strictly to a pact of friendship,
But cannot bear to reign as our kings reign.
If I must rule like them as ye direct,
I will die, rather, in my kingdom's downfall;
But if I may, unwed, reign without shame,
I wish for heirs only thy Rome or thee.
Choose, sir; or if ye cannot suffer me
As Rome's ally to rule my realm myself,
Thou needest but hold this place now in thy hands,
And I already am the Romans' prisoner.

POMPEY.   Madam, thou hast a soul too great for thee
Not to obtain an honorable peace;
And I shall make Rome ever pay thy virtues
Honor unless I there am reft of power.

                              (*Re-enter* CELSUS.)

Is it done, Celsus?

CELSUS.   Yes, sir; countless hands
Have punished that vile dastard's treacherous crime.
Flung to the raging people as thou badest,
He spake no word . . .

POMPEY.   Enough! Rome, then, is safe
From him; and those whom I too well made hate me,
Fearing naught from me, give me naught to fear.
Do thou agree, Queen, as to our dead hero,

Now avenged, that his spirit may rest in peace.
Come and give orders for a stately funeral,
Such as befitteth his illustrious name,
And raise in memory of his hapless story
A tomb that tells our sorrow and his glory.

Othon

(O T H O)

INTRODUCTION

If we may trust the words of Corneille himself, *Othon* (1664) was one of his favorites among his later plays; but it may have been the demands of verse which governed his selection when he wrote:

> *Othon* and *Suréna*
> Are not unworthy younger brothers of *Cinna*.

He tells us in his prefatory note to *Othon:* "If my friends do not deceive me, this play equals or surpasses the best that I have written. A number of people of fame and dependability have so declared it. . . . As for its verse, none of mine has yet appeared on which I have lavished greater pains." Thus *Othon* would seem to have been much admired by sophisticates, though never a general favorite.

Voltaire, on the other hand, admired only the first scene in the first act, which he considered the most deft presentation of expository matter that Corneille ever achieved,—surpassed in this respect, among French-classical tragedies, only by the opening of Racine's *Bajazet.* For the rest, he said, the play "is only a family affair; one feels concerned about nobody in it; it contains a great deal of talk about love, and this love leaves the reader cold." The last clause shows that *Othon* had, even then, long vanished from the stage. A modern authority, the late Daniel Mornet, refers to it as "now unreadable." [1]

Brasillach is far from finding it so. He calls it "a masterpiece of intellect and passion," and considers it Corneille's "best political play, superior even to *Nicomède*"; [2] yet more, he says that *Othon*, "written after a set-back [the failure of *Sophonisbe*], in a sort of cold rage, with a desire to triumph and astound, is, beyond question, one of the very great political dramas in all the drama of the world." Corneille, he says, here "thrusts before us" a "menagerie of monsters"; he "knits together and puts into a single day a tight-packed

[1] In his *Andromaque,* Paris, 1947, p. 75.

[2] In Brasillach's book on Corneille it can be clearly perceived that he has formed in his own mind a definite ranking list of this dramatist's better tragedies, in the following order of merit: 1, the *Cid;* 2, *Polyeucte;* 3, *Suréna;* 4, *Othon;* 5, *Nicomède;* 6, *Sertorius;* 7, probably *Attila,* but he may rank *Horace* and *Cinna* just ahead of that play instead of just behind it.

and powerful drama, without a parallel in French literature. 'These,' as he himself says, 'are only closet intrigues, which defeat one another.' . . . And this *Othon* is indeed a drama of *intrigue,* in the most exact sense of the word. The character of the protagonist is perhaps its weak point, for he ends by having no longer any existence save as the very center of the converging lines of the play. . . . But never did Pierre Corneille unfold more simply, in more austere and lucid verse, such a palace revolution." [3]

Brasillach would seem to stand alone, however, in his unqualified admiration for *Othon.* Petit de Julleville pronounced it an "obscure and confused play, devoid of the poignant interest which in *Héraclius* redeemed the same faults." [4] Hémon said that its "two intrigues, one political, the other amatory," are "quite clumsily connected and the impression of the whole will necessarily be ill defined," and that it is "a play admirable in some parts, singular in its totality." [5] Faguet said that its "maze of deliberations, of hesitations, of movements forward and backward and forward again, of feints and shifts" are followed "with a certain curiosity (because it is not obscure) but without any interest, for one cannot be fond of people who love or who refrain from loving only as it accords with their political advantage to do so." He would concede merely that there are "some fine things here and there in this unfortunate work," which "must be declared a failure." [6]

If Lemaître in his statement *"Othon* has greater worth" was comparing it with Corneille's *Sophonisbe* alone, that is faint praise indeed; but the comparison may have been with *Sertorius,* too—we cannot tell from the context. He finds *Othon* "fairly interesting," and says that it is "complex, subtle, deftly handled," but "not at all moving." [7] This appears, to judge from the following, to be also Merlet's view:

"If style were enough to make a tragedy live, *Othon* would still be appreciated; for there are verses in it which do not

[3] Pp. 400-404.
[4] P. xvii.
[5] *Théâtre de Pierre Corneille,* vol. iv, pp. 415, 482.
[6] Pp. 206, 207, 211.
[7] P. 331.

smack of a decline. But it was hard to make dramatic the intrigue contrived to give a successor to Galba. In this study there is at least the seriousness of history, and Corneille paints for us in striking colors the mortal agony of the Empire. . . . To this understanding of the characters, of the events, and of the causes that produce them, is added a conciseness of fervid eloquence which Tacitus would have envied. But the stage is not a rostrum, and fine speeches there are not enough." 8

Lancaster pointed out that Corneille "sought to combine the tragedy of well-meaning, but ineffective Galba with the drama of a courtier who had in him germs of greatness; but, unwilling to alter well-known historical events, he was unable to present in action the second and larger part of his undertaking. It is on this account that the play, though superior to *Sophonisbe,* was far from rivaling *Cinna.*" He thought that Corneille "might well have reduced the number of the intrigues that he represents" and given Otho a part in organizing the revolt, but that, on the whole, this tragedy "has very considerable interest, with its portrayal of court intrigue around an aging monarch," though "marred by Corneille's failure to express love convincingly." 9

Schlumberger, who is nearest to Brasillach in date, is also nearest to him in laudatory appraisal of this drama. *Othon,* he says, "is one of the best written" of the plays of Corneille. "Little fanfare, no lyricism, but an incisive and easy style, which lends itself to all the refinements of a closet intrigue very adroitly conducted. . . . Almost nobody in it says a word which can with certainty be taken at face value. . . . But there is nothing less heroic—I would even say, nothing more skeptical—than this play. Not the least grandiloquence, not a trace of an affected dignity which exaggerates the gestures. Without it we would not have had a very curious bit of evidence of the perceptiveness of Corneille. The complaint is made that we are not moved by any of the characters; but it is natural that a comedy (which is what *Othon* is, even though an old emperor is killed in it) should make us contemplate, without appealing to our sympathies, the behavior of an interesting menagerie." [10]

Here we find a distinction drawn which in part accounts for such diversity of views. For those who judge *Othon* as a tragedy, its lack of warmth and of any appeal to our sympathies makes it unsatisfactory; but such objections largely lose their force if this play is to be regarded as a bitter comedy. Before Schlumberger, Lanson spoke of it as one—"Here we have great political comedy"—and exclaimed in admiration, "With what dexterity Corneille has depicted these intrigues and the characters that take part in them!" [11]

I believe that a sense of deep feeling is conveyed to us once, and only once, in this play: in Plautina's renunciation of Otho at the end of Act I. She is perhaps the most invariably admirable in behavior of all Corneille's heroines, though of course she does not win our hearts like Chimene. Otho's wish to kill himself, rather than give her up, however, appears to me unconvincing; his love for her has not been shown to be fervent enough to prepare us for his having any such desperate impulse. Nor does Plautina's utter distraction upon learning of her father's death ring true; they were completely alien to each other in nature, and he had just exhibited the most callous and selfishly ruthless disregard for her; Corneille seems to have forced this final turn in the play that it might, as he says, "propose so many marriages without bringing any of them to pass."

[10] Pp. 214-218.
[11] *Corneille,* p. 89.

CHARACTERS IN THE PLAY

GALBA, *Emperor of Rome.*
VINIUS, *a consul.*
OTHO, *a Roman senator.*
CAMILLA, *niece of Galba.*
PLAUTINA, *daughter of Vinius.*
LACO, *prefect of the Pretorian guards.*
MARTIANUS, *freedman of Galba.*
ALBINUS, *friend of Otho.*
ALBIANA, *sister of Albinus; lady-in-waiting of Camilla.*
FLAVIA, *friend of Plautina.*
ATTICUS, *a Roman soldier.*
RUTILUS, *another Roman soldier.*
Two other soldiers.

The scene is laid in Rome, in a room in the imperial palace.

Otho

ACT I

OTHO and ALBINUS are discovered.

ALBINUS.   Our friendship, sir, makes me presume. I go
       Too far, and I am sure I shall displease thee,
       And thou wilt censure me as over-curious;
       But I would deem myself disloyal to thee
       If I concealed from thee aught I have heard
       Said of thy new love under this new reign.
         Folk are amazed to see a man like Otho—
       Otho, whose great deeds match his noble name—
       Deign to stoop to the daughter of a Vinius
       And with this consul link himself, this spoilsman,
       This plunderer, who can do anything
       With the Emperor, I admit, but all whose power
       Serves only to breed horror and destroys
       More and more, as men see it growing greater,
       The love they owe the virtues of his master.

OTHO.   Those whom thou seest amazed at my new love
       Have ne'er grasped what the Court is really like.
       Such men as I can never break free from it,
       No refuge or obscurity can hide them,
       And if they do not have the Emperor's favor,
       They needs must perish or find some protection.
         Men like me take their places round their sovereign
       Safely when he acts without others' guidance.
       Merit and noble blood are seen there plainly,
       But when the monarch lets himself be swayed,
       And when the great dispensers of his power
       Have for State policy only their own interests,
       These vile foes of all people high of soul
       Would hound us with the utmost cruelty
       Unless by instant and adroit subservience
       We should escape from their unresting rage.
         No sooner had the Senate chosen Galba
       Than I enforced his edicts where I governed.
       I was the first who gave to the new ruler
       An entire army and an entire province—

Hence thought myself one of his chief adherents.
But Vinius had outstripped the field already;
And Martianus the freedman, whose extortions
Thou seest, and Laco closed all means of access
To Galba, opened but at their good pleasure.
To advance myself, I therefore had to choose
One of the three. I saw them all alike
Seizing on every chance beneath a master
Who, laden with years, had little time to reign
And all three vying in eager emulation
To see which could devour his fleeting empire.
I felt a horror at these sole supports
Left me to seek. I sometimes hoped I could
Refrain from using them; but when Nymphidius
Was murdered here in Rome and was succeeded
By e'en that favorite who decreed his death,
Laco becoming the Pretorian prefect,
And when for peak and crown of such dark deeds
The same assassins then went on to stab
Varro, Turpilian, Capito, and Macer,
I saw 'twas time to take the needful measures,
That Nero's courtiers all were being killed,
And that I soon—alone now left of them—
Would in my turn fall without some protector.
　　In this dilemma I made choice of Vinius.
I sought alliance with him for greater safety.
The others had no sister and no daughter
To give me, and without so close a bond
Anything was to be expected from them.

ALBINUS.　Thy suit succeeded?

OTHO.　　　　　　　　　Yes, and marriage already
Would have made one mine and Plautina's lot,
Had not these rivals at the Court diverted
A master who without them does not dare
To decide anything.

ALBINUS.　　　　　　So all thy love
Is only policy, and the heart does not feel
What the mouth says.

OTHO.　　　　　　　　It did not feel it at first.
But what was policy now has become love.

Everything in her pleases me, everything
In her enchants me, and my former scruples
In her dear presence seem ridiculous.
Vinius is consul, Vinius hath power;
He is of high birth, and if he is nimble
In following that path oft trod by favorites,
Plautina hates this fortune-seeking in him.
Her heart is lofty, noble.

ALBINUS.   Whatsoever
Her virtues, *thy* heart should be somewhat torn.
Galba's niece will for dowry have the Empire,
And well may one for such a great prize woo her.
Her uncle must soon choose for her a husband,
And merit and blood confer a luster on thee,
Who to join unto them that of the crown . . .

OTHO.   Even if my heart could give up her I love,
And if Camilla viewed me with such favor
That I dared hope that she would hearken to me,
If, as thou sayst, her hand could make me master,
None of our tyrants tires of being that,
And it would draw them all three down upon me
If I aspired, unbidden by them, to win her.
Vinius especially, cut to the quick
By being thus wronged, would try hard to destroy me
And even before the gods avenge himself
Were I to turn my gaze unto Camilla.

ALBINUS.   Yet bear it in mind. My sister doth attend her.
There I can aid thee. It is a rare chance.
Anyone else would be enraptured by it,
And I would tell thee more if thou daredst love her.

OTHO.   Offer to others, not me, this vain lure.
My heart, wholly Plautina's, is closed fast
Against Camilla. My beloved one's beauty,
The shame of changing thus, the doubtfulness
Of the result, the certainty of danger—
All present hopeless obstacles to thy plan.

ALBINUS.   In less than no time miracles occur.
It would be sweet, perhaps, to his two rivals
To deprive Vinius of a son-in-law
Such as thou, and should one of them propose thee

By happy chance to Galba . . . 'Tis not that,
After all, I know anything about it;
They suspect me too much to talk with me;
But if I may tell thee what I really think,
I would propose thee if I were in *their* place.

OTHO.　Neither of them will do as thou wouldst have them,
And if they ever can find any pleasure
In making Galba choose them a successor
They will wish by this choice to be made safe
And will propose someone dependent on them.
I know . . . But I see Vinius approaching.

Enter VINIUS.

VINIUS.　Albinus, leave us here alone. I wish
To talk with him.　　　　　　　　　(*Exit* ALBINUS.)
　　　　　(*To* OTHO)　I think that thou'rt my friend, sir,
And that my daughter makes thee have the interests
Of all my family at heart. I need
A proof of this, and not one which consists
Merely of attentions that a lover pays her,
But something more substantial, which requires
A great man who is worthy to rule Rome.
Thou must stop loving her.

OTHO.　　　　　　　　　What! for proof of love . . .

VINIUS.　Thou must do yet more on this crucial day:
Thou must love elsewhere.

OTHO.　　　　　　　　　Ah, what dost thou tell me!

VINIUS.　I know that thy whole heart aspires to wed her;
But she and thou and I alike are fated
To perish, and thy change alone can save us.
Thou perhaps owest me something, sir: without me—
Without my influence, which opposed their purpose—
Laco and Martianus would have slain thee.
Thou must in turn shield me from a dire blow
Which, if thy heart will not give up Plautina,
Will include both of you in my destruction.

OTHO.　Amidst my sweetest dreams of love accepted,
To bid me thus to change my love—thou!

VINIUS.　　　　　　　　　　　　　Hearken.

The honor to us of a marriage with thee
Is so great torture to those two I spoke of,
That till now Galba, whom they both beset,
Hath held back the fulfilment of our wishes.
The obstacle they raised thereto will show thee
What hate and envy of thee and me are theirs;
And, as the looks they cast us prove, they soon
Will destroy us if we destroy not them.
This is a fact that is too manifest,
And on its basis I shall say the rest.
   Galba, old and infirm and without children,
Thinks that men scorn him for his age and weakness
And that none willingly can serve a master
Who has not time left to reward good service.
He sees on every side confusion reigning:
The army in Syria verges on revolt;
Vitellius advances with a united
Force of the troops of Gaul and Germany;
His own old legions grudgingly endure him;
And the Pretorians all murmur 'gainst him.
The base putting to death of their Nymphidius
Asks of them justice on the murderer.
He knows this, and intends to win them back
And calm their rage by means of a young emperor.
He hopes for stable, ample, tranquil power
By naming a husband of Camilla Caesar;
But he hath not yet chosen her this husband,
And I cannot be safe unless 'tis thou.
I therefore have extolled thy courage to him,
And Laco hath for Piso cast his vote.
Martianus spoke not save uncertainly,
But he will surely take the side of Laco.
Our sole salvation is to win Camilla;
If she speaks for us, they will speak in vain.
Those favoring either choice will be the same
In numbers; and if these are equal, Galba
Will please his niece. He hath delayed so long
Expressly to make up his mind. Divert
The impending thunderbolt from our heads to theirs.
I say again: 'gainst these great, jealous rivals

I can find safety, sir, in thee alone.
Whate'er I might expect from thy first preference,
Even more than for son-in-law I want thee
For master, and I see our shipwreck certain
If from their hands we must accept a prince.

OTHO. Ah, sir, on this point thou'rt too confident.
This is to be too sure of my obedience.
I heed no dictates save of my heart's passion;
Plautina is the goal of my ambition;
And if thy friendship fain would tear me from her,
The hate of Laco is less cruel to me.
What matters it, if I am so ill-fated,
Whether I die of grief or by his orders?

VINIUS. A noble heart, however much it loves,
Knoweth the need of being self-possessed.
Poppaea was at least as dear to thee,
And yet when robbed of her thou didst not die.

OTHO. No; but Poppaea was a faithless wife
Who wished only the throne and who loved me
Less than herself. The little that she loved me
Made Otho's bed only a step by which
To mount to that of Nero. She espoused me
Solely to win her way there, and contrived
To do so at the risk of harm to me.
Thus I was banished with a show of honor,
And was made governor, to be seen no more.
I love Plautina; in her heart I reign.
To order me to quench our love's fair flame
Is . . . I can say naught. There are other Romans,
Sir, who could better further thy designs.
There must be one whose soul yearns for Camilla
And who would gladly owe to thee the Empire.

VINIUS. I wish this fortune might be had by others,
But art thou certain they would be our friends?
Art thou more sure than I that they would please her?

OTHO. And dost thou think she would be mine more gladly—
Wed *me,* whom other vows . . .

VINIUS.   To hide naught from thee,
When I left Galba, I sought speech with her.
I wished to sound her mind about this matter;

I mentioned several men, to test her with them,
And at their names her coldness, downcast eyes,
And sad mien showed at once she did not want them.
At thine she blushed, and then began to smile,
And left me suddenly without a word.
It is for thee, who knowest what 'tis to love,
To judge what should be thought as to her feelings.

OTHO. I do not wish to; and without Plautina
Love is a poison to me, good fortune death,
And all the joys of sovereign power, if they
Cost me her hand, are fearsome tortures to me.

VINIUS. My soul would be entranced by such devotion
If this excessive love ensured our safety;
But we must have the throne or lose our lives,
And when we perish, what will love avail us?

OTHO. Ugly suspicions fill thee with vain fears.
Piso is not cruel; he will let us live.

VINIUS. "Will let us live"—and I advised thy choice!
If seeing us in Rome alarms not Piso,
Our common foes, who will assume his guidance,
Will end for him all danger from our presence.
When one is nominated, sir, for emperor,
He must, whatever happens, reign or die.
Agrippa Postumus was able to live
Only a little while under Tiberius;
Nero spared not the blood of his step-brother;
And Piso will kill thee for the same reason
Unless thou hastenest to kill Piso first.
There is no mean which in wise policy . . .

OTHO. Love is the sole thing that my whole heart follows.
It served thee nothing, sir, to nominate me.
Thou wishest me to reign; I only know
How to love. I could do more if my star
Destined me to reign someday with Plautina.
But to renounce thus one so dear and lovely,
And bind my life to one I do not love!

VINIUS. Well, if love sways thee with resistless force,
Reign still, for he who reigneth can divorce.
One on the throne indeed knows his true friends.
When thou'rt omnipotent, all things are allowed thee.

O T H O N

(PLAUTINA *has entered unperceived and heard their last words.*)

PLAUTINA (*coming forward, to* VINIUS). Nay, nay, sir! whatsoever heaven sends me,
I wish to have naught in a shameful manner.
Such vileness, which would give him back to me,
Would savor of the tyrant, not the emperor.
For thy security, since danger threatens,
I shall give up my love and all its sweetness
And conquer my dismay at this cruel duty
To save the life to which I owe mine own;
But though I do this violence to my heart,
I shrink from the base pleasure of unworthy
Hopes, and if I subdue and banish love
For right's sake, I will ne'er consent to have it
Again save rightly.

OTHO.   Ah, what bitter anguish
Her sense of right imposes upon me,
Sir! And by what means am I to obey thee?
See her—if possible, to know all my torment—
Not with a father's eyes, but with a lover's.

VINIUS.   I am well able to admire my daughter.
I see her charms, I see her many virtues.
I think they are sufficient, even, if someone
Takes our lives, to make someone else avenge us.
Our foes will deem her, hence, one to be dreaded,
And hence her death will be inevitable.
I see, however, that I shall gain nothing
So long as thy pained glance encounters hers,—
That we shall but waste time with futile words,—
And to avoid this I shall end them briefly.
Unless thou gainest the throne all three must perish.
Prevent that doom, await it, as thou choosest.
I leave to thee what concerns thee; but touching
Me and my child, my honor is at stake.
I am sole master of her life and mine,
And will dispose of them as I determine.
I fear not death but hate the humiliation
Of having it decreed me by a foe,
And like a Roman could shed all our blood

Unless the choice I look for stays my hand.
Galba will choose within an hour or two.
Ye both know what I am prepared to do.
Decide together as to this.   (*Exit* VINIUS.)

OTHO (*calling after him*).   Then stay, sir;
And if this mortal shame must be prevented
Take my example; judge if the dishonor . . .

                    (*He offers to stab himself.*)

PLAUTINA (*restraining him*). What, sir! before my face this sudden
    frenzy?
That brave act of despair, so worthy of Romans,
While they have courage is always in their power;
But were it worthy of gods, for thee and me
'Tis not yet time to give examples of it.
Nay, we must live—love shall compel us to—
To save my father and to protect me.
When thou beholdest my life bound up with thine,
Must thy unruly soul, in spite of me,
Hasten thy death to ope for me the tomb
And without my consenting speed my doom?

OTHO.   When from my heart I must tear all thy love,
Can I, save with my blood, put out its flame?
Can I unless I die . . .

PLAUTINA.   And did I bid thee
To stifle all the love I made thee feel?
If our unjust and cruel fate no longer
Lets us look forward to a happy marriage,
There is another love, whose innocent vows
Lift it above all commerce of the senses.
The purer its flame burns, the more 'tis quenchless.
It makes two hearts indissolubly one;
It hath true pleasures which delight the soul,
And seeks naught but to love and to be loved.

OTHO.   Such purity requires how great a nature!
How hard its practice, even for the noblest!
Madam, permit me in my turn to say
That he who loves desires all that which honor
Can grant to love, and fain would hope to have it,
And thinks himself loved little if he cannot.

PLAUTINA.   Yet love me without hoping it from me,

And grudge me not the honor thou'dst thus do me.
What pride Plautina's if she could say, O heaven,
That her heart's choice was worthy of the Empire,
And that a hero destined to be earth's
Master preferred to limit his ambition
To living 'neath her sway, and had it not
Been for a positive command from her,
He for her love would have renounced the crown!

OTHO.   Ah, but how little thou must love, to find
Happiness from thy pride in such sad glory!
If thou didst love me, thou wouldst feel distress
In seeing that I could hearken to others' vows,
And the necessity of my turning elsewhere
Would have made thee already share my grief.
But all of my despair nowise disturbs thee;
Thou canst lose Otho and not shed a tear.
Thou showest joy hereat, and lookest forward
To all the too-great woes that I must bear.

PLAUTINA.   Oh, how unjust to me thy blindness is!
To lighten *thy* woes, I augment my anguish:
I suffer, and for thy sake I impose
Upon myself the torture of dissembling.
All that thou feelest, I feel in my soul.
I, having the same love, have the same pain.
I have the same despair, but I conceal it
And seem unfeeling, to afflict thee less.
Do a like violence to thy love's desires:
Restrain display of them; forbear to show them.
In our besetting peril, act a part.
Pretend, to make thyself loved, different feelings.
Nowise do I forbid thee silent sorrow
Provided that thy face never reveals it
And that thine eyes, not governed by thy heart,
Triumph like mine over thine inward turmoil.
Follow and outstrip my example; go
Unto Camilla with glad, tranquil mien
Which will belie naught that thou sayst to her
And cause her to accept what thou dost offer.

OTHO.   Alas! alas! what can I say to her?

PLAUTINA.   My life hangs on it; empire, too, hangs on it;

Act thou accordingly. Time flies. Farewell, sir.
Give her thy hand, but keep for me thy heart;
Or if that is too much for me, give both,—
Carry my love with thee, and leave not thine
With me,—but if thou pitiest then my plight,
Let me have always thy respect and friendship,
And ne'er forget, when thou shalt be Rome's master,
'Twas I who forced and helped thee to be that.

(Exit PLAUTINA.*)*

OTHO *(alone)*. Why is it not permitted me to flee
By death so hard a task's dire cruelty!

A C T   I I

PLAUTINA *and* FLAVIA *are discovered.*

PLAUTINA. Come, tell me, then: when Otho wooed Camilla,
Did he appear constrained? was she receptive?
Did his suit make a great impression on her?
How hath she taken it, and how hath he urged it?
FLAVIA. I witnessed everything, but thy curiosity
Is too ingenious in distressing thee.
Whatever remnant of thy love for Otho
Still speaks within thy breast, forget him, madam—
Even his very name, if possible.
Thou for his glory's sake o'ercamest thy feelings;
Be proud of triumphing, after that self-conquest.
The account which thou hast bidden me to give thee
Means a new battle for thee, risking all.
Thy heart is not yet so well sundered from him
That he can love another and not wound thee.
Take less great interest in his success
And flee the unhappiness of learning of it.
PLAUTINA. I myself forced him to appear inconstant,
And looking on his conduct as my doing,
I take an interest, far from jealous, in it.
Let him wed, let him reign, it all delights me.
FLAVIA. I doubt it. Rarely doth a love so strong
Willingly let its ardor . . .
PLAUTINA.   How does that
Concern thee? Let me risk it; and without

Dissembling, tell me how he spoke of love.
FLAVIA. Blame but thyself, then, if thy soul, disquieted,
    Feeleth to my regret some secret pain.
      Otho addressed his compliments to the Princess
    More as a courtier would than a real lover.
    His artful eloquence, linking gracefully
    Excuses for his silence with his boldness,
    In too-well-chosen words blamed his respect
    For her as having so delayed his homage.
    His studied gestures and his well-weighed manner
    Left naught to chance. One could see planned effect
    In all his utterance. Appropriateness
    Ruled even his very sighs and marked throughout
    His speech, which sounded as though memorized
    And which 'twas easier to admire than credit.
      Camilla herself seemed of this opinion.
    She better would have liked less polished phrases.
    I saw this in her eyes, but her distrust
    Too little was in harmony with her heart.
    Her wishes, outraged by her just suspicions,
    Immediately destroyed them or disdained them.
    She fain would believe all, and if some caution
    Had managed to restrain the love which swayed her,
    'Twas evident, from the little she let slip,
    That she enjoyed allowing him to deceive her;
    And if sometimes his horror at being forced
    To act thus, made poor Otho sigh in earnest,
    At once her eagerness to reign o'er his heart
    Imputed to his love these sighs of grief.
PLAUTINA. And what was her response then?
FLAVIA.   She was courteous;
    But all Camilla's courtesy is love,
    While Otho's love is only courtesy.
PLAUTINA. And did she say naught of his fickleness—
    Naught of the faith he seems to have kept so badly?
FLAVIA. She put out of her mind such vexing thoughts
    And gave no evidence that she even knew
    That he had ever loved thee for one moment.
PLAUTINA. What did she tell him?
FLAVIA.   That she would, in duty,

Do whatsoever Galba bade her do;
And then, for fear of saying too much and showing
Her heart to him too plainly, she abruptly
Sent him unto the Emperor. He is now
Talking with him. What sayest thou of this
And of their meeting, which thy soul desired?
Wouldst have him be accepted or gain nothing?

PLAUTINA. To tell the truth, I myself hardly know.
As, either way, 'twould be a cruel blow,
I would prefer present uncertainty
And deem myself most blest if all my days
I still remain therein, unsure always.

FLAVIA. Yet one must needs decide and prefer something.

PLAUTINA. Let heaven decide all, without troubling me.
When its decree is once determined on,
We must conform our will unto its will.
Reason made me bid Otho to seek empire;
Honor forbids me to unsay my words;
And whether my choice was free or by compulsion,
'Tis good to persevere as one began.
But here is Martianus.   (*Enter* MARTIANUS.)
     (*Addressing him*)   What comest thou
To tell me?

MARTIANUS.   That on thee alone depends
The choice of who shall rule the Empire.

PLAUTINA.   What!
Galba would wish to abide by *my* choice?

MARTIANUS.   No;
But we are only three who form his council,
And if thou wishest *my* vote for thy Otho,
I come to offer it thee with humble homage.

PLAUTINA. With . . .

MARTIANUS.   With sincere and most submissive pledges
Which will go further if thou givest me hope.

PLAUTINA. What pledges? Hope of having what?

MARTIANUS.   This great service
Which with profound respect I offer thee . . .

PLAUTINA. Indeed? It will fulfil my dearest wishes.
But what dost thou desire for recompense?

MARTIANUS. The honor of being loved.

PLAUTINA.   By whom?

MARTIANUS.   Thee, madam.

PLAUTINA.   By *me?*

MARTIANUS,   By thee. I see thee, and my soul . . .

PLAUTINA.   Thy soul, in doing me this courtesy,
      Ought to add to it a greater sense of fact.
      One cannot credit such displays of deference
      When something so unreasonable follows.
      Thy offer is good and well deserves reward,
      But thou in choosing one madest a mistake.
      If thou didst know me well, thou wouldst show better . . .

MARTIANUS.   Alas, my plight results from knowing thee
      Only too well. But, after all, thou knowest
      Thyself not, when thou thinkest thy spell so feeble.
      If thou couldst dream how great a prize thou art,
      Thou wouldst not doubt the love that thou inspirest.
      Otho can serve me as a proof hereof:
      He had loved none since seeing Poppaea's charms,
      For, although Nero tore her from his arms,
      Her image was preserved still in his heart;
      Death, death itself, could never drive it thence.
      Thou alone hadst the glory of so doing;
      Thou alone with one glance borest off the honor
      Of making vanish there his sweetest memories
      And being able to fill with new desires
      That heart insensible to the loveliest sights—
      And thou'rt astonished that mine longs for thee!

PLAUTINA.   I am much more astonished that thou darest
      To tell me so,—astonished to observe
      Thou hast forgotten that the prosperous
      Martianus once was Icelus the slave,
      And that he changed his name but not his face.

MARTIANUS.   It is this wrong done me by Fate that swells
      My heart: when I am what I am despite it,
      Men see my native worth in what I am.
      Sheer chance, which we control not, rules our birth;
      But since achievement comes from our own efforts,
      The shame of origins that are ill-matched with it
      All the more honors us when we rise above them.
      Whatever blot my ancestors have left

Upon my lineage, ever since Rome bowed
To masters, these have always chosen men
Like me for their chief posts and secret councils.
They have in our hands placed the public welfare
And left earth's governance to our discretion.
Patrobus, Polyclitus, Narcissus, Pallas—
All have deposed kings or bestowed realms on them.
On casting off our shackles, we mount thrones;
'Neath Claudius, Felix had three queens to wife;
Yet when in me love offers thee a husband,
Thou treatest me as a slave, unworthy of thee!
   Madam, in whatever station thou wert born,
'Tis much to have the ear of the earth's lord.
Vinius is consul, Laco is a prefect;
I, who am neither, am in fact yet more;
And of such consuls and such prefects I
Can, if I wish, make mere dependents. Galba
Hearkens to me; and I thereby am now,
Though without these great names, next him in power.

PLAUTINA. Forgive me, then, sir, if I was mistaken.
Naught in thy slavery warrants my haughty pride.
I have just come to see I am, instead,
Unworthy of the honors thy love bringeth.
To have cast off thy shackles is a glory
Beyond a consul's or a Pretorian prefect's;
And if I still cannot be thy love's prize,
'Tis now respect, not scorn, that will not let me.
I have been told that nature oft, however,
Preserves in those like thee its earliest tincture,
That those among our Caesars who have hearkened
To them have stained their names by some base conduct,
And that, to rid the Empire of such shame,
The world needs a real hero for its ruler.
That is what made me want its throne for Otho;
But this wish is not meet, from what I learn.
Let heaven decide, and to thyself be just.
Disdain a truly Roman heart's caprice.
A hundred queens would vie to wed with thee;
Felix had three, and he was not thine equal.

MARTIANUS. Madam, once more I say, accept my love.

Reflect that power supreme is in my hands,—
That my vote, not yet cast, according as
It shall incline, will make an emperor
Of Otho or of Piso. I have thus far
Done nothing but prevent the marriage that
Would have linked Otho's fortunes with thine own.
I could have ventured something more. Do not
Drive me to do so by rejecting me.
To let me, when thou givest up Otho, take
His place, may accomplish more than one good end.
For never hope that thou shalt yet be his.

Enter LACO.

LACO. Madam, Galba at last grants thy desires.
    I have today prevailed on him to give
    His sanction to the marriage of thee and Otho.
PLAUTINA (*to* MARTIANUS). What sayst thou, sir, to that? Canst thou permit
    This marriage which Laco comes to offer me?
    The earth's lord hath now spoken; wouldst thou gainsay him—
    Thou, who art after him the next in power?
    Must I stoop to this husband, or must I
    By thy command aspire to wed but thee?
LACO. What riddle is this, madam?
PLAUTINA.   His great heart
    Hath just made me an offer of its love.
    He told me Otho never could obtain me,
    Half saying that to refuse *him* would destroy us.
    But thou assurest me of the opposite,
    And I scarce know what answer I should make.
    As it is sometimes well to explain one's stand,
    At other times 'tis better not to try to.
    Great ministers of State, agree together,
    And I can tell you then what I decide.
               (*Exeunt* PLAUTINA *and* FLAVIA.)
LACO. Thou lovest Plautina, eh? 'Twas her betrothal
    Which bound thee to me against Vinius?
MARTIANUS. And if Plautina's glance hath charms for me,
    Can aught herein cause thee anxiety?

The blissful moment that makes me her husband
Would through me reunite Vinius with thee.
Concord once more reigning in our three hearts
Would root out there all jealousy and hatred.
The power of us all three, by all three strengthened,
Would have its bond in me, his son-in-law
And thy friend, and if he dared aught against thee . . .

LACO.   Thou'dst be my friend, but be his son-in-law,
Too; and old friendship is a frail support
Against new love, amid affairs at Court.
Whatever an adored wife cares to ask for,
Vain or of brief duration is resistance.
Her own time doth she choose, and so well choose it
That one hath power to refuse her nothing.
Art thou thyself sure that this tie will stay her
From adding, if need be, thy death to mine?
Remember, hearts sundered unwillingly
Learn easily how they may be reunited.
Otho has not quenched all his love for her.
He knoweth how wives are taken from their husbands.
That art is common knowledge now, because
Of him; his master Nero taught it to him.
After all, unless I am wrong, with her . . .

MARTIANUS.   In Vinius I have hope, if not in her.
My offer to him to cast my vote for Otho
Will instantly cause him to favor me.

LACO.   What! thou wouldst give us Otho for a master?

MARTIANUS.   And who in Rome would be a worthier one?

LACO.   Oh, as to being worthy, yes, he is—
More so than anyone. But in addition,
To be entirely frank, he is too shrewd
For us. He knows too well how to apportion
His virtues and his vices. Under Nero
He would participate in every pleasure,
But Lusitania beheld this same Otho
Govern like Caesar and be as just as Cato.
In Rome wholly a favorite, in his province
Wholly the master, he was here a base
Courtier and proved himself there a great ruler.
His pliant spirit, looking to the future,

Can pay court and hold Court equally well.
We would be nobodies 'neath such a sovereign:
Never would he depend on us entirely:
His hand alone would bestow lordly gifts,
His choice alone distribute lands and honors;
He would alone steer with the helm he grasps,
Weigh and conclude, hear and determine all;
And whatsoe'er renown our office gives us,
As soon as he would fain be rid of us
He could destroy us with a single glance.

But Galba—see what power he leaves with us;
In what posts under him his weakness puts us!
Our orders govern, we give, we take away;
Nothing is done that we oppose; since naught
Can be obtained except through one of us,
We find more court paid unto us than him;
And we would be quite independent of him
If Vinius did not share in our good fortune,
Our sole grief being that he disputes it with us.

Now Galba's age makes his death near at hand.
For fear 'twill spell our ruin, we must have
A new support, and one as weak as he.
It must be one who, satisfied with titles,
Lets us be still the supreme source of power.
Piso is of a simple, lowly nature.
Though he has high birth, he lacks character—
I mean not virtue, which hates evil doing;
His strict integrity is to be admired;
He is a wholly noble, upright man;
But in a monarch that is naught or little.
A monarch needs discretion, needs wise insight,
Needs enterprise no less adroit than bold,
Which is impressive, dazzling, and charms all—
He needs a thousand traits which Piso hath not.
He will himself beg us to rule the Empire,
And will know only what we please to tell him.
The more we keep him in subjection to us,
The more will he exalt us over him;
And that is just the master we must have.

MARTIANUS. But to set such a man, sir, on the throne

Is to serve ill the realm, bring shame to Rome.

LACO. Rome and the realm—what matter they to us?
What matters it if their fame shines bright or dimly?
Let us make our position safe, and scorn
All else. No thought, no thought of public good
If it to us be dangerous! Let us have
Hearts that are jealous for our greatness only,
Live only for—think only of—ourselves.
Again I tell thee: to set Otho o'er us
Is to expose our heads to dreadful tempests.
He will owe all to us, so he will say,
But if through us he reaches his great goal,
Vinius alone will benefit thereby;
And *he* proposed it, 'twill be held his doing,
And death or exile or humiliations
Will be the real thanks given to thee and me.

MARTIANUS. Yes, our security requires Piso's triumph.
Obtain for me his promise of Plautina.
I pledge thee, at this price, my vote for him.
Compulsion, when she scorned me so, is just.
Thus let us first enjoy his rise to power
And learn if he is one who dares gainsay us.

LACO. What! does love always make thee deem Plautina's
Charms and thy wedding her thy highest good?
Well, then, we must needs see whom 'twill be better
To hearken unto . . . But here now is the Princess
Camilla.

Enter CAMILLA *and* ALBIANA.

CAMILLA.   I most fortunately find you
Both here, and I would have a few words with you.
If I may trust a rumor I must speak of,
Ye carry somewhat far a minister's
Presumption. It is said that ye extend
Your sway unto my station, and that ye
Think ye can make what use ye like of me.

MARTIANUS. We, madam?

CAMILLA.   Must I needs obey you—I,
Whom Galba doth intend to make an empress?

LACO. We both know better what respect is due thee.

CAMILLA. Your crime is greater if ye have lost that.
　　　　　Speak! What has each of you twain said to Galba?
MARTIANUS. He wanted to confirm his views with ours,
　　　　　And since he means to choose now his successor,
　　　　　To leave the Empire in the worthiest hands,
　　　　　As to whom he shall give the throne unto,
　　　　　Vinius hath spoken and so, too, hath Laco.
CAMILLA. And know ye not, both Vinius and ye,
　　　　　That his successor is to be my husband,—
　　　　　That my hand's gift goes with this gift of empire?
　　　　　Would Galba break, on your advice, that promise?
LACO. It stands inviolate, and we have spoken
　　　　　According as the gods have given us insight.
　　　　　On such occasions they who watch o'er crowns
　　　　　Inspire men's counsels on a choice of rulers.
　　　　　We thought, moreover, that we could not wrongly
　　　　　Count the whole Empire's interests thy best interests.
　　　　　Thou wouldst not wish them to be contrary.
CAMILLA. Ye have not—thou nor he—considered aught
　　　　　Save yours. To offer Piso to me proves . . .
LACO. Dost thou, madam, find him unfit to reign?
　　　　　He lacks not virtues, intellect, nor courage;
　　　　　He hath, besides . . .
CAMILLA.　　　　　Besides, he hath your preference.
　　　　　That is enough to win him my rejection.
　　　　　In deference to his race, I say naught more.
MARTIANUS. Wouldst thou love Otho, who is Vinius' choice—
　　　　　Otho, whose heart, thou knowest, Plautina sways
　　　　　And who aspires to naught but marriage with her?
CAMILLA. Whether he loves her or leaves her for me
　　　　　Is no affair of yours, and this nice care
　　　　　Ye take for me gives you too much concern.
LACO. But the Emperor consents for him to wed her
　　　　　Today, and I have just contrived this for him.
CAMILLA. Did *he* beg thee to? Tell me, or if the wish . . .
LACO. A true friend does not wait for one to beg him.
CAMILLA. Such friendship charms me, and I must confess
　　　　　That Otho has till now had cause to prize it,
　　　　　And that the blest mischance of this rare service . . .
LACO. Madam . . .

CAMILLA.   Nay, hearken to me: have done with craft.
　　　　Risk not yourselves to make an emperor. Galba
　　　　Knows well the Empire, and I know my heart.
　　　　I know what I should do; he sees what he
　　　　Should do, and who would be the realm's best ruler.
　　　　If heaven inspires you, it will watch o'er us
　　　　And can hereon make us agree with you.
LACO.　If Piso doth not please thee, there are others . . .
CAMILLA.　Connect not here my interests with yours.
　　　　Ye have shrewd wits, but I have piercing eyes.
　　　　I see 'tis sweet for you to be all-powerful;
　　　　I shall not hinder you from still continuing
　　　　To be so quite as much as ye are now;
　　　　But as to him I wed, ye will not irk me
　　　　By finding that 'tis best that I should choose him.
　　　　I feel some fondness for myself, and care not
　　　　To sacrifice for you my life's contentment.
MARTIANUS.　Since he must govern with thee all the world . . .
CAMILLA.　Need I again tell you mine eyes are open?
　　　　I see into your hearts. I am determined
　　　　To say no more now; but I really could
　　　　Unveil their secret.
MARTIANUS.　　　　If the Emperor heeds us . . .
CAMILLA.　Beyond doubt he will heed you; beyond doubt
　　　　I shall accept the husband offered me.
　　　　He, whether he be pleasing in my sight
　　　　Or whether he be revolting to my soul,
　　　　Will be my master; I shall be his wife.
　　　　I shall acquire, in time, some influence o'er him,
　　　　And ye will then discover that I have it.
　　　　That is the little which I wished to say.
　　　　Reflect upon it.　　　(*Exeunt* CAMILLA *and* ALBIANA.)
MARTIANUS.　　　　This rage, which Piso draws
　　　　Down on us . . .
LACO.　　　　It alarms thee? Let her talk,
　　　　And let us waste no fears of being destroyed.
MARTIANUS.　Thou seest what haughty pride incites her 'gainst us.
LACO.　The more she shows it to me, the more I see
　　　　Her weakness. Let us make a prince of Piso;

And she herself, however furious
Now, will, as thou shalt find, have need of us.

A C T   I I I

CAMILLA *and* ALBIANA *are discovered.*

CAMILLA.   Thy brother told thee of this, Albiana?
ALBIANA.   Yes, madam; Galba hath made choice of Piso.
    Thou art to be his wife, or, to express it
    Better, the slave of Laco, unless thou
    With bold and lofty spirit dost refuse.
CAMILLA.   And what becomes of Otho?
ALBIANA.   Thou shalt see
    His head confirm the triumph of thy three foes—
    That is to say, assure thy hand to Piso
    And the Empire to those tyrants who will make him
    Reign in name; for as he hath in his favor
    Only a line of ancestors, Martianus
    And Laco are to be our real masters,
    And Piso will but be a sacred idol
    Which they will ever keep above the altar
    To speak as they desire. His probity,
    As stupid as it is intractable,
    Will force his lips to utter their commands,
    And the first sentence he pronounces will
    Rid them of Otho, who might else dethrone them.
CAMILLA. Gods, how I pity him!
ALBIANA.   He is to be pitied
    If thou abandonest him to all that he
    Hath to dread, but since death will end his woes,
    I greatly fear to see thee deserve pity
    More than he.
CAMILLA.   Marriage gives us o'er a husband
    Some power.
ALBIANA.   Octavia died through that belief.
    Her blood, not yet cold, shows thee to what fate
    A second Tigellinus might consign thee.
    This great choice gives you both good grounds for fear.
    The more I think, the more I tremble for you.
CAMILLA.   What can I do, Albiana?

ALBIANA. Love, and show . . .

CAMILLA. That love is stronger in me than obedience?

ALBIANA. Let thy thoughts dwell on Galba less than Laco,
Who flouts thee and besides makes a slave flout thee.
Let them dwell on thy perils, and perchance
Duty will find 'tis in accord with love.
We owe complete obedience to authority,
Madam, but we owe something to ourselves—
Especially when we see dangerous orders
Given us in great sovereigns' names by others.

CAMILLA. But Otho—does he love me?

ALBIANA. Does he! Ah, madam!

CAMILLA. 'Twas thought Plautina had his entire heart.

ALBIANA. 'Twas naturally thought so, but quite wrongly—
Or else would Vinius have proposed his name
And cheated hopes of him for son-in-law?

CAMILLA. Feigning to love her, what could he intend?

ALBIANA. To come near thee and gain at Court a sure,
Free opportunity for a worthier love.
By winning the good will of Vinius
He hath contrived to arouse a different hope
In *him*—of a more certain, higher station—
If through thee Otho, by his aid, were emperor.
Thou seest how Vinius undertook this task
E'en while to thee Otho declared his love.

CAMILLA. But he hath waited full long to declare it.

ALBIANA. My brother hath till now assured thee of it.

CAMILLA. Meanwhile, thou'st led me to take some steps first,—
To let Albinus try to make him speak,—
And even Vinius, when he named him to me,
Might easily perceive I could love Otho.

ALBIANA. This is the penalty which the scrupulous
Observance of respect that must be shown
Toward those of thine high rank imposeth on them.
It stays men's wooing, keeps them with downcast eyes,
Holds their desires pent in, stifles their sighs,
Locks up their tender feelings in their bosoms;
And such the lot is of a princess that
Whatever love she can inspire or feel,
She must divine or cause to be divined.

However little one may say to her,
One fears he said too much to her, and scarcely
Doth one dare risk avowing that he loves her;
And to o'ercome this hampering respect
For her, she must despite her pride half offer
Herself. Dost thou not see that Otho would
Be silent still, had I not through my brother
Emboldened him?

CAMILLA.   Thou thinkest, then, that he loves me?

ALBIANA.   And that it would be sweet to him if thou
Wouldst have the love for him he hath for thee.

CAMILLA.   Alas, how readily doth my love believe
What pleaseth it! In vain my reason speaks,
In vain it fears, in vain doth doubt do all
It can do. My love wishes to believe thee,
And does believe thee—only because it wishes
To do so. I perceive that 'gainst Plautina
Or me there is a ruse employed, yet blithely
Do I insist on shutting fast mine eyes.
I pity her who is deceived, and it
Is I, perhaps, who am, and who deliver
Myself to endless sorrow. It may be
That at this moment when 'tis sweet to me
To hearken to thee, he vows love to Plautina.
Perchance . . .

Enter ALBINUS.

ALBINUS *(to* CAMILLA).   The Emperor cometh here to find thee,
To tell thee of his choice and justify it.
If thou dislikest it, thou must needs be steadfast,—
Must needs resist with brave and faithful heart,—
Must . . .

CAMILLA.   I know how to do what I should do.
Go and find Otho, that he may see me do it.

Exit ALBINUS. *Enter* GALBA.

GALBA.   When my son's death left my house desolate,
Dear niece, my love then took thee for a daughter.
Seeing in thee all left me of my family,
I eased my grief by giving thee their place.

Rome, which hath since burdened me with its empire,
When 'neath the weight of years I scarce draw breath,
Hath seen my love for thee make me accept it—
Less to sit high-throned than to raise thee high.
Not that if Rome could be so thoroughly
Reborn that she could do without a master,
I would not think it meet, in that glad moment,
For me to initiate her restoration;
But this great empire is too vast for her;
One mind must rule her, or so huge a body
Totters, and her unconquerable horror
For the word "king" still leaves her so submissive
Unto an emperor that she cannot bear
(Having been thus ruled) either complete freedom
Or complete servitude. She wishes, then,
A master, and the fate of Nero showeth
What she desires in him who wears the crown.
Not Vindex, Rufus, nor I caused his downfall;
His crimes alone did that, and heaven vouchsafed it
To prove to sovereigns that they hence should be
Worthy of the choice which it hath made of them.
Until this great event we were like chattels,
Inherited by members of one house
In shameful slavery. Rome hath thus regained
Instead of liberty the right to give
Elsewhere the power; and to leave after me
Upon the throne a great man is now all
That I can do for Rome, and to take care
Of her best interests will take care of thine.
This master she must have should be thy husband,
And patriotism joins with paternal love
To give thee one befitting thee and her.
Julius and the great Augustus made
Choice in their family, or among those allied
With it, of heirs to whom to leave their office.
I without thought of any ties of kinship
Have chosen like them, but from the whole Republic.
I chose thus Piso; he is of Crassus' blood;
He is of Pompey's, too; he hath their virtues;
And those famed heroes, in whose steps he follows,

Will unite such great names with those of *my* race
That there can be no marriage so becoming
Which can lend greater dignity to the Empire.
CAMILLA. I have endeavored to respond to thy
Fatherly love by an affectionate
Respect, by cherishing and revering thee,
Sir; and I see the better by thy choice
How much thou lovest me and how much I owe thee.
I know who Piso is, and how great-souled;
But if I may display to thee some frailty,
However worthy he is of Rome and me
I fear to pledge my heart and my fidelity
To him, and I confess, as to my marriage,
I somewhat am like Rome, which gave me birth.
I do not ask for complete liberty
As she hath bowed her fearless pride; but if
Thou forcest upon me complete servitude
I shall, like her, find its yoke over-harsh.
I am too ill-versed in affairs of State
To know what such a mighty prince should be;
But does Rome have but one man in her walls?
Hath she but Piso who is worthy of her?
And cannot two in all of her domains
Be found whom thou'dst vouchsafe to let me wed?
  Nero waged cruel war upon all manhood
If he destroyed it throughout earth's four quarters,
And if, to give us worthy emperors,
Piso alone with thee escaped his fury.
There are more heroes in so vast an empire;
There are some who would joyfully be hailed
As thy successor, and who could, without
Shaming thee, join unto the noble art
Of reigning that of winning every heart.
Men fear stern government from unbending virtue.
This, just when 'tis admired, oft proves revolting;
And since thy choice must give to me a husband,
It would be well if he were somewise gentle,
If in him were displayed a lover's graces
Equally with a master's haughtiness,
And if he were as apt to show affection

As to make all the Court here quail before him.
Oft-times a little love in monarchs' bosoms
Accompanies well their noblest attributes.
'Tis not that I would offer opposition;
I like to obey thee, sir, without contending.
To reward a sacrifice for which my heart
Is ready, let my husband owe me something.
In this submission wherein I find my pleasure,
To have a choice or two is some slight freedom.
Thy Piso may be able to attract me
If he no longer needs must be my husband;
And he would in his love feel surer of me
If I, he saw, preferred him to some others.

GALBA.   This lengthy answer combines delicately
No small adroitness with its loving deference.
If thy refusal is wrong, 'tis sweet and courteous.
Speak frankly, then: does Otho suit thy fancy?
He was suggested to me; what hast thou
To say of him?

CAMILLA.   Didst thou at once reject him
As not fit to be emperor?

GALBA.   No; but later,
Consulting my best judgment, I have found
I had to give my preference to Piso.
His virtues, sturdier, not to be corrupted,
Will bring us an incomparable era,
As did Augustus, whereas the other man,
Immersed in vice by Nero, would bring back
That luxury in which he moulded him
And all those evils of vile licentiousness
With which he dared to stain his power supreme.

CAMILLA.   Otho knew how he must conduct himself
With such a monster till time rid him of him.
He who is politic adapts his life
To the habits of his prince; but Otho was
Wholly himself when he was in his province,
And his great qualities, by what he accomplished,
Were there seen promptly—not his assumed vices.
His fame hath in thy reign grown daily greater,
But Piso never hath had post or army,

And as he hath till now had no employment
Only on faith can we account him worthy.
I gladly for the sake of his heroic
Forefathers would believe he has their traits,
Will follow in their footsteps, and will equal
Those of them with the most illustrious names;
But I would believe more some great deeds by him.
If he in long exile seemed without vices,
The virtues of men banished are oft feigned.
Without gain to thyself, thou hast recalled him.
But Otho was the first to have thee crowned;
He, when there were two sides, declared for thine.
While Piso owes thee all, thou'rt in *his* debt.

GALBA.   Thou makest it *thy* task to acquit me toward him;
But as the Empire needs a different mainstay,
Thou'lt concede Piso is for Rome more suited.
That I have named him should assure thee of it.

CAMILLA.   For Rome and for the Empire I believe it
Since thou dost, but I doubt if Otho is
For me less suited.

GALBA.   Doubt it, then. Such doubt
Indeed is worthy of a heart which fain
Would bring back Nero's odious times again,
And, seeing that Otho most resembles him . . .

CAMILLA.   Make choice thyself, and I shall with shut eyes
Accept it. Let thy goodness alone order
My fate, and I will blindly give myself
To him to whom thou givest me; but when thou
Consultest with Laco and with Martianus,
I deem a husband from their hands a tyrant,
And if I dare speak freely at this juncture,
I look on Piso as their creature, who,
Reigning by their decree and lending them
His voice, will force me to obey their will.
I want no throne where I shall be their captive,
Chained by their power; and whate'er betideth,
I would prefer a husband capable
Of being an emperor, rather than a husband
Who is one but who tolerates a mentor.

GALBA.   To constrain hearts is not my purpose. Let us

Say no more of it. There will be other women
In Rome whom Piso will not woo in vain.
Thy hand is thine to give, the Empire mine.

(*Enter* OTHO *and* ALBINUS.)

Is it true, Otho, that thou lovest Camilla?

OTHO. No doubt my rashness is without avail,
But if I dared, sir, with a kinder fate . . .

GALBA. Nay, nay; if thou lov'st her, she loves thee, too.
She does thee such good offices with me
That to reward thy services I give her
To thee. Hence, though I promised Laco for thee
That thou today shouldst be Plautina's husband,
The noble ardor of a love so great
Makes me revoke my word and take thee for her.

OTHO. Thou seest me speechless and confused with joy.
When I foretold myself a prompt rejection,—
When I expected but thy righteous wrath,—
I am most fortunate not to have displeased thee!
And far from censuring my too high ambitions . . .

GALBA. Thou still know'st not how much thou owest her.
Her heart aspires so fervently to wed thee
That to be thine she hath renounced the throne.
Choose then, together, with your common preference,
Some place at Court, or else some governorship.
Thou needest but to speak.

OTHO.   Sire, if the Princess . . .

GALBA. Piso will not wish to gainsay my promise.
I have named *him* Caesar, to make him emperor.
Thou knowest his virtues; I answer for his feelings.
Farewell. To observe the customary forms
I shall myself present him to the army.
As to Camilla, for your happy union,
Be thou assured, she shall have all my wealth.
I from this day shall make her my sole heir.

(*Exit* GALBA.)

CAMILLA (*to* OTHO). Sir, thou canst see now my heart's inmost
    depths,
And vainly would I wish to hide them from thee
After what love hath made me do for thee.
What Galba was at pains to tell thee for me . . .

OTHO.　How now! would Otho make thee lose the Empire,
　　　Madam? He better knoweth his small worth.
　　　'Tis not at such a price that thou shouldst buy him,
　　　Scorning it loftily. He should oppose
　　　This act whereby thine over-generous heart
　　　Humbles thee for his sake, and by an act
　　　No less magnanimous give back to so noble
　　　A soul the throne which thou deservest. Whatever
　　　May be the cause of such whole-hearted love . . .

CAMILLA.　I am not one to stress what I have done;
　　　And in this outcome which delights our hearts
　　　Thou owest me much less than thou supposest.
　　　It seems that I for thee renounce the Empire,
　　　And that blind love hath made me give it up.
　　　I love thee, yes—but if the throne is sweet,
　　　I think I make it surely mine by giving
　　　Myself to thee. As long as Galba lives,
　　　Men's reverence for his white hairs will maintain
　　　His sway—at least it seems so. Piso hopes
　　　To reign; but someday Rome will in her turn
　　　Perhaps allow herself to make her choice.
　　　Whate'er then leads her to select an emperor,—
　　　Whether 'tis noble blood she seeks or merit,—
　　　Our union shall win votes in any case;
　　　For I have lineage, thou hast ability.
　　　With such a famous name as thine to make thee
　　　Desirable, Galba's heir will seem right worthy.
　　　That title will be loved in such a husband,
　　　And if I am thy wife the throne is mine.

OTHO.　Ah, madam, put from thee this futile hope
　　　Of seeing us someday again considered.
　　　If Piso's rule must be accepted, Rome
　　　Will while he lives have eyes no more for me.
　　　She vainly murmurs 'gainst unworthy masters;
　　　She suffers them, however base or evil.
　　　Tiberius was cruel, Caligula brutal,
　　　Claudius weak, Nero wicked beyond any.
　　　He by his great crimes did destroy himself,
　　　But all the rest were reckoned rightful sovereigns.
　　　Claudius, in fact—the spiritless, blind Claudius—

When once his eyes were opened, straight went mad;
And Pallas and Narcissus, having made him
Do so, gave cruelty free scope with his sanction.
He reigned, however, though he was detested,
Till Nero found it irksome to obey him;
And that most monstrous foe of Roman virtues
Succumbed but tardily to men's common hate.
By what they dared do, judge what Piso, governed
By Laco, will when thou refusest him.
He will be vexed to realize—he, who loves thee—
That marrying thee gives me claims to the throne.
Anyone would on that ground be thy suitor,
And power supreme indeed emboldens love.
If Nero, though my friend, took my Poppaea,
Judge thou what scruples, to possess himself
Again of that hand which was taken from him,
A man will feel about the foulest deed
Done 'gainst his rival both for love and empire.
There is no exile—is no Lusitania—
Which till I die will shelter me from Piso,
And all too well I know the Court to doubt
One moment his hate's fervor or the outcome.

CAMILLA.　And this is that great soul, thought to be fearless!
Peril, I see, frightens thee like all others;
And with the fairest prospect of attaining
The throne and having me, thou wilt risk naught!
Thou standest in dread of Piso! Then, pray, tell me:
If thou art known to have loved me openly,
And thou and he crave the throne equally,
Are ye less rivals if thou dost not wed me?
How wouldst thou have it that his hate should cease
For one who strove 'gainst him for power and love,
And that he willingly should forget, when sovereign,
That thou mayst in thy heart still nurse great hopes?
Deceive thyself no longer; he hath seen there
Thy love and thy ambition, both, and he
Can do whate'er he will 'gainst thee unless
Wedding me gives thee Galba's aid 'gainst him.

OTHO.　So be it! He will, for having loved thee, kill me;
His hatred will delight my burning heart,

And I would spare no drop of all my blood
If it is only thus that thou mayst reign.
Permit my honest love again to tell thee,
However, that of which it dares not keep
Silent to thee. With Piso in the estate
In which he is, thou must renounce the Empire
This very day, or else acquire it with him.
Before deciding which, think well on 't, madam.
Thy interest, and naught else, makes my love speak.
There are unnumbered joys in such high rank,
Whereof thou mayst have thought less than thou shouldst.
Thou in one moment someday mayst perceive them;
And if I dared speak further of Poppaea
I would say that she loved me once a little
But that a throne soon wakened other longings.
Heaven gave thee a nobler, lovelier nature,
But thou'rt a princess and, like her, a woman.
The horror of seeing another in the station
Due thee, and just regret for stooping so,
Will secretly impel thy soul to seize
On even the least hope of regaining power.
One does not always wish to shut one's eyes,
But sovereignty hath ever charms for them.
Love passes or grows cold, and howso strong,
It cannot always master thirst for empire.

CAMILLA.   What sort of love I have aroused in thee
I know not, sir; but it is fond of arguing
About the Empire; it is strong enough
In this respect, I find, and even strong
Enough to show that it knows all the charms
Which power hath, and, from what thou sayst to me
About the choice to make, that it hath deigned
To give more than one fleeting thought thereto.
I fain would think, like thee, 'tis firm and genuine
And tells me only what it needs must speak of;
But to be quite frank . . .

OTHO.   Ah, dear madam, hearken . . .

CAMILLA.   Yes, I shall hearken to Piso in these matters,
To whom thou sendest me; and as for thee,
To give thee somewhat greater joy, thou'lt hearken

Unto Plautina, back to whom I send thee.
I am not jealous, and say this without anger:
Thou lovest but power, and I loved but thee.
Fear naught; I am a woman and a princess,
Yet am these without arrogance or frailty,
And for thy blindness I feel too much pity
To crush thee further with my enmity.

(Exeunt CAMILLA and ALBIANA.)

OTHO.   How plainly this prepares my ruin, Albinus!

ALBINUS.   All is lost if thou goest, sir, to Plautina.

OTHO.   Still I shall go to her. In this plight wherein
I find myself, I cannot heed the counsels
Of any heart except one wholly mine.

A C T   I V

OTHO *and* PLAUTINA *are discovered.*

PLAUTINA.   What counsel wouldst thou have me give thee, sir?
I feel no less confusion from like grief,
And my heart, quite wrapped up in thee, is not
Sufficiently detached for it to find
A remedy for the ills that I foresee.
I can but weep; I can but pity thee.
   The choice of Piso in itself would give us
Reason to fear the worst; my father told thee
That he would leave to all three of us only
The hope of dying together as we chose;
And we should fear still more a passionate woman,
Angered by having in less than one day's space
An offer of marriage made her and retracted,
By homage which had not the looked-for sequel,
And by her vain loss of a throne for thee.
She with that throne was one thou couldst adore;
For thee did she renounce it, and had then
Nothing to make thee love her. Where will the shame
Of seeing she lost the Empire and thee, too,
Not carry her in her righteous wrath—a shame
So much the greater and more keenly felt
As she had counted on her return to power,
Thinking her hand through thee would soon regain

What for thy sake her heart seemed to disdain?

OTHO.   I then can only die. I wished to, madam,
When without stain I might, because I loved thee,
And I should wish to when thy cruel decree
Hath made me criminal and deserving of death.
Thou badest me offer marriage to Camilla.
Thanks to our bad luck, that misdeed proved useless.
I shall die wholly thine, and if, to obey thee,
I seemed to love thee ill—seemed false to thee—
My hand, made ruthless by that hest, before thee
Will in my blood wash out my perfidy.
Begrudge me not, in my cruel fortune, madam,
The glory at least of dying a true Roman,
After it pleased thee to make me unable
To have the bliss of dying a true lover.

PLAUTINA.   Far from condemning such a noble impulse,
I wish to make it my own joy and ambition.
People renounce life for less great misfortunes.
Be sure of me with Arrius my example:
I have a heart as brave, a hand as steady;
And when 'tis necessary, I can strike.
Yet if thou'dst deign, sir, to constrain thyself
I might, with everything to fear, still hope.
Camilla is angry, but can be appeased.

OTHO.   Wouldst thou condemn me, then, to wed her, madam?

PLAUTINA.   Why can I not, myself, forbid that step?
But if thy life can be assured thus only,—
If there is else no way . . .

OTHO.   Ah, let us hasten
To meet death, or, if we must try to avoid it,
Let us submit to Laco's tyranny
Before subjecting me to ignominy.
I would prefer the former's worst extremes
To seeing myself alike without a throne
And thee, and to the shame of nuptials which
Declare me infamous—for Camilla's preference
For me is held a crime, and she is robbed
Of the Empire by the hate felt for that troth
Which her love made her wish to plight with me.
Not that this throne had charms for me without thee!

For thee I sought it, though with some misgivings;
And had I not by Galba been disdained,
I would have had the scepter, thou'dst have reigned.
Thy wishes, which are rightfully my sovereigns,
Would have alone governed Rome's vast domains.
Thy hests . . .

PLAUTINA.   Then 'tis for me to make thee emperor.
I could. The way filled me at first with horror,
But I can conquer that and, by bestowing
My hand, assure thee of both life and empire
And thus repair the crime of showing a pride
Which robs thee of a throne and opes thy coffin.
I would have gained Martianus' vote for thee
Could I have suffered his presumptuous wooing.
His love . . .

OTHO.   Martianus knew his place so ill
That he dared . . . ?

PLAUTINA.   He hath not yet quenched his love.
Whate'er the grounds were for the choice of Piso,
I need to say but one word to change all.

OTHO. Couldst thou so far stoop as to listen to him?

PLAUTINA. For thee I would go further, and accept him.

OTHO. Take counsel with thine honor. It can tell thee . . .

PLAUTINA. That 'tis my duty to give thee the Empire.

OTHO. That one still scarred by fetters he hath worn . . .

PLAUTINA. Ought to delight me if he brings thee safety.

OTHO. Canst thou indeed see all the humiliation
Involved?

PLAUTINA.   I can see none in saving, sir,
Thy life.

OTHO.   To wed him even before mine eyes!
And to complete my misery . . .

PLAUTINA.   Give thyself
To Camilla, or I give myself to him.

OTHO. Let us die, madam,—die, each for the other,
With all my honor and all thine preserved.
To make our death one for the gods to envy,
Be again wholly mine, as I am thine;
Or if, to save in thee all that I love,
Thou art resolved, because of my ill fortune,

To make elsewhere disposal of thy hand,
At least have no less care than I for honor,
And wed instead of me some noble rival
Only. I, if thou doest that, shall die
Of grief, but I would die of rage if thou
Weddest instead of me a former slave.

(Enter Vinius.*)*

(*To* Vinius) Oh, sir, prevent Plautina . . .

Vinius.   Sir, thou canst
Prevent whate'er thou wilt, if thou hast courage.
Despite the trying rigor of our fortunes
Heaven puts our entire fate now in thy hands.

Plautina.   What dost thou tell us?

Vinius.   What I have just seen.
That to be emperor he hath but to wish to.

Otho.   No more of empire, sir, without Plautina!

Vinius.   Seize on a throne which heaven destines for thee,
And choosing, thyself, the wife with whom to share it,
Assist thy happy lot to be accomplished.
    The army hath seen Piso, but with murmurs
Which seemed to relish ill the wrong done thee.
Galba presented him to the soldiers curtly,
With no suggestion of forthcoming largess.
By the appeal of fictive promises
He could have roused in them a moment's joy;
But he liked better to say loftily
He knew how to recruit them but not buy them.
His haughty harshness, shown unseasonably,
Recalled the horrors of his ruthlessness
When all his path from Spain to Rome was strewn
With Romans sacrificed to his new fortunes,
And after all lands with their blood were stained,
His entry here was marked by further carnage.
    Sir, during the whole time Piso harangued them,
Thy name sped on their lips from rank to rank.
Four of the eagerest came to tell me of it
And promise thee the army and the Empire.
Then hasten to the Square, where thou wilt find them;
Follow them to their camp, make sure of them.
Seizing the right time can accomplish all things.

OTHO. If this same adverse star which hath to me . . .

VINIUS. Do, without more words, what must needs be done.
　　　　A moment's tarrying can bring all to naught.
　　　　Thou'lt be arrested on the least suspicion.

OTHO. Ere I go forth, suffer me to protest . . .

VINIUS. Go! When thou'rt emperor thou canst say the rest.

　　　　　　　　　　　　　　　　　　(*Exit* OTHO.)

　　　　(*To* PLAUTINA) This is not all, my daughter; a more certain
　　　　Good fortune, howsoever he may fare,
　　　　Will put the Empire in thy hands.

PLAUTINA.　　　　　　　　　　　　Wert thou,
　　　　Then, flattering Otho with vain hopes?

VINIUS.　　　　　　　　　　　　　By no means.
　　　　What I have told him was entirely true.
　　　　I look to see thee reign with thy beloved
　　　　Otho; but do thou hope no less from Piso.
　　　　Galba gives thee to him. Vexed with Camilla,
　　　　Whose love hath brought to naught what he intended,
　　　　He wants this marriage to punish her, unite
　　　　Again with me Laco and Martianus,
　　　　And thus avert the evil auguries
　　　　From the strife seen among his ministers.
　　　　Thus on both sides all works to thine advantage:
　　　　The luckier man will bring to thee his love;
　　　　Thou, sharing not his risks, wilt share his glory,
　　　　And at thy feet wilt see the one who triumphs.

PLAUTINA. What! could my heart, which thou hast given this hero,
　　　　Love him no more if he should not be crowned;
　　　　And if ill fate consigns us unto Piso,
　　　　Could I indeed for Piso wish to live?

VINIUS. If what we both wish does not come to pass,
　　　　Thou still canst do as thou hast done already.
　　　　She who hath given Otho up to crown him
　　　　Can give herself up, in her turn, to reign.

PLAUTINA. If I have done a noble act to crown him,
　　　　Ought I to do a shameful one to profit
　　　　By his death? I renounced him without selling
　　　　Myself to anyone; and thou wouldst have
　　　　His death bestow my hand,—wouldst have me, swept
　　　　Off my feet by the splendor of high rank,

Clutch at one reeking with his blood,—wouldst have me,
Triumphant and in bliss through his misfortunes,
Be the reward of cutting short his life!
Nay, sir, we shall this day have the same fate:
Thou'lt see me reign with him or die with him.
To do one of these things is my sole wish.

VINIUS.　How ill thou knowest what sovereign power is!
If thou couldst make but a brief trial of it,
Ne'er wouldst thou think it could be bought too dearly;
Thou'dst gladly see a thousand lovers perish
Were all their blood required to win it for thee.
Love Otho, if he can assure thee of it;
But love thyself, if need be, more than him,
And without caring where the lightning strikes,
Let the gods choose on whose head it shall fall.
Take at whatever life's expense the scepter.
Reign without qualms with whosoe'er shall reign.

PLAUTINA.　How strange thy maxims of behavior are!
My heart would, if it dared, deem some are wicked.
Sir, I can love and keep my plighted faith;
I can do what I should for one I love;
I can, for his good, sacrifice myself;
And I can die on seeing that he hath died.
But I have not the power to force myself,
In tears, to cull the fruits of his disaster.

VINIUS.　Yet hold thyself ready to do just this.
Change thou thy feelings, or at least thy speech;
And, to accord thy heart and fortunes better,
Hope for thy lover, but wed him who triumphs.
Farewell. I see the Princess here—Camilla.
Whate'er thine inward turmoil, appear tranquil.
Profit by her mistake; perceive more clearly
Than she the luster of the throne she loses.

Exit VINIUS. *Enter* CAMILLA *and* ALBIANA.

CAMILLA (*to* PLAUTINA).　Wilt thou permit me to pay duteous homage,
Madam, to my empress, as I come to do?
PLAUTINA.　I have no right to bid thee not to do so,
But this is not the place where thou must seek her.

CAMILLA. When Galba giveth thee for wife to Piso . . .

PLAUTINA. 'Tis not yet time for thee to feel, hence, jealous.

CAMILLA. If I loved either empire, though, or Piso,
    I could already be that with some reason.

PLAUTINA. And I, madam—if I loved either Piso
    Or empire, I would have some reason for not
    Refusing them; but thy example teacheth
    Hearts such as mine that sometimes noble scorn
    For that which might be theirs becomes them best.

CAMILLA. What! carest thou naught for empire and for Piso?

PLAUTINA. That which thou scornest do I, too, disdain;
    That which doth please thee seems as sweet to me:
    I take such pride in being governed by thee.

CAMILLA. If I loved Otho, then . . .

PLAUTINA.   I, too, would love him,
    If when I gave my hand I gave the crown.

CAMILLA. Is one without the throne not worthy of him?

PLAUTINA. That do I leave to thee, whom he loves now.

CAMILLA. Thou best of all canst know the truth about it;
    And as your passion hath been mutual,
    The example thou affordest leaves no doubt
    That one without the crown cannot deserve him.

PLAUTINA. The example I afford leaves no doubt that
    Unless thou hast the crown he may forsake thee.

CAMILLA. He found in thee, without it, such attractions . . .

PLAUTINA. All loves are not alike.

CAMILLA.   Indeed, thou hast
    Charms so exceptional . . .

PLAUTINA.   Charms quite aside,
    Love oft is unpredictable. With different
    Loved ones, one cares for different things. To some,
    One gives oneself; to some, one sells oneself.

CAMILLA. One who knew Otho well could in such matters,
    As a friend, give me confidential counsel.

PLAUTINA. And one who values him enough to lift him
    So high, can tell me, if she will, his worth,
    That if my love hath warrant to be reborn . . .

CAMILLA. I judged him of some worth before I knew him,
    And when I knew him I sent him back to thee.

PLAUTINA. Anyone sent by thee is always welcome.

I accept the gift, and deem that I without
Shame, having it from thee, can value it.

CAMILLA.   He came to thee to bring thee back his heart?

PLAUTINA.   He knows his place too well to disobey thee.

CAMILLA.   He left thee soon, and his ingratitude . . .

PLAUTINA.   Hast thou hence, madam, some anxiety?

CAMILLA.   Nay, but I fain would know how he obeys me.

PLAUTINA.   Sometimes our curiosity betrays us,
Extorting from the heart a hint whereby
It often says more than it means to say.

CAMILLA.   Mine does not say all that thou thinkest.

PLAUTINA.   Regarding
All that I think, it tells me quite enough.

CAMILLA.   Often the great concern love makes one feel
Infers more than is said or than is true.
If thou knewest what is my most ardent wish . . .

PLAUTINA.   I give thee choice of Otho and of Piso—
The latter gladly, since I lack ambition;
And as for the other, if I must send him back
To thee my love, I own, thereat may murmur;
But as thou knowest, 'twould fain defer to thee.

CAMILLA.   I can make shift without this deference.

PLAUTINA.   Doubtless;
But if I may believe appearances . . .

CAMILLA.   Let us have done; further talk would be tiresome.

PLAUTINA.   Martianus, whom I see, can entertain thee
Better. Permit me to withdraw and shun
An insolent slave who by his love hath vexed me.

(*Exit* PLAUTINA. *Enter* MARTIANUS.)

CAMILLA.   From what she says, thou lov'st her, Martianus?

MARTIANUS.   Despite her proud disdain, her glance hath charmed me.
Yet as for the Empire, 'tis still thine to have.
Galba hath yielded; Piso worships thee.

CAMILLA.   And this results solely from thy great influence?

MARTIANUS.   Disown not what my zeal for thee hath done.
My efforts have dispelled the Emperor's wrath
And sent Plautina home to obey her father.
Our new-made Caesar wished to marry her,
But I convinced him he should think not of her;
And Galba, to whom ties of blood speak loudly,

Will now let Vinius bestow her elsewhere.
He gives thee back the crown, Piso his love.
Prize more the glory and delight of empire
And the felicity of which thou wert robbing
Thyself by too precipitate dislike,
And deign to bear in mind for thy best interests . . .

CAMILLA. I see my error, and I can repair it;
But I desire—for ne'er was I ungrateful—
That first my gratitude shall be displayed.
I will do naught till thou hast been made happy.
Thou lovest, thou hast said, this haughty creature,
And Piso ne'er shall see my hand in his
Till he hath made Plautina give thee hers—
If all the scorn with which she hath requited
Thy love hath not made thee have other wishes.

MARTIANUS. Ah, madam, marriage formeth such sweet bonds
That little time is needed to end hatred,
And my good fortune could at least avenge thee
Upon Plautina and the ingrate Otho.

CAMILLA. I preferred him—that ingrate—to the Empire.
I told him so too plainly to deny it;
And love, which teaches me a lover's weakness,
Unites thy dearest wishes and my anger
To make me wreak my vengeance on Plautina
And soon complete it with his own destruction.

MARTIANUS. Ah, if thou wishest that, I know hands ready;
And I so warmly espouse all thy quarrel . . .

CAMILLA. Oh, what keen joy is this thou givest me!
These hands thou offerest me—let me behold them
That I may give them orders and set the time.
It is my wish that my desires shall be
All satisfied before the eyes of Otho,—
That he shall see the marriage of his heart's mistress
Deliver her he loves into thine arms,—
That he may ere he dies know this despair.
After that, thou wilt see me speed his death.
Till then, refrain from undertaking aught.
Thou mayst expect all good things from the power
Given me. Go; prepare for these glad moments,
But carry out nothing save at my commands.

(*Exit* MARTIANUS.)

ALBIANA. Thou wouldst slay Otho? Thou canst do that, madam?

CAMILLA. How ill thou knowest my heart's inmost thoughts!
Seeing the foul design of his base rival,
I can by this ruse frustrate its achievement
And make him love me. I shall be delighted
For him to know how well I guard his life.
Go, find for me thy brother, that through him
Otho may learn from me the risk he runs,
To what his blind course will expose him, and
That he hath now no safety but in flight.
It is the most my wrath can grant my love.

ALBIANA. Sweet the return from wrath to love will be.

Enter RUTILUS.

RUTILUS. Oh, madam, hear thou what disaster threatens.
Fifteen or twenty rebels in the Square
Have just now proclaimed Otho emperor.

CAMILLA. Is Otho not aghast at their presumption—
He who well knows such outbreaks end in nothing?

RUTILUS. They lead—or rather, carry—him to the camp,
And all the populace massed round about them
Quake at their daring course and let them pass.

CAMILLA. Does the Emperor know of it?

RUTILUS.   Yes, madam; he
Summons thee; and to prevent promptly what
Is to be feared, Piso will swiftly follow
Hard on the footsteps of these mutineers
With all the soldiers he can find.

CAMILLA.   Since Otho
Wishes to perish, let us let him perish.
Let us go urge Galba to visit on him
His deserved punishment. If the return
From wrath to love is sweet, in sooth the path
Is easily retrod from love to wrath.   (*Exeunt.*)

A C T   V

GALBA, CAMILLA, RUTILUS, *and* ALBIANA *are discovered.*

GALBA (*to* CAMILLA). Again I tell thee, dread my vengeance if

Thou even hast in the least connived with him.
There is no pardon for high treason; the more
One loves the hand, the more one hates the crime;
And when it goes so far as sacrilege,
Not sex nor ties of blood afford protection.

CAMILLA.　These undeserved suspicions would soon vanish
If thou wouldst note who by this crime would profit.
Otho, who in his heart adores Plautina—
Otho, who does not want me without empire—
If he can win the victory and dethrone thee,
Which one of us two women will he crown?
Could I plot Piso's overthrow, which would
Lose me the throne and seat Plautina on it?
Trust my self-interest, if thou doubtest me;
And with such surety, knowing my good faith,
Direct toward Vinius all of that mistrust
Which would unjustly tarnish my fair fame.

GALBA.　Vinius is by his loyal zeal acquitted.
See what he in one day hath done for me.
He offered to me Otho for thee, whom
He wished to be his son-in-law; I gave Otho
Back to his daughter, and he was glad to have him;
I wanted her for Piso, and my wishes
Were law to him; I put thee in her place,
And found him much pleased; when his friend revolted,
He fanned my wrath 'gainst him; he gave Plautina
To Martianus at my request. Shall I
Suspect a man of criminal designs
Who sets himself to do whate'er I wish?

CAMILLA.　One who doth wish alike whate'er is asked
Of him, in secret often wishes something
Else in his heart, and, as his soul's own master,
Is without loyalty except that which
He gives himself.

GALBA.　　　　　　　This marriage is, however,
The final proof of loyalty which is always
Unsullied, inviolable, and complete.

CAMILLA.　Thou'lt see in the result how it will act, sir,
And how Plautina really will obey.
Certain of her resistance and perchance

Trusting to see his beloved Otho soon
Master here, as he views the future for thee,
He glibly promises more than he would do.

GALBA. Duty can cut in twain the strongest friendship,
But love can easily prevail o'er duty;
And its flame, never more than half extinguished,
Means to a woman what no friend means to men.
Vinius approaches. Let his daughter be
Brought to me.   (*Exit* RUTILUS.)
              I will punish any crime
In all the family if I can ever
See that I have no grounds for doubt about it;
But until then I would be loath to strike.

                              (*Enter* VINIUS *and* LACO.)
I see besides him Laco. Well, what tidings?
What learned ye in the camp, as to our rebels?

VINIUS. The naval forces and the Illyrians
Have joined with wildest fervor the Pretorians.
Only the troops recalled here from the Nile's
Banks have not been infected by their madness.

LACO. These mutineers are only common soldiers;
No leader shares the guilt of their vain crime.
Hence have no fear of an armed mob wherein
Dissension is perhaps already kindled.
As soon as it is known the populace
Demands with loud cries that this plot's devisers
Shall be proscribed and clamors for the head
Of the perfidious Otho, consternation
Will calm the tempest, and thou, sire, hast only
To show thyself in order to recall
Everyone to his duty with one glance.

GALBA. Shall we go, Vinius, and by my presence
Hasten this natural, good hope's fruition?

VINIUS. Stake only in the last extremity
The dread power, sire, of thine authority.
When 'tis effectual, all gives way before it;
But if it fails, there is no other help.
There should be, for the use of sovereign power,
Complete security or black despair;
And, frankly, we are not in a position

To risk all, any more than to fear the worst.
If men are rushing into monstrous crime,
Let their impetuosity but slacken;
'Twill be abortive, and fear of punishment
Will turn against the leader his most zealous
Adherents. 'Tis wise counsel to act slowly.

LACO. A ruler worthy of the name acts boldly,
And I do not believe this counsel wise,
When Otho takes the crown, to watch him do it.
If men are rushing into monstrous crime,
We must curb their impetuosity
Before their spirits, which just fears make waver,
Can be emboldened by our negligence
And get the better of those prudent promptings
Whose aid we look for when it is too late.

VINIUS. Always doth thy advice bring mine to naught.
The mere sound of my voice makes thee dissent,
And so long as thy influence is exceptional
I need but speak for thee to contradict me.
Piso, whose fine choice is thy worthy work,
Would be mere Piso still, had *I* endorsed him.
Thou hast set Martianus against Otho
Only because my lips proposed his name,
And thou wouldst see—like others—proof enough
Of just how much superior is thy counsel
Hadst thou not sworn to be till death the foe
Of all advice which is not given by thee.

LACO. Thou'rt Otho's friend—and that tells the whole story—
Who, having wanted him for son-in-law
And chosen him for master, perchance now
Cherishest hopes thou mayst, at one same time,
Have him for master and for son-in-law.

VINIUS. I was his friend, and I was proud to be so,
Till he committed such a wicked act,
Which some would say resulted from despair
Wherein thy power, despite my efforts, plunged him.
I wanted him for son-in-law, proposed him
For prince; to neither choice couldst thou agree.
Thereby the fortunes of the State now prosper,
And thou canst see how it must therefore thank thee!

GALBA.   How hapless is that ruler when the zéal
    Of those he listens to takes diverse courses,
    And they, with fondness each for his own judgment,
    Urge, acrimoniously, different counsels!
    But am I not deceived? Can I call "zeal"
    This hate in which both stubbornly persist,
    Who, despite all the evil they foresee,
    Consult and trust themselves alone concerning
    My interests? Nay, do better, and believe—
    In our great peril—thou, that Laco serves me,
    And thou that Vinius loves me. Hate but Otho,
    And both of you remember that today
    Ye have but him to speak against.

VINIUS.   Then I
    Dare again tell thee, as thy loyal servant,
    'Tis ill to goad so many angry people.
    The good ones, for their mutual support,
    Must have time to grow calm and to collect;
    The wicked ones must have it to recognize
    How impious 'tis to differ with their master.
    Piso can meanwhile stay them in their frenzy,
    Cause them to fear thy vengeance, give them also
    A hope of mercy at their least repentance
    For their presumption, and if thou must finally
    Go to his aid, what thou art now advised
    To do thou canst do always.

LACO.   That I doubt,
    And *I* think *I* speak as thy loyal servant—
    I, who have no friends in the hostile faction.
    Shall we, sire, wait till Piso comes back, flouted,
    To bury us 'neath the wreckage of thy rule;
    Till here thy foes, for battle ranged, fall on us;
    Till in this palace they besiege thy Court;
    Till Otho goes up to the Capitol
    Before thy very eyes to render thanks
    Unto the gods for the empire he usurped;
    And till, with brow decked by thy crown, this traitor,
    All too successful, doth dispose of thee?
    Let us go, sire, go sword in hand, to uphold
    The authority of the Senate and the people

Of Rome,—go risk before the eyes of Otho
Death at our loyal soldiers' head (a death
For him more damning and for us more worthy)
And by this noble effort let us show him . . .

GALBA.   How now, niece, how now! is it sweet to reign?
Is it sweet to hold the tiller of an empire
And see its chief supports always at variance?

CAMILLA.   The more one hears of contradictory counsels,
The more light his for making a good choice.
That is what I would say, were I not doubted;
But I am Piso's and I reverence thee.
And yet I cannot hold back these few words:
Hadst thou believed me, all would be serene.
Plautina, now brought here, will think like me.

(*Enter* PLAUTINA *and* RUTILUS.)

She seems afflicted with keen sorrow.

PLAUTINA.   Madam,
I do not hold it back. Otho is dead.
All who come from outside bring us this news,
Nor wilt thou at his death be so delighted
That 'twill not cost thine eyes, like mine, some tears.

GALBA.   Is it true, Rutilus; or do vain hopes cheat me?

RUTILUS.   The tale is widespread, sire; none knows its author.
All hope him dead; 'tis common talk he is;
But how and by whose hand—that no one telleth.

GALBA.   Come, Laco, come; make it, thyself, thy task
To bring us a sure witness of the fact;
And if he can be found who dealt the blow . . .

Enter MARTIANUS *and* ATTICUS.

MARTIANUS.   Seek him no longer: here he stands before thee,
Sire. It is by his hand this rebel, punished . . .

GALBA.   Atticus' hand ended this great disturbance!

ATTICUS.   Loyalty nerved my hand; heaven guided it.
'Tis for thee, sire, to check all further trouble,
Prevent disorders, and restrain the cruelty
With which the victors set upon the vanquished.

GALBA.   Let us go quickly. Be consoled, Plautina.
Think only of the husband I shall choose thee.
Vinius will let thee have him, and thou wilt

Accept him when thy first sighs have been vented.
   'Tis thou, Martianus, whom I leave to guard her,
As it is thy hand she will take in marriage.
Be tactful with her grief and do not vex her.
   Vinius, thou needst not follow where I go,
And if some remnant of thy former friendship . . .

VINIUS.   Nay, 'tis a friendship, sire, which I abhor.
My heart is wholly thine, and ne'er had friends
Save as they were submissive to thy sway.

GALBA.   Come, then, but tax not thy fidelity.

               (*Exeunt* GALBA, VINIUS, LACO, *and* RUTILUS.)

CAMILLA.   Lovers, when talking, hate all others' presence,
Madam. I shall return to my apartments
To give thanks to the gods for such an outcome.

               (*Exeunt* CAMILLA *and* ALBIANA.)

PLAUTINA (*to the departing* CAMILLA).   Go there to hide the tears
   thou must let flow.
Otho's death stabs thy heart, as it does mine;
And if thy dearest wishes had been heeded,
Today we should have seen him crowned with thee.
   This is what comes of having too much loved me.
This, this is the result . . .

MARTIANUS.   If thy heart, burning . . .

PLAUTINA.   Vile slave, shalt thou intrude upon my grief?
Shalt thou attempt to lighten my misfortunes—
Thou, who darest offer me a baser love?

MARTIANUS.   'Tis right thy noble heart should grieve just now,
But also right thou shouldst not weep too sorely
A loss quite easily and soon repaired.
'Tis time a subject loyal to his sovereign
Should by good fortune take a rebel's place.
Thy emperor wishes it, thy father grants it;
Thou shouldst for both constrain thyself a little
And banish from thy soul the shameful memory
Of ill-placed love which sullies thy fair fame.

PLAUTINA.   Dastard, thou art not worth my stooping so
Far as to answer thee, to contradict thee.
Be silent! Leave in peace a heart engrossed
In thoughts still dearer than they are unhappy.
Break in upon my tears no more.

MARTIANUS.   Take me.
      What, after Otho's death, canst thou do better?
PLAUTINA (*while two soldiers enter and speak in whispers to* ATTICUS).
      Whatever hopes thy insolent arrogance nurses,
      Know thou that I can punish its excesses
      And pierce with mine own hand thy heart or mine
      Rather than suffer this degrading marriage.
      Know what thou art, if possible; or know
      What *I* am.
ATTICUS (*interposing*).   Pray thee, let me . . .
PLAUTINA.   Canst thou find
      So much audacity as to speak to me,
      Thou murderer of a hero I would see,
      Were it not for thee, rule the world, and himself
      Be ruled by me—thou, whose blood-reeking hand
      Consigns me to despair?
ATTICUS.   If thou lov'st Otho,
      Madam, know that he liveth still; and thou
      Wilt long behold his life safe if he dies
      Only from blows that I have boasted of.
PLAUTINA.   Otho still lives?
ATTICUS.   He is triumphant, madam,
      And master of Rome as thou art of his heart.
      Thou soon wilt see him at thy feet to offer
      To share with thee a lot which he loves only
      With thee, of which he would disdain the glory
      If thou wilt not become his victory's guerdon.
         The army at last accords his great worth justice.
      Piso's head hath been brought to him; and ill
      Now can Camilla do what she had meant to,
      Or she thanks gods of other realms for thee
      And wearies heaven with her futile prayers
      In favor of one whom it regards no more.
MARTIANUS.   Accursed man! Thus, then, thy lying promise . . .
ATTICUS.   He who doth promise treachery may lie.
      Had I not said I would commit this murder,
      Someone else by thy orders would have done it,
      And all I promised thee was but a ruse
      To place in Otho's hands Laco and Galba
      Himself. Galba hath naught to fear. All men

Respect him, and 'tis only under him
That Otho seeks to reign. But as for Laco
And thee, I see small likelihood that either
His life or thine hath similar assurance
Unless this lady's graciousness is such
That she will soften a conqueror's just wrath.
   Around the palace were two cohorts stationed,
Who have already seized its gates for Otho.
Here, I am in command; my orders, madam,
Are to obey thee and to hold him fast.
Take him hence, soldiers; he offends the sight.

MARTIANUS.   Gods! Was disaster e'er more unforeseen!

               (*Exeunt* ATTICUS *and soldiers with* MARTIANUS.)

PLAUTINA (*alone*). My heart is troubled. I know not what forebodings
Prevent my tasting fully this good fortune.
I seem most loath to give my joy free rein,
And though this happiness ends all my misery
I pass from one extreme to the other only
With some slight, vague uneasiness still left me.
I feel . . . But why comes Flavia here, dismayed?

               Enter FLAVIA.

FLAVIA. To tell thee of the wrath of angry heaven,
Or rather, Fate's insensate jealousy.

PLAUTINA. Can Otho have been given into Galba's
Hands, and inconstant Fortune in the midst
Of our success have cheated our fond hopes?

FLAVIA. Otho is free. He reigns. And yet, alas . . .

PLAUTINA. Is he so badly wounded he may die?

FLAVIA. Nay; all, on seeing him, throw down their arms;
And yet his triumph is to cost thee tears.

PLAUTINA. Explain, explain; for what, then, must I weep?

FLAVIA. Thou seest I tremble to declare it to thee.

PLAUTINA. Is it so bad as that?

FLAVIA.   I with my brother
Saw from a balcony . . . Why must I tell thee?
Why hast thou not divined, on seeing my grief,
Madam, that Vinius . . .

PLAUTINA.   Yes?

FLAVIA.   Hath just been murdered.

PLAUTINA.   Kind heaven!

FLAVIA.   The cruel hate of Laco for him . . .

PLAUTINA.   Oh, all too true presage of unknown woe!
   Laco . . .

FLAVIA.   'Twas he who dealt the fatal blow.
 Both went with Galba, keeping pace with him,
 When, turning, all three, at the first street-corner,
 They found that Otho held that avenue.
 Their consternation made them go back, only
 To see this palace seized by our adherents,
 And Laco then forthwith, aflame with rage
 To find their path blocked everywhere by Otho,
 Cast upon Vinius a glowering look,
 Without a word approached him, drew a dagger . . .

PLAUTINA.   The false wretch! Oh, what grief o'ertakes me, Flavia!

FLAVIA.   Thou understandest; I shall tell what followed.
  This caitiff turned on Galba with like frenzy.
 "Die, sire," he said, "but die an emperor.
 Accept this blow now as a final homage
 Which a brave spirit owes to thy fair fame."
 Galba fell; and that monster stabbed himself,
 Mingling his vile blood with their noble blood.
 The unhappy Otho at the dreadful sight
 Vainly rushed forward to prevent the deed.
 All thy victorious lover thus could do
 Was to shed tears over the dying Vinius
 And clasp him dead. But he is here, and he
 Will make thee realize best how torn his heart is.

Enter OTHO.

OTHO.   Madam, knowest thou of the crimes of Laco?

PLAUTINA.   I have just learned my father is no more.
 Fly, fly, my lord, from one grief-stricken. Better
 Enjoy a day that proves so fair for thee.
 Thou'rt emperor; spare thyself the pain of seeing
 My father . . .

OTHO.   Oh, I am more dead than he!
 And if thy love gives me not back the life
 The wretch who pierced his breast hath robbed me of,

I come to thee but as a hapless lover
To adore thy loveliness till my last moment.
For thee alone love made me seek the victory;
Without thee I cannot abide its glory;
I will be master of the Empire only
To place it and myself in thy dear hands.
It is for thee to say what I shall do.

PLAUTINA. It is for me to grieve, to weep my father—
Not that I lay on thee, in my great sorrow,
Things wrought by Laco and by our evil fortune;
But now . . .

OTHO. Speak, if thou canst, as one who loves me.
Our hearts' love . . .

PLAUTINA. Press me not; I grow more dazed.
Thou seest my duty, and thou knowest my promise.
In my dire plight, answer thyself for me.
Farewell, sir.

OTHO. Please, yet one word further, madam.

(*Exit* PLAUTINA.)

Enter ALBINUS.

ALBINUS. Thou art awaited at the Capitol,
Sire. All the Senate have come there expressly
To swear before the face of Jove to obey thee.

OTHO. I shall speed thither; but for whatever honors,
Albinus, I am destined, they will have
No sweetness to my heart without Plautina.
Let me at least go, in my love's behalf,
To gain for hastening to them her command
Or her approval, that I, on my return,
May make, with spirit somewhat less perturbed,
An effort to console Camilla, swearing
To her on this ill-fated day to prove
A faithful friend to her I cannot love.

Attila

INTRODUCTION

Produced in March, 1667, *Attila* was moderately successful at first, but was soon forgotten amid the enthusiasm over Racine's *Andromaque* the following winter. It passed from the stage after the seventeenth century. No one has ever considered it a masterpiece or one of the very best plays of Corneille, as Brasillach does *Othon* and *Suréna*. But no modern critic has scorned it as Petit de Julleville scorned both of these plays or as Faguet scorned *Sertorius*.

Of those whose opinions we have been noting, the earlier ones are the least favorable to *Attila*. Hémon pronounced it "a tragedy bad as a whole, very good in spots"; [1] but this is the least kindly of their verdicts. Merlet said that "if one could expunge from this work some jarring details and absurd loves, it would deserve more than a passing memory, were it only on account of the keen sense of the period to which the play transports us." [2] Faguet called it "a very praise-worthy tragedy" and "a very ambitious play, rather well handled and in the grand manner." He thought it "really excellent" up to Act IV. "It is entirely in the manner of *Othon* with this difference, that it has for its central figure an Otho who is an insolent and arrogant man instead of being something of a sniveler. From the fourth act on, the play becomes strange and a little ridiculous because Attila becomes an incoherent monster." [3] Faguet then summarizes the scenes which he says he does not "understand at all"; but he fails to show how there could be any difficulty in understanding them.

A little earlier, Lemaître had written of this play: "*Attila* is not without picturesqueness or power. . . . The parallelism of the scenes is as perfect and as artificial as that in *Rodogune*. And Ildione and Honoria resemble Plautina, who resembled Sophonisba, who resembled Viriate, who resembled Cornelia. As for the King of the Huns, the poet has made him a brute, proud, pompous, cruel, and subtle, who is conscious of being the instrument of a mysterious power—an ogre who feels himself an agent of Providence. A very striking conception. . . .

[1] *Théâtre de Pierre Corneille*, vol. iv, p. 525.
[2] P. 183.
[3] Pp. 214-215.

(Hugo would have made of him a gigantic triptych for *la Légende des siècles.*)" [4]

The figure of Attila has been an especial point of admiration by others, too—and a source of dissatisfaction, also. Schlumberger says it "would be in place in a fresco of Michelangelo." [5] Lanson said it was "as bold in its conception as Hugo's *Cromwell*," though "too much at variance with French civilization of the seventeenth century" to be sufficiently appreciated in Corneille's day, whereas today we perceive the "incongruity of the subtle study of love" associated in this play with "the name of Attila and confused by all the images which that name evokes."

"But," he went on to say, "along with the man in love, the role of Attila contains a powerful study, unique in the seventeenth and eighteenth centuries, of a savage—proud, ferocious, and wily. The unity of the character would be re-established if one should see in the attitude of Attila in respect to love an effort of the savage to act like a man refined by civilization; this would perhaps be a little too subtle and modern." [6]

Attila, according to Brasillach, "is the last of the political plays of Pierre Corneille and one of the great successes of his pictorial poetry. Too bad that he ends it with a nose-bleed instead of letting Attila be killed by Ildione as in the pages of the historian Ammianus Marcellinus [*sic*]! But all the rest of it is happily conceived, and the scenes of comedy between Attila and the two women whom he thinks of marrying are disconcertingly ingenious . . . Without equalling *Othon* or *Sertorius,* it retains sufficient power, it mingles different manners with sufficient deftness, to seem to us worthy of being liked." [7]

Léon Lemonnier says of *Attila:* "This is, most certainly, one of the best fashioned of the tragedies of Corneille." [8] And Georges Couton declares: "No work of Corneille gives, perhaps, to the same degree the impression of power" as *Attila,* in which, he says, "*La tragédie matrimoniale* . . . mounts to a

[4] Pp. 331-332.

[5] P. 224.

[6] *Esquisse d'une Historie de la Tragédie française*, p. 99.

[7] Pp. 210-212.

[8] *Corneille*, Tallandier, Paris, 1945, p. 245.

crescendo of terror." He says, further, that "there is in *Attila* a study of the forces which tore at and dismembered the Roman Empire, together with an anticipation of the new political order which was to be born—and all this is not lacking in grandeur or incisiveness. . . . In so far as history tends to show what is unique in a period, *Attila* is the most thoroughly historical of all these plays"—that is, of all the dramas which Corneille wrote in the latter part of his career, beginning with *Œdipe* and ending with *Suréna*.⁹

In my own opinion, it is the best of the plays contained in this volume. True, its action flags a little from the latter part of Act I to the latter part of Act II, but the last scene of Act II is genuinely moving, and in the subsequent acts there is real and steadily mounting tension. There is also, throughout this drama, more warmth of emotion and a greater amount of violent passion than in any other tragedy written by Corneille after his youthful prime. Its protagonist, Attila, is the sole really gigantic figure that he ever drew, of far larger mould than any character in his most famous plays; the terror and the menace of him hang constantly over all; and the action works up to a fine climax when, dilating to demonic proportions, he glories in being "the scourge of God" and declares that he will give the two princesses to whatever two base-born fellows will kill Ardaric and Valamir for him. Explanations can, I believe, in large part remove or lessen the chief obstacles which *Attila* presents to a high appraisal of it.

The principal defect which is found in it is its portrayal of Attila's infatuation for Ildione, which is represented as too nearly the same sort of courtly love that Corneille's lovers feel in all his plays, and is expressed in too nearly the same gallant language as theirs. His Attila is in every other respect so vigorously drawn that he seems to us indeed the savage Mongolian conqueror, who would be ignorant of any love but sheer animalism—and therefore his passion for the Frankish princess appears wholly out of character, alike in its nature and in its expression. Yet even the grimmest lines of his portrait could equally well belong to a very different kind of man, not incapable of some refinements of speech and

⁹ Pp. 130, 136, 273.

feeling: one of the ruffianly, scheming despots or condottieri of the Renaissance, conscienceless and grandiosely ambitious, a Sforza or a Borgia, or even some wolfish, sardonic great French lord of the author's own lifetime. In view of the meager historical imagination then possessed by anyone, it is entirely probable that this was as near as Corneille came to divining what the real Attila, so remote from him in time and of so unfamiliar a race, was like. Corneille is indeed to some extent at fault in having drawn, consequently, a figure whom people living in any period with more accurate historical conceptions cannot identify in their minds with the famous king of the Huns, but we too are at fault if we think that this figure which he drew is not self-consistent or is like no men that ever lived or is without dramatic value.[10]

An undeniable defect in this play is, as Brasillach said, its denouement. This, albeit in accord with history and not without dramatic foreshadowing in the play itself, is quite out of keeping with tragic dignity in spite of Corneille's best efforts to veil the fact of the mortal "nose-bleed" with vague and grandiloquent descriptions. A variant tradition offered him the obviously right alternative, that Ildione should wed Attila and then seize the first chance to kill him as she had intended to do; but by thus playing Judith to his Holophernes she would no doubt have forfeited to some extent the sympathy of seventeenth-century audiences, in whose opinion her marriage vows, once taken, should have protected her husband against her, regardless of the circumstances.

The scruples which beset her, when the time for the deed she had planned drew near, seem absurd to us today in view of the situation; but the fact is that the dramatist displayed no small daring in representing her as continuing to cherish her purpose despite these scruples, as she evidently does when she persuades Attila to postpone his vengeance till the morrow. To let her carry out that purpose was more than could be expected of Corneille in the case of one of his most attractive heroines, which Ildione is.

Her reproof of Ardaric for asking her to use a word so

---

[10] In actual presentation on the stage a good deal of the difficulty could be overcome by making this "Attila" quite different in garb and appearance from any mental picture that we may have of the Attila of history.

"bold" as "love" in regard to her feelings toward him, has often been judged a ridiculous manifestation of fantastic delicacy, but only because it has not been understood. In the first place, she considered herself plighted to Attila, and betrothal was a far more solemn and binding thing in seventeenth-century France than now. More important still, in the France of that century an avowal of love evidently carried with it a conscious envisagement of—and was thought of as expressing a desire for—the physical consummation of love, as it does not carry now in even a remotely comparable degree. Not otherwise can the reluctance which the heroines of the dramas of those days exhibit about admitting their love be explained—or the "hate" which they feel for the suitor whose love they do not reciprocate. Ildione does confess her love for Ardaric when she sees that complete frankness between them is needed. That she does not do so as unhesitatingly as Honoria avows hers to Valamir shows a difference between them which Corneille wished to emphasize.

CHARACTERS IN THE PLAY

ATTILA, *King of the Huns.*
ARDARIC, *King of the Gepidae.*
VALAMIR, *King of the Ostrogoths.*
HONORIA, *sister of the Roman emperor Valentinian.*
ILDIONE, *sister of Meroveus, king of the Franks.*
OCTAR, *captain of Attila's guards.*
FLAVIA, *lady-in-waiting of Honoria.*
Guards.

*The scene is laid in the camp of Attila, in Noricum. It repre-
sents an open space among the tents.*

The names "Attila," "Ardaric," "Valamir," "Octar," and
"Flavia" are accented on the first syllable, "Honoria" on the
second, "Ildione" on the third. In the translation, "Ildione"
is made a classical name, with the final "e" a separate syllable;
the native form of this name is probably "Hildegonde," in
which also is the final "e" a syllable.

Attila

A C T   I

ATTILA, OCTAR, *and guards are discovered.*

ATTILA. Have they not come yet, these two kings of ours?
　　　Let someone tell them that they are too slow
　　　And Attila is tired of waiting for them;—
　　　That when I summon them, they should hasten to me.
OCTAR. But why, my lord, needest thou consult with them?
　　　Why call them to decide about thy marriage—
　　　Them who have here but the vain name of monarch,
　　　And whom thou leavest still among the living
　　　Only that thou mayst have two kings as followers
　　　Where'er thou goest?
ATTILA. 　　　　　　I can decide alone
　　　As to this matter, and I have not called them,
　　　Octar, with hopes that they can throw new light
　　　Upon it. I expect to see, ere *they* do,
　　　Whatever they point out to me, and tell
　　　Myself beforehand all that they can tell me.
　　　But whichsoe'er of the two princesses
　　　I choose, the honor done her is an insult
　　　To the other one and to that other's brother;
　　　And 'tis my wish to draw the deadliest blows
　　　Of their just anger on the head of him
　　　Whose counsel I accept, to have an excuse
　　　For failing in appreciation, and be
　　　Able, if necessary, to provide
　　　A victim for that anger. This it is
　　　Which now compels me to consult these kings
　　　And let them make this great and perilous choice.
　　　　After all, I would love to have a pretext
　　　To encompass their destruction, and I promptly
　　　Would use any occasion offered for it.
　　　Their rank grates on me, and I know not wherefore
　　　A king I rule dares call himself a king.
　　　So proud a title smacks of independence,
　　　Which even the least obedience mars and ends;
　　　And I am weary of seeing them both assume

The right, by virtue of the royal circlet,
To treat me as an equal.

OCTAR.   But, my lord,
Can it be that for both those princesses
Thou hast the same eyes, the same inclinations,—
That well-matched merit in them makes it not hard
For thee to bend thy undecided soul
To follow the decisions formed by others?
Or if it hath towards one of them some leaning
Unlike the course which thy two kings advise,
Wouldst thou desire to sacrifice thy dearest
Wish, to have ready an excuse to give
To that just anger of which thou hast spoken?
And howsoever just, is it so very
Formidable that great Attila
Should stoop to be constrained because of it?

ATTILA.   No; but the lofty ardor to o'er-run
So many realms requireth one to fight
Even more with his head than with his arm,
Disrupt the accord between his enemies,
Among them spread confusion and distrust,
And hazard naught where every risk is not
Eliminated as far as possible.
We were as strong as now we are when I
Invaded Gaul with half a million men.
If thou recallest, I then sought in vain
To separate the Visigoths and the Romans.
My failure to do this was my undoing:
Far from dividing them, I made their union
Closer. The terror of my name gave to them
New allies—Franks, Burgundians, and Alans;
And, not being able to sow dissension 'twixt them,
I found myself, with all my army, routed.
I have contrived to rally it; I seek vengeance,
But seek to have this in a way less dangerous.
    I offered peace unto the two most warlike
Of the five nations that were victors o'er me,
Treating with each of them, and since they both
Were ready to be bound to me by ties
Of marriage as I proposed, one of the two

Princesses whom they then sent in good faith
Will be my wife, and the other one my hostage.
If I offend one of two kings thus, he
Will feel fear for his sister in my hands;
Hence will I hold them both constrained—the one
By our alliance, and by fear the other;
Or if the one displeased persists in anger,
The fortunate one will fight in my behalf,
So that our conquerors' thrones, each by the other
Hurled down, will lie in wreckage at my feet.

    As for love, know my chief concern is not . . .
But Ardaric nears, and also Valamir.

                    (*Enter* ARDARIC *and* VALAMIR.)

    Kings, friends of Attila, my power's chief stay,
Who range so many lands beneath my sway,
And whose advice and valiant hearts and hands
Make me the terror of all the human race,
You see here in my camp the striking proofs
Two sovereigns give us of their dread of me.
In Gaul Meroveus and in Rome the Emperor
Have thought to shun mine anger by my marriage.
The peace negotiated with both at once
Was at this price agreed upon with each,
And almost on my envoys' heels their envoys
Have brought me the two princesses, their sisters.
The choice of one of these embarrasses me,
And now the time has come for it. Since they
Arrived, I have deferred it; it must be made,
And whichsoe'er I choose, I must offend
An emperor or the greatest of the kings.

    I said "the greatest," not that his victory yet
Hath placed Meroveus on that pinnacle
Of glory, but unless the prophecy
Of our diviners be quite false, his greatness
Is to attain the highest eminence,
And the firm-rooted power of his successors
Will through the centuries grow so formidable
That someday all the world will be ruled by them
Or at least tremble at the name of France.

    Ye, then, who know of just how much assistance

This or that ruler would be to our vast projects,
Lend light to me to see today from which
These would gain more support, and from which less,—
In pride of marriage ties, which of the twain
Would best avenge for me Chalons' dire plain,
And which of them, if cheated of his hopes,
Should more be feared by one who seeks world-empire.

ARDARIC. When heaven hath made thy power so great, 'twere useless
For us to weigh their capabilities.
All difference, more or less, which can be seen
In them doth not deserve thy least concern.
The treaties are enough to show they both
Fear thee and dare no more do aught against thee.
Thus, without losing time by being disturbed,
Thou needest but to consult thine eyes alone, sir.
Let thy choice be, on their report, for her
(As most deserving it) towards whom love inclines thee;
Believe what, with their aid, thy heart decideth;
And let which ruler wishes then take umbrage.

ATTILA. Love is with Attila not a thing to heed.
One who would rouse it in me would offend me,
And I would quite deliberately wed elsewhere
For fear that one would thus have too much power
O'er me. A wife beloved assumes a sway
Which ne'er a husband dares—or can—gainsay.
The common run of kings enjoy their chains,
Not those who make the world quake at their names.
Let all find bliss in thralldom to fair eyes;
For my part, I see in them only tyrants
Whose might I will defy; and by whatever
Charms they may captivate a heart, mine own
In spite of them seeks nothing but my greatness.
   (*To* VALAMIR) Speak only, then, of which choice would
      most aid me,
Which wrath is easier to o'ercome, which harder;
And do not tell me that between the two
Choices, like him thou seest little difference.
In an affair of State, were there one atom's,
A kingdom sometimes hangs thereon. The veriest
Scruple is not a thing to disregard,

And even the least advantage should decide us.

VALAMIR. Sire, in the turn which matters take, no great
Amount of talk is necessary here.
Only one's eyes are needed: to learn all,
To decide all, one need but open them.

    A mighty destiny begins, a mighty
Destiny ends; the Empire is about
To fall, and France now rises. She, in growing
Strong, can be unto thee a strong support,
The Empire in collapsing bury thee
Beneath its ruins. Thy soothsayers have told thee
Of this; seek not to stay the course of Fate,
Thou, who hast ne'er doubted their prophecies.

    To lend aid to a tottering, crumbling realm
Is but to see oneself crushed in its downfall.
Aid France, then; let Rome perish. To the great
Mandates of heaven add those of a great king;
Support these prophets of so fair a future,
Speed the event, and hasten what is fated.

ARDARIC. Yes, in thy choice of this great marriage, heaven
Hath given destiny into thy hands.
But if 'tis glorious, sire, to speed its course,
'Tis still more glorious to reverse that course,
So France, despite unfailing oracles,
May only with slow steps go towards her greatness,
And so the Empire, doomed by the new turn
Of Fate, may fall only upon thy tomb.
Can any glory equal thy deferring
That which these two States can expect from heaven
And showing thyself unto the wisest prophets
As master of events and destiny?
I will say more to thee. All they foretold thee,
They read most plainly written in the skies;
But can they assure thee that some jealous star
Hath not deferred it more than a whole century?
Such notable reversals wrought by Fortune
Are rarely but the work of a few years,
And what was prophesied thee of these realms
May be a future that affects not thee.
Consider, though, what still the Empire is.

It totters, it is crumbling, and all rend it;
From its own breast spring tyrants, but e'en yet
'Tis mightier than all its conquerors.
The slightest recollection of Chalons
Offers to thee proofs too well known of this.
Sangibar, Thierry, Gondebaud, and Meroveus
Would all have perished there but for Aëtius.
The Romans won the day in that great battle;
Bind them to thee by a most fitting marriage.
Since thou already canst without them do
Almost anything, there is naught which thou
Canst not do with their aid. When they have made thee
Master of these new kings, thou canst decide
At leisure just of whom thou'dst fain be master
And calculate in thine own heart if thou
Wilt let them be thine equals still.

VALAMIR.   The Empire
Is yet a power to reckon with, I grant thee;
But these are not the days of Theodosius,
And as he does not live in his descendants,
Rome is a power, the Emperor is naught.
His sons have sat on the two Roman thrones
As mere imposing effigies, mere shadows.
These sham but idiotically proud sovereigns,
Who dared not call on Romans to defend them,
Borrowed, that they might reign, strange helpers' aid
From nations looked upon as barbarous;
And Stilicho in the West, and in the East
Gainas, left but the name to these two monarchs—
A Goth in the one empire, in the other
A Vandal, ruling with like arrogance.
As everywhere this state of things aroused
Anger, on every side others seized power.
The second Theodosius did no better:
His sister was his guardian still when he
Was fifty years old, and throughout his reign
She was the soul of that great realm, and is
The moving spirit of it, even yet.
    Valentinian, while his mother lived,
Seemed to be what a sovereign ought to be,—

Appeared to rule,—but now 'tis clear that he
Ruled through his mother or she ruled for him;
And since her death he has too plainly shown
That if he reigns, Aëtius is his master,
So 'tis Aëtius' sister thou shouldst wed
If thou desirest to be allied with Rome.
This prince is weak, effeminate, stupid, envious,
Elated by good fortune, when the issue
Is dubious frightened, seeking pleasure only,
Leaving the power to whoe'er can seize it.
    The great Meroveus, unlike him, is
A noble king, athirst for glory, eager
To win men's admiration, who allows
None of his subjects to have any function
Or power they should not have. He well knows how
To rule and conquer, and if he already
Hath since his victory passed the Seine and Loire,
Not long will either the Garonne or Arar
Stay him if thou art willing to unite
Thy warriors with his. Then that same field
Which saw thy shame will see thy vengeance, greater
And swifter; and as thy reward for having
Contrived to take revenge, thou shalt have Gaul
To share with him, and thou canst demonstrate
Unto all Italy that when wisdom maketh
Alliance with valor there is naught it cannot
Do, and that now the time hath come when thou
Shalt rule alike the Tiber and the Po.

ARDARIC.   Then take the right to do so by espousing
A princess who will bring it as a dowry
To satisfy thy soul's imperious longings,
And thus shalt thou take what is hers instead
Of seizing realms to which thou hast no claims.
Her mother shared the power to such extent
That she could give Constantius a part
In governing the Empire, and if thou
Findest attractions in such sovereignty,
The daughter can confer it on her husband.
    Go with armed force to claim the portion of it
Which, when he died, her father left to her

To give; and with such warrant thou wilt see
Not a few Romans forsake Rome for thee.
Aëtius hath less power than men suppose.
Many around him envy him his greatness,
And thou wilt have for thee all who at heart
Dislike the Prince or weary of his mentor.
The Empire in its ruins is still fair.
If it lacks heroes, it hath high-souled women.
It offers one of them to thee, and with her
Part of its spoils. Couldst thou refuse so much?
Naught but herself doth Ildione bring thee.
Her dowry can include no claims to kingship;
The Franks allow none such through womankind.
But those Honoria hath are all-embracing;
Make them thine own, my lord; make surely thine
The throne of Theodosius the Great.
The brother hath no power; Rome loves his sister
And hates Aëtius. Thou canst do thy will.

ATTILA.   Is this the way to rid my soul of care—
Plunge it yet deeper in uncertainty?
And do ye champion, to dispel my doubts,
Deliberately these opposite opinions?
Each clings to his with equal obstinacy.
The more ye talk, the less can I decide;
And when I seek your aid, that I may waver
No more, ye both try to confuse me worse.
I do not ask of you such tortuous reasonings;
I need assurance, and not new misgivings;
When I entrust to you a fate like mine,
Ye wrong me, both, when ye reach no conclusions.

VALAMIR.   Sire, each of us says to thee what he thinks.
Each shows thee how important this choice is;
But neither jealously would have his counsel
Followed. Take his or mine; we are not envious.
Both spring from naught but loyal friendship in us,
Whose fervent zeal . . .

ATTILA.   Then make this zeal agree
And force me not to see in your dispute
More than I wish to see, and . . . I shall say
Naught further. Only tell me what impels you

To espouse the cause of this and of that princess.
By presents have their brothers made you each
A partisan of her whose side he takes?
Or is it fondness for the one, and hatred
Felt towards the other, that shapes both his advice
And thine? What aim to please me or to serve
Your fortunes . . . nay, but I again would probe
Nothing; and I believe that in my presence
None would have such audacity. Therefore,
If for your lives ye care aught, do yourselves
A kindness now. Agree, contend no further,
Or get from one of those two a refusal
To wed me, that we may because of it
Impute the breach of troth to her aversion.
Employ thus, both of you, that zeal and ardor
Which ye both say ye feel to serve my greatness.
As to this, I will credit what is done
To please me, and till then hold back mine anger.

> (*Exeunt* ATTILA, OCTAR, *and guards.*)

ARDARIC.   Shall we be always its unhappy targets,
And always see him treat us as his subjects?
VALAMIR.   To such humiliations let us shut
Our eyes, sir. Heaven someday must efface
All memories of it. So have my diviners
Told me; and if 'tis needful that I say so,
That day, perchance, is not far off. They tell me
They have a sure presage that it is not.
I will say more to thee: they tell me, further,
That a Theodoric, to be my descendant,
Will rule in Rome and make himself its king.
That is what forces me to speak in favor
Of France, advising Attila to choose
Alliance with her and marry Ildione,
That he may by this choice leave me Honoria
To wed, with all her rights.

> Oppose no longer

Greatness for Ildione. Let her mount
Attila's throne for my sake, and if I
Can ever do as much for thee . . .
ARDARIC.   Thou canst,

Sir, at this very moment. Let me briefly
Explain myself, thus following thy example.
Thou lovest, but thy love is policy,
And—since I owe thee frankness in my turn—
I have a real love for the other princess.
That is what forces me to speak in favor
Of the Roman Empire, that there may be left me
Her whom I long for. A firm friendship binds us,
But our desires are incompatible.
Let us see who must win, and if my heart
Must sacrifice its love to thy ambition,
Or whether 'tis not better thy ambition
Should sacrifice itself to my great love.

VALAMIR. 'Twould be a cruel sacrifice for me.

ARDARIC. And the alternative to me were torture.
Art thou loved?

VALAMIR. I at least have reason to hope so.
And thou, sir?

ARDARIC. I at least am listened to.

VALAMIR. What a sad blessing is a mutual love
When that one whom we love must wed another!

ARDARIC. The tyrant will, moreover, deem a crime
Thy love, which reasons of State alone have fostered.
We know too well how far his wrath will go,
Which hath not spared the blood of even his brother;
And since that time how many kings allied
With him he sacrificed to his savage pride!

VALAMIR. The followers of these illustrious victims
Follow, in him, one for his crimes unpunished;
And the dread license which he allows his soldiers
Wins him so many hearts, so many arms,
That our own subjects, leaving our domains,
Despite us serve him rather than their sovereigns.

ARDARIC. He talks as if already he suspects us,
And that suspicion we must needs allay.
Let us dispose my princess to reject him
As he desires.

VALAMIR. To make mine do so, will
Require small skill.

ARDARIC. If thou persuadest her

What woe is mine!

VALAMIR.   And if thou art successful,
Can I still hope for aught?

ARDARIC..   Ah, why can we
Not both be happy!

VALAMIR.   Why is my good fortune
Compatible with thine no more!

ARDARIC.   Come, let us
Each make an effort in his own behalf.

VALAMIR.   Come, let us leave to Fate the final outcome.

                                       (*Exeunt.*)

A C T   I I

HONORIA *and* FLAVIA *are discovered.*

FLAVIA.   I shall deny it not: yes, madam, Octar
Loves me. All I have told thee, I have learned
From him. Those two are kings, but in name only.
For them, this empty title carries with it
Scarce anything it should; and every day
The haughty Attila shows them that if he
Is not their king, he is at least their master,
And they are treated as his friends here only
In so far as they are subservient to him.
Both have great qualities and are high of heart,
But both of them are really hostages,
While their men, nowhere near them in the camp,
Are marshaled 'neath his sway like those whom he
Hath made his own; and, were their troops not ready
To follow him, these kings, kings though they are,
Would answer for it to him with their heads.

   His elder brother, Bleda, juster-natured,
Despite him treated them with complete equality.
He could not bear this, and in jealous hate,
To have no equal, took his brother's life;
And ever since that prince's blood was shed,
Every day blood gathers in his head
To punish fratricide and, trickling thence,
Pays for his brother's a strange recompense.
According as his wrath is great or little,

This daily punishment is worse or milder,
A fuller or more meager vein is opened,
And every fit of anger brings therewith
Its penalty.

HONORIA.　　　　What doth it serve me, then,
That I am loved? Why should I tolerate
A love which cannot take due vengeance for me?
Attila insolently brings to me here
A rival, and by hesitating 'twixt us,
Makes her my equal; and if, to punish him,
I take for husband a great king, I take
Only a great name, powerless to aid me.
Judge of how bitter this is for a princess
Who loathes alike presumptuousness and weakness,
And how I needs must look upon a lover
Who has for me, when outraged, only pity,—
Who can but love me, and whose heart's devotion
Can lend no arm to me to right such wrongs.

　　　Attila sent to Rome to offer marriage
To me, but in his camp cannot decide
Now between me and Ildione. Oh,
Flavia, alas, if such a hesitation
Insults me, what would an unworthy choice
By him in these great matters do, perforce!
And is this exhibition of a helpless
Grief not the last extreme of wretchedness!

FLAVIA.　Forestall him, madam. Show him to his shame
How little thou esteemest such arrogance.

HONORIA.　'Tis easy to defy him; words are soon said;
But how escape a tyrant whom they anger?
Shall I return to Rome, where I have left
My brother filled with hate and rage against me?
Save for the terror of a name so dread,
Never would he have let me go from durance—
Me, who for dowry claim half of his empire . . .

FLAVIA.　'Twould be to fly from one ill to a worse one.
Let no blind passioning thus work thee harm.
Thou canst in other ways flout Attila.
Wed Valamir.

HONORIA.　　　　Is this a way to flout him—

Marry a king of whom he makes a slave?
FLAVIA. Thou lovest Valamir.
HONORIA.   If I do love him,
    I do not want a king who is compelled
    To yield obedience; and if what thou tellest me
    Be true, however high my rank, to wed him
    Might be his doom and mine. But would I wish
    Attila, loving someone else, to be
    Insulted thus, here in his Court? 'Twould mean
    That I would be in Ildione's train,
    Where I would find myself reduced to shameful
    Subservience, and the blood of Roman Caesars,
    Which men have always worshipped, would do homage
    Unto the blood of kings of a day's standing!
    But tell me: doth his heart incline towards her?
    What sayeth Octar?
FLAVIA.   That he deems her fair,
    Talks of her gladly, avoids talking with her.
HONORIA. He talks with me, and, to be wholly frank,
    His words evince respect for me, esteem,
    And even some love, without the word being used.
FLAVIA. That seems to be a little more than he
    Feels for her.
HONORIA.   And perhaps it is much less.
FLAVIA. What! her whom he hath taken pains to shun?
HONORIA. Maybe he does so but from fear of losing
    His heart to her, and if he shuns not me
    That is because he can defend it better
    'Gainst me. Yes, he must fear her, and his pride
    Strives to retain some freedom in his choice.
FLAVIA. But which is it thy wish that he should choose?
HONORIA. My heart in either case will ache the same;
    Thus love, thus fair fame, have their charms for me.
    I shall die if he chooses me—or if
    He does not, and . . . But here is Valamir,
    And at the sight of him my pride doth waver,
    My love grows proud. Flavia, he hath more power
    Than I like o'er my heart. He would have all
    My wishes if I listened to him long.
    Tell him . . . But I must needs control my feelings.

3 3 1

(Enter VALAMIR.*)*

    Sir, dost thou know how I would fain be loved?
'Tis at my feet thou layest thy heart; dost know
What price I put upon myself? I speak
Frankly, and do not care to hide it from thee
That thy attentions could be pleasing to me,
Were it enough that thou shouldst be attractive.
But though they pleased me even a hundred times
Better yet, something more would still be needed
For thee to win me.
                Attila's troth is plighted
To me. I have his word for guarantee.
The princess of the Franks hath the same claims
Upon him, and he seems to hesitate
About his choice between us; but since I
Am who I am, I would do ill to doubt
What it will be. But he who plights his troth
Thus with two women doth insult them both.
I have a lofty heart; search thou thine own.
I have been wronged. Canst thou avenge me for it,—
Punish him for it?

VALAMIR.   Is it by blood alone
That I may win thy hand? And must my love
Meet thy requirements of it by my murdering
The greatest king on earth—a king whom thou
Hast wished to be thy husband? Can I not
Be worthy of thee save by crime?

HONORIA.   Nay, I
Say not to thee that 'tis by killing him
That thou shouldst win my love and pay me for it.
The kindly manner in which now he treats thee
Makes him deserve thy tender feelings for him.
Besides, thou shouldst not only love but fear him.
Yet it is Attila whom I must show
Disdain for. Couldst thou pluck me from his grasp,—
Defy with me the proudest of mankind?

VALAMIR.   That is not needful, madam. He respects thee;
And though thou mayst misdoubt his pride, I know
At thy least coldness, least sign of disrelish
For him, he will bestow thy hand on me.

HONORIA.　Have I such slight regard, then, for the blood
　　　　　Of Theodosius as to let a tyrant
　　　　　Dispose of it in me, and let one plighted
　　　　　Himself to me select a husband for me
　　　　　And give me to a king, as to his favorite?
　　　　　If thou at all dost love me, thou shouldst deem
　　　　　Naught means as much to me as my fair fame.
　　　　　Reign as doth Attila; I prefer thee to him;
　　　　　But never will I wed with one who dares not
　　　　　Repudiate his support,—who would abase me
　　　　　Thus to the station of his subjects. I
　　　　　Must have a king. Ask thyself, art thou one?
　　　　　And know that though thou standest first in my heart,
　　　　　I can love only a free, sovereign prince.
　　　　　Think by what marks, my lord, kings are distinguished.
　　　　　Breathe not a vow to me unless thou hast them,
　　　　　And be content that I vouchsafe to assure thee
　　　　　My heart prefers thee to all other monarchs.

(Exit HONORIA.*)*

VALAMIR.　What haughty pride, Flavia! What can a king
　　　　　Expect, whose every hope . . .

FLAVIA.　　　　　　　　　　　　　Let her alone, sir.
　　　　　Love will be master, and the very pride
　　　　　Which now disputes with thee dominion o'er her,
　　　　　Together with her hate's aid, will soon make thee
　　　　　Triumphant over her high Roman heart.
　　　　　The same pride which, despite her love, rejects thee
　　　　　Makes her hate Attila for promising
　　　　　Marriage with two princesses—not that this pride
　　　　　Within her would not be indeed too jealous
　　　　　To endure to see him wed with Ildione.
　　　　　Induce him to send *her* home to her brother—
　　　　　Back to the Franks—and thou wilt see that heart
　　　　　Suddenly bare itself completely, give
　　　　　Itself to him it loves, defying him
　　　　　Who angered it, and award the victory
　　　　　Where it hath been deserved. Be not disturbed
　　　　　By any trivial outburst of her feelings.
　　　　　Good fortune comes to us sometimes despite us.
　　　　　Love makes us happy when we least expect it.

I have said naught to thee without sound reasons.
Ardaric is bringing thee more pleasant converse.
Farewell. Time, like her heart, is on thy side.

Enter ARDARIC. *Exit* FLAVIA.

ARDARIC. What hath thy princess granted to thee?
VALAMIR.   Much
And nothing. She revealed some fondness for me
But knows so well how great a prize she is
That if the Frankish princess hath a heart
As proud and sets as high a price upon it,
Thou long wilt offer her thy crown in vain.
She hates my rival—this I cannot doubt;
Her heart is mine, I have good grounds for boasting;
I know that she prefers me to all others;
Yet what I have a right to hope, I know not.
    Go, see thy Ildione, sir; and mayst thou
Find there more light to read her heart, a soul
Better inclined to satisfy thy wishes,
A spirit more pliable. Octar comes from her tent.
Farewell.   (*Exit* VALAMIR. *Enter* OCTAR.)
ARDARIC (*to* OCTAR). Might I, in my turn, see the Princess?
OCTAR. No, unless thou wouldst wait till she comes back.
But, sire, to judge by what her people said,
Thou needest to wait for her only a moment.
ARDARIC. In the meantime, tell me: thou wert taken prisoner
In the last battle by the King of the Franks,
Her brother?
OCTAR.   Our defeat, sire, at Chalons
Gave me no great share of our common misfortunes.
Although I was this noble monarch's prisoner,
I fared not badly at his Court. Not irksome
Was my captivity, and I had always
Such kindness at the hands there of the Princess
That on returning here I felt I owed her
The greatest reverence possible in subjects.
ARDARIC. How happy is a king when heaven gives him
The hand of one so beautiful and wondrous!
OCTAR. Yet well thou knowest Attila is not happy.
He is embarrassed by too much good fortune.

ARDARIC.   Since he has eyes, he surely must choose her.
But thou hast highly praised her brother also.
Be frank with me: hath he the qualities
To make him thus admired by everyone?
Is it the truth I hear men say, or is it
Without good reason that all the world admires him?
OCTAR.   My lord, I know not what thou hast been told,
But what I saw is quite enough to make him
Admired. I saw him in both peace and war
Have at all times the bearing of earth's master.
I more than once have beheld warlike peoples
Disarm his wrath by their submission to him.
Everything this heroic king enjoyed
Was great and noble, and his royal care
Provided for his subjects in the midst
Of peace a school of war. Through such diversions
His lofty, restless soul made preparation
For the accomplishment of his wise plans;
And we should be right glad, if I may say so,
That they are not directed against us.
I have beheld him, covered with dust and smoke,
Set all his troops a glorious example,
Spread terror everywhere by the risks he courted,
Level strong walls as by a single glance,
And o'er the bowed pride of the haughtiest heads
Pursue the swift course of his many conquests.
Bid me not to describe so great a sovereign;
Too much, for tongues like mine, is what I saw.
But I cannot restrain myself from telling thee
How wonderful is the little prince, his son.

He shows a heart so high in his child's breast
That, though but five years old, he is a warrior
Already. Time is needed by his body
To grow; he has a manly soul e'en now.
He at the head of a whole troop of horsemen
Will put himself and lead them, sword in hand.
They glow with pride to go 'neath his command.
All of his father's majesty and all
His mother's grace and charm are in his face,
Whose sweet high-spiritedness reveals them all.

The love and reverence he, though young, deserves . . .
But here the Princess is, my lord. I leave thee.

Enter ILDIONE. *Exit* OCTAR.

ILDIONE. (*to* ARDARIC). Attila hath consulted thee. Dost thou, sir,
 Know what he finally will do with us?

ARDARIC. What wilt thou do, thyself, about my heart?
 Attila soon will choose. Thou must speak out.
 Should he choose thee, what wilt thou do for me?

ILDIONE. All that one can whose hand is plighted elsewhere.
 My heart prefers thee; and if I do not
 Love thee, at least I pity thee as I do
 Myself. I have the same woes, the same griefs,
 But I shall not forget my obligations.

ARDARIC. Thou art perhaps about to be released
 From them. If thou hast any heart at all,
 Thou canst accept the freedom thus allowed thee.

ILDIONE. I have a heart as resolute as any's
 To conquer my own feelings if I need to;
 But never shall I have one that will conquer
 My sense of duty.

ARDARIC.   One who plights his troth
 So with two women releases both from theirs.

ILDIONE. Thus I should think, like thee; and if I were not
 She who I am, sir, I would exercise
 On this account the right to end my sorrows.
 But high birth, which with its imperious claims
 Makes me a slave where others would be free
 To do aught, holds me powerless; and I
 Must, as a victim of State policy,
 Wait without shrinking, to be sacrificed.

ARDARIC. Must wait till Attila, whom thou hatest, chooses
 To sacrifice thee to a Roman woman's
 Pride?

ILDIONE.   Oh, how happy I would feel, to be
 Thus sacrificed! how I shall suffer if he
 Does not so choose!

ARDARIC.   How splendid it would be
 If thou thyself shouldst make that sacrifice
 And spare the shame of it unto thy crown!

3 3 6

I mean that of the Franks, if thou, not waiting . . .

ILDIONE. 'Tis for my brother to avenge and punish,
Nowise for me to break thus an alliance
By which he hath just joined the Huns with France,
Nor turn myself, from being the guarantee
Of peace, into a torch that kindles war
Which ne'er shall end. 'Tis Attila who must choose;
And may Honoria be the one more valued,
Or I the one less liked! May he decide
To break his troth with me! To pray thus, is
All I can do for thee and for myself.
If thou'dst have my own wishes, I am not
Niggardly with them; if thou'dst have my own
Regrets, my heart will be prepared to give them.
'Twould fain . . .

ARDARIC.   What good are wishes, which but leave
Both of us vain regrets? Canst thou expect
Attila not to choose thee?

ILDIONE.   Rome is still
Powerful, and it may be that he fears her.

ARDARIC. Unless Rome now be aided by thy coldness,
Thy beauty will prevail o'er all her grandeur.
I judge thus from myself; naught hath such power
Over me that thine eyes could not o'ercome it.
Arm them with cruelty, and, for pity's sake,
Divest them, madam, of half their fatal charm.
It still would be too great; however veiled
Their brightness, I can cherish no illusions.
Then do more: go so far as to reject him,
Or realize that Ardaric hopes no longer,
That he no more shall live, and that thy hands
Will, by this marriage, have broken his life's thread.

ILDIONE. Have I in such unhappiness so little
Part that, to see it, I require thy plainings?
Wouldst force me to the shame of shedding tears?

ARDARIC. If thou begrudgest me in my woe that sight,
Show to my anxious heart some other kindness,
And at least tell me, madam, that thou lovest me.

ILDIONE. Not to believe it unless *I* use words
So bold is for a noble heart a little

Ungenerous. Whatever shafts have pierced
My bosom in regard to thee, those words
Till now have not escaped my lips. But is
To hate thy rival, to endure my being
Loved by thee, to be filled with dread like thee
About this choice, to give thy hopes when wavering
All my desires, to give them if defeated
All my regrets—is this not all too plainly
To say what it becomes me not to say?

ARDARIC. But thou wilt marry Attila.

ILDIONE.   I shall do so
With many sighs; my heart . . .

ARDARIC.   What does thy heart
Do but deceive me, if it, even in daring
To do naught, is afraid it dares too much?
Nay, if thou hadst one, thou'dst take now that freedom
Which will perhaps be given thee from thy troth-plight.
I will not unsay what I said: my just grief
Cannot too often say thou hast no heart.

ILDIONE. I must explain, then, everything to thee.
Listen, and above all, sir, make no answer.
    I love thee. It is hard for me to speak
Those words; but since it matters so much to thee,
I force myself to. Yet I say again
That if thy Attila honors me with his choice,
I shall accept him seemingly as gladly
As if I gained what most my heart desired.
Not that I do not look upon his love
As the worst torture and the utmost outrage,
Nor that the cruel effort I must make
Does not increase my hatred and resentment;
But duty bids me show him such regard
That he cannot suspect the least repugnance.
    I then shall marry him and gain the glory
Of having done the thing I ought to do.
I share, like others, in the general hate
Which this proud tyrant loves to breed in all,
And hate him even more, because he seeks
To enslave my people, and because in spite
Of treaties, howsoever sacred, he

Who hath already murdered his own brother
Would be, if he someday had naught to dread,
Unlikely to show mercy unto mine.
Then if his choice tears me from him I love,
Gives me to him who fills my soul with horror,
Binds me to him who would lay waste all lands,
What woes, what interests have I to avenge!
My love, my hatred, and the common cause
Cry out for vengeance—all three—on one head;
And as his life will then be in my hands,
He has no less grounds to fear me than I have
To pity thee. Not a few other tyrants
Have by their wives been slain. It is not hard
For one high-souled to yearn to have that honor,
And it is glorious that the selfsame blow
Which breaks my chains avenges the whole world.
 That is what I am like; those are my thoughts;
That is what love prepares for him who wrongs it.
Be just to me, sir; and consider well
If thou must still say that I have no heart.

          (*Exit* ILDIONE.)

ARDARIC (*gazing after her*). May heaven preserve thee from the cruel
    test
  To which a heart so great would put a soul
  So fair! May Attila be kind enough
  To let me have thee by his gift, not thine.

A C T   I I I

ATTILA *and* OCTAR *are discovered*.

ATTILA. Octar, hast thou seen to it that my guard
    Is doubled?
OCTAR.   Yes, sire, and they all already
    Look at each other and ask each other wherefore
    These orders which I carried out . . .
ATTILA.   Does he
    Who hath two rivals, lack foes?
OCTAR.   But, my lord,
    As yet thou knowest not that thou hast any.
ATTILA. And to discover what indeed I know not,

I shield myself well from the foulest deeds
Despairful love inspires in men like them;
And, leaving to their bitterness no weapons
But helpless rage and ineffectual hate,
I make on this great day my triumph certain
O'er their resentment even as o'er their love.
What do our two kings say?

OCTAR.   With hearts dismayed
They see their tents by these new guards surrounded,
But they assume a tranquil mien.

ATTILA.   Each can
Go freely from his tent to mine.

OCTAR.   'Tis true,
But only alone and unattended. As
For the two princesses, who still are left
Each her own mistress to do what she will,
None but their servants can have access to them,
And I have kept the two kings and their agents
Thus from them. Feel no more anxiety,
My lord; I have them under close surveillance,
And wheresoe'er they bend their steps are watchers
Whom I have stationed, from whose eyes they will not
Escape. Thou shalt be told of all that these two
Kings and they do.

ATTILA.   Enough for that. Now listen
To other news. The mighty Roman general,
The illustrious Aëtius, whom alone
I feared, no longer lives.

OCTAR.   Who rid thee of him?

ATTILA. Valentinian himself. He thought Aëtius
Would soon usurp his throne, and, being moved
By the suspicions which I had contrived
To breed in him, himself, before his own
Eyes, had him slain. Rome loses in his person
More than four battles, and I see the way
Now opened for me to her very walls.
If I should bring Honoria with her claims
There, against such an emperor every voice
Would be for me; the terror of my name
And all men's hate, that such a heinous deed

Draws on his head, could make his sister's husband
Easily, without one blow, Rome's master.
OCTAR. Thy choice, then, falls upon Honoria?
ATTILA. I do the best I can to make it fall there,
And glory bids me to; but Ildione
Has, on the other hand, such attractions for me
That my confused heart wavers more than ever.
I feel still struggling in my sighing breast
The appeal of beauty against that of empire.
My reason is supported by my pride,
But neither can withstand one glance from her;
And when I have regained self-mastery,
To re-enslave me she needs but to appear.
O beauty, which dost make men in all places
Worship thee, cruel poison to the soul
And sweet charm to the eyes, what will become
Of my supreme authority if thou
Assumest in spite of me dominion o'er me,
And if this haughty pride, which everywhere
Bends all beneath my yoke, cannot assure me
That I shall not bow beneath thine?
                    (*To* OCTAR) Go, find her
For me—this lovely, fascinating princess.
Make her afraid that I shall choose as serves
Mine aims best. To compel her to flee hence,
Picture to her all the humiliation
My marriage will bring upon her. Venture further:
Cause her to fear she will be held a prisoner
Here, to safeguard me from her brother's wrath
And to give pause to all whom hope to win her
Might soon arouse against me. But what heart
Would not indeed be thus aroused? I see
Too many dangers, Octar, in her flight.
Her eyes, my sovereigns, to which all submit,
Could give me, with one glance, too many foes.
To save my heart from her, use other methods.
Cause her to hate me; paint me in darkest colors;
Tell her I love another,—that Honoria
Is to be honored in her stead, and lead her
To act, herself, ere this can happen. Make her

Disdain me and prefer to me another
Who has no power save that which I allow him—
Ardaric, or Valamir, no matter which . . .
But how behold her, whom alone I crave,
In other arms than mine?—desire that someone
Else should before my very eyes possess her?
Oh, but the cure is worse than the disease!
Tell her, let her know . . .

OCTAR.   What, sire?
ATTILA.   Nay, I know not.
All that I can conceive of tries me sorely.
OCTAR.   Till when wilt thou put off deciding, then?
ATTILA.   Octar, I see her. A new bolt to blast me!
O reason now confounded, pride brought low,
Why did ye not prevail before its blow?

                              (*Enter* ILDIONE.)

(*To* ILDIONE)   To come and force me to pay homage to thee
Here at mine own tent, madam, is to carry
Thy power too far. Is it, then, not enough
My heart is thine?
ILDIONE.   That is the way to make
Sweet hopes be born. Yet 'tis not this, my lord,
Which brings me here. There are new things whereat
I have good cause to be distressed. Thy guard
Is doubled, and I see that two kings here
Are closely watched by thy express commands.
ATTILA.   Art thou concerned for either one of them?
ILDIONE.   My concern is to share thine own, my lord.
I have a right to feel anxiety
When thou'rt in any danger; and, moreover,
I, too, am watched, unless I am mistaken.
Am I suspected by thee? and of what?
ATTILA.   Of being loved. Madam, thy charms, by which
I am enchanted, have smitten more than one king
If I may trust appearances. Some others
Have eyes and vulnerable hearts like mine,
And I for thy sake and my own forestall
Their insolence, which might use force against thee.
ILDIONE.   There are more kindly, easier ways to stay them
If I enchant thee as thou sayst I do.

ATTILA.   Ah, thou enchantest me too greatly—me,
Whose lordly soul would see the whole world tremble
Beneath my feet. I, who would be all-powerful,
No sooner see thee than despite my pride
I have no power even o'er myself.
I wish, I try in vain to shun by flight
This overmastering charm which doth attend thee.
My best success in doing so only drives
Deeper the shaft thine eyes sink in my heart.
One unexpected glance gives them a victory.
One thought of them makes me renounce ambition
And dominates my soul and fondest cares;
And with my mind on thee I quite forget
Attila. Madam, what would I do after
Marriage had put my whole fate 'neath thy sway?
When I might wish to punish, thou couldst pardon;
Thou wouldst refuse mercy where I would show it;
Thou wouldst conclude peace when I wanted war;
Thou in thy hands couldst wield the lightning's bolt;
And all my love fears to accept a blessing
Which leaves me able no longer to do aught.
   Abuse less thy resistless power, madam,
And cease to be thyself this one day. Cease
To be adorable, and let me choose
Her with whom I can easily recover
My self-possession. Do not let thine eyes
Shine with that brightness which doth conquer all,
Wherewith my pride no more is possible.
Reject me, flout me, and thyself give back
My soul thereby to me.

ILDIONE.   I had supposed
Honoria was to be preferred to me
Without such honeyed, gallant words; and I
Had not expected compliments which well
Might make me vain although humiliated.
Her honors beside mine are empty honors;
They are but forms, and I have thy heart's utterance;
And if thou turnest to her, it is because
She has less charms and makes herself less feared!
Who would have thought that the great Attila

Could be afraid, that such scant comeliness
Had power to constrain him, and that he
Whose mighty name fills all with dread did not
Dare risk his pride against me? Ere transferring
Elsewhere that timorous homage which till now
I had so well won from thee, let me know,
My lord, that I may carry out thy wishes,
How to disdain the greatest of mankind.
Tell me what scorn can satisfy him. Ah!
Should I offend him in the attempt to please him,
If too much love in him results in hate,
When I deserve hate what will happen to me?
   Go, my lord, go where thy ambition sends thee.
Honoria's dowry will be half an empire.
That is a firm support for doubtful merit
And makes mine naught. I have my person only.

ATTILA.   And that is more than the whole Empire, more
Than sovereign rights o'er everyone that breathes.
All that is great or precious in this empire
I shall take pride in holding as thy gift.
Make me accept it, and for recompense
What regions wouldst thou wish beneath thy sway?
If Gaul thou likest, thou shalt have part of it.
I will bestow it, conquered, on thy beauty;
And my love . . .

ILDIONE.   Whatsoe'er that love would do,
The conqueror's hand is better than his conquests.

ATTILA.   What, madam! couldst thou give me love for love?
One who sows horror, wakens little love.
What wouldst thou love in me? I am cruel, barbarous.
Only my pride and violence are exceptional.
Men fear me, hate me; everywhere they call me
The terror of mortals and the scourge of God.
Thou hast all too good grounds for a refusal
To wed me, which I wish for; and if 'tis not
Enough to add my prayers to them,—if nothing
Makes thee decide to break our plighted troth,—
Fear for thyself as I for myself do.
If with thy charms thou like a tyrant takest
My freedom from me, I can be one also

To her who thus would tyrannize o'er me.
Do not forget that I am Attila;
And when I have said that, all has been said.

ILDIONE.   Must I, perforce, decide? So be it! I venture . . .
Nay—spare me the rest. It takes such boldness!
I tremble, as do others, at the frown
Of Attila; and I cannot forget
Myself to that extent. I shall obey.
Those words, alone, say all that he desires.
If they are not plain, let him as he wishes
Interpret them. I have all feelings which
It pleaseth him to order me to have.
I shall accept the dowry he hath given me.
Gaul do I share already with my brother.
I desire everything that is necessary
Not to displease thee any more. But may I
Not know, that I may fail in naught, to whom
Thou givest me, when I obey so well?

ATTILA.   I dare not decide that. Again I shudder
When I conceive of so much bale at once.
To lose thee and to give thee to another
In the same instant is too much. Allow me,
Madam, to separate my miseries.
Let one ill thing prepare me for the other.
After my marriage, thine will be provided.
My self-denial is too hard already
Without the addition of the task of making
Someone else happy. Often a brief space
Of time will do more than one dares to hope.

ILDIONE.   I dare do more than thou, my lord, and do it
Without delay. Since we can all dispose
Of what is ours, thy heart is mine and I
Can give it, but I place it in the hand
Alone which it desires. Do thou treat me,
I pray, as I treat thee, and when this task
Becomes less hard for thee, before thou givest me
In marriage, consult my wishes as to that.

ATTILA.   Thou lovest someone!

ILDIONE.   Till thou weddest, my heart
Belongeth to the monarch to whom I

Was given. But when by his own will I lose
All hope of him, I shall have eyes to see
What I should see.

Enter HONORIA.

HONORIA.   Is thy choice made, my lord,
And didst thou, making it, so fear mine anger
Thou thoughtest thy life would not be safe unless
Thy guard was doubled and thou hadst me watched?
I had not deemed I was so dreaded here.
But I should not complain of such ill treatment
When I can see that fear of my resentment
Begins already thy just punishment.

ILDIONE (*to* HONORIA). Let not these new commands trouble thy
      soul.
'Twas I who was feared, madam, and not thou;
And this great choice, which stirs thy wrath, has fallen
Not upon me, but upon thee. 'Tis true
That but for me thou couldst not have obtained it.
His heart, so long as I had wanted that,
Would have refused to choose thee. It was mine
Utterly. Do not be alarmed to learn
It had succumbed to my poor charms. I make thee
A present of it. Take it as a proof
Of my good will or my devoted homage,
And, strong henceforth through both thyself and me,
Form with this lofty heart the nobler ties.

HONORIA. 'Tis, then, from thy hands that it comes to me,
Madam, and 'tis from thee that I must have it?

ILDIONE. If now thou dost not want it from my hands,
Fear lest tomorrow thou wilt vainly want it.
      (*To* ATTILA) She from thyself will surely love it better,
My lord, or thou wilt give it to another.
To bring to her this heart I won from thee,
Thou hast required of me scorn and rejection.
Let my respect for thee dispense with scorn;
Behold in all else my complete obedience.
I give thee back thy heart—can do naught more.
'Tis thou must make her take what I refused.

                              (*Exit* ILDIONE.)

HONORIA.   Take what she refused! I, sir?
ATTILA.   Thou, madam.
   Can it be shameful to become my wife?
   And when a name so glorious is assured thee,
   What matters it to thee who gives it to thee?
   What matters it how comes to thee that honor
   Of which Ildione robbed herself for thee?
   Whether by her refusal or my choice,
   Wilt thou the less tread on the necks of kings?
   My two peace-treaties have given to me two
   Princesses, one of whom will have my hand
   If the other had my love. The one will have
   My greatness, as the other had my preference.
   Thus Attila gives each a part of him.
   Murmur not thou, madam; Ildione did not.
   Her part satisfies *her*. Receive thine better.
   I adored her; I wish to marry thee.
   Why? It is thus it pleases me to do.
HONORIA.   And it does not please *me* for thee to do thus.
   I cease to value what another spurns;
   And though the treaties pledge me unto thee,
   Ildione's leavings are unworthy of me.
   Yes, though the whole world either serves or fears thee,
   I have but scorn for one whom she rejected.
   What honor is it to be thy wife when this
   She grants me as a favor or in pity?
   I know how high above her heaven set me,
   And am more glorious than she is fair.
ATTILA.   I love thy pride; it is as great as mine,
   Madam; and thus we are so much alike
   That if love springs from similarity,
   I well may love thee as my other self.
HONORIA.   Ah, if no more than thine my heart were high,
   Our pride would still be not enough alike
   For that. Mine is a queen's pride, thine a slave's.
   I defy scorn; thou lovest to be defied.
   Thy pride hath lapses, and mine, always haughty,
   Cannot endure love from one so unlike me.
   If love springs from resemblance, and thereby
   A noble passion can unite great natures,

How could I love thee when I everywhere
See loftier pride which more resembles mine?
ATTILA. Thou seest it here; if I am not mistaken
Someone else hath thy heart, which thou deniest me.
This high-souled eagerness to disobey me
Preserves that prize for lucky Valamir.
HONORIA. I am accountable to myself alone, sir.
I can without shame love him if I wish to.
He is a king, like thee.
ATTILA.   A king, indeed—
That I can grant thee—but not one like me.
In royal blood and title we are equal,
But some degrees of power separate us,
And from the throne where heaven hath pleased to seat me
'Twould be a long descent to Valamir.
This title which he boasts among his subjects
Puts him but half-way between them and me.
He does my bidding and he bids them do it;
If he rules o'er the Goths, I rule o'er kings.
HONORIA. And I have means to put him above thee
As soon as I have let him win my hand.
The only power thou hast is power usurped
O'er peoples taken by surprise and princes
Outwitted. Thou hast no authority
Except that given thee by thy crimes. But he
Will have from me naught save legitimate rights;
And were he in thy rage trod 'neath thy feet,
Greater than thou is he, if he is worthier.
ATTILA. His worth and all thy rights are not so wondrous
If I do not by force of arms support them.
They need me if they are to reach their goal;
But to be emperor I need thee no longer.
Aëtius is dead; the Empire hath
No man left to defend it now, and I
Can open without thee a path to Rome.
HONORIA. Aëtius dead! I have no tyrant left me,
And I again shall find in Valentinian
My brother; and a thousand valiant heroes,
Whom this false minister oppressed, will vie
In coming forward to see justice done me.

They will defend the Empire and uphold
My rights by aiding him whom for his merit
I shall have chosen. Men with noble hearts
Dare nothing under such a great vice-gerent.
Their highest qualities bring them only harm.
Their glory gives offense by making jealous
This man in power, who deems that he will be
Destroyed if he does not destroy them all.
But after he is dead, their spirits revive,
And, freed now from the shackles which restrained them,
Each takes his proper place and does his duty
Again. Aëtius' death will prove this to thee.
If I should bring them for their master thee,
A savage, thou wouldst see what sort of welcome
Their valor gave thee; but if I should honor
The imperial station with a Valamir,
None would be sparing of his blood to serve me.

ATTILA.   Thou makest me pity thee for so forgetting
Thyself,—for feeling so much love and showing it.
'Tis shameful, madam, for rulers like ourselves
When smitten by it to let this be seen.
Love has a right to reign o'er common souls,
But not o'er those who make and unmake fortunes;
And if these cannot tear it from their hearts,
They must needs master it, or at least hide it.
I blame thee not for having had my frailties,
But try no less than I do to o'ercome them;
And as I deem thee, only, worthy of me,
Account me, only, worthy of thy hand.
Thou lovest Valamir; I love Ildione.
I keep myself for thee; keep for my throne
Thyself. Have loftier sentiments like me.
Copy my virtues, not my flaws alone.

HONORIA.   Flaws?—rather say thy frenzies and their crimes!
Some touch of greatness may be mingled with them,
But one cannot, with honor, imitate thee.
Courage itself in tyrants is repulsive.
Shall I, like thee, assassinate my brother,
On all of my allies vent my wrath freely,
Bathe in their blood, and with a jealous pride . . .

ATTILA. If we give passion free rein, I shall go
  Further than thou wilt, madam.
HONORIA.   Noble natures
  Speak their minds freely.
ATTILA.   When I remember this,
  Be not surprised; and if I marry thee
  Remembering it, thou knowest the past; judge what
  The future is to be. I leave thee now
  To think of that. Madam, farewell.
HONORIA.   Ah, villain!
ATTILA. I am thy wooer still. Tomorrow I
  Shall be thy master.
    (*Peremptorily*) Take the Princess back
  To her tent, Octar.
HONORIA.   What!
ATTILA.   That is enough.
  Thou'rt going to tell me everything thou thinkest,
  But still think twice before thou tellest it to me.
  Reflect, it is through me that thou canst have
  The Empire, and without my aid thy claims
  Are only airy nothings.
HONORIA.   Heavens above!
ATTILA. Go, and at least learn how to talk to me.
HONORIA. Learn, learn thyself to change thy manner of speech
  When plighted to a daughter of the Caesars.
ATTILA. We can change that before this day shall end.
HONORIA. Tyrant, do what thou wilt; my turn will come.

A C T I V

HONORIA, OCTAR, *and* FLAVIA *are discovered.*

HONORIA (*to* OCTAR). Go, serve me well, and if thou lovest Flavia
  She will be thy reward for what thou doest.
  I pledge my word to that: her hand is thine
  When thou dost get me Valamir for a husband.
OCTAR. I wish I could. Under thy Valamir
  I would feel sure of having life and love.
  Though Attila often confides in me,
  These may 'neath him be lost in one bad moment.
  He needs but a suspicion, some annoyance,

Or mere caprice, to hate me and deprive me
Of them. He is not one whom I can sway.
To make him lean a little more towards that
To which his will inclines, to enlist him somewhat
More in the course which he hath chosen, is nothing
Which thousands cannot do as well as I;
But to propose directly, or seek gently,
To turn his heart against its own decisions
Or argue against his ideas for thine—
That do we dare not do, not I nor any;
And if I risked such dire disaster, madam,
I would destroy myself and serve thee ill.

HONORIA. But what makes him choose *me*, when he loves *her?*
OCTAR. Aëtius' death, and thy claims to the Empire.
He thinks he sees the road thus made smooth for him,
And from his heart all other dreams are banished.
He loves to conquer, but he loves not battles;
He wants his name alone to shatter walls;
And, being a great diplomatist even more
Than a great warrior, he maintains that fighting
Smacks always of the adventurer, he fain
Would have the dreadful torrent of his peoples
O'erwhelm with ease the nations that he crushes,
And though of blood most lavish, he is sparing
Of that which all his men would risk for him.
Then hope not that he e'er will give thee up,—
E'er will renounce this choice that irks thee so.
Yet if an unexpected chance is offered,
Be assured I shall seize the opportunity.

(*Exit* OCTAR.)

FLAVIA. Hast thou not, madam, overmuch committed
Thyself? and hath not the chagrin of seeing
Someone preferred to thee stifled the fear
Thy words expressed of having to pay homage
Unto the blood of kings of a day's standing?
HONORIA. I indeed told thee that my wavering soul,
Whate'er I did, expected the same torture;
And of two evils which are feared alike,
The one which happens to us always seems
The worse; the one that we experience

Becomes the more apparent unto us.
My shame in this great choice is all too patent.
Ildione has contrived to get the better
Of me. Hers is the honor, mine the anguish.
She hath the testimonial to her merit
And leaves me with the woes which she escapes.
Mark how insultingly and haughtily
She by refusing the great king has thrown him
Back upon me, the while she rapturously
Makes certain for herself the happiness
Of being his who hath her love. For doubt not
She is in love: the fact that Ardaric
Attempts to see her every day, the attentions
He showers upon her, and the pains he takes . . .

FLAVIA.   I will say further, Attila suspects him
Of loving her; he is proud and choleric;
And if he ever knows that Ildione
Secretly honors Ardaric with her favor
And Ardaric hath dared to lift his eyes
To her and hath solicited that love
Which he believes is owed to him alone,
I fear their hopes, instead of being increased . . .

HONORIA.   Then how much better 'twould have been, had I
Not told him I love Valamir; but when one
Is being insulted and is losing him
She loves, can she have instant self-control?
Let us turn Attila's anger, which I dread,
Against my rival or against her lover,
If possible, and thus thwart *their* love. Let us
Promise him at the price of thwarting it
My hand, and make his eagerness to wed me
The means of keeping her from being now
More fortunate than I. Let us prevent
Their triumph.

              What strange madness! Without loving
Ardaric myself, I feel a jealousy
About him! But I seek to avenge the wrong
Done me, and am, in rightly seeking this,
Jealous of Ildione's happiness
And not concerning him who causeth it.

FLAVIA. Attila is here, madam.

HONORIA.   Well, then, let us
      Show him that one born of the Caesars' blood
      Will brook no master and can with complete
      Propriety decline what anyone
      Else would show great temerity in declining.

Enter ATTILA.

ATTILA. All is made ready, madam. This great marriage
      Will in an hour or two conclude the day;
      But I would not constrain thee, and come only
      To learn if thou hast better perceived what
      Thy duty is.

HONORIA.   My duty is to preserve
      My honor against what will make too dark
      A stain upon it if thy kingly love
      Does not first manifest itself in taking
      Adequate vengeance for the outrage done me.
      Can I without shame know that thou didst ask
      Fair Ildione's leave to offer me
      Thy throne, and that . . .

ATTILA.   Always of Ildione,
      Never of Attila!

HONORIA.   My lord, if thou
      Preferrest me, punish her. Espouse my cause
      And make thy love restore thy wife's fair fame.
      Ildione treats me with too great disdain.
      Suffer the like from me, or pay her for it.
      On what grounds wouldst thou think rejection of thee,
      If noble in her, becomes a crime in me?
      And after the refusal of us both
      To wed thee, why should mine deserve to be
      Punished, when hers is praised? Wherefore can she
      Defy thee to thy face as I must fear
      To do, and what right hath she to condemn me
      To marry one whom she herself hath spurned?

ATTILA. To justify my orders and my wishes,
      I thought a simple " 'Tis my will" sufficient;
      But note—since everything must needs be weighed—
      Of thee and Ildione, which offends me

And which obliges me.

                                        Where her refusal
To wed me serves my aims, thine works against them.
Where hers obeys me, thine attempts to balk me.
One shows respect, the other is defiant.
Thine shames me, hers does me a favor. Then
Can I have only at her life's expense
The honor of enthroning thee beside me?

HONORIA.   Can one not take revenge except by murder?
I do not want her death or even her ruin;
And there are punishments more just and mild
Which better would prevent her triumph o'er us.
I say "o'er *us*," for she offends against us
Both equally, and what thou offerest me
Makes us twain one. As a reward for breaking
Faith with thee, Ildione arrogantly
Makes disposition of both me and thee.
As a reward for all the haughtiness
With which she mocked me, she is free to marry
Her happy lover, with whom she is to have
The satisfaction of depriving me
Of him I love and placing me in *thy* arms.

ATTILA.   Who is her lover?

HONORIA.   Dost thou still not know
She adores Ardaric and he does her?

ATTILA *(lifting his voice)*. Bring Ardaric here to me!
                             (To HONORIA*)* But how dost
thou know . . .

HONORIA.   'Tis but a figment of my jealous fancy,
And I am misinformed, as thy pride tells thee
When she flouts me and when she plays with thee.
To credit thee, she does not serve thee ill
When she disdains thee for thy rival's sake.

ATTILA.   'Twixt Ardaric and me, such is the difference
That her mad choice will punish her enough.

HONORIA.   What! If his power is less than thine, hast thou
Not robbed him of it over his own army?
A real king whom an adverse fate oppresseth,
Howe'er oppressed he be, is still a king.
That name remains his in the worst of straits;

He even in chains is any monarch's peer;
And Ardaric's hand suffices for my rival
To have the right to treat me as an equal.
If thou wouldst punish her affront to us,
Reduce her to a marriage with a subject.
Seek not a harsher penalty for her
Than that of seeing thy wife be her sovereign;
And I myself can ask thee then to give me
The power to make her serve me and obey me.

ATTILA.   I can find, madam, a fit punishment
For her. Consent, thyself, to the same justice.
Since one who spurns a king should wed a subject,
Choose, in one hour from now, Octar or me.

HONORIA.   Octar, or . . .

ATTILA.   Noble natures speak their minds
Freely. That is a fact which thou hast taught me.
Ponder without complaining, then, thy choice,
And thank me for thus following thy precepts.

HONORIA.   Propose Octar for *me!*

ATTILA.   What canst thou find
To say 'gainst him. Is he, in thy opinion
Not fit to rule the Empire? If he was born
Without a crown and never had a realm,
Others have mounted from a lower station
To that great throne. Caesars, even the best,
Have first been artisans, bandits, or slaves.
Time and their native worth have made them famous,
And our good Octar hath the selfsame virtues.

HONORIA.   Nay, make no jest of Octar unto me.
I could indeed espouse him without shame,
Tyrant, and thou at least shouldst recollect
That if he is not worthy, he can become so.
If one lacks princely blood, one can perform
Great services, have humble aspirations,
Be capable of self-sacrifice, achieve
Glorious and surprising deeds, exhibit
The virtues of a hero—and the crimes.
Example can do much. With thy instruction
He hath acquired the habit of wrong-doing.
Being thy creature, he must be like thee.

When I have made him bold, begin to tremble.
Thy life will be in *my* hands when he wishes
To win my favor; and thou canst feel no
Security, if I once arouse his hopes.
Thy rival comes. Farewell. Discuss with him
Whether thy Octar loves me or will be
Faithful to thee.

>   (*Exeunt* Honoria *and* Flavia. *Enter* Ardaric.)

ATTILA (*to* Ardaric).   Sir, I no more am troubled
About my choice. This evening, I shall wed
The Roman princess. I must now decide
Only to whom I can most safely trust
The other one, angry as she is. The king
Of the Burgundians formerly sent envoys
To ask her hand for Sigismund, his son;
But *our* suit was more favorably heard.
Could he assure us of complete security?

ARDARIC.   His realm on one side bounds that of Meroveus.
A pact between the two could soon be formed,
And thou wouldst see a husband take up arms
For his wife's sake, a brother for his sister's,
With equal ardor. Their alliance would be
Too easy and too strong.

ATTILA.   The Visigoths'
King made a like request. As he is not
So near Meroveus, they would find it harder
To act in concert. The Burgundians,
Moreover, separate their lands and make
A barrier for us between these two monarchs.

ARDARIC.   Yes, but between them the Burgundians
Would presently be crushed, and a direct
Road would unite them then; and both these kings,
Gaining thereby control of the whole country,
Would so much the more zealously defend it
As they would have the more to lose and as
A righteous wrath no longer would be needed
To league so many sovereigns then against thee.
The princess Ildione is both proud
And beautiful. She needs must have a husband
Who can control her better and whose interests

Are unto thee subservient—and not one
Chosen among thy foes. The stubborn hatred
A proud and lovely woman feels will wage
A never-ending war 'gainst him she hates,
And if her husband hearkens at all to her . . .

ATTILA. Then she must needs wed Valamir—or thee.
Couldst love her? Speak without dissimulation.
I know Honoria loves Valamir.
It may be that my marriage irks him somewhat,
And I feel sure of thee more than of him.

ARDARIC. Thou honorest me with too great trust, my lord.

ATTILA. Speak, then: couldst find this union to thy taste?

ARDARIC. Thou knowest my chief joy is to do thy pleasure.

ATTILA (*calling loudly*). Go—someone—for the Princess. Bring her
    here.

    (*To* ARDARIC) I wish thee to receive her hand from mine.
But tell me, pray, while waiting till she comes:
How wouldst thou prove thy loyalty to me?
What wouldst thou be prepared to do for me?
For she is fair, indeed. She might corrupt
Anyone, and make even thee seek my death.

ARDARIC. Wouldst have me slay for thee proud Torismund?
Stain with the blood of Sigismund the Arar?
Lay at thy feet the crowns of both these kings?

ATTILA. Hide naught from me. Thou lovest Ildione
And dost propose these glorious tasks much less
Against my enemies than against thy rivals.
This prompt enthusiasm and sudden hatred
Are all too certain proofs of jealous love.
Concern for me is but concern for it.
Didst thou not love her, thou wouldst be less eager.
Observe how quickly we can hate a rival,—
How, being such, he sins against our love,—
How just his death is, even if he does nothing;
And without going hence, rid me of mine.
Postpone the punishment of doubtful wrongs
And serve my wrath before thou servest thy hate.
Would I be safe to expose myself, through kindness,
To all the efforts of a supplanted lover?
Wouldst thou thyself espouse a wife and leave

Before her eyes the master of her heart?

ARDARIC. If he is to be feared, he must be banished.

ATTILA. When he is to be feared, he must be killed.
This is a king whose men, mingled with ours,
Would make too many follow him to exile,—
Who would oppose us in our best-laid plans
And swell the squadrons of our enemies.

ARDARIC. Is it a crime to cherish the fond hope
That thou wouldst give thy preference elsewhere?

ATTILA. Yes.
For him, for thee, for any other king,
It is a crime to aspire where I aspire.
To snatch a heart whose troth is pledged to me
Is, as it were, to seize a fortress given me;
And thou wouldst be as culpable as he
If I did not regard thee otherwise
Today. I owe like justice to like crimes,
But choose for thee a loving punishment.
For putting in thine arms her whom thou lovest,
Is it too great a price to slay one justly?

ARDARIC. But thou dishonorest thy wedding day,
My lord, by seeking with such blood to stain it.

ATTILA. Is there a greater honor it can have
Than to behold, according to my choice,
Which of two kings I wish to immolate
Unto my love, and how in making that
Sacrifice which will expiate their offense
One of them will perform it and the other
Will be the victim? If thou dost not dare
Thus to win her thou lovest, thou shouldst fear
That Valamir will be less scrupulous
And will not think it is too barbarous
For him to have at such a price Honoria,
Nor feel a horror at his dearest longings
If their fulfilment doth require thy death
Alone—for I can still espouse *thy* princess
And let *him* be the object of my kindness.

(*Enter* ILDIONE.)

(*To* ILDIONE) When thou didst, as I wished, reject me thou
Badest me consult thy wishes ere I gave thee

To anyone. This I resolved to do.
Then tell me, madam: would thy heart accept
The love of Ardaric?

ILDIONE.   It is for me
To obey if thou desirest it; but, my lord . . .

ATTILA.   He raises some objections, but I know
Thy power o'er him is unlimited.
Bring his irresolute soul to overcome them,
That in one hour, amidst my Court, your wedding
And mine may bring this great day to a climax.

                                        (*Exit* ATTILA.)

ILDIONE (*to* ARDARIC). Why dost thou sigh? Whence is thy sadness
    born?
Hath sheer surprise struck dumb all joy, or dost thou
Delay expressing it till thou canst show it
Better, and must thou still dissimulate
Before the tyrant? He has gone, sir. Let
Thy gladness—let it to its full extent—
Be shown, that I may see how much thou lov'st me.

ARDARIC.   Thou wilt sigh, madam, in thy turn, unless
Thy heart, despite its better nature, can
Be as inhuman as this savage man.
        He chooses me for thee. 'Tis a great honor,
But one made dreadful by the price at which
He sells it. Canst thou take my hand in marriage
If it must cost the life of Valamir?

ILDIONE.   What, sir!

ARDARIC.   Be not dumbfounded by this news
Until thou knowest whose arm must murder him.
'Tis mine which Attila destines for this deed,
Madam.

ILDIONE.   He chooses *thee* to murder him?

ARDARIC.   He makes of me his executioner
To slay another king, to whom he makes
The selfsame fell proposal as to me.
Thou at the price of Valamir's head must needs
Be had, Honoria at the price of mine:
His cruel favor lets *me* decide which.

ILDIONE.   For what crime would his wrath punish two kings?

ARDARIC.   Their crime is that they love two princesses

And more deserve the love of these than he does.
He makes your favor a misfortune for us—
Of such a cause for joy the deepest sorrow.

ILDIONE.   Is there a baser pride, a viler baseness?
He fain would have me cost thee life or honor
And serve as grounds for the unhappy choice
Of being a murderer or being murdered!
He offers thee my hand as a supreme
Blessing, but only if thou'lt make thyself
Unworthy of it; and if thou wilt not win me
In this way, thou canst not thyself shun death.

ARDARIC.   'Tis well to die, if need be to shun crime.
Dying for honor's sake, one lives again
In men's thoughts,—triumphs o'er the cruelest fate.
By such a death one makes himself immortal.

ILDIONE.   An immortality which triumphs in fancy
Would please us best if seen in the far future;
And when such triumph is fatal to our love,
The glory of it can but ill console us.

ARDARIC.   Thou wilt avenge my death; and my glad soul . . .

ILDIONE.   To avenge a death does not restore to life.
The tyrant's death will leave me still unhappy.
Shedding his blood will not dry up my tears.

ARDARIC.   To save a life mortal in any case,
Shall I make infamous and loathsome all
The rest of it; and is it not much better
To satisfy his fury and deserve
Thy tears, instead of causing thee to feel
A horror of me?

ILDIONE.   Thou wouldst make me feel it
Beyond doubt, after doing such a deed,
Enough to treat thee as a deadly foe.
But Fortune often hath propitious changes
Which lead, though we do naught, to great events.
Heaven is not so kind to villains always.
After long leniency it visits justice.
Go, talk to Valamir, and see with him
If there can be some cure for all your troubles.

ARDARIC.   Madam . . .

ILDIONE.   Nay, go. Our ills brook no delay,

And the same dangers threaten both of you.

ARDARIC. I go, but in our plight we only can
Lament together and decide on nothing.

(Exit ARDARIC.)

ILDIONE *(to herself)*. A truce, sad eyes, a truce today to weeping.
Take, 'gainst the monster, your most dangerous charms.
See if ye can again enchant and rule him,
And turn against him all he tries to do.
Resume your place usurped now in his heart;
And lead anew my victim to the altar,
Who hath escaped from me; and once again
Awake that wrath which his uncertain choice
In favor of my love lit in my breast.
How easy all seems when one might not do it!
But when the time for action comes, how trying
And difficult it is! How readily
Our sex opposes to a noble course
Its natural gentleness and timidity!
What! pledge my faith with no thought but to break it,
And wed a husband but to slay him? Heaven,
That seest me tremble at the mere name "husband,"
Make me more ruthless or this tyrant kindlier!

ACT V

ARDARIC *and* VALAMIR *are discovered. Both are swordless.*

ARDARIC. 'Tis thy diviners, sir, that have destroyed us.
By them the door to all our ills was opened,
And the deceitful charm of their predictions
Has made ambition's lure too sweet to thee.
Thence came that love, fostered by policy,
Which a proud tyrant deemed in thee a crime.
Without the flattering hope of a bright future
Honoria would not have been so attractive
To thee. 'Twas this that made her in thy sight
Adorable, and thus begot real love
In her, which binds her to thee and arouses
A frenzy which thou seest stops at nothing.
Unless I slay thee, I must perish. Thou
Hast a like chance or sufferest like injustice.

Thus thy soothsayers alone force us to die,
And that is all that they have done for thee.
VALAMIR.   I have just come from them. Far from unsaying
What they have said, they still assure my race
Of the same empire. Knowing Attila
Is in the highest degree infuriated,
They yet are not disturbed by his mad rage.
Whatever he decrees me, they are confident.
Heaven hath shown them its immutable
Decisions; nothing can keep these from being
Carried out, and for monarch Rome will have
That great Theodoric who will be descended
From me.
ARDARIC.   Do they wish thee, at my life's cost,
To make the way smooth for this hero's conquests?
VALAMIR.   Sir, such words wrong me worse than Attila did.
ARDARIC.   How else canst thou escape his hate? How else
Canst thou possess Honoria? And whence
Will this son, if thou losest thy life, be born?
VALAMIR.   I see myself, like thee, at death's grim portals,
But I still hope for what is past my knowledge.

Enter HONORIA.

HONORIA.   Know ye how far the rage of Attila
Goes, and how frightful its ferocity
Is, Princes? This proposal which he makes you,
Offering happiness to one of you,
Is but a snare set to destroy you both.
He wishes, through the hope held out to each,
The blood of one to stain the other's hands.
Whichever serves him would be handed over
Then to the troops of him whose death he wrought,
Whereby, denying he ordered it, this tiger
Would glut alike his anger and their vengeance.
Octar loves Flavia and hath told her this.
VALAMIR.   Euric has only just gone—his lieutenant.
That minion was deputed to disarm us
By the suspicious tyrant, who is afraid
Of getting his deserts; and as he rightly
Thinks we are outraged, he took this precaution

Ere having speech with us again. Had he
Delayed a little longer, we would have
Gone to surprise him in his tent and balk
His villainous designs while he still left us
Each free to carry at his side a sword.
He promised both of us our weapons back
When he knows what he can expect of us,
What our intent is, or, to put it better,
When we decide that one shall slay the other!
Meanwhile he hath reduced to impotence
That brave despair by which one ere one's death
Takes satisfaction for it, punishing
The wrong before 'tis done him and believing
That to die thus is to die less completely;
For though we would have died by his guards' hands,
Death is a fairer thing when boldly courted.

HONORIA.   He comes, sir.

Enter ATTILA *and* OCTAR.

ATTILA.   How now, my illustrious friends!
What can I hope for 'gainst my mighty rivals?
Will neither vouchsafe to himself the bliss
Of winning his princess by destroying one
Who hath offended me? What! love and friendship
Equally cold! Neither loves me enough
To hate my rival! Neither has a heart
Enough enthralled by her he loves, to wish
For happiness at a single life's expense!
What friends! What lovers! What dull-metaled princes!
Seek, seek at least your safety. If the two
Other considerations cannot move you,
Let dread of death, where they are powerless, do so;
And if ye pay no heed to love or friendship,
Make a brave effort, each to save his life.

VALAMIR.   To add to ruthlessness such jeering mockery
Is to be barbarous to the last extreme.
Thy brother and six kings were murdered by thee;
Our turn hath come to suffer a like fate;
And we indeed deserve the worst of deaths
For having exposed ourselves to the same treatment

And every day enduring some new wrong.
Punish us, take revenge—but who will slay us?
If thou'rt a king, remember we are kings.

ATTILA. Ye? Beside Attila ye are two mere men.
When I am ready to abate your pride,
Your heads will fall at the least glance from me.
I show you mercy in asking for but one's
Life; let the sword and Fortune decide whose;
And he who dies at least will have from me
The honor of perishing by a king's hand.
      Then, princely gladiators, of whom I make
A noble spectacle on this great occasion,
Display a courage worthy of your rank.

ARDARIC. Thine own hand is more wont to shed such blood.
Thou doest it an affront in borrowing *our* hands.

ATTILA. To avenge my wrongs I shall find others; but
If ye renounce the objects of your love,
Refusing me one head may cost you two.
I now revoke my mercy. Let your crimes
Make victims for me of two kings, my rivals;
And these rare beings, so little worthy of me,
Will be a fit reward for those who lend me
Their hands to slay you.
          (*To* ARDARIC) I will give her thou lovest
To whosoever will strike off thy head
Before me.
          (*To* HONORIA) And, as thou wilt be the payment
For Valamir's, we shall at such a price
Have many executioners to choose from;
And for the further punishment of such loves
Our choice will fall only upon the basest.

HONORIA. Thou couldst be vile and cruel to this extent?

ATTILA. Still more, at need, yet always Attila.
Always the happy object of men's hate,
Wielding the despotic power lodged in him,
Always . . .

HONORIA.   Go on; say thou'dst be everywhere
The terror of mankind, the scourge of God.
Paint us with insolent pride the dreadful picture
Of rivers of blood in which in thy fell fury

Thou'st bathed. Show . . .

ATTILA.   How thou wastest bitter words,
Reproaching me with what is sweet and glorious!
    This God of whom thou speakest, though often stern,
Not always arms himself with all his anger;
And when he empties on the world his vials
Of wrath, its deluge every time is different.
Of old he made all oceans overflow,
And drowned all lands beneath a flood of waters.
His hand holds in reserve a fiery deluge
For the last moment of our last descendants;
And *my* arm, which he makes today his sword,
Covers the earth now for him with a deluge
Of blood.

HONORIA.   When with the hand of tyrants he
Punishes us, he keeps his thunderbolts
For these great criminals, with whom he afflicts
All nature, till their frenzy fills the measure
To overflowing. It may be that he
Is now preparing at this very moment
His blow of chastisement for thy foul deeds,
And that when in thy rage thou wouldst destroy us
He hath his arm raised to fall on thy head
And would by this example force to tremble
Whoe'er henceforth desires to be like thee.

ATTILA.   Well, while I wait for this change in my fortunes
I shall, till it occurs, serve as his agent
And carry out all his will regarding thee
And these two kings who have rebelled against me.
By new fell deeds shall I requite your crimes,
And die in my turn only after you.

HONORIA.   Does not thy blood, which falls in great gouts daily,
Seeking thy brother and six murdered kings,
Tell thee plainly enough their spirits call thee;
Or must those summons be by me repeated?
    See, see that blood flow now which comes to warn thee,
Tyrant, that thou must perish soon and join them.

ATTILA.   'Tis naught; and if there is in store for me
No bolt from heaven besides this, I shall have
A long time to prepare myself for going.

3 6 5

Others would make thee tread that path before them,
But I shall let the doom thou threatenest take
Its course, and shall requite thee differently
When the mood seizes me to punish thee.

(*Enter* ILDIONE.)

(*To* ILDIONE) Why comest thou, madam, and what em-
boldens thee
To wish to see my death, here prophesied me?
Comest thou to take the part of these two kings,
Rebel like them or storm at me like her,
Or wouldst thou beg aid of my righteous wrath
Against thy Ardaric, who no longer wants thee?

ILDIONE. He would not merit my love or my esteem
If he dared hope to win me by a crime.
That he so properly refused to do it,
Pleases me, and I come not here to blame him.
No, my lord; 'tis mine own renunciation
I come here to retract,—to have my glance
Resume its sovereign sway over thy heart,—
To make thy wishes meet with mine again
And take from thee once more the freedom which
Thou hast misused.

Is this, then, the reward
Promised so solemnly for my obedience?
I left my people, hoping to be thine;
By thy command I gave up that fond hope;
I forced myself to accept him whom it pleased thee
To choose for me—and what thou biddest would make him
One whom I could not cherish. In reverencing
Thy mandate and accepting this king thus,
I see only opprobrium for him
And only shame for me. Restore, restore
To me that power o'er thee which would no longer
Let thee make disposition of thyself.
Turn thy whole soul back to its first desire.
Take her who loves thee; fly from her who hates thee.
Honoria hath her claims, but that of pleasing
Thy fancy is, thou knowest, no trivial claim;
And for thine aid Meroveus hath arms
Stronger than all claims when it comes to blows.

ATTILA.   Nay, I no more can see that curst Honoria
              Save with the horror that I would a Fury;
              And all which heaven hath made that is most winsome—
              All that is best—I think I see in thee.
              But in thy heart another love doth murmur
              When . . .
ILDIONE.   Thou couldst credit such a lie? What have
              I said, what have I done, except obey thee?
              And wherein could I have betrayed such feelings?
ATTILA.   Ardaric would be a husband thou wouldst love.
ILDIONE.   Thy hand's gift of him made him lovable;
              And I just now accepted him for husband
              Only on that express command thou gavest me.
              Thou hadst ere then seen that, despite my love,
              To make thee emperor . . .
ATTILA.   Thou speak'st falsely, madam;
              But love as I behold thee doth so sway me,
              I shut mine eyes and will no more resist thee.
              Do not abuse thy power o'er me, though.
              Remember, I have still some other longings.
              Vengeance is dear to me as well as love.
              Leave me some power to act in my turn, also.
ILDIONE.   Wouldst thou with blood stain this great day, my lord?
              Wait, wait at least until our marriage is over.
              Suffer its festive torch to burn unsullied,
              And leave affairs of State until tomorrow.
ATTILA.   'Tis thy will, madam; I must needs content thee.
              But thus my wrath will only be so much
              The greater; for the hours it is postponed
              By thy command will fan its flames the hotter.
HONORIA.   See, rather see by thine own instance, sire,
              How blind a lofty heart is when it loves,—
              To what extent love, which can seal thine eyes,
              Masters and moves the kings who best resist it,—
              What power it hath over the haughtiest spirit;
              And if thou foundest mine too arrogant,
              See me, for love's sake, lay aside completely
              My very just pride for a lover's safety,
              And, with that pride now melted by my tears,
              Stoop to entreat thee, yielding to my fears.

To have reduced me in my wrath to this,
Should be a triumph sweet enough, my lord.
Let my crushed pride suffice thee as thy victim.
Wouldst treat thine own example as a crime,
And, when thou lovest one who doth not love thee,
Condemn the promptings of a mutual love?

ATTILA. Nay, rather should we imitate each other—
Thou follow my example, and I thine.
As thou wouldst have this lady wed a subject,
Carry out in her place a course so proper.
I have already bidden thee to do so,
And feel too much respect for thy injunctions,
Most fittingly imposed on her, to dare
To punish otherwise thy contumely.
If thou lov'st Valamir, buy his life thus.
Dispose at this price of a hand thou owedst me.
    Octar, lose not the Princess from thy sight.
    (*To* ILDIONE) Thou, who commandest me to wed thee, madam,
Come with me to the temple; and ye, kings,
Follow me.

                    (*Exeunt all but* HONORIA *and* OCTAR.)

HONORIA.   Thou hast seen, to touch his haughty
Heart, I have wept, prayed, and tried everything,
Octar; and as the fruit of such abasement,
The cruel wretch treats me still more arrogantly.
If any hope is left, it lies in thee.
Wilt seize thy chance? Thou dost command his guards.
The night and sleep leave all things in thy hands.
Flavia is the reward of two kings' safety.

OCTAR. Ah, madam! Attila, since thy threats against him,
Hath put so bold a plan beyond my power.
With heart mistrustful, he now carries out
All of his wrath's dire will through my lieutenant.
It was through him he had both kings disarmed;
And by thy words he was so much alarmed
That he expressly bade me not to leave thee
Today, to give me no way to come near him.
Were I to quit thy side, 'twould cost my life;
And if he once discovers I love Flavia . . .

HONORIA.   That will I tell him, if thou dost not act,
Wretch, who unblushingly refusest to do so!
If thou wouldst still live, go and find some courage.
Thou seest his anger claim, each hour, its quarry,
And thou with all thy valor, which thou art
Afraid to show, waitest with folded arms
To be in thy turn slain. Kill him or die.
Forestall his blows, thou coward, or fall beneath them.
Avenge the whole world, or be one more victim.
If love and glory have no power to move thee,
Die as a traitor, or at least for me.

(*Enter* VALAMIR.)

   (*To* VALAMIR) But what, sir, lets me see thy face again?
VALAMIR.   My eagerness to tell of joy unlooked for.
The tyrant is no more.
HONORIA.   He is dead?
VALAMIR.   Hearken
How his own savagery hath punished him
At last and gracious heaven hath just confirmed
What in our ill plight thou foretoldest him.
   Scarce had we left here, full of woe and horror,
When Attila began to bleed again
Because of his dire rage—now copiously.
The blood that gushed forth flowed in such great streams
That he himself was thunderstruck. Yet though
Thus taken unexpectedly, he cried:
"If it will not stop, ye shall with your lives
First pay me for the life that it will cost me!"
   Immediately upon these words he lost
All voice, all strength. His senses suddenly
Took leave of him, his throat was swollen, its passage
Was, by the blood now thickening in it, closed
Or at least greatly narrowed. The fierce reek
Of that blood so confined seemed to have stifled
His anger and himself, too, and already
He by the fatal pallor of his brow
Revealed that but a remnant of life's warmth
Held death in check,—when he believed he saw
His brother, and thereon his strength and fury
Were instantly renewed. He thought he saw him

Followed by the phantoms of six kings, whom he
Wanted to slay a second time; but such
A swift return of his most savage passions
Was a last effort of exhausted nature,
Which, ere succumbing to the touch of death,
Flares in one final blaze and then is quenched.
It was in vain he railed at that dread vision;
His wrath, reborn, at the same moment killed him.
The impetuous vehemence of his new transports
Now opened every channel for the blood
Confined within him. Its spasmodic force
Breeched or broke open all his veins, and these
In bursting became fountains, every one,
By which both blood and soul sought exit, thus
To end his frenzy and safeguard us from it.
His lifeblood in long streams spread o'er the ground.
Each moment weakened him; he could do naught.
Each throe dealt justice unto those whom he
Had slain, and mercy unto those he threatened.
Whate'er he meant to say, he could no longer
Now utter anything but sobbing noises.
He shuddered, staggered, stumbled, and fell dead;
And his last rage, that drained the cup of horror,
Finally avenged mankind for all his rages.

Enter ARDARIC *and* ILDIONE.

ARDARIC.   Yet more remains to tell: the general hate
Of him, now there was nothing to fear from him,
Was eagerly displayed. All longed to serve
More humane sovereigns, and they wished to have them
In us. This wonderful deliverance sent us
By heaven makes many nations glad alike.
Our danger's end fulfils their common wishes.
For all four of us to attain the highest
Degree of happiness, we have but to see
Our love find favor with the Emperor
Of Rome and with the great Meroveus.
The Princess of the Franks imposes this
Condition on me.
HONORIA.   As for me, I need

Only mine own consent.

ARDARIC (*to* VALAMIR).   Let us not lose
  Time in this change of fortune. Let us give
  All necessary orders, fill again
  The vacant throne, and see upon what terms
  So many people wish us for their kings.

VALAMIR (*to* HONORIA). Wilt thou permit me, madam, to do this?
  And may I think that thou at last accountest
  My love a thing to prize?

HONORIA.   Go, sir, and rest
  Assured the changes in our destiny
  Have changed in no wise my heart's love for thee.

Pulchérie

(P U L C H E R I A)

INTRODUCTION

Pulchérie met with little success on its appearance in 1672 and has been little esteemed since. Its highly unromantic denouement, in which the heroine renounces for the good of her country the young man whom she loves, and contracts a nominal marriage with an old soldier, could not please an audience, as Corneille ought to have known. Petit de Julleville said of it and *Suréna,* which followed it, that "these last children of his tragic vein are utterly tiresome. They are purely tragedies of love, where the only question is whether the hero will marry the heroine or not; and yet neither he nor she succeeds in interesting us in their cold, verbose passion." [1] And, more recently, Brasillach has said that in *Pulchérie* Corneille "carries still further the extravagances of *Pertharite* ... he returns to his psychologizing, shows us an impossible woman, who is in love but is over-proud, who loves a handsome captain, and, out of sheer pride, not to yield obedience to love, prefers to wed an old man. ... But for us, is there not a certain weariness and monotony in returning always to these well-worn grooves of Corneillian love, to this inhuman, unreal, and cruel world ... to this resumption of barbarous themes exalting the Will? ... The scene in which the father and daughter confess their love to each other is one of the most beautiful, most suffused with soft and golden light, that Pierre Corneille has ever written ... For this scene, and for two or three others, *Pulchérie* abandons the world of *Héraclius* and of *Pertharite* for the world of Chimene and of Pauline ..." [2]

Between the dates of these two pronouncements by Petit de Julleville and Brasillach, others have been somewhat more kindly. Thus Lemaître: "*Pulchérie* is just another political comedy, which could not possibly have any great warmth. But this Byzantine virgin, in her almost hieratic pose, is nevertheless a figure which lingers in the memory." [3] And Lanson: "*Pulchérie* is not, perhaps, a moving play, but it is a very pretty thing." [4] And Faguet, with stronger commendation:

[1] P. xviii.
[2] Pp. 457-459.
[3] P. 338.
[4] *Corneille,* p. 90.

"*Pulchérie* is another very praise-worthy work and one which contains—bear in mind that this must be said to the very end —verses as beautiful as those of the author's youth." [5]

Lancaster is perhaps the most favorable of its critics. After analyzing the characters in *Pulchérie* appreciatively, he goes on to say: "The technique of the play is excellent. The exposition is made in discussion, not in narration of earlier events. . . . The plot advances steadily, with each motif helping or retarding Pulcheria's decision, and the questions at issue are settled only in the last few lines of the play. There are no monologues, no confidants, few examples of *préciosité*, while repartee is effectively employed . . ." [6]

Brasillach must never have read *Pulchérie* with any great attentiveness, we are forced to conclude from his complete misunderstanding of its heroine's motives and from his calling the world of this play unreal. On the contrary, its peculiar excellence is that the problem it presents is a real one, a natural one, not marred by the sense of being contrived like the situations in so many French-classical tragedies. Its quiet tone is of course deliberate with Corneille—deliberately in contrast with the emotionalism of Racine's *Andromaque* and *Bérénice*. *Pulchérie* was the first play that he wrote after the latter of these two dramas of his rival, and deals like *Bérénice* with a royal marriage in which considerations of State oppose the dictates of the heart. "It is thus"—Corneille seems to say— "thus with dignity and intelligence that such unhappy situations should be dealt with, not by tearing a passion to tatters." One divines, however, the presence of true emotion in its characters; with them strong feeling seems restrained, not absent. They all are subtly and consistently portrayed; their conduct is natural; and the action progresses to the final denouement without being open to serious criticism at any point. *Pulchérie* seems to me, therefore, one of the best of the later plays of Corneille.

[5] P. 228.
[6] Part III, pp. 581-582.

CHARACTERS IN THE PLAY

PULCHERIA, *sister of Theodosius the Younger, the recently deceased emperor of the Eastern Roman Empire.*

MARCIAN, *an elderly senator, who had been Prime Minister under the late emperor.*

LEO, *a young soldier in love with Pulcheria.*

ASPAR, *a prominent general.*

IRENE, *Leo's sister.*

JUSTINA, *Marcian's daughter.*

The scene represents a room in the imperial palace in Constantinople.

The names "Pulcheria" (with *ch* like *k*) and "Justina" are accented on the second syllable; "Marcian," "Leo," and "Aspar" on the first syllable. "Irene" is pronounced as a word of two syllables, as in English and French.

Pulcheria

ACT I

PULCHERIA *and* LEO *are discovered.*

PULCHERIA. I love thee, Leo, and make no secret of it.
Such love as mine hath naught that one must hide.
I love thee not at all with that mad passion
Which dazzled eyes make master of one's heart—
Not with a love born of the senses stirred,
To which one yields oneself without due thought,
And which, since it consists but of blind cravings,
Grows less when favored and dies amid its joys.
My love for thee, pure and unshakable,
Makes thy great worth its basis, reason its guide,
Honor its aim, and fain would 'neath thy sway
Put all men and myself this fateful day.
    The fact that Theodosius was my grandsire,
Arcadius my father, and I governed
The Empire for my brother fifteen years,
My habitude of reigning, and my horror
Of doing so no longer, have made me wish
To have the selfsame power with a husband.
I deemed thee suitable for that high station;
And midst the expectations which my preference
Fondly assured me would be realized,
I have found naught in all the tasks I gave thee
That hath belied the hopes with which I chose thee.
Thy great deeds were fast bearing us toward the throne;
I had constrained my brother not to oppose
Thy mounting it; he let thee share my power,
And I was disposed wholly in thy favor.
But this unhappy prince hath died too soon.
The Empire must be placed in someone's hands.
The Senate meets to choose a head for this
Huge, tottering body, which the Huns, Goths, Franks,
And Vandals drag down, tearing at its flanks.
    Everywhere I see factions forming, each
Weighing its chances and intriguing. Gratian,
Procopius, Areobindus, Aspar—any

Of these may rob thee of the name of Caesar.
They all have merit, and the last feels sure
His father Ardaburius is remembered
Still, who o'erthrew in single fight Mithranes,
Won our entire success for us 'gainst Persia,
And giving new courage to our eagles thus,
Ended the war alone before both armies.
My wishes, influence, friends are on thy side;
But save with empire, no more love, no marriage!
Whatever happiness our love may offer,
There needs must be, for Theodosius' blood,
The throne or exile; and if by the outcome
My hopes are cheated, I shall go to seek
Asylum in Judea, with Athenaïs.

LEO.   Then I would follow thee, madam, and, at least
Not envying my rivals' triumph o'er me,
Unless thou gavest me some happier fate,
Die there of grief for being unworthy of thee—
Yes, die before thine eyes, adoring thee.
Perhaps thou'dst wipe away some of my tears;
Perhaps thy noble heart, which dares not soften,
Would there resist so ill my final sigh
That some unlooked-for show of grief and love
By thee would follow hence my soul, despite thee.
My death, which would forever end my pain,
Would be far sweeter than my present plight.
Thou lovest me but, alas, what love is thine,
Who art preparing, perhaps, to love another?
What serve these wishes which will come to naught
Unless thy lofty pride be satisfied?
What can this love avail whereof thou'rt master,
This love whose thirst is wholly for the throne,
Ambitious slave of empire, of a title
Which at will kindles it and quenches it?
Oh, it is nowise thus that I love thee;
In the worst exile thou'dst be the dearer to me:
There would mine eyes, unceasingly fixed on thee,
Make my love my sole care; and my attentions,
All centered on that noble vassalage,
Could every moment pay thee complete homage.

To be a happy lover, must I give
The world place in my heart, which wishes only
To love and serve thee? must the worthiest efforts
Of such true love be turned to various ends?
Ah, what grounds hath my heart for fear if I,
Unless I am emperor, shall be loved no more!

PULCHERIA. Thou shalt be always loved; but high-born folk
Do not always make love result in marriage.
Love in two hearts desires but to unite them;
Marriage is needed to maintain their honor;
And I confess to thee, in the fairest lives
Pride of birth can indeed be tyrannous.
Often the dearest wishes can but torture.
One's duty to oneself battles with love.
'Neath duty's stern yoke love groans vainly . . . Oh,
Had I but had a senator for father!
But in my family women were the noblest
Spirits. Eudoxia and Placidia wedded
Emperors. I cannot be less proud in heart.
Despite my love, I want the selfsame lot.
I think it is assured me, yet I tremble
To see my happiness hang on one decision.

LEO. Why shouldst thou tremble? Whoever is named emperor,
Thou hast thy lover or else at least a great man
Whose name, adored by populace and Court,
Will make thee honored and will o'ercome thy love.
Thou canst love, when they have this great name, men
Like Aspar, Areobindus, and Procopius;
And their rank's splendor, which so rouses envy,
In them will as in me have charms for thee.

PULCHERIA. How cruel and how unjust thou art to me
In saying I love the name of empress solely!
Whate'er my pride of birth requires of me,
Thou alone art my joy and happiness.
Hateful would any other emperor's grandeur . . .

LEO. But thou wouldst wed him, be it with joy or sadness?

PULCHERIA. Nay, press me not so hard; believe with me
The Senate's blessed choice will make me thine,
Or if it should be adverse to our wishes,
Heaven will inspire me to do what I ought to.

LEO.   It will inspire in thee some discreet sorrow
        Which needs to expend for me only one sigh.
        Yes, with such mighty rivals . . .

PULCHERIA.   All of them
        Love someone.

LEO.   A crown lifts a soul above
        All tender feelings. When one takes the throne
        Of the great Theodosius, one must needs
        Place on it what remaineth of his blood.
        He will desire—this rival of mine, whoever
        Is chosen—to secure unto himself,
        By wedding thee, thine own rights to the Empire.
        If he could plight his faith with someone else,
        That is because he deemed thy heart too partial
        To me; but seeing himself upon the throne
        And me in the dust, he will hope everything
        From thy proud nature, and if he lays before
        Thy feet what charms thine eyes, he will become
        The being whom thou viewest most favorably.

PULCHERIA.   Sir, thou mayst try my patience somewhat far.
        I have a proud soul; and such great foreknowledge
        Requires, for me to endure it, even more
        Fondness in me than thou hast yet seen pride.
        I blame thee not for what love makes thee feel,
        But one can fear and still not say so much.
            Yet I abide by all that I have promised.
        Thou hast my wishes, and thou hast my friends;
        Thou hast the votes of all the friends of Marcian.
        He hath, old as he is, more worth than age;
        And if he sought the throne, his glorious deeds
        Would give thy mightiest rivals much to dread.

LEO.   Our empire hath, 'tis true, no greater man.
        Renounce power, madam, and I will propose him.
        If he can win, o'er me, the imperial station,
        At least I fear not he will win thy hand.
        He might, if virtues could; but he is old.

PULCHERIA.   Whate'er he be, my favoring thee enlists him.
        He 'neath my brother loved to do my will,
        And I have just made sure that I can still
        Depend on him.

I see Irene here. Aspar
Finds her fair. Make him, since he loves her, aid thee;
And as, in this case, naught should be neglected,
See what thy sister can contrive for thee.

(Enter IRENE.*)*

Irene, wilt thou help me to crown thy brother?

IRENE. Thou hast but little need of such weak help,
Madam, and the Senate . . .

PULCHERIA. Give it, none the less.
Join to my prayers thine, to my efforts thine,
And let us in this situation show
What love when seconded by sisterly
Affection can accomplish. I shall leave thee
To think on this. *(Exit* PULCHERIA.*)*

IRENE *(after a pause, to* LEO*)*. Thou sayest nothing to me,
Sir. Art thou waiting for me to speak first?

LEO. To tell the truth, I know not what to say,
My sister. Aspar is my friend. He loves thee.
The question is, Who is to be made emperor?
And if one now must hesitate between us,
The Princess favors me; merit is his.
To ask him to renounce the throne for *my* sake
Is a request unworthy even of notice;
And if I could exact this of his friendship,
I would rob thee of what he should share with thee.
That is what forces me to hold my peace.
To all my thoughts I can reply for thee;
And since I suffered him to possess thy heart,
I needs must suffer thee to seek his triumph.

IRENE. I know not yet what I could hope for from him.
As for the throne, he surely hath a right
To aspire to it. He may obtain it o'er thee—
O'er everyone—but whether he would let me
Share it with him, this I make bold to doubt.
He loves me seemingly, really trifles with me,
About our marriage never lacks excuses,
And likes thee so much that, to credit him,
He can be happy only if *thou* art—not
That thy good fortune doth concern him deeply,
But knowing what love the Princess hath for thee,

He would fain see how her plans thrive, and nowise
Wed me unless I am his sovereign's sister.
  Thou seest he thus for two years hath delayed.
Besides, he takes great care to please Pulcheria,
Carrying out her commands in all details;
And in the service thou'st had under him,
That thou wert constantly exposed to dangers
Hath almost wholly disabused me touching
His feelings toward us both—though possibly
A friend's zeal for thy glory or a rival's
Hatred alike would make him risk thy life.
The time has come when he must show his colors,
And most exceptional will his friendship be
If he, when put to proof, attempts to serve thee,
Ambitious as he is, 'gainst his own interests.
He may make promises, but whatever he
May promise thee, we should no less feel anxious.
He will enlist such scant support for thee
That he himself will be elected emperor
Despite his wishes; and then, however love
Protests in my behalf, he will be forced
To favor one of Theodosius' blood—
The Senate will desire him to turn from me
To have the Princess in his family's lineage!
  His heart will go where'er the scepter shineth.
If Marcian gains it, he will love his daughter.
His friendship for thee and his love for me
Will give place to the hope he may succeed him;
And in one word, my fortunes still are dubious.
If thou'rt not happy, I cannot be happy,
Nor have more lover than thou'lt have a friend
Unless he sees thee 'stablished on the throne.

LEO.   Thou think'st ill of a hero who doth love thee.

IRENE. I deem I know him no less than myself;
But heed me, and the Empire, sir, is thine.

LEO.   My sister!

IRENE.   Yes, thou'lt have it in spite of him
Or anyone.

LEO.   Let us lose no time: make haste
To tell me how; make haste to open for me

The path that leads to it, and if thy good fortune
Depends on mine . . .

IRENE.   This way thou'lt risk no failure.
Ask nothing for thyself; there are too many
Others whose deeds shine brighter than thine own,
Whose higher posts have won them more distinction,
And who have—frankly—served the Empire more.
In nobleness of heart thou mayst surpass them,
But opportunities and age thou lackest;
Thou hast commanded only under generals,
And hast not yet the importance of thy rivals.
Propose the Princess. She hath advantages
Which will at once unite all votes for her.
During her brother's life, she ruled for him;
Her mandates have alone sustained the Empire;
For fifteen years it was obedient to her.
Contrive that she be kept in supreme power,
But on condition that she take a husband.
Would her choice fall on anyone but thee?
Would she want from thee any finer thing
Than a respectful love which makes thee wish
To owe to her all that thou mayst become?
Her love will hence be greater than before,
And thou wilt serve thyself in serving her.

LEO.   Oh, what good counsel this thou givest me is!
Did ever sister help her brother more?
Marcian will joyfully heed that suggestion.
He hardly speaks ere his advice is followed,
And since he hath unto the Princess promised
Zealously to make every effort for me
According to the orders she hath given him,
He as her servant will make greater efforts
Still for her than for one she loves.

IRENE.   If he
Aids thee at all, go, thy success is certain.

LEO.   Aspar approaches. Make some overtures
To him, my sister. See . . .

IRENE.   He is a person
Who must be dealt with carefully. To tell
Our plans to him would be to endanger all.

He is ambitious, clever, and very able.

(Enter ASPAR.)

LEO *(to* ASPAR). Sir, thou wilt pardon me if I quit thy presence.
    To leave thee with my sister, whom thou'lt find
    More pleasing, will supply best what I owe thee.
ASPAR. Thou art considerate, but on this occasion
    I need, sir, a brief conference with thee.
      The world's fate is to be decided by us:
    The matter concerns thee, and perhaps me;
    And if my friends do not unite with thine
    We, being divided, may yield place to others.
      Let us in concert act; and, nowise jealous—
    Thou of me, I of thee—in seeking power
    Swear that whichever of us is selected
    Will make his friend his colleague in his reign;
    And, to assure us of succeeding, let us
    See to which one of us two it is shrewder
    To throw our influence,—which name would more likely
    Attract all other votes. I for my part
    Am wholly ready, as I here attest . . .
LEO. Thy name is weightier for the choice than mine,
    Nor can I doubt thou wouldst use well thy power.
    I would, from any other, fear ill treatment,
    But would not have with thee the least misgiving,
    And, as thy friend, would like to pledge to thee
    My word about this; but 'tis for the Princess,
    Sir, to dispose of me. I can act only
    With her consent and dare do naught without it.
ASPAR. Had we to choose the most devoted lover,
    Thou'dst be victorious over all, 'tis certain.
    But this is not the issue now before us.
    The most beguiling act of gallantry
    Cannot . . .
LEO.   What wouldst thou? I adore Pulcheria,
    And with no other reason to deserve her
    My hope lies in that fact, which I am proud of.
ASPAR. The throne, and not one's lady, is at stake.
LEO. I shall submit thy offer to the Princess.
    She knows, better than I do, the realm's needs.
    Farewell. I shall before the Senate tell thee

What she says.   (*Exit* LEO.)

IRENE.   He is much in love.

ASPAR.   Yes, madam;
And I confess the Princess with some reason
Is pleased thereat; but I on this occasion
Would have preferred that love should better go
Hand in hand with ambition and that his
Affections should less let themselves be moved
Nor make us likely to destroy each other.
Thou seest I wished to have an understanding
With him. Wouldst thou still love me if I could
Renounce for him my hopes—I, who should have
So much the greater care as to my fortunes
As love should make them common to us both?

IRENE.   Sir, when my love for thee gave thee my heart,
I thought not to wed one who would be emperor.
Thou couldst, without such rank, find bliss with me.
But of my brother's fate Pulcheria
Is mistress, and her pride of race can suffer
No husband, naturally, who lacks that title.
Ere my dear Leo can espouse the Princess
'Tis necessary that he should combine
With his devotion sovereign power, and that
The highest rank show to the best advantage
The greatness of his merit and his love.
Couldst thou love me sufficiently to follow
The only course to make my brother happy—
Thou, who in *thy* love hast been able, without
Any vexation, to refuse to be so
One moment ere he was, and wouldst deserve
To be made to know better that if he
Could not be happy, thou couldst hardly be?

ASPAR.   Thou goest too fast and wilt ere long insult me,
Speaking as the Emperor's sister who would fain
Leave me. I love thee, and no truer love . . .

IRENE.   Is this to love me: to undo my brother?

ASPAR.   Wouldst thou have me for him undo my hopes?
Is this to love *me:* to make happiness
Cost me so much? I, as men know, have taken
By storm three camps and twenty walled towns; I

Have in the last ten years won seven battles;
And have I gained a name so glorious only
To obey one who hath held command but under
Procopius or me—only to make him
My master, and myself to bow my head
Beneath a shameful yoke, in a crown's stead?

IRENE. I am more reasonable, and do not ask thee
To take so low a place for a friend's sake.
Pylades would have done more for Orestes,
But such acts are no longer customary.
A lofty soul disdains them; times have changed.
One thinks himself obliged to love himself
More; and his heart, persuaded by the current
Virtues, hates those old heroes' strange ideas.

ASPAR. My glory is the issue, and past times . . .

IRENE. It does not lie, perhaps, where thou imaginest;
And whatsoe'er thy just hopes make thee think,
To risk rejection is to risk dishonor.
The Princess is all-powerful, or at least
More powerful than thou. Thou wilt draw down
Her hate and anger on thee. Her own love
Is here involved, and her proud soul . . .

ASPAR.   Let me
Be emperor, and I shall not fear her hate.

IRENE. But if another should be chosen and mount
Before thine eyes, despite thee, to that station,
What woe, confusion, and humiliation
Would leave thy fair fame tarnished evermore!
Nay, hearken to me: go not unto the Senate.
Let the renown of thy brave deeds speak for thee.
How glorious it will be if, unsolicited,
They bring the crown and lay it at thy feet,—
If thy deserts alone decide their choice
Without thy presence having begged their votes!
If Leo, Marcian, or Procopius wins it,
Thou wilt have ne'er had much ambition for it,
And thou wilt disavow all friends of thine
Whose zeal in thy behalf hath been too active.

ASPAR. Madam, I hardly could avoid undoing
Myself if I had to conform to these

High sentiments. I find a great acuteness
In them and still more artifice. I can say
This quickly and without dissimulation:
To show thyself so wise in these things is
To be a loyal sister and a dangerous
Woman in love. Time presses. Fare thee well.
I must see friends who can accord my honor
And duty. Heaven through them will lend me light
To satisfy the claims of both completely
And do with joy all that I owe to thee
And thy dear brother, the Princess, and myself.

(*Exit* ASPAR.)

IRENE (*alone*).　False man, thou hast not yet attained thine ends.
I have perceived thy feelings, learned thy hopes,
And seen thy love for me is mere illusion;
Yet thou'lt turn from it but to thy confusion.

A C T　I I

MARCIAN *and* JUSTINA *are discovered.*

JUSTINA.　Our noble princess, then, is empress, sir?
MARCIAN.　Justice hath been accorded to her virtues.
Leo proposed her, and when I spoke like him,
The Senate was, I saw, wildly delighted.
Its diverse voices suddenly were at one,
And it was rid of all those troublesome,
Turbulent hopes of all the rival aspirants
Which the desire to reign had roused in them.
JUSTINA.　Thus 'tis assured that Leo will be emperor.
MARCIAN.　The Senate, I confess, was loath to choose him,
And against his competitors' great names
His youth had given him but lukewarm supporters.
He lacked not worth, nor did his lofty heart
Not promise everything in a few more years.
Such exploits never have been seen so early.
But more experience, the foremost tasks,
The title of commander of an army—
All of those things, in short, that swell one's fame—
All require time, and love will do today
What his renown would someday do for him.

JUSTINA. Alas!
MARCIAN.   Alas! . . . What secret woe compels thee,
    Daughter, to sigh o'er what thy father tells thee?
JUSTINA. The picture of the realm in such young hands
    Made me sigh thus, because of pity for it.
MARCIAN. One sighs but rarely for the public weal
    Unless some hidden grief is mingled with it.
    The one conceals the other, with false semblance.
    None ever, at thy age, pities the State.
JUSTINA. A sigh at my age seems to reveal love.
    But thou has sighed, sir, in the selfsame way;
    And if I dared to tell thee, in my turn . . .
MARCIAN. 'Tis not for one so old to sigh from love.
    I know that; but all have their weaknesses.
    Mightest thou love Leo?
JUSTINA.   Dost thou love the Princess?
MARCIAN. Forget, for my sake, that thou hast divined it,
    And heed not the suspicion a sigh gave thee.
    In men like me, love is without excuse.
    The least self-scrutiny breeds self-contempt
    For it; one loathes oneself, and this affliction,
    Which one dares not disclose, is even harder
    To hide than to endure; but to confess it
    To thee is to confess it unto none.
    The role which thy respect and thy affection
    Give thee, and all that filial ties bring with them,
    Impose on thee an everlasting silence.
    I love, and for ten years my love and my
    Concealment of it have done equal violence
    To my sad heart. I hear the voice of reason,
    I know it gives good counsels, and the more
    I hearken to them, the worse I follow them.
    At least a hundred times a day am I
    Cured and have a relapse, a hundred times
    Rebel, a hundred times succumb anew—
    So this forced calmness, which I vainly practice,
    Doth vanish in this matchless creature's presence.
JUSTINA. But why thyself give her the crown, when thus
    Thou givest her person to her belovèd Leo?
MARCIAN. Know thou that one as worn with age as I

Dares not desire or even accept aught. Love
Binds him unselfishly to her he loveth,
And hoping for himself and his own interests
Nothing, he serves her.

JUSTINA.   But since thou aspirest
To naught, why dost thou sigh?

MARCIAN.   When one aspires
To naught, one still is jealous, and the quenching
Of one's desires through life's decline doth not
Prevent one's looking on with envious eyes.
When one hath merits well deserving honor
And someone younger must instead be happy,
What bitterness the briefest backward glance
Towards our good years breeds in our tortured souls!
"Why was I not born later by some decades?"
I say. "I for his blessings might have hoped
Had heaven not, as regards the Princess, set
Against my extreme love my lack of youth.
Of all the hearts it forceth to adore her
Is mine the only one that cannot hope?"
    When I was young, I loved and was found pleasing;
Sometimes some lady sought, herself, to win me;
I could aspire to those of highest rank;
But I was young; alas, that time hath passed!
The memory killeth, and one cannot face it
Without, to tell the truth, a sort of frenzy.
One thrusts it from him, thinks of countless things;
The shaft lodged in his breast sinks ever deeper,
And love's fires, which, for shame, one tries to extinguish,
Redouble through his efforts to subdue them.

JUSTINA.   Instructed in love's mischiefs as thou wert,
Thou mightest have prevented its recurrence,
'Gainst all its wiles been better on thy guard.

MARCIAN.   Have I regarded it as thou dost now—
I, who imagined that my waning vigor
Made me safe, even in beauty's presence? I
Undertook, without fear, to serve the Princess,
Proud of my white hairs and in weakness strong;
And when I thought only to do my duty,
I grew to love her without knowing it.

3 9 1

My heart, where carelessly this flame was kindled,
Perceived it only through my jealousy:
All who came near her wished to take her from me;
All who spoke to her wished to rob me of her.
I trembled lest she seem to them too fair;
I hated all of them as worthier of her,
And could not bear that someone should be blest
By his possessing that which I would envy
Anyone's having, though I hoped for naught.
   What torture to adore a lovely being
And know oneself less able to be loved
Than any of one's rivals! To love her more
Than all of them combined, and yet not dare,
However fervently his love's flame burneth,
To hope as they do! Someone would have guessed
My love by seeing my anguish, if my fear
Of this discovery had not made me flee
Such pain. However much the august Pulcheria
Enraptured me, I delayed seeing her
Till there was need to serve her. I did more.
I fostered Leo's hopes. The Princess loved him.
I had her confidence and dissuaded her
From giving herself to him till he should be
The master or sustainer of the Empire.
Thus, to prevent a marriage fatal to me,
I, without making Leo happy, ruined
The others' prospects, and put love's fruition
Far in the future, hoping I might die
Ere that sad day.
                        So stands it with us, daughter,
And I at least have had the joy of opening
The sole path to his triumph. I shall die
The moment they are wed, but die at least
With the sweet thought that they owe all to me.
   I have so long concealed the woe that preys
Upon me that despite myself at last
I had to give vent to it, and its keenness
Is less great from my telling thee about it.
Do with thine likewise. 'Tis my turn to listen.
JUSTINA.   One word suffices to withhold naught from thee:

The same star ruled the birth of sire and daughter.
That tells thee all. Let my imprudent impulse
To speak out now defer to modesty.
   I am young, and love found a tender soul
Which had no care nor art for its defense.
The Princess loved me, told her secrets to me,
And thus supplied love with sure weapons 'gainst me;
And all the reasons which confirmed her love
Were but so many shafts that pierced my breast.
Instinctively I followed her example.
"A lover worthy of her is worthy of me,"
I thought. "If he loved me as he loves her,
I would respond to his devotion better."
The more she pictured to me his rare virtues,
The more was I beguiled by cherished visions.
The certain presage of an illustrious future,
Which was so plainly graven on his face,
And his renown, which I beheld each day
Increase, deserved my love the same as hers.
I saw them in accord as to their marriage,
But we had not yet reached the day for that.
"Some obstacle still unforeseen will shatter
Their blissful ties," I said unto myself
Further, "and time puts out love's fairest flames."
Thus was I led into sweet reveries
Wherewith until this day my love was nourished.
My soul, unwilling to despair of aught,
Told itself charming stories constantly.
   How dear to dream is when one's smitten heart
Is utterly wrapped up in the beloved one!
Thou knowest this, and how at every turn
A vague, sweet feeling troubles the heart's peace.
Our restless sleep, out of its cloudy fancies,
Incessantly evokes enchanting pictures
And on their unsubstantial basis gives
Birth to desires which we, when we awaken,
Deem wonderful and never disavow.
   Thus on the point of being plunged in misery
I hid the thought of that by self-deception;
But such fond error needs must be renounced.

I am in the same plight as thou, sir, art.

MARCIAN.   Thou canst love someone else, and that is something
    That one who loves at my age dares not venture.
    Choose whom thou wilt, I can obtain him for thee.
    But I see Aspar coming; let us hear him.

Enter ASPAR.

ASPAR (*to* MARCIAN).   Thy preference hath united ours. Thy voice,
    sir,
    Hath done more than a hundred others could have.
    But there are murmurs, and I fear the choice
    That will be made now by the Princess will
    Not be approved by everyone.

MARCIAN.   And what
    Leads some to fancy, when it is still uncertain,
    That 'twill be grievous and objectionable?

ASPAR.   Her love for Leo. He will be her choice.
    No one doubts that.

MARCIAN.   I think, like all, he will be.
    What can be said 'gainst him, and what misgivings . . .

ASPAR.   He is quite young. Men fear his inexperience.
    Consider, sir, how much is risked hereby.
    He who hath but obeyed can ill command.
    He ne'er hath had an army, or a province.

MARCIAN.   Good subject never yet became bad ruler;
    And if in him heaven answers ill our prayers,
    The august Pulcheria knows enough for two.
    'Twould not surprise me if we saw her do
    As she did fifteen years with Theodosius.
    He was a weak prince, immature of mind,
    Yet with her aid he governed very well.

ASPAR.   We have six generals here who have led armies,
    Whose nature is accustomed to command.
    Would they be willing to obey the orders
    Of one who up to this time obeyed them?
    'Tis indeed hard to be, sir, 'neath a master
    Whose master one hath been and still should be.

MARCIAN.   And who will guarantee that these six generals
    Would 'neath one of their equals unite better?
    Jealousy is more natural to great men

The more a like worth summons them to greatness.

ASPAR. I can unite them, sir, if thou wilt let me.
There still, there still are names more eminent. I
Know who would please them. If I must say more,
Sanction my efforts and I will make thee emperor.

MARCIAN. Me, at an age at which the tomb awaits me!
A two-days' sovereign is not what is wanted.
I know a crown's weight and my strength too well
To be responsive to such vain lures still.
Time, which hath tired alike my mind and body,
Would make the smallest task too much for both;
And my death, which thou wouldst thereby see hastened,
Would re-arouse the ambitions of these rivals
And be immediately the sad occasion
Of causing discord in the State again.

ASPAR. To shun the evils thou wouldst thus expect,
Thou with a son-in-law couldst share thy burden,
Install him on the throne, and name him Caesar.

MARCIAN. That son-in-law should have thy qualities;
But thou lov'st elsewhere, and 'twould be a crime
To render faithless any heart so noble.

ASPAR. I love, and do not feel my love could change;
But someone else would tell thee that, to aid thee,
Although his love was sheer idolatry,
He to his country's good would sacrifice it.

JUSTINA. Someone who loved me for the public good
Would find my heart not unappreciative,
And I would thank him in the whole Empire's name.
But thou art constant; and, if I need say more,
Whate'er the public good ever requireth,
'Twill not be I, sir, who will make thee change.

MARCIAN. Let us recur to Leo. I scarce know
What harm the choice of him could make us dread.
Whoe'er sees thee the husband of his sister
Will fear, if not him, his defender; also,
If thou still reckonest me as aught, my counsels
Will have their weight, as under Theodosius.

ASPAR. As to that, we may both fail in our efforts.

MARCIAN. That would be to find death in a good cause.
It could but cost me a life nearly over,

Which age and its afflictions soon will end.
    But thou, who viewest differently this danger—
Longer hast thou to live and more to do.
I shall not stay thy zeal to serve the Princess
From being displayed as much as thou considerest
Fit. Thou canst warn her of what thou believest,
Explain what thou foreseest from this choice,
And tell her frankly whom she should select.
Truth pleases her, and thou mayst please her. I
Shall in that case change like her my opinions
And hold myself ready for her commands.

ASPAR.   Among truths there are some which nobody
Tells bluntly to crowned heads, and which require
Of us some wile, some influence, that none
Can find except a prudent minister.
Thou better wilt display these evidences
Of loyal zeal. In broaching unto thee
This subject, I have done my duty toward her,
And having nothing more to bring me here,
I leave the field to thee, and go. Farewell.

                                           (*Exit* ASPAR.)

MARCIAN.   A dangerous spirit! He how easily
Would fail in love and pledged faith to Irene!
Of Leo's rivals, he is the most jealous,
And he revolves plans which he tells not widely.

JUSTINA.   He hath for goal only the Empire's good!
Dethrone the Princess; have thyself elected:
This is an unexpected lover for me,
Who will relieve thee of the cares of State!

MARCIAN.   He is a man—remember this someday—
A man to ruin all unless forestalled.
But Leo comes to tell us of his bliss.
Steel thyself to be nobly firm of heart,
And whatsoe'er emotions trouble it,
Midst all its turmoil control well thy face.

Enter LEO.

LEO.   Who would have dreamt of it! I am undone.
MARCIAN.   What sayest thou? Have I heard thee rightly?
LEO.   I

Am hopelessly undone, beyond denial.
I have just seen Pulcheria, and seen only
An ingrate; it was when I thought to win her
That I have lost her. I undid myself
By serving her.

MARCIAN.   Explain thy words, sir; speak
In confidence. Hath she made some other choice?

LEO.   No, but she hesitates. She does not wish
To make me despair yet, but she takes time
To think about whom she shall choose. No longer
Am I her choice, since she defers her choosing.
Love is not king when one deliberates.
I can no more promise myself her hand—
I, who have only love to plead my cause.
Ah, madam . . .

JUSTINA.   Sir . . .

LEO.   Couldst thou have e'er believed it?

JUSTINA.   When love deliberates, it is sure of victory;
And when it hath its basis in real merit,
There are no reasons which do not plead its cause.
Often it likes to rouse some slight impatience,
And feigns to draw back when advancing most;
That moment's bitterness makes its fruit the sweeter.
Love; let her act whose heart is wholly thine.

LEO.   "Wholly mine!" My ill fortune is too real.
I have foreseen the blow and feel it crush me.
The more she would assure me of her love,
The greater fear I felt of her ambition.
I knew not which was stronger of the two.
Ambition hath prevailed; 'tis all too true.
If her heart still speaks to her in my favor,
Her throne disdains me in her heart's despite.
    Sir, do thou speak for me; speak for me, madam.
Ye can do aught with her; ye read her thoughts.
Paint well to her my love; recall hers to her;
Remind her of our happiest hours together;
And if ye know how ardently I love her,
Make her remember that she loved me likewise.
She herself hath intrigued to crown me emperor;
I without that great title was unworthy

Of her, but if I have it not—this title
Which fascinates her—what, sir, is the reason
Except her changing mood? Should her pride arm her
Against me, when to see me on the throne
Needs but her wish? The Senate hath supported
My nomination of her only that
Thus all my greatness might be her love's work.
It knew how long she hath vouchsafed to love me,
And when it chose her, thought 'twas choosing me.
    Ah, go, sir, go; keep her from being faithless.
Make me as emperor be thy dependent.
How freely would I give *thee* that high station
If thou couldst crown my love's desires without it.
For really my love wishes but her person
And is ambitious but by her command.

MARCIAN. We shall go—both of us—and show her, sir,
That she should use her sovereign power better.
In the meantime, temper thine excessive anguish.
Regain thy spirits by talking with Irene.

LEO.   Irene? Her counsels have betrayed, undone me.

MARCIAN. She did her loyal best to aid her brother.
How could she have foreseen the way Pulcheria
Hath in her pride treated thy love? I speak
Thus of it, but that is only 'twixt ourselves.
Less wayward and more kindly shall we make her
And bring her heart and her choice back to thee.
Go.

LEO.   Why art thou not between her and me
The arbiter! Farewell. Through thee alone
Can I retain some remnant still of hope.

                                 (*Exit* LEO.)

MARCIAN. Thou seest, Justina, this blest obstacle
Whose miracle thy heart seemed prescient of.
On this occasion I do not forbid thee
To base a little hope on their dissension.
But let thyself not have a soul so brazen
As to be treacherous to their love at all.
My soul is so involved in their misfortune
That now I hope to live some moments longer.
But with what countenance to make them know

The perils of a love which we saw form,
Of which we both have been the confidants
And perhaps moulded the most ardent features?
We are responsible thus for all their troubles.
As friends who truly love them let us serve them.
Genuine love seeks nothing for itself.
Come; I shall go on as I have begun.
Take my example: show that noble natures
Find in their good deeds what can make them happy.
Let duty well done be its own reward,
Nor e'er deserve any reproachful word.

ACT III

PULCHERIA, MARCIAN, *and* JUSTINA *are discovered.*

PULCHERIA (*to* MARCIAN). I have told thee my commands. Go, sir,
  I pray thee.
  Save my sad heart from the blow threatening it.
  In this dear cause enlist thou all the Senate.
MARCIAN. They well know, madam, how fond thou art of Leo,
  And name him plainly enough when they permit thee
  A choice thy love hath made already for thee.
PULCHERIA. Why, then, doth their decree not bid me wed him?
  To leave the choice to me is not to choose him;
  'Tis, sheltered from the storm, to await the outcome.
  If I am praised for it, it will be their work.
  If I am blamed for it, they had no part in it.
  Doubtful of its result, they flee its hazard;
  And when I want their warrant for it before
  The whole world, they want me to be responsible
  Solely. They leave me thus to mine own choice.
  If there are malcontents, I alone make them;
  And I alone must needs abate the murmurs
  Of those to whom this choice will seem injurious,
  Prevent revolt by them, and pacify
  Unruly folk who envy our good fortune.
MARCIAN. Aspar hath seen thee; his embittered soul . . .
PULCHERIA. He saw me, and I saw chagrin possessed him;
  But he tried tirelessly to make me realize
  What dangers there would be in my heart's choice.

Good counsel sometimes can be had from hate;
One can find fruit in that which giveth pain;
And whoso would succeed in weighty matters
Lends ear to all, derives from all some profit.

MARCIAN.   But thou hast promised, and the pledge that binds thee . . .

PULCHERIA.   I was Pulcheria, and I am the Empress.
    I from this throne, foe to my sweetest longings,
Regard love as it were one of my subjects.
I wish that the respect it owes my crown
May stay the attempt it makes against my person.
I wish it to obey me, not betray me,—
To set all an example of obedience,—
And, jealous for my sovereign power already,
To bow all to it, assume it o'er myself.

MARCIAN.   So Leo, then, who was so dear to thee . . .

PULCHERIA.   I love him but so much the more if I
Must disengage myself from him.

MARCIAN.   Would he
Be in thy sight less worthy of the Empire
Than when thou urgedst the Senate to elect him?

PULCHERIA.   'Twas necessary that he should be seen
By them as I see him, that they be convinced
Like me of all his worth, and that by signal
And public approbation of him, my love
Be shown to accord with wise State policy.
    I would already have fulfilled the hopes
Our fond love cherished, if the Senate's choice
Had sanctioned my so doing. I would have taken
The course which I must now forbid myself;
And if no more I dare to stoop to Leo,
I would have been proud, had I seen him emperor,
To reach the throne by giving him my hand.

MARCIAN.   Thy heart will cleave to him against all others.

PULCHERIA.   If *he* has thoughts like these, they are not thine.
Nay, sir, 'tis Leo, his quite natural anger,
His misery, that doth speak through thee. Thou makest
Loan of thy mouth; *thou* art not capable
Of giving me counsel fatal to my honor.

MARCIAN.   But have his rivals more worth?

PULCHERIA.   No, but they

Have higher posts, greater rank, and more fame;
And if my love governs this solemn choice,
I shall begin my reign by showing weakness.

MARCIAN.   And art thou very sure that veering thus
Will lend more luster to thy dignity?
Forgive the word "veering," if 'tis too blunt.
The people may have less respectful hearts.
They like to censure those who make their laws,
And even will say thou dost not keep thy word.

PULCHERIA.   I told thee what acquits me of that charge:
I *was* Pulcheria, and I *am* the Empress.
I shall say more: Leo hath made some jealous,
Who hold him not in such esteem as we do.
Howe'er remarkable are his first brave deeds,
An emperor's virtues go not with his age.
He is young; this they deem so great a fault
That the word's utterance cancels all his merits.
Then if I make this choice, I seem to make it
To rule in his name just as in my brother's.
And thou: since thou 'neath *him* servedst in ways
In which thy counsels ruled no less than I,
Or more, wilt thou not give them grounds for saying
That thou desiredst but a phantom emperor,
And that with such a choice thou wilt feel flattered
By keeping in thine own hands all the power?

MARCIAN.   That is not *my* aim; and if I must tell thee
What heaven suggests to me on Leo's choice,
In the blest hour when he becomes thy husband
I leave Byzantium and bid thee farewell,
To go and take in quiet solitude
Good thought upon the death that soon awaits me.
That is how I aspire to rule the Empire.
Thou badest me to assemble now the Senate.
I go to do so.

PULCHERIA.   What! doth Marcian leave me
When he is needed to make my crown secure?
He whose great heart, wisdom, and loyalty . . .

MARCIAN.   All the reward I seek is thus to die.

(*Exit* MARCIAN.)

PULCHERIA.   What hath he said, Justina? Why should he

4 0 1

By such departure jeopardize the marriage
He wishes of me? Hath he made himself
The advocate for Leo to me only
The better to disdain to serve me 'neath him?
Doth he hate him? doth he fear him? and why else . . .

JUSTINA.   Whoever weds thee, he would wish the same.

PULCHERIA.   If he were of an age to seek my hand,
As he would be the worthiest of all,
What seems the case would have some likelihood;
But his years must have left his heart impervious.

JUSTINA.   How know we, madam? Is there 'neath the skies
A heart safe from the power of thine eyes?
The experience which they have of conquering hearts
Hath found men ever ready for their chains.
Age shelters no one from thy darted glances—
Not that I know of their effect on Marcian;
He hath told me like thee that thy great marriage
Will send him far from here to end his days,
And if I venture to have vague suspicions
I speak in general and know nothing more.
But, as to Leo, hast thou decided to
Destroy him through thy sovereign power today?
For not to wed him will indeed destroy him.

PULCHERIA.   To show thee with what anguish his mere name
Fills me, let me make known to thee, in favor
Of his love, what a loving heart is mine,
As I have shown thee how high-souled I am.
Leo is my one joy, my one desire.
I can choose no one else, nor dare choose him.
Clinging three years to one sweet dream, I by it
Am every hour and everywhere possessed.
Nothing but death will tear it from my breast.
I know not if aught can e'en after death;
If heaven lets us still love in the tomb,
Then I shall love him in my tomb the same.
Throne which dazzles me, titles which beguile me,
Can ye be worth to me all that ye cost me;
And is your loftiest pride of pomp enough
To match the happiness ye rob me of?

JUSTINA.   And thou canst think of marrying another?

PULCHERIA.   It is not that, thou knowest, which I resolve.
   If honor will not let me give myself
   To Leo, love is able to defend me
   From anyone else. Oh, how strong that love is!
   Protect me from it, if thou canst. See Leo.
   Talk with him. Win, thyself, his heart. To take him
   From me would do me now a service that
   Can snatch me from the brink of an abyss.
   I fear him—fear myself—unless he plights
   His faith elsewhere, and I too utterly
   Am his so long as he is wholly mine.
   Dost think thou couldst do this in friendship for me?
   Hath this brave youth naught which could make thee love him?
   I to thy beauty's power will add my power . . .
   Speak. What dost thou decide to do?
JUSTINA.   My duty.
   Mine is a race that makes me vain enough
   To expect a husband from my sovereign's hand;
   And since I love naught but my maiden freedom,
   If that must needs be lost for thy protection,
   I shall dare . . . Here is thy dear Leo, madam.
   Dost wish . . .
PULCHERIA.   Let me take counsel with my heart
   Better. I do not yet know what I wish.
   Await new orders and defer all efforts.

              (Enter LEO.*)*
   What brings thee back, sir? Is it an impatience
   To add unto my woes that of thy presence
   And give my heart o'er to new strife? Do I
   Suffer too little when I see thee not?
LEO. I come to learn my fate.
PULCHERIA.   Doubt not of that.
   I love thee and I pity both of us.
   That pictures my whole plight unto thee. That
   Is all I now feel, and if thy affection
   Felt any touch of pity for my misery,
   'Twould spare mine eyes the fatal sight of thee
   Which will undo me, kill me, and kill thee.
LEO. Thou lovest me, thou sayest.
PULCHERIA.   More than ever.

LEO.   Oh, I would suffer less if thou didst not love me!
Why love me still only to pity me?
PULCHERIA.   How hide love's flame which I cannot extinguish?
LEO.   Thou smotherest it, at least, beneath proud scruples,
Which cause alone the woes we both shall die of.
Lament not thine, for thine are voluntary;
Thou hast but those thou choosest to make and have;
And 'tis no question of one's dying of them
When one hath power to end them if one would.
PULCHERIA.   I alone cause my woes which I lament?
Was it, then, for myself I sought the crown?
Did I take every care, enlist my friends,
Except in thy behalf? Have I thus sought
Anything but to see thee hence my husband?
What! thy respect for me opposed my efforts,
Shattered my plans—and I alone cause all?
'Tis having given me more than was my due
That hath undone me, and undone thee, too.
Thou, if thou lovedst me, shouldst have trusted me
And not involved my duty and my honor.
These are two foes which thou hast made for us
And which not all our love will e'er appease.
Vainly thou overwhelmest me with sighs
And with endearments. Vainly my sad heart
Feels deep concern o'er thy unhappiness
And gives thee, for our mutual longings' sake,
Endearments for endearments, sighs for sighs.
When to a love so sweet I do this justice,
A loving woman speaks; hear now the Empress.
That title is thy work; thou toldest me so.
Thy hopes rejoiced in doing me such a service
And blindly raised an insurmountable
Obstacle to themselves when they believed
That what was done would make their triumph certain.
Supported by my aid, sure of my heart,
Thou shouldst have offered me an emperor's hand
To lift me, as thy fortunate subject, to thee.
My joy and honor would have been unmarred;
But can I do the like for thee, when Empress?
I have to name a ruler, choose a husband:

That is the task imposed on me, or rather
The penalty I must pay for sovereignty.
I know the Senate with united voice
Respectfully hath left me a free choice;
But it expects of me the greatest man
Who now draws breath in this Rome or the other.
Thou art that, I am sure; and yet, alas!
'Twill be someday believed, but . . .

LEO.   None believes it.
There still are needed, madam, time and service,
And fortunate caprices, too, of Fate,
And favorable fame enrapturing all
The world, to win thy great heart's admiration.
Yet marvel at a lover's self-beguilement.
I thought thine honor somewhat less fastidious.
I thought to accord thee better what I owe thee
By having all from *thy* hand than by offering
Thee all with mine, and that, with one who loves,
Her love for me would take the place of merit
In me.

PULCHERIA.   It would; but would it with the Empire,
Which with wide eyes waits for this solemn choice?
Perhaps the Senate still dares not select thee,
And if I take that risk, will dare gainsay me;
Perhaps 'tis planning to make overtures
Elsewhere because of the humiliating
Refusal it now waits to give our love;
For let us realize that inexorable
Duty requires for me the most illustrious
Husband, not the most lovable; and the more
My rank exalts me, the more its dignity
Makes this and lofty pride essential for me.

LEO.   Suppress this pride, which all thy heart opposes,
Madam, and for the sake of both of us
Take some risks. Love and so great pride accord
Not well, and to risk naught is not to love.

PULCHERIA.   Did I but risk my life, I would agree,
But 'tis too great a thing to risk my honor;
And if I shut mine eyes to mine own peril,
I see that thus I risk too much *thy* life.

Ah, if the public voice had seconded
Thy hopes by urging me to give thee preference,—
If of those names which fame brings to me proudly
The one most dear to me rang out most loudly,—
I would abide by its renown how gladly
And let thee have my person and the Empire!
But crowning thee would make too many people
Of great note jealous of thee. In my heart
I think thou dost surpass them all; *I* set thee
Above the greatest; but they are better known.
Thy worth has not like theirs been widely shown
And the world, dazzled by their illustrious name,
Dares not expect of thee the same as them.
   Thou lovest, sir, and thou inspirest love.
With women that is everything; thereby
One catches them, one steals away their hearts.
But on a throne to sit, and win respect there,
'Tis not enough to inspire love and to love.
The most securely 'stablished throne soon totters
When through love's work it seems to have been seized;
And to retain a place so coveted
One needs ability in greater things
Than loving. Stoop not to the shame of tears.
They are weak arms 'gainst such compulsive duty;
And if by their aid thou shouldst win a crown,
I would deem pitiful one bought by weeping.

LEO.   Ah, madam, was thy soul so haughty when
Thy love concerned itself in my behalf?
Didst thou then say that governing demanded
Other ability than that of loving?
Had but the Senate joined its voice to thine
I would have seemed as worthy as another,
Or worthier. This great art of reigning would
Have come with all those votes, and thou thyself . . .

PULCHERIA.   Yes, I would have accepted their decision,
Sure that the Senate, jealous of its choice,
Would have upheld this against all the world.
Those who would rise up against thee and me
Would dare not against so august a body;
Scorning what love led *me* to do, they would

Respect in it the Genius of the Empire.

LEO. But the chance offered thee to trust thy wishes . . .

PULCHERIA. Is but a kindly, deferential refusal
To grant them.

LEO. What fantastical ideals
Of honor, what uncompromising adherence
To merciless policy, makes me in that heart
Entirely mine but vainly won by me
The man most loved and least esteemed?

PULCHERIA. Nay, hold!
My love springs purely from esteem. I see
A great soul, great abilities in thee,
And valor worthy of my forefathers;
And if the Senate saw thee with my eyes . . .

LEO. Have done, pray, with the Senate! Tell me, madam,
To what more fortunate man I must give place,
Whom I must imitate to obtain someday
From a proud emperor a fit love's reward.

PULCHERIA. 'Tis hard for me to choose; choose him thyself,
This fortunate man; say whom thou'dst have me love.
But thou hast pain enough, without being jealous.
I love thee; and if this choice cannot fall
On thee, at least, whate'er be ordered of me,
None ever shall be master of my person:
I swear it to thee and leave my heart with thee.
Expect naught else unless thou beëst emperor—
And I mean emperor as thou must become one,
By being the Senate's choice to rule the land,
Which makes thee of this mighty realm the mainstay
And by the general vote sanctions our marriage.
I reassembled it but to elect thee
Or else let me alone govern the Empire
And not subject me further to its choice
Unless for thee is lifted every voice.
Farewell; I fear that I can curb no longer
The weakness which thy sight, sir, fills me with,
And that my agony, which equals thy
Anguish, will cost me some unworthy sigh.

(*Exit* PULCHERIA.)

LEO (*to* JUSTINA). I have held in too long; 'tis time I vented

My wrath. I have not called her an ambitious
And faithless woman, but at last the subject
Gives place to the outraged lover, and excesssive
Respect to a natural outburst of my feelings.
    Thou tell me, madam, was there ever seen
Faithlessness blacker in the heart or more
Brazen outwardly? Was there ever seen
More studious effort to apply one's reason
To aid, unworthily, such treachery?
The arrogant woman casts not down her eyes
But glories in her conduct. This she dares
To speak of to us as a noble victory
Over herself: honor and duty solely
Determine what she does, and if she were
More faithful to me she would have to blush!

JUSTINA.   Her sufferings are at least as great as thine.
For thy sake she will not choose any other
Husband; she herself swore this unto thee.

LEO.   More self-deception, and the merest trifling!
Only too many circumstances are there
In which new oaths result in new oath-breakings.
One who knows how to reign breaks them with pride
And never lacks a hundred reasons of State.

JUSTINA.   If thou wouldst rouse in her some jealousy,
Sir, and thereby confuse her mind, then love—
Not stifled yet—might call thee back to her.
Her pride would find it hard to let thee go.

LEO.   Thinkest thou I have a soul so base that I
Would stoop to trickery to escape misfortune?
I am young, and I pay court here too badly
To join to that defect false shows of love.

JUSTINA.   Oh, how attractive a defect is youth,
And how those wiser who are jealous of thee,
Proud though they be, would gladly buy it back
With all they now, or will, think they deserve!
But if thou deemest it wicked to feign love,
Take really thy most tender regards elsewhere,
Punish by thy disdain the haughtiness
Shown thee, and place thy heart in surer hands.

LEO.   Thou seest me sacrificed to her high station,

Madam, and thou wouldst have me justify her!—
Have me, after her scornful treatment of me,
Show her a similar unfaithfulness!

JUSTINA. Love, without thought of that; and do not trouble
Thyself about whether thou justifiest
Or punishest thereby this heartless woman;
But know that if she treated thy love badly,
Someone else might accept thee joyfully.
The honor it would be to win thee from her
Would make thy heart a nobler, fairer prize.
The more worth one would need to cause thy love
To change, the greater would the glory be
Of her who doth await thee—for perhaps
The Princess thus herself compels to love thee
Her unto whom thou sayest "I love thee" next.
Farewell. That is enough to think of now.

(*Exit* JUSTINA.)

LEO. O heaven, deliver me from my soul's confusion!

A C T   I V

JUSTINA *and* IRENE *are discovered.*

JUSTINA. No, thy dear Aspar doth not love the Princess.
'Tis but her rank that all his heart adoreth;
And if my father had been chosen Caesar,
The noble Aspar would ere now have wooed *me*.
He has said as much already in my presence,
And all the interest that he hath in her—
All his desire to rouse fear or disdain
In her—is due to his desire to reign.
    Pulcheria hath eyes that read his secret,
And deemeth him not thy brother's friend but rival;
Yet as she wavers, she hearkens readily
To whatsoe'er supports her own opinion.
That is all *I* know.

IRENE.   I am not surprised
By what thou frankly tellest me of Aspar.
Thou sayest naught that I did not say of him
When recently I described his character
To Leo. I divined his hidden motives,

Even foreseeing what he revealed to thee.
　Since I in vain love one who doth not love me,
I must with honor escape from this bad plight.
I must—like him—be politic, find a brave
Face amid my misfortunes, give our rupture
An aspect to my credit, and preserving
A seemly outward show, stifle my sorrow.
But tell me, what will happen to my brother?
What can his great love hope for from the Princess?

JUSTINA.　She loves him, deeply—far more than she wishes—
But does the best she can to break with him.
Must I needs tell thee all? I have been bidden
To attempt upon him artifice and wiles.
She will owe much to me if I can shake
His love for her—will let me have his heart
If I can steal it—and I have in fealty
Already tried to, and made some slight progress;
But thou canst judge how, as a faithful lover,
He hath repulsed such importunity.
However little thou likest to aid my efforts,
Thy help would constitute a signal service.

IRENE.　'Tis not a service to expect of me,
To lead him to keep ill his plighted faith;
Yet if I could persuade him to love thee,
What good then would his change of feelings bring him?
Couldst thou, who lovest him not at all, accept him?

JUSTINA.　Leo is not a man one could refuse;
And after marriage vows are sealed, so often
A perfect love is born of such a union
That if I saw in him some fondness for me,
I would hope soon to love him, in my turn.

IRENE.　Too much thou tellest me and too little. Is
This love still to be born? Is it born already?

JUSTINA.　It may be. Let us not go into that
Before the proper time. That time may come,
And I await it.

IRENE.　　　　　And thou aidest Leo's
Love for the Princess?

JUSTINA.　　　　　　　I concern myself
In his behalf sincerely; and if *my* voice

Were heeded, he would have the happiness
Of winning her hand as he hath won her heart.
But I shall follow the directions given me
And let him woo me, if he should lose the crown.
Here is the Princess.

Enter PULCHERIA.

PULCHERIA.   What is thy poor brother
    Doing, Irene?

IRENE.   What men in such plight do.
    He sighs, complains.

PULCHERIA.   Of me?

IRENE.   Of his ill fortune.

PULCHERIA.   Doth he perceive now that 'tis common to us
    And that like him I accuse Fate of cruelty?

IRENE.   I cannot see into his inmost heart,
    But outwardly he in his grief respects thee.
    He speaks not of thee.

PULCHERIA.   Ah, I like not that.
    Modest reproaches would befit his woes.
    To say naught of me is to blame me greatly.
    Hath he forgotten me and in his soul
    Effaced already such a fervent love?

IRENE.   Thus ought he to find solace for his misery,
    Madam, and I do what I can to help him.

PULCHERIA.   Ah me! my love hath not become so little
    That I can bear it for him to forget me!
    Make him, Irene, make him find solace, rather,
    In knowing I suffer as much as he, and more.
    That is a fact I need for him to know,
    To mingle with my pain some fruitless joy—
    If that sad sweetness can be called a joy
    Which a true heart can cherish despite misfortune.
    The heart which once hath felt such love is always
    Moved by it, and even if one loves no longer
    'Tis sweet to be loved.

JUSTINA.   Dost thou still remember
    Giving him to me, and the kind care, madam,
    With which thy tortured soul . . .

PULCHERIA.   Bear with the love

4 1 1

Left in me, which confuses and o'ercomes me.
I made thee no irrevocable gift,
But I will say now: take his heart from me,
Win his love, rob me of it, if thou canst.
Too little have I played the part of empress.
Let us resume therewith the attendant glory
And grief. I shall have both of these, most cruelly,
Unless the Senate deems my love can be
Reconciled with the welfare of the realm.

IRENE. Is it not to degrade thy sovereign power
To take of others what thou canst take thyself?

PULCHERIA. Irene, thou'dst needs have the same eyes as mine
To see the least part of what I foresee.
Spare me the pain of telling thee to what
Disorders I could by my choice expose
The Empire. I have spoken of them already
So much that my exhausted spirit could not
Bear now to paint again the picture of them.
Thy brother hath a great, brave, noble heart;
Yet that he is a little young is reckoned
Such a defect that if, with all his virtues,
He hath but me in favor of him, to make him
Emperor is to destroy him and myself.

IRENE. What mandate doth exclude youth from the throne?
What star links weakness with our loveliest years?
Worth and not age hath to such rank the right;
And but for the respect thy blood inspireth,
I would say Leo equals Theodosius.

PULCHERIA. Beyond doubt; yet their case is not the same.
Weak though that prince was to rule such an empire,
He had advantages thy brother hath not.
Sovereignty was with him hereditary.
He had it from his grandfather and father.
He reigned from childhood; none were jealous of him;
Esteemed by few, he was obeyed by all.
Leo can have his title to be ruler,
But not the blessings of a like obedience—
So would the throne, if my love placed him on it,
Make for him enemies of my foremost subjects.
  All who in peace and war have been illustrious

Aspire to be the master of the world.
All regard empire as the prize that each
Alike seeks for himself if no one hath it.
Full of their fame, proud of their services,
How unjust to them would they deem my choice
If through my stubborn love and its desires
This fell on him whom they esteem the least!
Leo is worthy to become their emperor,
But since 'tis love which helps me to perceive it,
All those who dare against us to rebel
Will say I only have imagined it.

IRENE.   'Tis in vain, then, we pray and hope for him?

PULCHERIA.   I love him, and to see him gladdens me;
But unless heaven enlists the Senate for him,
I mean to give up all for the realm's good.

IRENE.   How it would thrill my soul to imitate thee
And sacrifice to the realm all my life's joy!
Madam, name Leo Caesar or else let
Thy great choice fall on the illustrious Aspar.
I love him and despite my love would proudly
Make my heart's lord be lord of all the world,
And weeping for my brother in his pain,
Console myself by seeing my lover reign.
Of the two dearest men on earth to me
Set one or the other on thy father's throne.
Deign . . .

PULCHERIA.   Aspar would be worthy of such honor
If thou, Irene, hadst over him less influence.
'Twould shame me sorely if I should, as his wife,
Make him reign without reigning in his heart,—
If I had but that name, thou all the power,
And my Court's deference were divided 'twixt us.

IRENE.   Fear not that, madam; however much he loves me,
He cares for power more than for his love.

PULCHERIA.   I think as thou dost—that his master-passion
Concerns the realm more than thee, me, or Leo.
I understand thee and speak frankly to thee.
I see his plans and what must be feared from him.
Dost love him?

IRENE.   I did love him when I thought

That *he* loved *me*. I saw in his appearance
Something that charmed me quite; but since time made me
Better perceive the nature of his love
I almost have quenched mine and freed my heart.

PULCHERIA.   Say on! Such as he is, wouldst care to wed him?

IRENE.   Yes, or at least be able to reject him.
After two years, my honor is involved.
The affront would be too gross, the stain too black,
If in the situation now existing
He dared regard me as unworthy of him.
His aim is higher, and, as he now loves thee,
Though perhaps not so much thee as thy crown,
I have seen naught in me that still could hold him,
And offered him to thee, to act ere he did.
'Tis thus I thought to assure my own position
By falsely seeming most magnanimous.
I gave thee something that I could not keep,
Which my fair fame lets me give thee alone.

PULCHERIA.   Rely on me. Here is thy Aspar.

Enter ASPAR.

ASPAR (*to* PULCHERIA).   Madam,
I have already sounded more than one
Heart as to thy intentions, and I deem it
My duty to acquaint thee better with
What was set forth to me regarding them.
    I hope for Leo's triumph, and I am doing
All I can for him, but I foresee therewith
A certainty of discontent which may
Be limited merely to some ill feeling
But may go even further than sedition.

PULCHERIA.   Thou knowest who said this. Speak; let him be punished.
I shall ask justice on him from the Senate.

ASPAR.   It is perhaps someone thou mightest choose
If thou hadst need to turn elsewhere thy wishes—
Someone whose choice would be so satisfactory
That we should have to fear no adverse faction.
To name him unto thee would be to undo him,
To rob the Empire of a stout support,
And to deliver to his certain ruin

A brave man who deserves not yet thy hate.

PULCHERIA. One ill addresses me with such advices,
Which, without naming anyone, name more
Than ten. I like not these assiduous acts
Of loyal zeal that only fill the mind
With vague chimaeras and, by offering me
Naught but obscurest warnings, give to me
All things to fear and nothing to prevent.

ASPAR. The nation's need is oft a mystery, half
Of which is to be told, half left untold.

PULCHERIA. 'Tis also oft naught but an airy phantom
Which those with hidden aims make speak and act,
And which doth fade when those who for their interests
Shaped it and raised it choose that it shall do so.
If thou art jealous for the public welfare,
Leave that to me, who better than thou see it.
Marcian, like thee, to speak to thee quite frankly,
Finds in the choice of Leo grounds for fear;
But he advised me whom I should mistrust,
And I can, if I wish, rid myself of him.

ASPAR. Whom names he?

PULCHERIA.   Aspar, 'tis a mystery, half
Of which is to be told, half left untold.
If Leo is so hated, get permission
At least for me to reign without a husband.

ASPAR. I could not. 'Tis a thing unprecedented.

PULCHERIA. The chance to show true zeal in my behalf
Is that much greater; thou wouldst show it best
By getting for me what hath ne'er been granted.

ASPAR. Yes; but whom wouldst thou have the Senate give thee,
Madam, if Leo . . .

PULCHERIA.   Leo, or else no one.
Conform thy thoughts to these alternatives.
Thou lov'st Irene; she will be thy reward.
I leave her with thee, that thine ardor may
Kindle from the flame that in thy heart burns for her.
Justina, come with me.   (*Exeunt* PULCHERIA *and* JUSTINA.)

IRENE.   Sir, this reward
Promised thee should not greatly stir thy soul.
Mine own, won wholly by thy once true fervor,

Can be no prize meet for thy lofty spirit;
And love so makes thee master of my heart
That giving me to thee doth give thee nothing.

ASPAR. This is true, madam, and I shall dare say further
That giving me a heart which brings not empire,
A heart which would decree a vile subjection
For me, doth give me nothing worthy of me.

IRENE. Unworthy though I am of troth so dubious,
Would I decree for thee any subjection
That could be vile? If Leo owed the Empire
To thy support—he who would make thee in it
The next to him in power—wouldst thou have need
To blush for having made him master of it,
Sir, thou who seest that *thou* canst not be that?
Set thyself—I consent—above all love
If thus thou hast some chance to mount the throne.
Were lover false to gain that glorious station,
I could admire him for it, love him more,
And see with joy a great and noble ambition
Triumph over a long and ardent fondness.
The most enchanting thing must yield to empire.
Reign; if my heart grieves, I will disavow it.
Thou dost not, sir, believe my words, and yet
Thou soon wouldst reign had my advice been followed.
Learn to what lengths I went in thy behalf.
I just now myself offered thee to the Princess,
And would renounce for thee my dearest longings,
To set thee on the pinnacle of greatness.
Thou knowest her answer: "Leo, or else no one."

ASPAR. Generous and good is such an act of love,
But generosity cannot cost one much
When what one offers is sure to be rejected.

IRENE. Thou seest the pain that I invited by it,
But dost not wish to owe the least thing to me!
Oh, if I dared to call thee, sir, an ingrate!

ASPAR. The offer was indeed exceptional,
And bright would shine its luster—dazzlingly—
If thou hadst had the skill to shake, however
Little, the resolution of the Princess.
She is now empress and can with a mere

    " 'Tis my will" make Leo a blissful monarch.
    What need hath he of me, he who can wholly
    Sway her?

IRENE.   Insult not, sir, a love so great.
    Tired of its cruel restraint by reasons of State,
    It might not heed the Senate slavishly.

ASPAR. It need but speak; whate'er thou thinkest, the Senate
    Will show naught but respect and deference;
    And, to judge by the way things take their course
    Now, Leo may for three whole days be emperor.

IRENE. Three days are quite enough to accomplish much.
    The Court hath in less time seen countless changes.
    A prince whose word is law can in less time
    Repay true friends and false friends as he should.

ASPAR. The love which speaks thus seems not very tender,
    But I love thee too well to understand thee
    And yet will say, without embarrassment,
    That 'tis too soon for thee to utter threats.

IRENE. I do not utter threats, sir, but I love thee
    More than myself, more even than my dear brother.
    True love is timid and fears for the beloved one
    On seeing him conceive a dangerous purpose.

ASPAR. Thou dost, I think, love me—at least thou mayest—
    But in what fashion dost thou show it? Doth love
    Inspire such eagerness to see thy brother
    Reign, whatsoe'er the cost be to thy lover?

IRENE. It makes me with regret fear thy destruction.
    Reign; I have said I opened the way for thee
    To do so. Thou hast worth and I lack charms.
    Scorn me, forsake me, but harm not thyself.
    For Leo's welfare have I so few fears
    That I must needs have other cause for tears?
    'Tis woe enough that I yearn vainly for thee;
    Do not compel me, sir, to weep thy fate.

ASPAR. Keep, keep thy tears for those who should be pitied;
    I, since thou lovest me, have naught to dread.
    Whate'er anxiety my rashness causeth,
    Thy hand, which waits for me, ensures my safety,
    And 'gainst the most inexorable wrath
    'Twill give me an inviolable asylum.

IRENE. Thou mayst want that, and thou too late mayst want it.
Do not expose thyself, sir, to that risk.
I doubt if I would always love thee so;
I might not be the mistress of my hand.
I speak to thee frankly, and cannot jest
When we must needs strive for the public good.

ASPAR. And I, too, wish to answer thee quite frankly.
   I have for thee a love that ne'er will die;
And midst my pride, which thou thyself approvest,
The claims of Leo's friendship still are felt.
But never will that friendship nor that love
So fond (whate'er solicitude or efforts
Thou mayst find pleasure in expecting of them)
See me persuaded in my soul that I
Ought to obey one whom I have commanded
And whom, if I may trust the heart that loves thee,
'Twill be my right still to command much longer.
I, who for honor's sake will not consent
To such abasement, find in all my peers
The selfsame feelings. They have made the Princess
The ruler of the Empire. Let her wed
Leo; all are prepared to give their sanction;
But I will not vouch for their long obedience
Unless he promptly will associate
One of us with him. That is nothing new,
And I suggest now to thee only what
Was done for Theodosius the Great.
It was in this way that the Empire fell
Into that family's hands who have been so
Proud of their birth and jealous of their rank.
By their example plan to give thyself
Thy just deserts, and make me emperor
To become empress. Thou hast power, madam;
Use it well, and for thine own interests link
Thyself with mine.

IRENE.   Could Leo thus dispose
The Princess' heart? It is a great, proud heart;
To share the power would offend it. She
Wants all or nothing, and in her high station
Will quench her love rather than fall from that.

We, being near her, might in time do more;
But let us not now urge that power be shared.

ASPAR.   Thou mayst want that, and thou too late mayst want it.
Do not leave long to chance our destiny.
I shall await this new proof of thy love.
Farewell.

IRENE.   Farewell. Ambition, sir, is very good;
But with such thoughts thou art not, I discover,
Either a real friend or a real lover.

A C T   V

PULCHERIA and JUSTINA are discovered.

PULCHERIA.   The more I think, the more I feel disturbed:
I fear that I may lose a love so perfect
And that if Leo should be made my husband
This longed-for blessing would be less sweet to me.
I know not if my new rank changed my nature;
I tremble when I think of being his wife
And of the fact one cannot wed the dearest
Lover without thus making for herself
A master at the same time as a husband.
I would reign, rather, with that independence
Which a true sovereign prudently makes sure of.
I would that heaven might inspire the Senate
To let me rule the realm alone and spare me
This master, and I ever contemplate
Semiramis and Zenobia enviously.
Zenobia was o'erthrown; Semiramis
Appropriated her son's name and garb,
And 'neath the mask of a long guardianship
That garb and that name both reigned more than she did;
But I am not less jealous of their lot.
This was indeed to reign—reign with no husband.
The one's defeat only preserves her memory;
The other one's disguise mars not her glory.

JUSTINA.   How soon would matters wear a different aspect
Did but the Senate take the side of Leo!
How soon . . . But I see Aspar with my father.

PULCHERIA.   Let us from them learn what fate heaven decrees me.

Enter MARCIAN *and* ASPAR.

MARCIAN. Madam, the Senate deputizes us
To swear to thee 'twill follow all thy wishes.
After it placed the Empire in thy hands,
To prescribe aught to thee would be an outrage;
And it respectfully a second time
Begs thee alone to give thyself whatever
Master thou wouldst.

PULCHERIA.   It could have chosen him.

MARCIAN. It would not be so bold; and on that point,
Madam, it craves indulgence.

PULCHERIA.   Wherefore, then,
Doth it make this step requisite for me?

MARCIAN. To lend more power to thine authority.

PULCHERIA. Such is its loyal zeal I must content it
And do its will better than it hath deigned
To content *me*.
                    My sex makes contradictory
My lot. To rule I must enslave myself,—
Mounting the throne, must enter into bondage
And take commands from one who pays me homage.
  Go; in a few days I will let you know
This choice the Senate's mandate makes my duty.

ASPAR. 'Twould reckon it a great, exceptional favor
To know that, madam, ere adjourning finally.

PULCHERIA. What! not one moment to take thought about it?
But I would do wrong to defer it further.
'Tis best for my first act of sovereignty
To show a worthy instance of obedience.
Aspar, do thou withdraw. Thy turn will come.

                                        (*Exit* ASPAR.)
  (*To* MARCIAN) I have been told, sir, that thou lovest me.
Might it be true?

MARCIAN.   Madam, who told thee this?

PULCHERIA. Thy services, mine eyes, thy soul's confusion,
The exile that my marriage was to impose
On thee. Are these, sir, witnesses thou canst
Refute?

MARCIAN.   Then, madam, I must confess my crime.

Love is born easily of esteem and zeal,
Which in the presence of a radiant being
Await not our consent to do their work.
For me to love is shameful, as it is
For thee to be loved by a man whose life
Already hath been lived and who lives on
Only regretfully since he hath seen
How far his ravished eyes have made him thus
False to his duty. My heart, which so great age
Had left without a fear, hath been delivered
Thereby into the power of thy charms.
In vain, in vain have I resisted them,
In vain kept silent after having yielded.
I have been forced to love, been forced to own it.
For more than ten years I have pined and yearned
Without thy being able, from the greatness
Of such long anguish, to surprise in me
One tear, one sigh. But of a truth my worn
Aspect results even more from love than age.
Someone must be made happy, and quite soon.
Spare me the misery of beholding this,
If I by exile seek to ease my woes
And punish a love worthy of thy hate.
Farewell. Live happily, and if many jealous . . .

PULCHERIA. Go not hence, sir. I shall outwit them all;
And since none will excuse me from this choice,
'Tis made, and such a one as none imagines.

MARCIAN. Whoe'er it is, 'twill be my death's decree,
Madam.

PULCHERIA. Once more I say, do not go hence.
Sir, up to this time thou hast served me well.
Thy wisdom hath caused all my life's renown.
Thy life hath been consumed in aiding me.
Thou needs must do yet more, must needs . . .

MARCIAN. What?

PULCHERIA. Wed me.

MARCIAN. I, madam?

PULCHERIA. Yes; that is the greatest service
Which thou, in loyalty, canst do thy empress.
Not that in offering myself to thee

I to thy love respond to the extent
Of wanting sons and grandsons. My grandfather,
Whose great deeds' fame still resounds everywhere,
Would in truth wish his line to end with me,
Whereof I am the last and worthily
Would seal the tomb of such a mighty emperor.
Let none suggest again that I should hazard
My honor to leave Caesars of the blood
Of Theodosius. Am I obligated
Unto my race to do myself dishonor—
I, who have seen our blood become degenerate
And know that if it breeds illustrious
Princesses, now its princes are but weaklings?
   'Tis now not as if Leo, chosen emperor,
Had won my hand to give me back my rank;
My love, for that end, would be justified.
But since I have, without him, been named empress,
I owe to that great rank too noble aims
To let one of my subjects share my bed.
I wish no more a husband, but I needs
Must have a seeming one who can augment
The number of Caesars for me: one
Who, satisfied with being above kings,
Will give me counsel and enforce my laws,—
Who, really being only my prime minister,
Will check whate'er should in my realm be dreaded,
And to control the unthinking populace,
Appears my husband, yet is so but in name.
   Thou understandest me; I have said enough.
Lend me thy hand; I shall give thee the Empire.
Let us thus blind the people, and in private
Live as though we were nowise wife and husband.
If this is not to possess her thou lovest,
It is at least to be her spirit's master,
Take her from all thy rivals, stand above them,
And be the luckiest of those who love her.

MARCIAN. Madam . . .

PULCHERIA.   I owe thy great deeds this reward.
I pay the realm's debt and my brother's to thee.

MARCIAN. Would anyone have e'er thought, madam . . .

PULCHERIA. Go, sir,
    And let the assembled Senate see the Emperor.
    It hath remained here to receive its sovereign.
    Go; make thyself known unto them from me;
    Or if thy wish and mine do not agree,
    In kindness to my sex say nothing to me.
MARCIAN. Let me before thee kneel . . .
PULCHERIA. Nay, go, I say.
    I do myself a kindness, more than thee;
    And having bared my heart to thee, I wish
    Neither to be rejected nor be thanked.
    Send Aspar in. (*Exit* MARCIAN. *Enter* ASPAR.)
    (*To* ASPAR) What doest thou with Irene?
    When wilt thou wed her? Doth that question irk thee?
    Thou sayest naught?
ASPAR. No, madam, and I owe thee
    This respect for thy graciousness to me.
    He who says naught, obeys.
PULCHERIA. I like an answer.
    Silence at Court means one is politic.
    When rulers speak, those in agreement praise them,
    And 'tis by saying naught that one gainsays them.
    Time will enlighten me about what I
    Suspect. Meanwhile, learn I have made my choice,
    As I was bidden, of a husband. Leo
    Dissatisfied thee, and I have suppressed
    My love that I may give to thee a master
    Admired at Court and worshipped by the army,—
    One whom the chief upholders of the Empire
    Would glory in electing: it is Marcian.
ASPAR. What! old and worn out as he is?
PULCHERIA. Though he
    Be old and worn out, I shall wed him. I
    Like him. I have my reasons. But he will need
    A son-in-law to share with him the cares
    Which he must take upon himself—to be
    A staff for his declining years and bear
    Half of his burden as his deputy.
    Whom wouldst thou judge appropriate for this office?
    A second time thou seemest petrified.

ASPAR.   Madam, both Areobindus and Procopius
Have given their hearts elsewhere—made other vows.
Save for that, I would say . . .

PULCHERIA.   And save for that,
I would confer on Aspar this great honor;
Yet even if he were a man who could
Renounce with ease love's happiness, Justina
Hath not a soul so shameless that she would
Accept a heart blackened with faithlessness,
But would regard him as an inconstant spirit
Ready always to turn where Fortune smiles.
Knowest thou none whose faithful ardor . . .

ASPAR.   Madam,
Thy gracious will can better choose for her.
As it hath taken us by surprise with Marcian,
It can again surprise us. I shall leave thee
To make thy mind up.

PULCHERIA.   Go; as to Irene,
If thy heart feeleth naught which doth restrain thee
Leave thy long love doubtful no more, or I
Shall in two days make disposition of her.

                                    (*Exit* ASPAR.)

    That is not all, Justina; I would fain
Make Leo the successor of thy father.
Wilt thou assist me? Wilt thou lend thyself
To the achievement of that worthy purpose?

JUSTINA.   My hand and heart are wholly in thy power,
Madam. Canst thou doubt my obedience after
It hath already cost me by thine orders
Advice against thee which should have assured thee?

PULCHERIA.   Let us proceed. Here he is. I will answer
For Marcian's consent; his heart too wholly
Is mine to be opposed to what we do.

Enter LEO.

LEO.   Well did I tell myself that thy new pledges,
Madam, would be mere trifling.

PULCHERIA.   Thou beginnest
In a way . . .

LEO.   I shall end in the same way,

False woman! I am not the Leo now
Who loves thee. Nay, I am not . . .

PULCHERIA.   Understand . . .

LEO.   I have no wish to understand aught. I
Bring thee here neither reverence nor fealty.
I come in the mad fury of distraction
Solely to earn the death that I desire,
And all my paroxysms of righteous rage
Give utterance only to my horror at thee.
Yes, as Pulcheria and as the Empress,
Thou'st shown me naught but trickery and injustice;
If thy false kindness hath deceived me, thy
Oaths have reduced me to despair.

PULCHERIA.   Oh, Leo!

LEO.   By what power which I cannot comprehend
Art thou with one cry able to compel me
To lay aside my anger? With one glance
Thou overcomest it, and when I behold thee,
Straightway do I forget thy faithlessness.
My lips refuse to call thee "perjurer";
My grief is not allowed the faintest murmur;
The terrible despair that brought me hither
Gives place now to the secret joy of dying
Before thine eyes. I shall indeed die there,
Madam, and not of anger but of love.
With my last breath accept my humble homage,
And if thy haughty pride of place permitteth,
Accept it, I implore, with some regret.
Never did love approach mine own in fervor;
Never did vain hopes flatter a heart more.
I ne'er deserved that they should come to aught,
Nor that a love so true should find fulfilment,
But when thou saidst, "Whate'er be ordered of me,
None other shall be master of my person,"
I had a right to trust thee; yet, alas,
Thou'lt be tomorrow in another's arms,
And thou forgettest, this same day, what thou
Didst graciously command me to believe!

PULCHERIA.   Nay, I forget it not; I know what I
Should do. Have thoughts that give me greater credit,

And charge me not with having broken my word,
When I have sacrificed myself to keep it.

LEO. What! dost thou not wed Marcian tomorrow?

PULCHERIA. Knowest thou the terms on which I give my hand
To him?

LEO. What matters it to me upon
What terms such happiness will be bought?

PULCHERIA. Have done,
Have done with the distress thine error gives thee,
And learn thou that with me the name of husband
Involves no privilege which can make thee jealous;
For notwithstanding this false-seeming marriage
I took an oath to die as I was born.
Marcian will have my hand and nuptial vows
Only to keep me still untouched and sovereign,
And all the power that our wedlock gives him
Will never make him master of my person.

Is this to break my word? Dost thou not see
How I serve thee in making him my husband?
It is for thee that in his hands I place
The Empire; 'tis to keep it safe for thee
That I chose to select him. Make thyself
Worthy like him of this custodianship
Which his advancing years will soon give thee.
Imitate him, and following in his footsteps
Make thine beyond doubt his place after him.
Learn 'neath his tutelage the art of reigning,
Which almost no one else could teach thee better,
And to make surely thine what I wish for thee
Bind thyself to him as his son-in-law.
I give to thee Justina.

LEO. To me?

PULCHERIA. To thee,
Whom I had promised to myself for husband.

LEO. 'Tis not enough to lose thee, then,—to see
Thy hand, mine rightly, laid in another's hand.
I must love someone else!

PULCHERIA. Thou must be emperor
And with the scepter thine prove my heart wise—
Yes, show the world, in the brave man I love,

All that which makes a brow deserve a crown;
Rise, like myself, superior to thy feelings;
And, as I plan, reign finally in thy turn.
Justina well deserves thee; she is young
And comely; all thy rivals for my hand
Would gladly be the same for hers, and empire
Hath as a dowry such attractions I
Can but this moment promise 'twill be thine.

LEO. Yes, madam; thee aside, she hath no peer.
She is the greatest ornament of thy Court,
With qualities to make herself adored.
But I had until now, alas, the right
To aspire to thee. Wouldst thou that I before
Thy face should wrong one with such shining merits,—
Should without loving her invite her love,—
Leaving my heart with thee, should ask for hers,
And promise her all things yet give her nothing?

PULCHERIA. Knowest thou not that there are marriages
Which heaven without one's choice makes very happy?
When it would have these take place here below,
It bears us where we had no thought of going,
And when it decides on them finds a way
To make us joyfully accept its mandates.

LEO. But not to love thee henceforth! To turn from thee
All my thoughts!

PULCHERIA. Love me; I consent to that.
I will say more: I wish it—but as empress,
No longer as a woman who loves thee.
Let passion cease and loyal zeal increase.
Justina, who now hears me, will consent
For me to keep a place within thy heart.
I know hers thoroughly. Be thou more willing
To learn to love her as she should be loved,
And let thyself be led by one who knows
Better than thou the path to make for thee
A destiny illustrious and sweet.
Trust that to the Empress and to her who loves thee.
One loves thy virtues; the other will reward them.
I should have power enough over Justina
And thee to say to both: "I speak; obey."

LEO (*to* JUSTINA).   I do obey, then, madam, this command
      To offer thee a heart not its own master;
      But I in truth know not when I can give thee
      What I can offer only by constraint,
      And thus to offer a heart held by another
      Cannot create a love deserving thine.

JUSTINA.   It is enough mine, when in such good hands,
      For me to fear no real nor long disdain,
      And I would pledge thee my sincere affection,
      Had but my father given his consent.
      Time will do all, sir.

Enter MARCIAN.

MARCIAN (*to* PULCHERIA).   With united voice,
      Madam, the Senate doth accept thy choice.
      Its members, joyful o'er thy kindness to me,
      As one man eagerly await the day
      On which the ceremonies will take place.
      Their oath of fealty, sworn to avoid delay,
      Hath just associated my name with thine.

PULCHERIA.   I meanwhile have without thee made disposal
      Of thy Justina, sir; and 'tis for Leo
      That I have destined her.

MARCIAN.   Could I have chosen
      A more illustrious husband for her than
      The man thy love selected for thyself?
      He can have under thee unbounded power
      In the Empire and find tasks for him to do
      Which will make all admire him, that we may
      By thy command and with the assent of Aspar
      Install him on the throne and name him Caesar.

PULCHERIA.   Let us all go and make our preparations
      For the twin marriages, arrange their pomp
      And circumstance, and set the day for them.
      Fain would I do the same for Irene and Aspar,
      But I have given that fickle man two days
      And leave my favor doubtful until then,
      His fortunes hanging on those of Irene.

Suréna

INTRODUCTION

No other tragedy of Corneille, unless it be *Pompée,* has been so diversely appraised as *Suréna.* Its reception when it was first acted, in 1674, was so little favorable that he never wrote another play. It was not one of his dramas which continued to be performed after 1700; and as late as the end of the nineteenth century Hémon coupled it with *Agésilas* as "the sorriest, perhaps," [1] of his tragedies and Petit de Julleville spoke disparagingly of it and of *Pulchérie* in the same breath, as we have seen.

Merlet, a short time earlier, had said: "One feels that the end is approaching with *Suréna,* which was, so to speak, the last tragic cry of an expiring genius. A dramatic idea and two well-drawn characters, Surenas and Eurydice, are the only good things in this poem, whose too-leisurely action betrays the weaknesses of old age." [2] But Lemaître was only half in agreement with this verdict, for he mingled praise with censure; he called *Suréna* a "slow-paced but charming tragedy"; and though he said of its heroine that "her irresolution fills three whole acts—which none the less seem a trifle long," he pronounced the end of the play "perfectly beautiful." [3]

Faguet was its first important champion. *"Suréna,"* he says, "although both over-loaded and a little too long drawn out, is, if not of the first rank, at least very close to the first rank among the works of Corneille. . . . Its sentiments are naturally expressed; it is extraordinary *and* plausible, very well constructed, arousing both curiosity and sympathy, which grow ever stronger, and, as always, mingling with some weak verses some marvelous ones." [4]

This favorable turn of critical appraisal is continued by Dorchain ("Read reverently this fine tragedy, and you will be well rewarded" [5]) and by Lanson, who in his *Esquisse* speaks of "great beauties and new beauties in *Othon, Attila, Psyché, Pulchérie,* and *Suréna,*" and has some good words for

---

[1] *Théâtre de Pierre Corneille,* vol. iv, p. 497.
[2] P. 188.
[3] Pp. 339-340.
[4] Pp. 238, 240.
[5] P. 457.

Suréna, especially;[6] it reaches its climax with Brasillach. "*Suréna,*" he declares, ". . . which perhaps only the *Cid* and *Polyeucte* surpass in beauty, is the masterpiece of renunciation . . . And it is because we discover there, sometimes with surprise, accents so new and so beautiful, that *Suréna* should remain among the most revelatory masterpieces of Pierre Corneille." He admires its "melancholy, noble unfolding" . . . "As soon as the drama begins, it is placed under the sign of accursed planets, and these lovers, so perfect and so lovely, this Surenas, this Eurydice, walk their way to the catastrophe, or rather they let themselves drift toward it, almost without a struggle, and we are sure that Surenas will be killed in the street as soon as he shall have passed through the door, and that Eurydice will die. We are sure of it, and yet they could save themselves, but they will do nothing about it; they will not resist; for stronger even than all constraints the bitterness of living, the weariness of struggling, from the very first scenes have possessed them utterly." [7]

Schlumberger is scarcely less enthusiastic. He, too, finds in this neglected play "some of the most consummate beauties of Corneille and indeed certain beauties which are to be found only there." "What magnificent opportunities it would afford a great actress!" he exclaims. "In fact, I know of only one role, that of Phèdre, which surpasses in love's agony the role of this Eurydice of whom no one speaks." He quotes the entire scene between her and Pacorus in Act II, as "the finest example of that art which Corneille called '*pointilleux,*' which substitutes for an overt struggle, for direct attack and for invective, a veiled, diplomatic struggle in which every word says more than it seems to say." There must here be revealed "by hesitations of the voice, by tremblings, the anguish that shudders in each verse. I know it is against all the traditions of the theater, especially solicitous about movement and rapidity, but here Corneille shows them to be wrong." [8]

Some modern critics remain lukewarm toward *Suréna:* Lancaster does not accord it especial praise among its author's

[6] Pp. 97, 99. *Psyché* is a production with music and spectacular effects, in which Corneille collaborated with Molière and Quinault.

[7] Pp. 460-464.

[8] Pp. 258-262.

later works as he does *Sertorius* and *Attila,* but says only that
its third act "is worthy of Corneille's earlier tragedies," and
that "there are also interesting scenes in the two acts that
follow," and in a later volume that it "has in the treatment
of the two women's love the same warmth he had put into
Polyeucte, but he did not sufficiently develop his suspicious
and jealous king, or avail himself of all the possibilities that
lay in his hero's character";[9] Martin Turnell thinks *"Suréna*
falls a long way below Corneille's finest work." [10] But most of
them, without going as far as do Brasillach and Schlumberger,
very definitely admire the play. Lemonnier says that in it
"Corneille has completely regained his powers and has almost
matched the masterpieces of the beginning of his career." [11]
And here is Couton's opinion of it: "One would say unre-
servedly that this is a masterpiece if the characters of Pacorus
and Orodes had been drawn with more incisive, less timid
strokes. With the recurrence of old, very Corneillian notes,
and with the Racinian influences which show in the elderly
Corneille a mind still quick to seize upon novelties, its appeal
is great." [12]

Whatever the right estimate of this play—and the truth
surely must lie at some distance from either of such extremes
of praise and censure—it was almost inevitable that in an age
in which, unlike all previous times, *Bérénice* has enjoyed
especial favor among the tragedies of Racine, *Suréna* also
would presently come to be highly esteemed. These two
dramas have much the same merits and much the same faults.
Both are simple in plot as compared with the norm of their
respective authors—*Bérénice* by far the simpler, of course,
but Corneille's plots are habitually far more complicated than
Racine's. Both plays are distinguished by subtlety and delicacy
rather than by vigor and power; the poetry of both has an
elegiac note; both are lacking in action in the usual sense of
the word—theirs being largely inward, psychological. The
action of *Suréna* consists in the hero's and the heroine's grad-
ual betrayal to others of the secret of their love, despite their

[9] Part IV, p. 146; Part V, p. 66.
[10] *The Classical Moment,* New Directions, n.d., p. 244.
[11] *Corneille,* p. 288.
[12] P. 216.

efforts to conceal it. The chief difficulty with both plays, for people who are not steeped in French-classical tragedy to the extent of becoming insensitive to characteristic unadmirable traits and behavior of the dramatis personae, is the difficulty of sympathizing at all with those figures for whom sympathy is needed to secure a suitable dramatic effect.

CHARACTERS IN THE PLAY

ORODES, *King of Parthia.*

PACORUS, *his son.*

SURENAS, *a Parthian general, who had formerly restored Orodes to the throne, and later had destroyed the Roman general Crassus and all his army.*

SILLACES, *another Parthian general.*

EURYDICE, *daughter of Artabazus, King of Armenia.*

PALMIS, *sister of Surenas.*

ORMENE, *lady-in-waiting of Eurydice.*

The scene represents a room in the palace of Orodes, in Seleucia, the capital of Parthia.

The names "Pacorus," "Sillaces," "Palmis," and "Ormene" are accented on the first syllable; "Orodes," "Surenas," and "Eurydice" on the second syllable. The final "e" in "Eurydice" and "Ormene" is a separate syllable.

Surenas

A C T   I

EURYDICE and ORMENE are discovered.

EURYDICE.   Speak not to me of happiness and marriage!
    Thou knowest not to what I am condemned,
    Ormene. It is here the terms of that
    Treaty which two kings chose to make must needs
    Be carried out—for which the preference
    Is given to this proud city, this Selucia,
    O'er Hecatompyle. The Queen and also
    The Princess have left there to give the Court
    Its brightest luster in this lovely place.
    The King expressly summoned them; the Prince
    Waits for them only; and these climes have never
    Seen such great pomp. But of what good to me
    Are all their preparations, if my heart
    Hath been enthralled and is not free to hope,—
    If it in all these shows of public joy
    Finds cause for perturbation and for sadness?
    I love elsewhere.
ORMENE.   Thou, madam?
EURYDICE.   Ormene,
    I have kept silent till I could recover
    Complete self-mastery. When I did not dream
    Of ever seeing again him who had won
    My love, it was locked up within my bosom.
    Absence and reason seemed to dissipate it.
    Lack of hope helped me to deceive myself.
    I thought my heart was tranquil, and stern duty
    Prepared it at my royal father's mandate
    To accept his choice made for me. But, O gods!
    What torment if I have to take a husband
    Before the eyes of him I love!
ORMENE.   Before
    The eyes of him thou lovest!
EURYDICE.   'Tis time to tell thee
    Both what woe crushes me and whom I love.
    Troubles poured out in words thereby grow lighter,

And mine would fain find solace thus in thee.
     When the avaricious Crassus, the Roman general,
Tried to o'ercome the Parthians on their plains,
Thou knowest that he sought my father's aid,
And that Orodes did the same a few days
Later, and sent as his ambassador
That very hero who had had the power
To avenge him and restore him to his throne.

ORMENE.   Yes, I then saw Surenas speak for his king
To thee, and Cassius do the same for Rome.
I saw these States, in all their haughty power,
Eagerly beg the aid of Artabazus,
The Court divide as to whose cause to side with,
And the ambassadors prolong their stay.

EURYDICE.   Both paid me visits, as they did the King;
And soon I learned how different was their merit.
One, swollen with pride and lifelong scorn of monarchs,
Seemed to think giving us orders was a favor.
The other, by the due respect he paid us,
Avenged that slight done royalty in us.
Love, too, had part herein, and all his converse
Appeared to offer me *his* heart and ask mine.
He won it; and mine eyes, which he held spellbound,
Met his with sudden, mutual understanding.
These mute interpreters revealed unto him
What I had forced myself to hide from him;
And the same glance which told me of his love
Read in my look the secret of my soul.
I matched his longings with desires as tender;
An unforeseen accord mingled our sighs;
And sweet love, staked upon a word let fall,
Found in each breast a heart completely yielded.

ORMENE.   But is he a king, madam?

EURYDICE.   He is not,
And yet he can retrieve for kings their realms.
The goodliest of all Parthians in both features
And mind, the mightiest, wealthiest, and bravest,
The noblest—add thereto his love for me
And he outworths a king who is king only.
View not askance a love in which I glory,

And let me finish telling my sad story.
    Our love, hid 'neath the mask of courtly usage,
Throve by the long delays of treaty-making.
No one guessed aught from this great man's attentions.
But choose we had to between Rome and Parthia.
My father had his reasons for favoring Rome;
I had mine for the opposite course, and even
Lifted my voice in vain; I was not heeded,
And in this great decision no one deigned
To weigh or take account of what I wished.
    We were for Rome, then; and Surenas, baffled,
Carried thence the chagrin of being wrongly
Rebuffed. He seemed to me much moved thereby,
But he controlled his feelings; he, instead
Of hating us at all, felt pity for us;
And as his heart remained entirely mine,
Our parting was not that of enemies.
    What served it that we cherished hopes now ended?
My father chose ill; this the sequel showed.
Surenas destroyed Crassus and his son,
And 'gainst Armenia was Orodes victor:
He fell upon us like a thunderbolt.
    I had foreseen the woes this war would bring us,
But not, alas, among its consequences
What fatal blessings peace reserved for me.
The two kings, in concluding it, have made me
The victim of it. I have been brought here
To wed a noble prince—for his high worth
Is not, indeed, unknown to me, and would
Arouse love in a heart not given already;
But when this heart is won, and the place in it
Is filled by somebody, his rival's virtues
Make no impression on it and they all
Vex me, and the more nearly he is perfect,
The more obnoxious in my sight he is.
But I shall be obedient; I shall wed him;
And yet more . . .

ORMENE.   What more can be?

EURYDICE.   I am jealous.

ORMENE.   Jealous! To crown thy woes, which I so pity?

EURYDICE.   Thou seest those I endure; learn those I fear.
　　　　Orodes hath now summoned here the Princess
　　　　His daughter; and if he desires to have
　　　　Him who is mine a member of his family
　　　　And with two marriages make notable
　　　　The same day, picture my unhappiness.
　　　　Now I have told thee of my love.
　　　　　　　　　　　　　Ah, heaven,
　　　　'Tis quite enough that thine almighty power
　　　　Before the eyes of him I love consigns me
　　　　To other arms than his; condemn me not
　　　　To see him *I* love in another's arms.
ORMENE.   Thou'rt too ingenious at conceiving causes
　　　　For grief.
EURYDICE.　　　When we have found we are ill-fated,
　　　　Naught meets our gaze that does not make us tremble.
　　　　The falsest of appearances confounds us,
　　　　And all that one conceives, all one imagines,
　　　　Forms a new poison for a distempered soul.
ORMENE.   Dost thou find these new poisons so delicious
　　　　That thou must make one from a foreboded marriage?
EURYDICE.   The Princess is to come here; she is fair;
　　　　The Romans' vanquisher is worthy of her;
　　　　And if he sees and meets her, and the King
　　　　Wishes it . . . I have said too much. Already
　　　　All my heart, shaken . . .
ORMENE.　　　　　　Try as hard to solace
　　　　Thy woes as thou dost to believe a baseless
　　　　Suspicion is a certainty. Consider
　　　　How best their bitterness might be assuaged.
EURYDICE.   I do whate'er I can—without avail.
　　　　I dare not see Surenas, who dominates
　　　　My thoughts, and who may deem my soul ambitious.
　　　　Thou knowest how I have made friends with his sister.
　　　　In her I think I find him, and some sweetness
　　　　There is in this, but it is scant and faint
　　　　And tortures me with vainly trying to hide
　　　　My love of him. She surely knows of it,
　　　　And by her manner she asks me to confess it
　　　　As I should blush to do. Her brother loves her

Too much for him to have hidden aught from her.
Act thou not thus, but be more faithful to me.
Enough that in my heart I find some solace
With thee. Yet thou canst tell me nothing of him.
Thou knowest not what he does nor what he thinks.
A sister is more natural to confide in.
She knoweth whether he blames or pities me,
Shares in my pain or laughs at my distress,
Thinks I had part in causing him to lose me,
Keeps his heart still mine, or is just to me.
    I see her. Force her, if thou canst, to speak.
Force me, if need be, to conceal naught from her.
Shall *I* dare speak, great gods, or can I do so?
ORMENE. Love, when it wishes, granteth itself license,
And when its will is weary of constraint
It grows so bold that it leaves naught unspoken.

Enter PALMIS.

PALMIS. Madam, I bring good news to thee. The Queen
    Arrives this morning.
EURYDICE.   And Mandane with her?
PALMIS. Beyond doubt.
EURYDICE.   And Surenas waits for her
    With much joy and with a contented heart?
PALMIS. With all the deference that she should expect.
EURYDICE. Nothing more?
PALMIS.   What more could a subject give her?
EURYDICE. I am most curious. I would fain know better
    Just what a subject *can* owe to kings' daughters;
    But subjects round whom the whole realm revolves
    Oft set themselves apart from all the others,
    And he is one such, who, if I may judge,
    Could oblige more by showing less respect.
PALMIS. Of that I know not, nor do I think my brother
    More learnèd in such mysteries than his sister.
EURYDICE. Enough of this! What of the Prince?
PALMIS.   Canst doubt
    He is in ecstasies, like a true lover;
    And could he feel aught but the sheerest bliss
    When seeing at hand the happiness he desires?

EURYDICE.   Perchance 'twill not be happiness for him,
  And I have feared therein some cause for woe.
PALMIS.   What woe could mingle bitterness with the sweet
  And full fruition of his consuming love?
  What bitterness hath power to mar such joy?
  Thy hand now given . . .
EURYDICE.   The hand is not the heart.
PALMIS.   He reigns in thine.
EURYDICE.   Indeed he does not, madam!
  I know not even if he ever will.
  From this, judge whether he is to be happy.
  But let us speak out, please, and conceal nothing.
  My secret—dost thou know it?
PALMIS.   I know my brother's.
EURYDICE.   Thou know'st mine, then. Does he do what he ought to?
  Does he now hate me? Does he, justly angered,
  Without regret feel towards me as he should?
PALMIS.   Yes, madam, he feels towards thee everything
  A lofty soul should feel—both loyalty
  And love—towards her who most deserveth them.
EURYDICE.   He loves me still?
PALMIS.   "Loves" is too weak a word.
  He suffers mutely; and should I accuse thee,
  Ever doth he defend thee and excuse thee.
  "She is a daughter," says he, "and a princess.
  I know a father's rights, and a king's rights.
  I know her unescapable obligations.
  I know what stern yoke, from her earliest childhood,
  Her birth and station have imposed upon her.
  Her heart is not exempt from love or hate;
  But though it hate or love, it must obey.
  She gave me all that she was free to give me—
  For which my gratitude must be eternal."
EURYDICE.   Ah, thou augmentest too much, by these sweet words,
  My love for him and hatred of the Prince!
  But let us say no more. In this sad plight
  The more I hate, the more I suffer; and
  I suffer no less than I love.
PALMIS.   Then let us
  Not make thy sorrows worse but change the subject.

I know thy secret; know thou also mine.
'Tis not for thee alone that Fate prepares
Long agony by means of this great marriage.
The Prince . . .

EURYDICE.   In heaven's name, name him not to me!
His name alone lays worse than death before me.

PALMIS.   Such utter hate!

EURYDICE.   'Tis but the consequence
Of mortal grief wherewith his sight o'erwhelms me.

PALMIS.   Well, then, this prince whom thou art pleased to hate
And for whom thou wilt to thy heart be faithless—
This prince, who loves thee, loved me.

EURYDICE.   The false man!

PALMIS.   Our longings were the same, our passion mutual.
I loved him.

EURYDICE.   And the wretch breaks ties so dear!

PALMIS.   Madam, is there a heart that could withstand thee?
Is there a vow 'twould not renounce for thee?
If he is false to me, thine eyes excuse him—
Thine eyes, which even o'er me have so much power.

EURYDICE.   Thou, loving him, remainest thine own mistress.
The blessing of thy being free consoles thee
For the wrong done thee by a breach of faith;
But I become a slave; 'tis my ill fortune
That I, when I lose him I love, must love
Another.

PALMIS.   Dost thou deem my fortune better?
Thou losest thy lover, but his heart is thine,
While I have such a cruel fate that I
Lose all my lover's heart in losing him.
My prize escapes me while thou makest more conquests,
Taking mine when they free themselves from me;
Thy sway grows wider while mine shrinks to nothing.
Naught is left me of all that I was proud of.

EURYDICE.   Take back thy conquests; make thy sway o'er them
Stronger; establish it o'er crowned heads. I
Shall not be jealous. I prefer the glory
Of mine own choice, the sweetness of my love,
To any hundred kings. Surenas' hand
Is worth more than a crown. But tell me, pray,

Is it true he loves me? Tell me; and if it is,
Why does he flee the sight of me?

PALMIS.   He is here,
Madam; and he, better than I, can tell thee.

EURYDICE.   Just heaven, to see him makes me sigh already!
Love, exercise less power over me!

                            (*Exit* PALMIS. *Enter* SURENAS.)

    I sent thee word, sir, ne'er again to see me.
Thy presence confounds me, who would do my duty;
And that which was the one joy of my heart
Can give me nothing now except new tortures.
Canst thou reck naught of this; and if I suffer
So much in seeing thee, dost thou suffer less?
Do we both suffer less by being together?
Go, find delight in having beheld me tremble;
And, pitying me at least, while thus triumphant,
Make me no more risk unbecoming sighs.

SURENAS.   I know what seeing thee will cost my heart,
But he who seeks to die must seek what killeth.
Madam, the hour approaches, and tomorrow
Thy marriage vows will make thee obligated
Forever to forget me. I have only
This day, this moment, left me of my life.
Forgive the love which yields it up for thee,
And let a sigh now breathe forth at thy feet,
For my last joy, a soul entirely thine.

EURYDICE.   And dost thou, sir, deem mine will be so hardy
Thou fearest not that it will take flight that moment,—
That the same sigh which will cut short thy life
Will cut short also the sad course of mine?
Live, live, sir, that I long may pine, and, thus
Languishing, long pay tribute to thy love.
To die before thine eyes would be too sweet;
I have not yet suffered enough for thee.
I wish deep sorrow slowly to consume me,
In long-drawn draughts to taste its bitterness,
And, without death's release, always to love,
Always to suffer, and always to die.
    But wouldst thou pardon this dolorous and ill-fated
Love if it should confess to thee a frailty?

Couldst thou, sir, be induced to alleviate
This crushing woe of mine by one small favor?
SURENAS.   What favor can be granted by a wretch
Crushed by his love itself, once favored by thee?
Can I do anything in my present plight?
EURYDICE.   Yes, thou canst spare me very bitter pain.
Wed not Mandane. She comes here to wed thee.
Of this have my suspicions made me certain.
Add not, my lord, to all my misery
That of thy being united with the family
Whose will doth tyrannize o'er me,—of thy
Giving into their hands the one thing left me,
Thy heart. That would be more than I could bear.
I want to keep it and, despite thy king,
Dispose of that heart which cannot be mine.
SURENAS.   Full of a love so great and pure as ours,
Blind to Mandane's charms, blind to all others',
As I no more have eyes to turn toward them
I have no longer heart nor hand to give.
I love thee and have lost thee. After that,
Is there a marriage that I could endure?
Are there still ties where happiness might be
Attained by one to whom thou wert so dear,
And whom thou madest unable, since he loves thee,
To find aught 'neath the sky that he could love?
EURYDICE.   Such protests are not what I wish from thee.
Thou owest descendants to posterity;
And thy illustrious ancestors, whose place
Thou tookest, deserve to live on in their race.
I would not have it end and I should think
'Twere vile if the least wish for that escaped me.
SURENAS.   Let all die with me, madam. What care I
After my death who treads the earth above me?
Will my illustrious ancestors perceive
The darkness of their tomb pierced by new rays
Of glory? Will they breath again the air
In which they shall be made to live once more
By these descendants who may find it hard
To follow in their steps and who perchance
Will but dishonor them and will have the same

Blood as theirs only to become degenerate?
When we have lost the light of day, such life
Is but a fancied blessing, and the briefest
Moment of longed-for happiness is better
Than such a cold and vain eternity.

EURYDICE. Oh, no, no! I am jealous, and my impatience
To rid my soul of all its fears will make me,
So long as thou art free to wed, believe
That thou reservest thy hand to obey thy king.
Mandane still will have the right to win thee;
Thou yet wilt wed her if thou'rt able to;
And I, who hate her, will not cease to tremble
So long as thus my woes may be redoubled.
A different marriage must assure me of thee.
Bring to it, if thou canst, only indifference;
But if thou then wert to be false to me
With a new love, I still would wish that thou
Shouldst love, in order to do what I bid thee.
I wish that finding thee a wife should be
My last work, that thy marriage might appear
As an eternal token of thy homage,
That my will should direct it, that I should
Be seen to be the mistress of thy heart
And of thy destiny, and that Mandane,
Despite the hope which hath been given her,
Unable to attain unto thy person,
Should be reduced to stooping to those helpless
Kings to whom, when thou wouldst, thou canst give orders.
Fear not thou mayst regret the loss of her.
There is no Court 'neath heaven not open to thee,
And everywhere thy glory shines so brightly
Thou wilt not lack kings' daughters for thy marriage.

SURENAS. Though they should make me master of the world,
Absolute monarch over land and sea,
My heart . . .

EURYDICE. No more! The way that thou beginnest
Could not enough content me in my anguish,
And from a heart that wishes still to be
Swayed by me, I want nothing but obedience.

SURENAS. Unto whom wilt thou give me?

EURYDICE. I? Alas,
> Why can I not deprive Mandane of thee
> And give thee unto no one! And against
> All the suspicions of this heart that loves thee
> Wherefore can I not reassure myself?
> But farewell. I have lost my senses.   (*Exit* EURYDICE.)

SURENAS (*to himself*).   Whither
> Am I to turn, ye skies above, if I
> Must ever—without cease—love, suffer, die?

A C T   I I

PACORUS *and* SURENAS *are discovered.*

PACORUS.   Surenas, thou hast served too well my father
> For me to think thou'dst be to me less loyal;
> And on the eve, then, of a marriage that
> Should be most sweet to me, I put my trust
> And hope in thee. Palmis dislikes this marriage,
> Naturally, but I can repair the wrong
> It does her; and thou knowest that in forming
> Such unions, princes are not their own masters.
> When ye twain wish to fix your love on someone,
> There shall be kings for her and princesses
> For thee; and solemnly I swear to you
> That neither 'gainst the Prince nor 'gainst the King
> Shall ye have reason for complaint.

SURENAS.   My lord,
> Treat me no more as one who seeks reward.
> I never served from hoping to be paid.
> Glory sufficeth, and the prize thus gained . . .

PACORUS.   I well know what I owe to one who doeth
> His duty, and if thy great heart would fain
> Accept it not, mine can be satisfied
> Only when I have given it.
>   I wed
> A princess who hath winsomely combined
> All graces, both of body and of mind,
> In the most radiant and charming concord
> That can adorn a soul or deck a face.
> I say no more of that; for thou, who knowest her,

Knowest sufficiently her loveliness.

    This princess, then, so beautiful, so perfect—
I fear that she doth not have what I want
Most of all, love; or that her heart's desires,
Rather, turn not just where I wish them to.
Thou, who long sawest her, and whom thy faithful
Service detained long near her father and her,
Withhold not from me any light thou hadst
Upon these matters when thou wert at their Court.

SURENAS.   I saw her only to win o'er her father.

    That, sir, was my whole task, my sole concern.
I felt, because of her, sure of his choice;
But Rome's intrigues had the more potent voice.
However, having no interest in discovering
Aught except what might serve or injure Parthia,
As I confined myself unto my mission,
I may have not seen what another could have.
Had I foreknown that when the war had ended
She was to have the honor of thy love,
I would have taken more pains, and have looked further;
But I did not, adhering to my orders.

PACORUS.   What! thou hast no ideas about this thing
I fear? Did not some envoy ask her hand?
Did no prince there, no worthy subject, show
His purpose by assiduous attentions?
For in our realms 'tis sometimes true that subjects
Are at the Court who are the peers of princes;
And love, besought by someone who is present,
Awaits not always kings one ne'er hath seen.

SURENAS.   During my whole stay I saw naught I liked not.
I never noticed any constant meetings,
Any suspicious homage, any converse
So intimate that if I were in love
I would be jealous of it. But what gives thee
Such gnawing fear, my lord?

PACORUS.   The more I see her,
The more constraint I see in her. She seems,
As soon as e'er I venture to come near her,
To have a something which she fain would hide
From my sight. Not that she hath asked for any

Deferment of our marriage. But this is not
Loving me; this is but enduring me;
And I can win no kindlier reception
From her than that which obligation prompteth.

SURENAS. Fear nothing from all this. Still quite bewildered,
Still trembling at the very name of marriage,
Homesick with thoughts of native land and kindred,
She hath a hundred different griefs to vex her.

PACORUS. 'Twould seem, to see her, that her grief takes pains
Perversely to affront the general joy.
Restless, distrait, untouched by the sweet feelings
Which love's fruition breedeth in one's heart . . .

SURENAS. All that will end, sir, when her nuptial vows
Have placed the hand in thine that is thy due.
Thou'lt see her grief in less than one day gone
And all her virtues turn to love alone.

PACORUS. 'Tis a great risk to build assuredly
On such a slender, dubious hope. And what
Happiness and rare quality can this love
Have which depends entirely on her virtue?
What charms will be in this love if it gives me
That only which the saddest marriage does not
Refuse to anyone: a slave who loathes
Her chains, in which her vows alone retain her?
   To make its bonds loved, marriage must do more
Than merely authorize modesty to be silent.
It must, to bring us happiness, entail
Giving without compulsion, and furnish sweet
Sanction to one who wishes to give all.
How will it be, great gods, if my affection
Should find my princess filled with dearer memories,—
If her heart cannot free itself from them,—
If in mine arms she longeth for another!
I must, must clarify my status with her.

SURENAS. My lord, I see her. Now is a good time.
But if thou learnest from her anything
Which proves thy fears were just, what wilt thou do?

PACORUS. I am not sure; and, to be frank with thee,
I think I love her too much to compel her
To wed me; but so great chagrin might seize me

That I would marry her to punish her.
A lover scorned oft thinks he does right well
To thwart the happiness of the man preferred
To him. But she is here. Go; leave me with her.
I fear I might be shamed too much before thee.

(Exit S<small>URENAS</small>. Enter E<small>URYDICE</small>.)

What, madam! Come thyself to see me? This
Acme of graciousness which thy heart now shows me . . .

E<small>URYDICE</small>.   I sought here Palmis, whom I fain would comfort
In the misfortune which impends for her
And cannot be postponed.

P<small>ACORUS</small>.   Nay, let me talk
With thee of matters that are more immediate
Still; and bethink thee that 'tis time for thee
To bare thy thoughts to me. 'Twould be a great
Mistake for thee to keep them hidden from me.
I love thee, and tomorrow marriage is to
Unite us. Dost thou love me?

E<small>URYDICE</small>.   Yes, my lord.
My hand will certainly be thine.

P<small>ACORUS</small>.   The hand
Matters but little if the heart doth murmur.

E<small>URYDICE</small>.   What harm could my heart's murmuring do if it
Murmured so softly that nobody heard it?

P<small>ACORUS</small>.   Ah, madam, thou shouldst speak to me more frankly.

E<small>URYDICE</small>.   Wed me, my lord, and let me remain silent.
Such doubt is an offense, and licence granted
Sometimes draws down on one all too much frankness.

P<small>ACORUS</small>.   That is what I desire. Let freely spoken
Words justify today my hopes or fears.
Oh, if thou only knewest my feelings toward thee!

E<small>URYDICE</small>.   I will do what obedient hearts do, what
Duty demands, and what thy love expects—
Which I am doing now.

P<small>ACORUS</small>.   Thou mightest do more.
Thou mightest deal fairly with me and find pleasure
In showing that we both have one wish only.
Thou mightest ever say: "Yes, Prince, I love thee,
And with a fervor as intense as thine.
I feel the same love, have the selfsame wishes;

What thou desirest is all that I desire;
Nor will our noble longing be assuaged
Until a blissful marriage crowns our aims."

EURYDICE.   To address, my lord, such loving words to thee
    I needs would know as much of love as thou dost.

PACORUS.   Genuine love, when the heart feels it, teaches
    One instantly all that one ought to say.
    Its language is not difficult for those
    Whose hearts burn with it, and if thou canst not
    Speak that, thou feelest none.

EURYDICE.   Supply my lack, sir,
    And tell thyself all that a heart can feel
    The moment that it loves. Compose for me
    That moving speech. I will subscribe to it
    Provided I may say naught.

PACORUS.   What thou sayest
    Is clear indeed. I easily understand it.
    For want of love, mayst thou have hate? I do not
    Wish to believe it, and from one so lovely . . .

EURYDICE.   My lord, know what my feelings toward thee are.
    If good will pleaseth thee,—if thou lovest esteem,—
    I would account it wicked to withhold them.
    As for my heart, if I may speak to thee
    Frankly, I do not feel it yet is thine.

PACORUS.   So, then, this treaty that two kings have made . . .

EURYDICE.   If it has bound us to each other, solely
    To the hand's gift its power was limited,
    And never hath my heart made any pact
    With thee. Yet, though not owing it to thee, I
    Am doing my best to become fonder of thee
    And more responsive to thee. Whether time
    Can so dispose it, I am not aware;
    But whether it can or not, sir, thou canst wed me.

PACORUS.   I can, I should, I wish to; but with this
    Unfortunate coldness wherewith thou rewardest
    My love, is there some other love?

EURYDICE.   Ah, what
    Is this thou venturest to ask me, Prince?

PACORUS.   That upon which my happiness depends.

EURYDICE.   Is it a thing that can escape my lips?

Pacorus.   It *has* escaped them, since my words so move thee.
　　　Hadst thou not given thy heart to someone else,
　　　Thou'dst find it much less hard to say thou hast not.
　　　To reassure me as to what I dread,
　　　Thou wouldst have answered willingly my questions.
　　　That which one doeth without remorse or shame,
　　　Madam, costs naught to say, requires no effort,
　　　And with no blush suffusing all one's face . . .
Eurydice.   Nay, 'tis not for myself I blush with shame.
　　　If my heart made a choice, it made one goodly
　　　Enought to honor me even in my grave;
　　　And if I should avow it, thou'dst have reason
　　　To think I would be proud of it forever.
　　　I blush, but 'tis for thee, who darest to ask me
　　　What anyone ought to try not to believe;
　　　And I cannot conceive how thou couldst so
　　　Unwisely wish me to disclose it to thee—
　　　Thou, who upon the eve of marriage entered
　　　Upon for duty's sake, shouldst fear to learn
　　　Too much regarding this.
Pacorus.　　　　　　　　　But hast thou made it—
　　　This choice whereof thou'rt obstinately silent
　　　Or fain wouldst tell me with such deviousness?
Eurydice.   I have not said so; but if thou compell'st me
　　　To speak, 'twill cost thee more than thou imaginest.
Pacorus.   So be it! Let me know, whate'er it costeth,
　　　Who this great rival is whom I must dread.
　　　Is he a hero? Speak! Is he a prince?
　　　Is he a king?
Eurydice.　　　　　He is the man, of all
　　　That I have known, most worthy of my love.
Pacorus.   Though great his merit, thy praise goes somewhat far.
Eurydice.   Thou needs must pardon love's enthusiasm.
　　　As thou hast forced me to explain too much,
　　　If I show lack of due respect, 'tis *thy* fault.
　　　It is so natural to admire a loved one
　　　That one would have all others, too, admire him;
　　　And 'tis so sweet to boast of his high worth
　　　That never doth one fear to exaggerate it.
Pacorus.   This is to say a great deal.

EURYDICE.   Learn yet more:
　　Know that the course which duty sets for me
　　Cannot compel me now to give to thee
　　Tomorrow what had else been thine—my hand.
　　Promise it to thyself now only after
　　Thy worth destroys this love within my breast
　　And when my heart, won by thine own attractions
　　Becomes assured that it loves none but thee.
　　And tell me not that 'twas with my consent
　　That that day was appointed for our marriage.
　　I know the importance of it, and defer it
　　Regretfully; but since thou torest my secret
　　From me, there is no king, no father, prayer,
　　Or empire that I shall not dare refuse
　　Though at the peril of a hundred deaths.
　　That is what I must now not hide from thee.
　　That is the price of having made me speak.
PACORUS.　To all thy kindness, madam, add one more favor:
　　While waiting for this love of thine to end,
　　Tell me at least who is thy blissful lover
　　That reigns so absolutely in thy heart,
　　And what traits have enabled him to win it.
EURYDICE.　Urge me not so much, sir, to tell thee this.
　　If once I named him to thee . . .
PACORUS.   Go on.
EURYDICE.   Nothing
　　Could keep me then from wedding him tomorrow.
PACORUS.　He is here, madam?
EURYDICE.   He may be, my lord,—
　　So well disguised that none could recognize him.
　　Perhaps he is close by me, as a servant;
　　Perhaps he found a place in the King's household;
　　Perhaps he had to find one in thy following.
　　Fear he is any of those thou scornest to fear,—
　　Is any unknown man whom thou mayst meet,—
　　And, more than all else, fear to learn too much.
　　I said too much; 'tis time to end this talk.
　　Treat Palmis, whom I see, with greater justice,
　　And may her charms now be again attractive
　　To thee until time teaches me to love thee.

(Exit Eurydice. *Enter* Palmis.*)*

Pacorus *(to* Palmis*)*.   Madam, in heaven's name, come not to reproach me.

    I have, without thee, folk enough to fear,

    And I would soon be crushed beneath their blows

    Were it not that thou art sent me for my refuge.

    Accepting it, I turn thereto; this joy . . .

Palmis.   Hadst thou but gone back to it without being

    Driven back to it! Thy love availeth naught

    For either me or thee if thou resumest it

    Only by another's orders.

Pacorus.   Is it, then,

    Naught that for thee my heart obeys those orders?

Palmis.   No; this is but through spite which thus thou seekest

    To gratify.

Pacorus.   Since when hath the return

    To someone of a heart like mine conferred

    So little honor that it counts for nothing?

Palmis.   Since it is shameful to love a faithless man;

    Since one whom a rejection drives away,

    A glance recalls; and since inconstant lovers

    Ne'er give their hearts without still being ready

    To carry them elsewhere again.

Pacorus.   I *am* one;

    I own it, and deserve the humiliation

    Of thy not valuing my unsure return.

    Be generous: if my inconstancy

    Hath changed thy love to keen resentment, let

    A wrath so fierce and so legitimate

    Give place to pity for a crime so luckless.

    My punishment is enough without the shame . . .

Palmis.   My lord, thy crime is great, but I am kindly.

    I know that those of royal birth, though masters

    Of all men, owe obedience to the State.

    Its interests prevail with them o'er theirs,

    And when those speak, the heart forthwith is silent.

Pacorus.   Nay, madam, let me disabuse thee. I

    Do not deserve the grace of that excuse.

    My fickleness alone made me inconstant.

    No reasons of State prescribed my conduct for me.

None to conclude a peace more advantageous
Forced me to make my love the price of it.
I gladly did so, and the blacker guilt
Mine was, the more will thy forgetting it,
Which I now beg for, compel me to owe thee
All of my heart . . .

PALMIS.   'Twixt lovers who were estranged
Guilt is forgotten when amends are made.
Though it hath pleased thee to be false to me,
I say, despite myself, I cannot hate thee.

PACORUS.   Be wholly generous to me; give me all
Again of such pure love, such tender ardor . . .

PALMIS.   Then give me, sir, thyself some light for guidance.
Tell me some sure means to hold fast thy love,
And if there is a way . . .

PACORUS.   "*If* there is"? Yes,
There *is* one to make steadfast my heart's wishes;
And if the bond which love once made so sweet
To us constrains me not, thou canst preserve it—
None else. There is, to keep me 'neath thy sway,
An aid to give, a secret now to tell me.
The Princess loves another; I no longer
Can doubt it; but I know not to what rival
She hearkens. Thou'rt too intimate with her
For her not to confide in thee entirely.
Clear up this question, and receive my promise
That none but thee shall reign within my heart.

PALMIS.   What guarantee is this, alas, of faith
So dubious? Will heaven make it less
Likely to be forsworn? And those sweet ties
Which thou hast broken—will they be less easy
To break anew? My lord, if thou desirest
To reawaken all my affection deeds,
Not promises, are needed; and thy pledges
Are without power to tempt me, for thy hand
In marriage alone can rightly make me speak.

PACORUS.   My hand in marriage alone! When sheer confusion
Fills me,—when hate, love, honor, all incite me,—
When I am given o'er to vain thirst for vengeance,—
Ah me! am I in any state to wed thee?

PALMIS. And I, my lord—without thy hand in marriage,
Can I make free with what the Princess deigned
To entrust to me, her heart's own secret? I,
To tell that, would needs owe thee more than her,—
Needs be thine other self,—and marriage only
Can break the silence in which my lips are sealed.

PACORUS. Oh, thou no longer lovest me!

PALMIS.   Would I might not;
But of what use to wish to love no longer?
I have for thee too much love, and I feel it
Revived more ardent, stronger, now than ever.
Yet if . . .

PACORUS.   Love me no more, or name my rival.

PALMIS. Heaven preserve me from e'er loving thee
So ill! 'Twould be to give to thee new wars,
Kindle 'twixt thee and him undying hatred . . .

PACORUS. What matters that to me? and what have I
To dread from him so long as I still have
Surenas on my side? Whoe'er he be,
This rival, he alone is to be pitied.
The Romans' conqueror need fear naught from kings.

PALMIS. I know it; but, my lord, what can enlist thee
In taking vengeance—punishing this man?
If he, when charmed by such a lovely princess,
Has through great worth won her esteem and love,
What god, what guardian spirit, could have told him
That thine own heart would burn with love for her?
By what signs was this rival then to know it
And to defer to a love's fires not yet
Kindled, foresee for thee chains of a love
Which was not that of which thou worest them then,
And thus read better than thou couldst thy future?
If he hath seen the prize his that he longed for,—
If he hath found a union of hearts easy,—
If he possessed himself of what thou soughtest not,—
Is that to be like thieves and murderers?

PACORUS. I see well, madam, thou and thy precious brother
Abound in reasons to conceal this secret.
I speak, beg, promise, but I make no headway.
Thus thy best interests are preferred to mine.

Naught is more natural, but . . .

PALMIS.   My lord . . .

PACORUS.   Farewell.

I cause thee too much joy with my soul's turmoil.

But heaven will tire of treating me so harshly.

PALMIS.   Sir, if thou wouldst, four people could be happy.

(Exeunt severally.)

A C T   I I I

ORODES *and* SILLACES *are discovered.*

SILLACES.   I, as thou badest, have seen him and ere thee
Have tried to learn the cause of his indifference
To all things. He seemed so reserved, restrained . . .
But thou wilt judge of this, sire, when he comes.
Yet I may say that his reserve suggests
A troubled and unhappy heart, that his
Calmness seems too deliberately assumed
To be derived from real tranquillity,
That his impassive manner hides disquietude,
And that his unconcern is somewhat studied.

ORODES.   How greatly, Sillaces, such cold composure
Must needs disturb a king who oweth so much
To him that he cannot repay him! Service
Beyond all recompense so obligates one
That it is almost an offense. In secret
It doth asperse whate'er one hath of greatness
And fills one with the shame of being ungrateful.
Too much aid is embarrassing; too much
Zeal is annoying; and excessive merit,
Power, and distinction tend to breed dislike.
Surenas, none else, brought me back from exile;
He, and none else, restored to me what I
Had lost, my throne; and now he hath destroyed
Crassus for me. To do as much for him,
What can I give him? Half my realm? The whole
Of it was his if he had not preferred
Only to be its mainstay. While I wept
My being robbed of it, he captured cities;
While I invoked the gods' help, he won battles.

I shudder, blush, and am indignant now
To think of it, and fear that someday he
May with his own hands pay himself in full;
And amid all of his great name and fortune
That fortune weighs me down, that great name irks me.
How happy a king is who ne'er can see
Among his subjects nobler men than he,
And knows of none so glorious in renown
As he and none so worthy of his crown!

SILLACES.   My lord, to extricate thee from this plight
The sole wise course is one of two extremes.
Whate'er Surenas did, whate'er he hopes for,
Kill him or make of him thy son-in-law.
Powerful through his high estate, and more so
Through his great office, if he became by marriage
Another king's support,—if, in the quarrels
Which heaven may bring to thee, a wife should make him
Espouse her father's cause,—what will it serve thee
To murmur at this then, my lord? Thou must,
Thou must make certain of him or destroy him.
There is no middle ground.

ORODES.   Thy thought is mine;
But if he does not wish the one, could I
Desire the other? To reward his great
Deeds and his having made me king, his death . . .
The word alone makes me grow pale with fright.
Never speak of that; let the whole realm perish
Sooner than stain my soul to this extent,—
Sooner than bow to reasons of State which could
Call such a vile deed right.

SILLACES.   But why didst thou
Give him the Romans for his adversaries,
Sire, if thou art so jealous of his glory?
Why didst thou take the field 'gainst Artabazus
And leave to him the chance for greater exploits?

ORODES.   The outcome quite belied my expectations.
I knew the far-famed valor of the Romans
And, thinking their defeat impossible
Without me, to lead up to that I first
Assailed this king. I reckoned that he could not

Resist both battle's fury and the offer,
Too, of a son-in-law, and that his people,
Aghast at war's dread horrors, would persuade him
To relish such a gracious treaty—while
Surenas, sent to meet the Romans' onset,
Would hold them but at bay or face disaster
And for myself reserve the victory's honor,
I either seeing him fall or saving him.
I was successful in my first endeavor,
Concluding an alliance; but Surenas
Conquered, and hence thwarted my hope. I scarcely
Had signed the peace with Artabazus when
I learned of Crassus' death and Rome's defeat.
Thus of so great and swift a triumph I
Had all the fruit and he had all the glory;
And though much more successful than I could
Have wished, I think it was to my misfortune
To be so absolute in power. I filled
All Asia and all Europe with alarm
Yet owed naught to the work of mine own arm;
And though my neighbors all fear for their lands,
Their fear was given them by another's hands—
And I, too, fear and see no remedy
Save in a base and ruthless policy
If my Mandane, sought by many kings,
Must bide a subject's choice or his rejection.
SILLACES. Rejection! Fearest thou, sire, he will refuse her?
ORODES. And may it not be that he loves another,
And that he, filled with just pride as he is,
Hearkens to his heart's will more than to my wishes?
He is here. Go!   (*Exit* SILLACES. *Enter* SURENAS.)
          Thy services, Surenas,—
Who would have dreamt it?—torture me to think of.
I am ashamed, and nothing can console me,
Because I see no gift that can requite them.
Supply my lack of a fit recompense,
Which thy great exploits leave me powerless
To give thee, and if there is anything
Which thou wouldst value, offer me the means
To seem a little less ungrateful to thee.

SURENAS. When I have served thee, I have been repaid,
Sire, and have done but what a subject should do.
The honor of that abides with me and is
The sole reward I seek for all my efforts.
Yet if 'twould please thee, sire, for me to ask
The grant most fitting for a king whose soul
Is ever noble, even the best of men
Can make some false step, and if I should ever
Do so, vouchsafe me not to notice it.
Keep for me grace always prepared to extinguish
Even the most righteous wrath that one could fear;
And if . . .

ORODES.   My gratitude be limited
To pardoning errors which cannot be imagined,—
Which ne'er will be committed? Shall I await
A crime to show thee how much I esteem thee?
Heaven is kindlier, offering me a way
By happy union of thy blood with mine:
That shall reward all thou hast done for me.

SURENAS. I long have cherished the rash hope of this;
But since the Prince at last . . .

ORODES.   He loved thy sister,
But the realm's welfare robs her of his heart.
At this price was the peace-pact with Armenia
Made, but the wrong can easily be repaired.
I know kings who would wed her, and tomorrow
Mandane, whom I now expect, will give
Her hand to thee. She is the one thing Fate
Leaves in my power to offer thee, whose arm
By dint of mighty deeds gave me a crown.

SURENAS. Nothing can equal this surpassing honor;
But if thou wouldst permit me to speak freely,
I would say, sire, that as a loving father
Thou owest this princess a throne worthy of her;
That the disparity between her and me
Would lower her destiny without bettering mine;
That such a union, howso high her state,
Leaves me a subject and makes her one also;
And that, despite my exploits, from this marriage
Instead of sovereigns subjects would be born.

How couldst thou wish, my lord, that she should give me
A hand refused to more than one crowned king,
And that a being worthy of the vows
Of many monarchs should at thy command
Descend to this unworthy choice? What scorn
'Twould mean for me, what shame for her! Nay, sire,
Hearken to a faithful servant: if thou wishest
Thy blood to lend more honor unto mine,
The union of my sister and the Prince
Is necessary. Mingle my blood, sire,
With that of thine own royal forebears only
That thus thy subjects may be given masters.
    Thy Parthians have been gloriously victorious
Too long to want kings born of those they conquered.
If this thou knowest not, all the army murmurs
About it, and the people ill endure
Any such thought. What bitterer yoke, they say,
Could Artabazus have imposed as victor
Even on a spineless folk? I silence them;
But, sire, to tell the truth, thou hast not so much
Attacked him as brought him a son-in-law;
And if thou hadst consulted their desires,
Thou'dst rather have had war than such a peace.

ORODES. Is it with the intent thyself to head them
That thou already askest of me a pardon?
Did they make thee the bearer of their vain
Wishes, that Palmis may be the prouder queen?
Naught is impossible for a man who gives
His sovereign back his throne and triumphs o'er Rome.
But all 'neath heaven changes, and the mightiest
Never are sure of being always happy.
My word is pledged; it is inviolable.
The Prince now loves Eurydice as much
As she deserves being loved; and, frankly, I
Should give him this support 'gainst what Phradates
Will venture to attempt 'gainst him, for all
That Mithridates tried to do 'gainst me
Pacorus must in turn fear from Phradates.
That turbulent spirit, envious of his power,
Although his brother . . .

SURENAS. He knows I know my duty,
And he forgets not that to quell rebellion,
Dethrone a tyrant . . .
ORODES. These things are heroic;
But does thy having enabled me to reign
Render my daughter one thou mayest disdain?
SURENAS. Disdain her, sire?—when I, zealously loyal,
Dare not regard myself as worthy of her?
Release me from the service that I owe thee;
And to deserve her I shall go and win
A scepter for myself. If there is naught
That is impossible for a man who gives
His sovereign back his throne and triumphs o'er Rome,
From what king could I not wrest easily
A kingdom, for Mandane's sake, to give her?
Select for me thyself, my lord, a conquest
To crown her brow with, when I take her hand;
And after that tell me if I disdain her
In wishing to make of her a queen or perish.
But, born a subject, I am this too gladly
To risk my life except to serve my master
Or e'er consent that such a man as I am
Should sully by his marriage his king's blood.
ORODES. I shall not ask what thy respect disguises;
But let us speak, for once, with utter frankness.
Thou art my vassal, but so great a vassal
That naught is arduous when thou undertak'st it.
Thou hast, beneath me, two whole provinces
With folk so fearless, peoples of such spirit,
That I have sway over so many subjects
In but as far as thou art faithful to me.
They follow thee who hast been ever loyal,
But they would follow thee, wert thou a rebel.
Such is thy name that every neighboring monarch
Would fain, like me, be linked with thee by marriage.
Thy victories, which have become habitual,
Make Rome uneasy in her very walls.
For show, or to defy my wrath if need be,
Thou hast ten thousand followers everywhere.
That is too many for a train of servants;

And, if I must explain my meaning fully,
I cannot think thee really 'neath my sway
Unless the ties of marriage bind thee to me.

SURENAS. By what crimes, or by what imprudence, sire,
Can I have merited such lack of trust?
If heart or arm of mine could be won over,
Crassus and Mithridates would have spared
Nothing. They both . . .

ORODES.   No more of Mithridates
Or Crassus now! Surenas, I love well
To see thy glory manifest to all.
I love to tell how much I owe to thee.
But though I think of this, thou shouldst forget it.
If heaven through thee hath given me back my kingdom,
I can spare thee the task of saying so;
And if that work doth prove thy zeal exceptional,
I am no ingrate; do not overstress it.

SURENAS. Sire, I recur to Palmis. If my duty's
Claims are too weak assurance of my fealty,
Is there a surer, stronger bond than having
One's sister to be queen, one's nephews kings?
Set on the throne my flesh and blood, and seek
No other bonds to make thy interests mine,
That all the world and all the future may
Find no way to disjoin us.

ORODES.   But can I,
Surenas, do this when my word is pledged,
And midst the preparations for this wedding?
Can I restore to Rome, which is my foe,
A friend whom by the peace I took from her?
If Pacorus gives up the happiness
He hopes to have, what will the Princess say?
What will her father do?

SURENAS.   As for her father,
Leave that to *my* care. I will answer for him,
And I perhaps could answer for her also.
Despite the unfortunate peace-terms which were sworn to,
She now hath spoken her mind unto the Prince.
If I may tell thee with what feelings she
Awaits tomorrow and those terms' execution,

She loves another.

ORODES.   Whom?

SURENAS.   That she doth not care
To tell, yet of her love she makes no secret
And wishes to delay the pact's fulfilment
At which the people take offense and murmur.

ORODES. Is it for the people, is it for thee, Surenas,
To tell me from whose blood to give them kings?
And must I, to see all my hests obeyed
Throughout my realm, take counsel with my subjects?
If the Prince wishes to resume once more
His love for Palmis, I am willing for him
To turn now from the Princess, and we later
Shall see how we can mend the breach that may
Result from his so doing. As for thee,
Who feelest thyself unworthy of my daughter
And fearest to become one of my family
Because of thy respect for us, choose a marriage
Which would be proper for thee, and which would
Above all leave me no cause to feel anxious.
Being in suspense about this matter vexes
My soul. I want it settled by tomorrow.

SURENAS. Sire, I love no one.

ORODES.   Whether thou lov'st or not,
Thyself make some choice or let me choose for thee.

SURENAS. But if I love where I should be ashamed to,
Can I reveal my secret unto thee?

ORODES. Goodbye, Surenas, till tomorrow. Let us,
If possible, decide today regarding
This marriage, be it with or without love.
In the meantime, do thou go and see the Princess
Eurydice. Subject her heart's caprice
To duty's yoke again, and do not force me
To say, as king, unto her fair self such
Civilities as would not please her. Palmis
Now comes, by my command. I wish to learn
What part she fain would take in thy designs.

                          (*Exit* SURENAS. *Enter* PALMIS.)

(*To* PALMIS) Surenas hath surprised me, and I would not
Have thought that with such merits he could have

Combined such cleverness; but the less it is
Foreseen, the more this cleverness impresses.
He hath found reasons to refuse my daughter,
And good ones, for they have been so persuasive
That in declaring himself unworthy of her,
He now hath convinced me!
                            Dost thou know whom
He loves? It is beyond all likelihood
That he would take this stand unless some preference,
Unless some loved one whom his noble heart
Hath fondly chosen, shuts fast that heart against
E'en his king's child.

PALMIS.   I thought that he loved no one.

ORODES.   He himself told me that. The Princess, though,
Avows—yes, openly—that she is in love.
Thou art her friend, and knowest who thus reigneth
Utterly in a heart not hers to give.

PALMIS.   If she confides some secret to me, sire,
    Have I a right to tell it to another?
Can one hear confidences without the seal . . .

ORODES.   I deemed it could be broken for a king,
Yet I prefer that it should be so sacred
That in my own behalf it keeps thee silent.
But thou at least canst tell me of thyself.

PALMIS.   Ah, as for *my* heart, I will bare it to thee.
I love him whom I loved; my feelings change not.
I make no secret of them.

ORODES.   Thou still lovest him?
Feel some shame o'er this; speak less boldly of it.
To love where one is not loved is but weakness.

PALMIS.   Nay, sire; to feel love for one's prince displays
Greatness of soul, not weakness; and to keep
A heart for him which once he cared to merit
Is not so shameful that I may not boast of it.
'Twill always be my pride; and that heart, thrilled
With happy memories of my being loved,
Will never stifle this dear flame of love
Which his high worth and vows to me enkindled.

ORODES.   Do better; avenge thyself. There are kings, madam,
Worthier of such true love than is this ingrate.

PALMIS.   I would be sundered thus from him I love still,
And 'neath the guise of reigning cause mine exile.
I want always to see this ingrate, fatal
To me—not for the sad delight of looking
Upon him (that false pleasure is beneath me
And is not worth renouncing a king for it)
But there are joys that a forsaken woman
Tastes in the midst of grief that saps her life:
I shall now see this faithless man made anxious,
Fearing a rival unknown but greatly loved,
Find 'neath my very eyes the punishment
For his misdeed, avenge me through his marriage,
And see me in his woe only with heart
Torn by remorse and brow made red with shame.
The merciless knowledge of my fondness for him
Which love will clearly show on my pale face
Will taunt his heart; and when we meet each other,
My tears and sighs will call to mind his own,
But they will serve only to make him know
That he could have been happy but can be so
Now nevermore,—only to make him rue
His faithlessness too late,—and, to say all
In but a single breath, make him regret me.
    These are the sole joys that my heart aspires to;
These are my sole intents against this ingrate;
These are the sole pleasures I hope to have;
These all my feelings which thou soughtest to learn.

ORODES.   It is to treat sovereigns like common folk,
Trying to inflict on them such grievous tortures,
As if, to please thee or to trouble them,
Love could ascend with them unto the throne!
Our need is for a marriage, to give us princes
To be the throne's maintainers, the land's hope.
Therein kings' strength lies; and, in their high fortunes,
To have no heirs to avenge them breeds rebellion.
Interests of State, which lead to these great nuptials,
Blind us to beauty and shut our hearts 'gainst love.
Policy, nothing else, is what impels us.
We follow that, and love fares as it can.
If we can have it, good! if not, no matter!

About these things thou canst believe my word.
'Tis not in a king's nature to grow jealous
Or be concerned whether one's heart is his.
Becloud thy mind no more with these vain fancies,
Which are the pleasure but of vulgar spirits,
Madam, and though the Prince suffer or not,
Accept one of the kings whom I can offer thee.

PALMIS. Pardon me, sire, if my dismayed heart nowise
Wants any of these kings who would love no one.
I thought the Prince loved me; and 'twas so sweet
That I prefer that memory to a husband.

ORODES. Let us say no more of it. Tell thy brother,
Who is as dear to thee as thou'dst be to me,
That he hath shown only too marked . . .

PALMIS.   What, sire?

ORODES. I believe I have made that clear to him.
Let him think on it. Farewell.   (*Exit* ORODES.)

PALMIS.   Oh, how ominous!
And what does this obscure threat really tell me!
Save these two lovers, heaven, and avert
Any suspicions which their love hath roused.

A C T   I V

EURYDICE and ORMENE are discovered.

ORMENE. Yes, now the half-disclosure of your secret
Brings thy Surenas to destruction's brink.
This I have learned from Sillaces; and, frankly,
I fear that he hath orders to arrest him.

EURYDICE. None would dare, Ormene; none would dare.

ORMENE.   Believe
Thy brave heart somewhat less, as to that, madam.
A hero, when he is arrested, hath
Only his own two arms, and an excess
Of glory often is a frail support.

EURYDICE. I know that merit is subject to men's envy,
And therefore hate assails the fairest life;
But on what grounds canst thou presume to think
One might . . .

ORMENE.   He loves thee and hath made thee love him.

EURYDICE. Who says that?

ORMENE.   Thou and he; the crime is his
And thine alike. He hath refused Mandane
And doth not wish to wed anyone else.
'Tis known thou lovest; none knows who is thy lover,
Madam; all these things tell too plain a story.

EURYDICE. These are but vain suspicions which thou airest.

Enter PALMIS.

PALMIS. Madam, at every gate guards have been posted.
None enters, none goes out, save by the King's
Command.

EURYDICE.   What of it? and what cause for fear
Findest thou in this?

PALMIS.   Either some great storm is
About to fall on us, or it is being
Prepared to fall, madam, on some great head.
I tremble for my brother's.

EURYDICE.   Wherefore tremble?
Would one who owes him all, desire to crush him?

PALMIS. Thinkest thou the King is so insensitive
That such an open refusal of his daughter . . .

EURYDICE. Great prior services might make him feel
That he should recompense ere punishing.

PALMIS. He should; but after such an insult rarely
Does anyone ever think of gratitude;
For services are by such slights effaced,
So that one's eyes no more behold the past.

EURYDICE. Thou'rt indeed timorous, for a hero's sister.

PALMIS. And ought a loving woman to be braver?

EURYDICE. Loving a hero, she would fain be like him
And see, like him, his perils without quailing.

PALMIS. Thou but deceivest thyself: the thought of them
Dismayeth her who loves; to picture them
Racks her; in her concern over his fate
She cannot, save with turmoiled bosom, wait
For it to be decided. Manlike powers
To show heroic fortitude are not
Virtues on which our sex can plume itself;
Or if to such a point it carries bravery,

What it calls "love" is without tenderness.
Thou'dst display *some* dread if thou lovedst my brother;
There would escape from thee some sigh, some tear,
Which would at least reveal a jealous fear
That more than thou his sister would seem moved.
   O gods! I set the example, and thou canst
Reject it! *I* give it to someone who
Disdains to follow it! Would one have ever
Thought to behold the ties of blood thus prove
Stronger at any time than the ties of love?
But I was wrong. Thy loss is less. Another
Lover is easier got than a new brother;
And if I lost the one that heaven gave me
And got another, would *he* be a Surenas?

EURYDICE. And would I, losing this endangered lover,
Then find a new Surenas to replace him?
Thinkest thou that I, exposed to such disaster,
Inwardly sigh and tremble less than thou dost?
My courage is purely a result of pride,
Which, great though that appears, my heart would fain
Not hearken to. 'Tis soft, and only with
Regret doth pay its tribute to this pride,
Rightly unyielding, which it belies in secret.
Yes, if I must reveal my soul to thee,
I think I see already his destruction
Being prepared for my belovèd hero,
And in my mortal anguish I no longer
Dare to aspire to aught but to die with him.

PALMIS. Thou with less passioning well mightest do much more.
To save my brother's life, accept my lover.
Since thou must wed him in the end, try now,
As good sense bids, to bring thyself to do so.

EURYDICE. My love is far too strong for such "good sense."
It hath been wholly bared, wholly avowed.
The Prince too well knows what is in my heart
To accept my hand as 'twere the greatest blessing.
I love another, and have too openly
Told him this, for me to unsay it till
That love hath died because of him. I said
O'er much, but though it mean destruction, I

Shall by my words abide—yes, to the end.

PALMIS. And so thou wishest this hero to be slain?

EURYDICE. Could anyone stoop to such a crime?

PALMIS.   'Tis he
　　Who is to pay for all your stubbornness
　　And both your hearts' refusal to be parted.
　　Make the Prince happy, and he will be safe.
　　Let him accept Mandane, and he will
　　No more be reckoned guilty of anything.

EURYDICE. Let him accept her, and tell me naught of it;
　　But, if his heart may still be ruled by me,
　　Let him not love her till my hate's cessation
　　Hath toward her brother's love inclined my fancy.
　　Make him, thyself, resolve to disobey me.
　　Force me, if possible, myself to hate him.
　　By dint of logic bring me to turn from him;
　　Bathe him with tears to render him unfaithful;
　　From pity, from affection, try thy best
　　To make my heart love him a little less,
　　And I will do the rest. Howe'er one loveth,
　　When love's flame dwindles, of itself it dies.

PALMIS. The Prince comes, madam, and hath no great need,
　　In his love for thee, of an unwelcome witness.
　　Thou canst without me flatter his hopes better,
　　And better turn his homage to our uses.
　　What I foresee gives me sufficient pain
　　Without my hearing his vows proffered to thee.

　　　　　　　　　　　(*Exit* PALMIS. *Enter* PACORUS.)

EURYDICE. Is it for me, sir, that your gates are guarded?
　　Or to insure my flight have I an escort?
　　Or do this marriage's last preparations . . .

PACORUS. Madam, like thee everyone hath his secrets.
　　Those whom thou honorest with thy confidences
　　Are silent loyally as thou bidst. The King
　　Follows thy example; and if this annoys thee,
　　Thou canst conjecture, as we must conjecture.

EURYDICE. Whoe'er conjectures will oft be mistaken.

PACORUS. If I conjecture ill, I know on whom
　　To lay the blame; because thy love is only
　　Too clear, and if I know not whom thou lovest,

I know in whom thou dost confide about it.
He is the guiltier. A lover may
Not speak, but in a subject of the King
Such secrecy is criminal. One who knoweth
An obstacle to the welfare of the realm
Commits a felony when he conceals it.
This confidant, then . . . Thou understandest me, madam,
And in thine eyes I read thine inmost thoughts.

EURYDICE. If I confide in him, he is my friend,
And I at least, my lord, owe him some pity.

PACORUS. That feeling is proper; I even would fain believe
A heart like thine rightly takes pride in it.
But this confusion, madam, and this emotion—
Have they no cause more powerful than compassion?
And when the threat of danger to him moves thee,—
When such prompt pity fills thee for his sake,—
Does not such dearness of him make it doubtful
Whether he is thy confidant or lover?

EURYDICE. What matters it? and why confuse the two
When really 'tis for thee alone I tremble?

PACORUS. What! thou in thy turn thyself threatenest me?
Carried away by thy blind love . . .

EURYDICE.   I am
Less carried away and blind than thou supposest.
To make thee confess that, let us talk freely.
     Sir, I look on thee as my destined husband.
My hand could be, and will be, only thine.
This I have promised, this my heart desireth.
When I can, I will make thee master of it.
And if he whom I love delays my bringing
Myself to do so, he yet can hope for naught.
I will be thine alone, whome'er I love,
Unless thou dost compel me to forsake thee.
But if I must have time to learn to love thee,
'Tis only through esteem that I can learn to;
And if thou makest me lose all esteem
For thee,—if thou dost not in thy impatience
Stop short of crime . . . Thou understandest me, sir,
And I have shown thee well enough wherefore
I have for thee at heart such deep concern:

Thine honor is mine also, and I tremble
Lest thou shouldst stain it ineffaceably,—
Lest some fierce outburst of unworthy feelings
May make the whole world loathe thy name, and lest
Thou shouldst attempt to end thine anxious fears
By dreadful, infamous ingratitude.
After that, could I keep my plighted faith
To thee as though thou still wast worthy of me,
Take without horror the crown offered me,
Still reeking with the blood of him who gave it
To thee, and be defenseless 'gainst the Romans
When thou hast no one to repulse them for thee?
Crassus was beaten, but Rome is not destroyed.
Others have rallied those left from his rout.
Fresh squadrons will restore their warlike spirits,
And thou hast need still of his vanquisher.
    That is why I must fear for thee—I whose fortunes
Shall soon be linked with thine, and who would needs
Be vile if I were willing to be wedded
Save to a king whose memory men could love.
PACORUS.   Thou canst prevent all that thou fearest, madam.
Thou needest but be a little more obedient
And do tomorrow what thy father promised:
Lover and confidant then will have no foes.
That is what all my heart anew begs of thee,
By the fond homage of the truest love—
That patient homage, ever flouted, which
Cannot win from thee what thou owest me—
By all the cruelty of thy stubborn pride,
By all my pain . . .
EURYDICE.   And I—have I no feelings?
Is my heart torn with a less cruel strife?
Sir, I am loved and thou art not. My duty
Will surely remedy thy ills, but cannot
Permit a cure for those I am possessed of;
And to end thine requires a moment only,
While mine must needs endure perpetually.
PACORUS.   'Tis sometimes hard to find that moment, madam;
And if the King grows tired of waiting for it,
Think what a monarch in his wrath can do

PACORUS. Thou hast refused Mandane with respectful
          Arguments so well framed they breed suspicion.
          Ere she was offered thee, thy reasons were ready,
          And none hath seen a seemlier rejection.
          But all this seemliness roused no fewer blushes.
          Thou shouldst have promised everything, and left it
          For her to act; thou shouldst have hoped her pride
          Would make her not obey her father's wishes,—
          Incensed her by such lukewarm, clumsy courtship
          That she before thee would have had the honor
          Of saying "No." Thou hast preferred to try
          A ruse which might replace Eurydice
          By Palmis, through this ruse incur my anger
          And show whom thou reservedest for thyself.
          But thou wouldst better have applied thy skill
          To leading back the Princess to her duty.
          Thou so wert bidden, yet I am the more hated.
          That truly is obedience in a subject!
SURENAS. My lord, I see this clearly: whether I
          Be loved or thou be loved,—whether thou be
          Not loved or I even do not love,—all
          Alike is held a crime of mine, and I
          Alone am answerable to the King for Palmis,
          Eurydice, and myself. As if I had
          Over a heart aflame with love the power
          Men see me have over an army corps,
          And 'twere not easier to o'ercome the Romans
          And to bestow crowns than to manage hearts!
              Can I, without committing a new crime,
          Tell thee that sovereignty o'er human hearts
          Hath not been given thee, and that love is jealous
          Of its authority and recognizes
          No king, no sovereign power, over it.
          It loathes all uses to which force would bend it;
          When one constrains it, it becomes rebellious;
          Yet I am treasonous not to triumph o'er it,
          When thou thyself, sir, canst not master it!
          Change its caprice by thy command, so that
          Eurydice will love thee, Palmis hate thee;
          Or make *thy* heart so docile to thy bidding

To avenge contempt for his authority.

EURYDICE. My life is in his hands, and he can show
How brave he is by glorious deeds against me!

PACORUS. Speak better of him, prithee, and fear naught
Save for the safety of the man thou lovest.
Thy weakness the King knows: with what confusion
A lover's danger fills the stoutest heart.

EURYDICE. That is my weakness—true; but if I love,
I have a lofty soul and can display it.
This great king, though, chooses a pretty way
To make me follow joyfully his orders.
Think better of it, prithee; and consider
That one forced step which leaves the path of duty
Can lead us far. With the first step once taken,
The sole step hard for us, love breaks its chains
With ease, masters in turn duty then scorned,
And long takes pride in having snapped its yoke.

PACORUS. Madam . . .

EURYDICE.   Sir, after this I shall withdraw.
If thou hast something still to say to me,
To avoid an unwise show of pride, I leave thee
To finish saying it to my confidant.

> *(Exeunt* EURYDICE *and* ORMENE. *Enter* SURENAS.*)*

PACORUS. Surenas, I have a complaint to make,
And have good grounds for making it.

SURENAS.   Of me,
My lord?

PACORUS.   Of thee. The time is past for feigning.
In spite of all thy shifts, the truth is known.
I thought that thou wouldst be more honest with me—
Me, who placed utter confidence in thee
And wished no other's counsel. Love is always
Indiscreet through its very cautiousness.
In keeping silent it betrays its secret.
Its care, in hiding that, shows what it hides,
Telling by silence what it fears men's knowing.
Hide thine no longer, then; everyone knows it,
And all thy cleverness hath spoken 'gainst thee.

SURENAS. Since the complaint is made by thee, 'tis just,
Sir; but I still am ignorant of my crime.

That 'twill forsake Eurydice and love Palmis.
All thy control over thyself or them
Will make my conduct so much the more criminal;
But if o'er them and o'er thyself thou'rt helpless,
See me no more as treasonous in loving.

PACORUS. I pardon love the crimes which it inspires,
But cannot excuse those which it refuses
Obstinately to confess and which, concealed
With care, are long committed and around
The King set secret malcontents. A subject
Who finds himself the rival of his master,
Whatever pains he takes to hide that fact,
Can heave no sigh that is not treasonable,
His love then being a crime against the State.
He stands in need of mercy, and most of all
When he is well enough beloved to be
Able to revolt against the crown and thus
Become inimical to the public welfare.

SURENAS. Yes; but though he be made his master's rival,
If he loved *first*,—if he, despite his love,
Gives up, though he is loved, her he adores,—
If he renounces hope, quells his heart's passion,—
Does he deserve no mercy or compassion?

PACORUS. He who gives up his love is worthy of praise;
But he who denies feeling it, gives up
Nothing; and such pretense of courtliness
Deserves naught but a real and long resentment.

SURENAS. Just now, my lord, thou spakest to me of mercy,
And thou proceedest already to utter threats!
For noble hearts, mercy is hard to accept,
And there is naught in threats which can dismay them.
While now outside the walls my men are scattered,
While the guards here within by Sillaces
Are set, and while the populace are waiting
For my arrest, if someone will command it,
It can be made. If 'tis my sword that is
Desired,—if 'tis my head that is desired,—
Say the word, sir, and both alike are ready.
All of my blood, every drop, is my king's;
And if I die he will lose more than I shall.

4 7 5

I lived for glory while I had to live,
And leave posterity a great example;
But if thy jealous wrath makes me its victim,
I shall perhaps have lived too briefly for thee.
PACORUS.   Surenas, those of *my* rank do not like
Such words. These haughty virtues are false virtues.
After so many great deeds and rare exploits
The King can have no doubt of thy deserts.
He doth not wish to lose thee; spare thyself
From wakening his anger and incurring
My hatred; give the example of obedience
Unto thy peers, rather than of a love
Which would undo thee. It is natural
For mighty spirits to show themselves intrepid
And give more heed to pride than to true virtues,
But oft these mighty spirits act more wisely
By being, when need be, masters of their love.
Accept this counsel from a loyal friend.
Tonight the Queen comes, and Mandane with her.
I ask not thy heart's secret. But remember
That when a king says, "I wish this . . ." Farewell.
These words suffice, and thou shouldst understand me.
SURENAS.   I do more; I see what I must expect.
I shall await it without fear, and I
In any event shall have as to mine honor
A care; do thou decree as to my life.

ACT   V

ORODES and EURYDICE *are discovered.*

ORODES.   Do not confess it to me. At this juncture
I find suspicions sweeter than sure facts;
Uncertainty pleases me, and I like to hear
Only what leaves me free still to feel doubtful.
Meanwhile, the gates are guarded by my orders,
The followers of thy suspected lover
Dispersed—for fear that he, in blind, mad passion,
Might go so far as forcibly to abduct thee.
The noblest virtue yieldeth to compulsion;
And for two hearts entwined, love hath such charms

That even the greatest wrath which takes its place
Aspires to naught but happy reconcilement.
'Tis all too clear to see what sequel this
Outrage would have for me; and that we may
Not come to that extremity, I have taken—
Whether or not thou likest it—my precautions.

EURYDICE.   To those precautions I am much indebted.
One with less prudence, sir, would never take them;
But in the doubt in which thy soul delights,
If I may show some interest in this hero,
His fate is more uncertain than thy mind,
And I have more than thou to keep me anxious.
I make no answer about being abducted;
My pride, my duty, all in me gainsays thee.
The noblest virtue may yield to compulsion—
I know that; and I know what charm love hath;
But against both a lofty spirit availeth:
One need fear nothing who knows how to die.
The Prince alone shall have me.

ORODES.   Yes; but when,
Madam? When is this day which all his soul . . .

EURYDICE.   After this evening he would be my husband
Had he not sought to peer into my heart
More than thou, sire. His curiosity
Concerned itself too much about a matter
From which he should have turned his thoughts. He knows
I love another, and he wished to know it—
Whence he must wait till duty makes me ready.

ORODES.   The longest delay, madam, hath some end.

EURYDICE.   Duty will triumph o'er the most constant love.
Noble hearts are drawn to it wondrously;
And when one fain would conquer self, one needeth
But little time. A day can do much towards it;
An hour may suffice. If one of those
Good moments which a heart dares not withstand
Doth not come always when we wish and seek it,
It often comes when we expect it least.
But I cannot promise to expedite it
So long, sire, as my breast is far from tranquil;
And I shall give myself up to my grief

Alone, while I am left in so great fear.

ORODES. Surenas' fate, then, fills thee with such fear?

EURYDICE. I feel the charm his virtues have for all;
I dread for him that which by all is dreaded,
An angry master and a jealous rival.
'Tis nowise love, however, which concerns me;
'Tis . . . But I fear that these words will offend thee
Yet more, and I had better keep to love
Than bring to light, now, my real cause for fear.

ORODES. Nay, madam, speak; show all thy fears. Can I,
Unless I know them, heal their wounds and choose,
In the thick darkness which thou makest thy refuge,
The proper remedy for the woes thou hidest?

EURYDICE. But if I told thee that I had a right
To feel anxiety for a throne to which
I someday must ascend as queen; that to
Destroy Surenas is to give up to Rome
A scepter which his hand restored to thee;
That 'tis to reawaken the ambition
Of Mithridates and expose with thee
Pacorus and Phradates; that I fear
That his death, robbing thee of thy chief support,
Would send thee back to the exile where thou'dst be
Without him—this, my lord, would be
Too great presumptuousness. I had to say it
To the Prince, but I ought not to say it to thee.
I ought to fear too long and great wrath for it
From thee; and love would easier find forgiveness.

ORODES. But, madam, is it thy part to be so
Shrewd in State-policy? Since thou canst be
Thus "silent," let us see where logic leads us.
If thy Surenas gave me back my kingdom,
Did he restore it to me not to obey me?
And dost thou find him thereby justified
To account me as his master but in theory
And wish me to obey him in my turn?
This theme would lead us far. Let us recur
To love, and if 'tis true that finally . . .

EURYDICE. Leave that to me, my lord; and I will conquer
My feelings. I am trying to, I hope to.

I will say more: I will make it my chief aim.
But I would have the time depend on me.

ORODES. This is indeed to speak as a queen, madam,
And I indeed like this impetuousness
Betokening a great soul. Thy noble pride,
Which naught can curb, shall well befit a throne
Whereto thou art to mount. Then as a queen
Give me an order which I can obey.
    Phradates hath arrived; this evening
Mandane comes. They will learn what regard
This fearless terror of Rome's mighty empire
Showed for her offered hand. 'Twill shame Mandane
To see him near. Phradates is hot-tempered
And will espouse her quarrel. When one so violent
And passionate is present, will Surenas
Be safe here in my Court? Can I assure thee
As to his life unless he withdraws hence?

EURYDICE. Drive from thy Court the realm's most glorious hero?
Thou canst do that, sire, and thou art his sovereign.
But I cannot endure his being exiled
On my account. For really these pretenses
Are quite beside the point. Whate'er the pretext,
I am not less the cause of all; and whoso
Claims that he fears Mandane might needs blush
O'er-much, fears only that I love Surenas.
Let him go; he displeases thee; take vengeance.
Punish him, banish him; he must bow unto
Thy will. To do my duty I shall wait
For his return. Till then, no love, no marriage.

ORODES. Couldst thou espouse the Prince before his face?

EURYDICE. I know not; but I do loathe violent courses.

ORODES. Prevent them, then, by giving thyself to us,
Or make him ask to be Mandane's husband.
This order once obeyed, I am content
And wish no more thy hero to go hence.
Let him be brought here. Be less haughty-souled.
Pride is not always proof of noble hearts.
I needs must have a marriage. Choose this or that one,
Or say farewell to him at least till thine.

EURYDICE. I shall keep every word I promise, sire,

And I would vainly promise ne'er to see him—
I, who well know that war, resumed, ere long
Will make him at least needed by the army.

ORODES. We will show then, in that extremity,
How we shall do whate'er must needs be done.
I leave thee with him. *(Exit* ORODES. *Enter* SURENAS.*)*

EURYDICE *(to* SURENAS). Sir, the King hath doomed
Me to wed Pacorus and thee Mandane.
Refusal by us cannot remain unpunished.
He requires one or the other, or thou wilt
Be banished.

SURENAS. Madam, such refusal is not
My crime in his sight. Though thou lovest me,
This is in no wise what inspires him now.
My real crime is that I have more renown
Today and greater qualities than he;
And that is whence his covert hate proceedeth,
Which time will but increase and render whole-souled.
The more one serves such ingrates, the more he
Makes himself hated. All we do for them
Goes to undo us. The sight of me offends him;
My glory irks him; and he probes my bosom's
Depths for some baseness, and attempts to raise
Himself by gifts or threats, from being the king
I made him, to become a master ruling
My heart—as though by gifts he could beguile me,
Or could crush me and not destroy himself!
I owe him, as his subject, all my blood,
All my possessions; yet though I owe him all
This, my heart oweth him naught, and it receiveth
His orders only as indignities,
Only as crimes against my fonder homage.
But we must needs now part forever, madam.

EURYDICE. Thine exile might last always?

SURENAS. For a man
Like me, one's virtues intercede in vain.
The envious never pardon merit. However,
My banishment will be no lengthy misery.
I shall not go far without dying of grief.

EURYDICE. Oh, take care lest thou makest me so believe it

That I shall die ere thee at the mere thought.
Live, if thou lovest me.

SURENAS.   What! live to know
That thou wilt finally have done thy duty;
That Pacorus—his crown, rather—will be master
Of a heart mine entirely, of thy person?
To think of it, kills me; and I hasten hence
Much less to exile, madam, than to death.

EURYDICE.   Had heaven but placed it in my power and thine
To belong to either no one or each other!

SURENAS.   Love had to see the difference in our rank
Doom thee to observe a treaty's cruel conditions!

EURYDICE.   That difference in our rank allowed me hope.
Thy valor and great name matched well my birth,
And Crassus made still worthier of my love
A man who had restored his king to power.
Amid the woes I saw befall Armenia,
My ravaged land hath victimized me only.
Slave of the State, a sacrifice to peace,
I had agreed to quell mine own desires,
Not dreaming that a love as great as ours is
Becomes unyielding in the loved one's presence.
For public weal I pledged my word, but oh,
I was not seeing *thee,* sir, when I pledged it!
Finding thee here hath made me know mine error.
I delay giving someone what is thine,
And the sole good that I can hope for is
Always to promise and always to delay.

SURENAS.   How happy I would be . . . But what do I say?
The vain, unworthy bliss my love aspires to!
Shut thine eyes to the woes I must endure.
Plan to live happily, and let me die.
A throne awaits thee, the world's loftiest throne,
Whereon one fears heaven's thunderbolts alone,—
Which rules the rest of mortals' destiny
And makes Rome tremble even within her walls.

EURYDICE.   I contemplate this throne and all its greatness,
And I see everywhere only thy work.
Its glory shows me merely that of chains;
In what awaits me I see what I lose.

Ah, sir!

SURENAS.   Make not the grief worse that o'erwhelms me.
Bring it not to the point of being unmanly,
But let me go forth with that constancy
Which breeds such jealousy and hath so much cost me.

EURYDICE.   Go forth, since thou needs must, with that high courage
Which merited my love and gives such umbrage.
I shall do like thee, and thou'lt have no grounds . . .
But I see Palmis, come to say farewell
To thee, and I can still enjoy, despite
What kills my heart, some moments of thy sight.

Enter PALMIS.

PALMIS (*to* SURENAS).   'Tis said thou wilt be exiled if thou wedst not
Her whom the King hath deigned to offer thee.

SURENAS.   Nay, but till Pacorus hath his wished-for marriage
He bids me go for some days to my home.

PALMIS.   Thou wilt go?

SURENAS.   I will go.

PALMIS.   But art thou certain
Thou'lt reach thy home, despite his wrath? Thou'lt be
Exposed to perils wherewith such disfavor
Threatens a man like thee; and if the whole
Truth must be uttered, on such long, long roads
Are there no poisons, are there no assassins?

SURENAS.   The King hath not forgot my services
Yet, to begin on me such great injustice.
He is too noble to slay his chief support.

PALMIS.   If so, are all those jealous of thee like him?
Is there no sycophant who would not refuse
To commit a crime for him and exculpate him?
Is there none who, with hope to play the courtier
Better thus, would without a qualm expose
Himself to a day's wrath,—which one pretends
In disavowing base acts of policy
Which one at heart is pleased with,—wrath which absence
Eludes while waiting for the moment when
All such feigned anger is allowed to vanish?

SURENAS.   Pretended wrath, which artifice creates,
Is oft too clamorous to cozen anyone.

If my death gratifies the King,—if sooner
Or later he desires it,—I prefer
That all know it results from crime, not chance;
That none ascribe it to the course of things
Which nature doth impose and Fortune governs;
That its perfidious author, though concealing
His hand in it, be loathed by all mankind;
And that undying hate be born of it
Which will make all his subjects become rebels.

PALMIS. I would want vengeance pushed to its last limits;
And yet the best-avenged dead do not come
To life, and all the world's unleashed mad fury
Would solace neither me nor her who loves thee.

SURENAS. What shall I do, then?

PALMIS.   Safety beckons.

SURENAS.   What
Safety?

PALMIS.   The marriage that was offered thee.
Thy life assured thus in Mandane's arms,
With nothing more to fear . . .

SURENAS.   And 'tis my sister
Who would doom me to this! 'Tis she who calmly
Bids me be faithless here before my princess!

PALMIS. When no least hope accompanies our love,
Must one be faithful at the cost of death?
(*To* EURYDICE) But thou doest naught to help me to per-
suade him—
Thou, who couldst with one glance decide it all?
Madam, dost thou find pleasure in his peril?

EURYDICE. I think I do well, madam, in keeping silent;
And when before my face thou makest disposal
Of all I have, 'tis all that I can do
To say naught. Force him, if thou canst, to nuptials
Which I abhor. I let thee speak; excuse me
From doing aught else. I raise no obstacles
To what thou doest, and my mind, bewildered . . .
I have explained enough. Require no more.

SURENAS (*to* PALMIS). What! dost thou think the name of son-in-law
Can shield me if my death has been resolved on,
When despite natural ties, though these are sacred,

Half of our kings have reigned by monstrous crimes,—
By brothers bathing in their brothers' blood,
Impatient sons speeding their fathers' deaths?
Where would Orodes be, himself, without me?
Did Mithridates prove to him more loyal?
Is Pacorus, think'st thou, surer of Phradates?
I know his heart ill if he strikes not soon,
And if his father and elder brother long
Enjoy the rank that I see dazzles him.
Then I no more can fight in their defense.
Refusing to wed is not my real offense.
My true crime is my glory, not my love;
I said 'twill with my fame grow greater daily.
I am the guiltier the more I serve them,
And if they wish my death I needs must die.
Each moment that my marriage might postpone it
Will lead them only to dissemble better
And 'neath the guise of gracious friendship make
Their deed more secret, easier, and blacker.
Hence, if I should in this match seek my safety,
I would to no avail act basely, stain
My name, and wish to have it thought I buried
My honor in my downfall's ruins.
                                      But, gods!
When I have served my king so well, can I
Have life snatched from me by his orders? Nay!
Orodes looks with favoring glance upon me.
Sister, thou seest I have not even one guard.
I am free.

PALMIS.   And I fear his wrath the more.
Had he set guards o'er thee, he for thy life
Would be accountable. But canst thou rejoin
Thy followers? Art thou free enough to flee?
Is each gate guarded save to some great end?
Thy safety but requires a hand in marriage.
    By all the affection natural to blood-ties,
    By all the tenderest feelings love doth bring thee . . .

SURENAS.   Tenderness would not suit a hero's love.
'Tis shameful for him to lend ear to weeping,
And midst the sweetness of the noblest passion

Some slight austerity becomes great natures.

PALMIS. What! thou couldst . . .

SURENAS. Fare thee well. Thy heart's confusion
Makes me fear thee more than I fear the King.

(Exit SURENAS.)

PALMIS *(to* EURYDICE). He goes straight to his death, and thou wilt
cause it,
Unless thy love opposeth his departure.
My pleas were wasted, and my steps to o'ertake him
Would be. But he will heed *thee;* thine would not be.
Do not withhold the words that will restrain him,
Madam.

EURYDICE. If he dies, my death will follow his.

PALMIS. I can say that, but that is not enough.
Thou lovest him so, and yet thou hesitatest!

EURYDICE. Is it to love him ill to wish to follow him?

PALMIS. 'Tis love's excess, which brings none dead to life.
How will our mortal grief for him avail him?
How will our dying after him serve us?

EURYDICE. Thou art alarmed too greatly. In his anger
The King does not say . . .

PALMIS. Would he tell thee all
That he intends to do? If he desired
His death, would he declare it from the throne
On which this hero seated him again?
Could he, without shame? and canst thou expect
To save Surenas' life when 'tis too late?
Lose no time; go! Wherefore delayest thou?
Perhaps this moment he is pierced with blows.
Perhaps . . .

EURYDICE. Thou fillest my mind with what dread horrors!

PALMIS. How now! thou dost not fly to him?

EURYDICE. Can I, madam?
Give him I love to her I fain would hate—
What love could do itself a wrong so great?
Know'st thou not that to send him to Mandane
Would be to kill myself with mine own hand?

PALMIS. Know'st thou not that thou must, or thou destroyest him?

(Enter ORMENE.)

EURYDICE.   I can resist no more; thou wilt not let me.
　　　Ormene comes to us, and can go tell him
　　　To wed ... Finish my words, and let me weep.
PALMIS.   She comes in tears.
ORMENE.　　　　　　　How much my news will grieve you!
　　　How for Surenas ...
PALMIS.　　　　　　　Hath he been arrested?
ORMENE.   Scarce had he left the palace, and reached the street,
　　　When from an unknown hand an arrow sped.
　　　Two others followed it, and I saw this conqueror,
　　　As if all three of them had struck his heart,
　　　Fall, in a pool of blood, dead on the spot.
EURYDICE.   Alas!
ORMENE (*to* EURYDICE).   Look to thyself. Thou next art threatened,
　　　And I e'en thought I heard some voice cry out
　　　To us that one is taught thus to flout monarchs.
PALMIS.   Ungrateful prince! vile king! Why hast thou thunder,
　　　Heaven, if thou sufferest what is done on earth;
　　　And for whom keepest thou thy flaming bolts
　　　If tyrants like these are not smitten with them?
　　　　　And thou, thou, madam, who with thy vain love
　　　And dauntless, haughty pride still seemedst unshaken,—
　　　Who in thy passioning couldst decide on nothing,—
　　　Hast loved him so much but to murder him!
　　　Go with such love as thine, see all thy work;
　　　Go, cull the fruit of it and taste its triumph.
　　　What! thou hast caused his death, and art not weeping?
EURYDICE.   I am not weeping—nay—but I am dying.
　　　Upbear me, Ormene.
ORMENE.　　　　　　　What sayest thou, madam?
EURYDICE.   Noble Surenas, receive all my soul!

　　　　　　　　　　　　　(*She sinks to the floor.*)
ORMENE (*to* PALMIS).   Come, let us bear her hence, to aid her better.
PALMIS.   Lighten, great gods, this weight of mortal grief;
　　　And in the woe in which my heart is plunged,
　　　Let me not die until I am avenged!